HOW TO CREATE
THE PERFECT WIFE

How to Create the Perfect Wife

Britain's Most *Ineligible* Bachelor and His *Enlightened Quest* to Train the *Ideal Mate*

Wendy Moore

BASIC BOOKS

A MEMBER OF THE PERSEUS BOOKS GROUP
New York

Copyright © 2013 by Wendy Moore

Published by Basic Books,
A Member of the Perseus Books Group

Books published by Basic Books are available at special discounts for bulk purchases in the United States by corporations, institutions, and other organizations. For more information, please contact the Special Markets Department at the Perseus Books Group, 2300 Chestnut Street, Suite 200, Philadelphia, PA 19103, or call (800) 810-4145, ext. 5000, or e-mail special.markets@perseusbooks.com.

Designed by Timm Bryson

Library of Congress Cataloging-in-Publication Data

Moore, Wendy, 1952-
  How to create the perfect wife : Britain's most ineligible bachelor and his enlightened quest to train the ideal mate / Wendy Moore.
    pages cm
  Includes bibliographical references and index.
  ISBN 978-0-465-06574-5 (hardcover) — ISBN 978-0-465-06573-8 (e-book)
  1. Day, Thomas, 1748-1789.
  2. Authors, English—18th century. 3. Marriage—Great Britain—History—18th century. I. Title.
  PR3398.D3M66 2013
  823'.6—dc23
                                        2012048149
10 9 8 7 6 5 4 3 2 1

To Peter, my perfect other half

CONTENTS

ONE

MARGARET

⇜ London, spring 1769 ⇝

S pring sunshine warmed the ancient brick walls of the courtyards and chambers in London's legal quarter. The jet of water that leapt up thirty feet from the fountain in Fountain Court sparkled in the light before splashing noisily into its basin. The seasonal warmth coaxed the blossoms to burst out on the trees and the young law students to burst out of their rooms and saunter in the gardens beside the river. But for one law student the arrival of spring brought gloom, not cheer.

Thomas Day read the letter from his fiancée in Ireland with incredulity. He had said goodbye to Margaret Edgeworth the previous autumn with every expectation they would be married this coming summer. All through the winter, Day had bent dutifully over his law books in earnest anticipation of his approaching wedding. Now Margaret had written to tell him that she wanted to break off the engagement and Day was mortified. Reeling in a mixture of horror and humiliation, he sank into a deep depression.

In truth the news should hardly have been surprising, for the romance had been shaky from the start. Although he was yet only twenty years old, Day had been romantically disappointed on at least one previous occasion and had been understandably wary of forming a new attachment. So when he first met Margaret, the younger sister of his ebullient Irish friend Richard Lovell Edgeworth, a year earlier there had been no immediate attraction. At loose ends after leaving Oxford University the previous year, Day had jumped at the chance to travel to Ireland for the summer with Edgeworth and Edgeworth's young son, Dick. On arrival at the Edgeworth ancestral home amid the flat fields and black bogs of County Longford, Day had greeted Margaret with initial disdain, and she had likewise shown scant interest in her brother's young friend. It seemed, indeed, that the two were opposites in every conceivable way.

At twenty-two, Margaret was considered one of the most attractive, intelligent and sophisticated women in the county. Brought up with a keen awareness of her long ancestry within one of Ireland's powerful Anglo-Irish families, Margaret had been introduced into the drawing rooms of landed society at an early age. Confident and refined, she had a gift for witty conversation and a reputation for impeccable style. One acquaintance would later say that if Margaret appeared on his doorstep dressed in rags and holding a begging bowl he would still have felt impelled to address her as "Madam."

Two years her junior, Thomas Day was not the most obviously eligible of bachelors. Although he was certainly clever, undoubtedly well educated and shortly due to inherit a considerable fortune, Day's personal attractions were decidedly marred by his comical appearance and unconventional manners. Tall and well built with curling black hair and large hazel eyes, he might have been considered handsome were it not for his stooped shoulders, the severe marks of smallpox that pitted his face and his general dishevelment. Scornful of the contemporary custom for cropped hair covered with a neatly curled wig, Day left his long hair lank and tangled. Eschewing fashionable dress, he wore plain, drab clothes that were invariably crumpled and askew. Even his close friend Edgeworth had to admit: "Mr. Day's exterior was not at that time prepossessing, he seldom combed his raven locks, though he was remarkably fond of washing in the stream." And as his unorthodox approach to personal hygiene might suggest, Day showed no regard for accepted etiquette.

At the dinner table Day's manners were considered so vulgar that they appalled Edgeworth's father. Whether Day merely slurped his soup or went so far as to rest his muddy boots on the table was left unsaid, but certainly Edgeworth senior took "a violent prejudice" against Day "in consequence of something in the manner of his eating and sitting at table, which appeared unsuitable to his rank in life." Over tea in the parlor Day made no attempt at small talk, preferring either to sit sulkily silent or to stand and declaim his dogmatic views loudly and at length.

Yet for all his slovenly appearance and boorish manners, there was evidently something about the youth that appealed to some men—Edgeworth for one—and occasionally some women. Day's commitment to enhancing human rights had struck a chord with fellow radicals, while his determination to help those worse off than himself had earned him many admirers. University friends at Oxford and fellow law students in London treated Day as something of an absentminded philosopher or a romantic rebel. He seemed not quite of his time. His espousal of chivalric virtues and classical heroes harked back to a past age; his opposition to class-ridden systems and traditional hierarchies seemed to anticipate a distant future. Certainly his ideas were out of pace with the consumer-driven, celebrity-obsessed, fashion-mad culture that was predominant in Georgian Britain.

At first, therefore, Day and Margaret appeared to have nothing in common. Repulsed by her brother's loutish friend and his daring ideas, Margaret kept out of his way as much as politeness allowed. Equally contemptuous of his friend's elegant sister and her polished manners, Day gave Margaret a wide berth. To Day, Margaret represented "a sort of being for which he had a feeling of something like horror," according to her brother Richard. And so for the first few weeks in the large country house the pair had maintained "an awful distance." But as they had spent more and more time together during uncomfortable meals and awkward social occasions over the early summer of 1768, they had gradually discovered some mutual interests.

Margaret found herself intrigued by the eccentric Englishman. She too had been disappointed in love—by a dashing but unsuitable English army officer—and Day offered a refreshing contrast to the fawning beaux who usually competed for her attentions. Managing to overlook his lack of grooming and poor social skills, she was moved by the powerful monologues Day delivered on improving the lot of humanity and had to admire his philanthropic plans. Drawing Day into conversation, Margaret's "easy manners, and agreeable conversation" had managed to "unbend" Day's aloof conduct, said Edgeworth.

At the same time, Day became entranced by his clever and attractive hostess. He discovered a shared interest in literature and nature as well as finding a few differences of opinion over the importance of etiquette and "aristocratic habits." According to Edgeworth, watching wryly from the sidelines, his smart little sister could always run rings around Day when arguing her point; it was only when he was alone with Day that Edgeworth found "Mr. Day's eloquence prevailed." As in the best of romantic comedies, the cut and thrust of verbal sparring led to heated passions.

At the beginning of August, Day cautiously proposed to Margaret and she tentatively accepted. When the pair announced their intentions to the assembled family, Margaret's brother had been as surprised as her father was horrified. Edgeworth senior refused point-blank to give the marriage plan his blessing, having taken resolutely against the scruffy English youth "from Prejudices too ridiculous to mention," in Day's words. But Margaret determined that she would go ahead regardless, and so the pair agreed that they would marry as soon as Day reached twenty-one the following summer. Postponing his return to London so that he and his future spouse could get to know each other a little better, Day stayed on in the Edgeworth country home as the summer faded. In retrospect this had not been such a good idea. For as Day outlined his vision of marital bliss, Margaret's ardor began visibly to cool.

Inspired by an admiration for the Stoics, the ancient Greek school of philosophy devoted to noble virtue and self-sacrifice, Day intended to live a frugal existence in a secluded rural retreat devoid of all comforts or diversions with only his future spouse for company. Impassioned by the ideas of Jean-Jacques Rousseau, the Geneva-born philosopher who urged a return to nature, Day believed that with the right partner they would both find joy and fulfillment in this austere isolation. And to gild his picture of happy married life, Day patiently explained to his fiancée that the "childish Passion call'd love" was only a figment of the imagination that no rational being should indulge. As Day told a friend at the time: "Love I am firmly convinc'd is the Effect of Prejudice & Imagination; a rational Mind is incapable of it, at least in any great Degree." Day believed that the woman he married should want to spend her life with him out of a strictly logical attachment—or an "Idea of Preference for me." Initially, through August, Margaret had been swayed by this image of a simple life in a rose-covered cottage with a saintly helpmeet. By September, as the days shortened and the autumn chill set in, she had got cold feet.

Confessing finally that her feelings had changed, and she now felt "perfectly indifferent" as to whether they married or not, Margaret volunteered—rashly or gallantly—to marry him still if neither of them found a more suitable partner within the next twelve months. Although he was naturally peeved at this sudden turnaround, Day grudgingly consented to the pact in the confident belief that Margaret would "scarcely find another Character she can coolly & deliberately think comparable to mine"—a statement that was probably true.

But just as Day was about to sail back to England in October, Margaret professed a rekindled warmth for him. "She is concern'd I am going to leave her, she acknowledges it, & that she loves me better than she herself thought," Day announced jubilantly to a friend. She would marry him after all, Margaret declared—so long as Day made a few efforts to smarten up his appearance—and the wedding plans were back on track. Leaving Margaret with a stack of books on metaphysics for her enlightenment through the winter, Day had returned to London to resume his law studies and looked forward to his June wedding with confidence.

Although none of their friends were in the least surprised by Margaret's last-minute change of heart the following spring, the news hit Day as a complete shock and a ghastly blow. He had suffered rejection before as a student at Oxford; then he had described the woman who spurned him as a "Bitch." But this time was far, far worse. Against his better judgment he had allowed himself to trust in a woman's promises again, and again he had been cruelly rejected. He had placed all his faith in obtaining the lifelong partner he had searched for to share his dream life and been rudely disappointed. He had told family and friends of his summer wedding plans and now he had to disabuse them. Disgusted by Margaret's fluctuating feelings as much as he was furious with himself for believing in her, Day reacted with bitterness and rage. He would later describe Margaret as "a toad, which I would not injure, but cannot help beholding with abhorrence." So as his fellow law students ambled and cavorted in the spring sunshine, Thomas Day languished in misery.

Many men his age, including some of his friends, had suffered similar romantic setbacks. Young men and women always had and they always would. As wretched as rejection could feel, most people eventually resurfaced and acknowledged that they had just not yet met the right partner. Day, however, refused to accept this view. Utterly baffled as to why any woman should want to reject him, at the age of twenty Day came to a startling conclusion. Since he had yet not found the right woman, the right woman simply did not exist.

Strangely, perhaps, this revelation did not put Day off the idea of marriage. His conviction that he should marry remained as strong as ever. Equally Day was just as firmly committed to his "Scheme of Life" exiled in a bleak rural hideaway with a lucky female partner. But his brief experience of romantic affairs to date now firmly convinced him that he would never find an ideal woman to share this lofty dream anywhere in contemporary society. His broken engagement confirmed his suspicions that women were universally shallow, fickle, illogical and untrustworthy. "These my Friend are the Prejudices & Caprices with which the whole Sex are infected"; he had complained to one friend during Margaret's earlier wavering, "nothing can please but what is extravigant, irrational." Yet he did not blame the female sex per se for these fatal shortcomings.

Women were the weaker sex physically and intellectually—that much was clear. But perhaps that deficiency was largely the result of their different upbringing and education, Day now reasoned. While boys were trained in boarding schools and universities to become future leaders who would one day occupy key positions in the church, law, medicine, business and government, girls were taught at home, or briefly in schools if they were lucky, chiefly to ply an embroidery needle, tinkle on a harpsichord and make pretty conversation at tea parties. Excluded from universities and law schools, and therefore denied entry into medical, legal and clerical professions, women were essentially trained to run an efficient household and make a man happy.

Yet while most people within eighteenth-century society unquestioningly accepted that women were inherently inferior to men, Day came to a boldly progressive view that women were potentially equally intelligent. "The Female Mind is doubtless susceptible of some Degree of Perfection," he argued. It was simply the way that women were brought up and educated in the fatuous, faddish, superficial world that turned them into giggling, flouncing creatures who changed their minds as easily as they changed their gowns, he decided. The pioneering feminist Mary Wollstonecraft would later applaud his liberal ideas on women's education. Yet Day was no harbinger of female equality.

Day wanted a lifelong partner who would be just as clever, well read and witty as his brilliant male friends. He craved a lover with whom he could discourse and wrangle on politics, philosophy and literature as freely as he could in male company. He desired a companion who would be physically as tough and hardy as himself. In short he wanted a woman who would be more like a man. But he was only human—and male. So for all his apparently egalitarian views on education, Day wanted his future spouse happily to suppress her natural intelligence and subvert her acquired learning in deference to his views and desires. He wanted a wife who would be completely subservient to his wishes at all times. How then would he ever obtain the woman of his dreams?

And then out of his pit of despair came a bold and daring plan. If only he could control a woman's education from the beginning, perhaps he could make for himself an equal—a woman who would be worthy of him. It was a scheme he had been nursing quietly for some years. He had returned again to this wild notion the previous summer during the shifting relationship with Margaret. At that point he had confided to a friend: "I am now going to try whether by taking a Woman's Mind before it is prejudic'd, it may be possible to prevent them [prejudices]." Then he had been diverted by Margaret's revived interest and put the idea to one side. Now he determined that he would go ahead with his experiment after all.

If the perfect wife did not exist then he would simply have to create her.

TWO

LAURA

❦ Stoke Newington, near London, c. 1753 ❦

The crowded room hushed as the small boy, dressed in infant's petti-coats, piped up with a question for the vicar. Bright and precocious, the young lad had learned to read early but had been puzzled by a partic-ular phrase he had come across in the Bible. When he had asked his mother for an explanation she had briskly swept the matter aside and sug-gested that he ask the parish vicar when he next visited the house. No doubt his mother hoped that he would soon forget his question, but there was no chance of that. Now that the vicar had finally come, an honored guest at one of his mother's tea parties, the boy pushed his way to the mid-dle of the room and loudly voiced his query: "Sir, I want to know who the whore of Babylon is?"

As the guests turned to stare, the embarrassed parson was at a loss for words. The boy was most probably not the first person to ask him for an explanation of the Mother of Prostitutes described in the Book of Reve-lation as sitting astride a scarlet beast with seven heads and ten horns. But he was almost certainly the youngest. Finally regaining his composure, the vicar replied, "My dear, that is allegorical." But the evasive answer, which might have silenced most of his parishioners, did not satisfy his young in-quisitor. "Allegorical!" the boy spluttered. "I do not understand that word."

Throwing a look of contempt at the cleric, Thomas Day ran to his mother and whispered loudly, "He knows nothing about it."

Thomas Day was born on June 22, 1748, in London's East End. He was the only child of a prosperous government official, also named Thomas, who had accumulated a portfolio of country estates, and his wife, Jane, the daughter of a rich London merchant. Since his father was in his late fifties and his mother less than half that age at the time of their wedding, the marriage was probably a convenient economic alliance rather than a love match. But when their son and heir was born two years later, he was very much a planned and wanted child.

The family lived in a large four-story house in Wellclose Square, a fashionable address close to the Port of London's Custom House, where Thomas's father held a lucrative post collecting export taxes. Baby Thomas was baptized by his proud parents on July 8 in the nearby church of St. George-in-the-East. But only a year later, his aging father died, leaving thirteen-month-old Thomas an enviable fortune in land and property to be held in trust until he reached the age of twenty-one. And so Thomas grew up in the secure knowledge that he would never have to work to earn his bread.

From his father, who bequeathed gifts to more than 150 friends, servants and tenants in his will, Thomas inherited not just a commitment to help people in need but also the money to fulfill that goal. From his mother—who had once stared down a bull she had surprised when crossing a field—Thomas inherited an intractable obstinacy and unshakable self-belief. It was a heady combination. Thomas grew into a solemn boy with a strong urge to do good and a fierce sense of self-entitlement.

Soon after she was widowed, the formidable Mrs. Day moved with Thomas to Stoke Newington, a village several miles north of the city's smog, "for the sake of her son's health." Whether or not the lad was especially sickly, his mother certainly felt a real need to protect her only child. As she established herself in village society, Mrs. Day enjoyed showing off her clever son's talents to guests. It was at one of her gatherings for local gentry that young Thomas had expressed his scorn for the village parson.

Thomas was devoted to his mother, and so his small world was turned upside down when she married again, this time to Thomas Phillips, a junior colleague and friend of the elder Day as well as an executor of his will. The event was climactic in seven-year-old Thomas's life. Unable to remember his father, he had developed an intensely close relationship with his mother. As a child he was naturally dependent on her, and yet, since he was his father's sole heir, she was financially dependent on him. Strong-willed and self-sufficient yet utterly doting and dedicated to his every whim, his mother represented a pinnacle of female perfection in her small son's eyes. No woman could ever hope to match this ideal. It was a perfect and perfectly exclusive relationship that fulfilled every emotional and physical need he could possibly encounter in his short sweet life to date. Although it was plain, since she had faced down that bull, that Mrs. Day was more than capable of looking after herself, in the mind of the seven-year-old boy who was technically head of the family, he was her protector against all threats and dangers. It is easy to imagine the young boy's alarm at the idea of a towering male force bearing down upon his beloved mother.

Thomas and his stepfather would never see eye to eye. As one of the guardians charged with supervising the boy's fortune and education, as well as now becoming his stepfather, Phillips played a dominant role in steering his stepson's upbringing and governing his expenditure. To his face, Day would always be respectful in accordance with the filial duty expected of children in the eighteenth century. Behind his back, he would sneeringly describe Phillips as "one of those common characters" who had improved his fortunes through a judicious marriage. Resentful of his step-father's control over his life, he would accuse him of a "busy teizing [teasing] interference in circumstances, with which [he had] no real concern."

Three certainly proved to be a crowd in the Day household. The moody young boy was promptly dispatched to a Stoke Newington boarding school while the newlyweds moved to a country house at Barehill, near Wargrave, in Berkshire. Thomas returned briefly to his mother's arms when he came home to recuperate after catching smallpox. Like many youngsters fortunate enough to survive the disease he was left with unsightly scars on his face. But at the age of nine he was packed off smartly again to spend the next seven years learning Latin, Greek, grammar and algebra at Charterhouse, one of England's oldest and most elite boys' schools, in the center of London.

One of about a hundred boarding pupils, young Thomas quickly learned his place in the school pecking order. Within the picturesque medieval quadrangles and sprawling grounds, thuggery reigned—among masters and pupils alike—as in any such school of its day. The headmaster, Dr. Lewis Crusius, had carved out a reputation for "ability and discipline," and the latter skill was studiously copied down the school hierarchy. So the masters administered regular floggings to erring pupils, the prefects beat the boys under their command and the older boys felt free to batter the younger ones in their turn.

Surviving this ritualized violence was regarded as an integral part of an upper-class boy's education. School floggings were public spectacles in which both the victim and the spectators were expected to withstand the experience with courage and stoicism. Customs such as tossing newcomers in a blanket or "roasting" small boys in front of a fire and the numerous inducements and punishments that surrounded the practice of "fagging"— in which younger boys were forced to work effectively as slaves for older pupils—were tolerated and indulged by the school administration. Along with these beatings and torments, the boys had to endure extreme physical hardship. Their meals were meager and unpalatable, the dormitories were draughty and crowded and the days were long. At Charterhouse, the boys were dragged from their shared beds at five each morning and only allowed to crawl back under the covers late at night.

Thrown into this brutal and austere regime, Thomas—the mollycoddled infant—not only survived but thrived. Rising early in the chilly dormitory to a breakfast of cold gray porridge, he drew strength from the philosophy and lifestyle expounded by the Stoics. As he was being pushed and shoved on packed classroom benches, he was inspired by the legendary heroes of classical literature and history and their feats of physical and mental courage. Like the Spartan lawgiver Lycurgus, young Thomas aspired to treat luxury and ease with contempt; like the former slave Epictetus, who became a Stoic philosopher, he steeled himself to accept adversity. If other boys grumbled at the discomforts, Thomas took pride in enduring hardship and relished the simple life.

Progressing through the forms, Thomas outpaced his schoolfellows in height and strength. He even gained a reputation as a champion at boxing in the officially sanctioned boxing ring where boys gathered to jeer at scuffles in the dust. Just like his mother facing down the charging bull, he learned to stand his ground against bigger and stronger opponents. In one match, the boys cheered Thomas on as he pounded another pugilist mercilessly with his bare knuckles. But just on the point of pummeling his rival into submission he suddenly dropped his fists and helped his opponent to his feet, announcing that the match was an uneven contest. Pride in his hardiness and physique would always compete with his sense of fair play.

No doubt his fame helped in attracting the admiration of older schoolboys. Thomas formed strong friendships at school that would last all his life and help to compensate for the lost intimacy with his mother. In particular, he made friends with John Bicknell, the clever son of a London law family, who was two years his senior, and with William Seward, the only son of a London brewer, who was a year above him. Indeed one version of the boxing story had Seward as the sorry loser of the bout. Sharing a passion for literature and classical history, as well as a youthful compulsion to right injustice, these three forged a firm bond.

A pale youth with delicate features, Bicknell left Charterhouse two years before Day to follow in the family tradition and embark on a career in law. Without the luxury of an independent income waiting for him, Bicknell needed a profession to earn his living. At sixteen he enrolled at Middle Temple, one of the four ancient Inns of Court between Holborn and the Thames, which trained young men to become barristers. Studying his law books just a short stroll from his old school, he remained Day's closest friend and confidant.

Together they nursed literary ambitions and dreamed of publishing success. With typical teenagers' contempt for convention and an urge to put the world to rights, they wrote a poem, "The Triumph of Politeness." A witty satire poking fun at vanity and fashion, it was published in a London newspaper in 1764, under the pseudonym Knife and Fork, when Day was still a schoolboy and Bicknell a law student.

Although Day left Charterhouse for Oxford University before he reached sixteen in 1764, at the same time as Seward, it was Bicknell with whom he remained close. As one contemporary put it, Bicknell was "in the strictest sense, the friend and companion of his youth." Ever ready to humor Day's increasingly strident views, whether on conduct he despised or individuals he disliked, Bicknell would always be willing to fall in with his plans. Like a knife and fork, they were a well-matched pair.

From the summit of Shotover Hill on the approach from London to Oxford, the first sight of the city's white spires glittering in the summer sunshine suggested a tranquil haven perfect for industrious study and philosophical contemplation. Arriving at Oxford in the summer of 1764 eager to indulge his love of the classics, Day soon discovered that appearances could be deceptive.

Like its rival, Cambridge, Oxford had become virtually moribund by the middle of the 1700s. With student numbers at their lowest-ever level and college funds almost depleted, academic study was notable by its absence. The colleges were half-empty, the professors were halfhearted and lectures and tutorials had become a rarity. Edward Gibbon, who would later write *The Decline and Fall of the Roman Empire*, had been admitted to Oxford in the decade before Day's arrival. Gibbon described the few classes he attended as "devoid of profit or pleasure" and summed up the fourteen months he spent at the university as the "the most idle and unprofitable of my life."

The decline and fall in standards at Oxford was indeed so profound that most students spent their days in an endless, carefree round of drinking and carousing. For students in the top two tiers of the university hierarchy—the nobles and the gentlemen-commoners who paid the highest fees—the day began at a leisurely hour when a servitor—a poor student on the lowest rung—brought breakfast to their rooms. The rest of the morning was devoted to dressing for dinner, which was served in the college dining hall at one or two in the afternoon. This was generally followed by several further courses—a gargantuan spread of puddings, cakes, fruit and cheese washed down with copious amounts of wine—which were usually consumed in a friend's rooms over the space of several hours. What remained of the day and night was spent in a spree of drinking wagers and drunken brawls in the coffeehouses and taverns that abounded within the city walls. With little time for study in this demanding timetable, any spare hours were generally taken up with private lessons to acquire social graces such as dancing, fencing and horse-riding, or with seducing women of the town in the lanes and parks that were notorious for lewd scenes.

For a healthy, normal, vigorous teenage boy, released from the austerity and discipline of an all-male boarding school, such temptations might have proven overwhelming. But not for Thomas Day. Arriving in Oxford in his black silk gown and velvet mortarboard a few weeks before his sixteenth birthday on June 1, 1764, Thomas enrolled at Corpus Christi College as a gentleman-commoner and looked forward to some serious study and philosophical enlightenment.

One of the oldest and smallest of the Oxford colleges, Corpus Christi provided a calm sanctuary of sunlit quadrangles and cool cloisters nestled in the shelter of the city's medieval walls. But the college's serene surroundings belied a reputation for misbehavior as outrageous as that of its rivals. One undergraduate had recently been forced to leave the university after lighting a bonfire of books and furniture in the Fellows' Common Room. Another student had been caught smuggling a woman into his rooms by disguising her in a scholar's black gown. And in the not-too-distant future, the college chaplain would be reprimanded, albeit mildly, for "misbehaviour, drunkenness, extravagance, and other irregularities."

Settling into his suite of rooms in the Gentlemen Commoners' Quad after the cramped and spartan regime of Charterhouse, Thomas could have been forgiven for succumbing to the pleasures of university life. As a gentleman-commoner, paying hefty fees to the college, he was entitled to all the privileges of his rank including the services of a personal servitor to bring him coffee and rolls each morning and to wait on him at dinner in the dining hall. To cover his expenses at Oxford, Day most probably received a quarterly allowance provided out of his trust fund. Although his future inheritance remained in the grip of his penny-pinching stepfather, these college funds would still have totaled what Edward Gibbon described as "more money than a schoolboy had ever seen." But despite all his newfound liberty and spending power, he made no attempt to indulge in university diversions, for the excesses Day encountered at Oxford only reinforced his distaste for the trappings of wealth and luxury. His enthusiasm for the stoical way of life remained as steadfast as ever.

Although he fraternized with his old school chum Seward and made some new friends among the more serious students, Thomas trod a singular path and cut a pompous figure. While his fellow scholars squandered their parents' funds on fine clothes, gourmet food and vintage wines, Day lived sparingly. While other students were fitted for embroidered silk garments and spent hours at the barbers being coiffed and powdered, Thomas wore dowdy and outmoded clothes and grew his hair long. He drank water instead of wine, dined on the plainest food, rarely ate meat and even considered vegetarianism.

Most controversially of all, Thomas liked to study. As other students caroused into the night, he pored over his books. And in the absence of lectures by tutors, Thomas spouted long speeches on any conceivable topic to anyone prepared to listen. He certainly could talk. Day liked to "descant at large and at length upon whatever became the subject of conversation," said one long-suffering friend. "From the deepest political investigation, to the most frivolous circumstance of daily life, Mr. Day found something to descant upon." As another acquaintance put it, "Mr. Day always *talked like a book*."

In male company Day's diatribes were grudgingly tolerated. In mixed company, his imperious lectures seemed discourteous and absurd. In particular, Day's insistence "even in the company of women, to descant on the evils brought upon mankind by love" did him no favors with the opposite sex. Childhood confusion at his mother's apparent betrayal in submitting to his despised stepfather had seemingly festered into suspicion of women in general. Like a brooding Hamlet, separated from his mother by a malevolent stepfather, Thomas was both enthralled and repelled by women. So while his fellow students smuggled girls into their rooms, Day was disgusted by their lascivious antics and felt awkward and uncomfortable with women.

Alone in his rooms, he poured his jumbled emotions into long, rambling letters to John Bicknell. Writing early in the morning with his hair wild and his stockings around his ankles before his servitor brought breakfast or late at night when the candle had almost burned down, Day complained about the shallowness of mutual friends and yearned for some deeper meaning in life. "An University is the finest thing in the World to compleat the Coxcomb & the Fool," he declared after meeting a friend of Bicknell's who was newly arrived at Oxford. "I ask'd him to drink Tea with me tomorrow. 'Sir I will do myself the Pleasure of waiting upon you but I never drink Tea,'" Day mimicked his friend's friend and then exclaimed, "surely Heaven never created a greater Poppy." Doubtless Bicknell regretted asking him to help a friend settle in.

Yet Day was easily hurt by supposed slights and craved companionship. "Explain the mystery of Seward's breaches," he demanded of Bicknell. When Bicknell tried to excuse their friend by blaming his aloofness on a quirk of character, Day curtly replied, "it is this Coldness of Disposition which I complain of." He shed few tears when Seward soon after left Oxford prematurely to travel abroad.

Instead Day made friends with other misfits. One of them was Richard Warburton-Lytton, a brilliant scholar and eccentric aristocrat who had inherited a late Gothic country mansion, Knebworth House, in Hertfordshire. Shy and nearsighted—he once mistook a statue on Oxford's Magdalen Bridge for a woman he thought was staring at him—Warburton-Lytton helped found the university's Grecian Club, which met to debate topical matters. A lifelong friend who venerated Day's "uncommon abilities," he would be inspired by Day's ideas on female education. Another new friend was William Jones, an expert linguist who would soon earn the nickname Oriental Jones. Having taught himself Hebrew and Arabic while still at school, he was busy translating the *Arabian Nights* back into its original tongue. Fellow radicals, both Jones and Warburton-Lytton were spellbound by Day and his eccentricities.

At Oxford, Day took charge of his own education. Without a set syllabus or the pressure of exams—for Day had no intention of taking his degree—he devised his own reading list. For lack of tutorials to discuss points of scholarly interest, he exchanged views with Bicknell. The pair fed their appetite for free thinking by snapping up the most controversial works of the moment. Day obtained an English translation of Voltaire's inflammatory *Dictionnaire Philosophique* soon after its publication in 1764. Back in his room, he devoured the *Philosophical Dictionary* with its dozens of entries on everything from adultery, kissing and love to tolerance, tyranny and tears. Burned in Paris and Geneva and banned elsewhere for its criticism of the Catholic Church, it was staunchly defended by Day. "I cannot say I think it calculated to do so much Harm, as to deserve a public

Execution," he told Bicknell. When he overheard a student in an Oxford bookshop applauding rumors that the book was to be banned in London too, Day angrily challenged him. In the manner of many censors, it turned out that the student had not read a word of the book.

Day was equally drawn to the views of the Scottish philosopher David Hume, who was condemned by many for his atheistic outlook. He admired Hume's book *An Enquiry Concerning Human Understanding*, with its rational approach to explaining how people reason and shape ideas. Scientific explanations for human emotions such as love seemed to make perfect sense to Day's logical mind. As he consumed atheistic texts, Day's skepticism about religion grew. The contemptuous child who had challenged the village vicar was ready to reject religious authority altogether. But in its place he needed an alternative philosophy—a new faith.

Engaged on a path of solo research, Day devoted his time to "the discovery of moral truths," which he pursued, according to one friend, "with the severity of logical induction and the depth of metaphysical research." Like any bright and inquiring adolescent, he was struggling to find a meaning to life. A clever young man about to inherit a fortune but with no interest in material pleasures, religious devotion or political pursuits— how was he going to spend his life?

Briefly considering a career in law, Day enrolled at Middle Temple, where Bicknell was already a student, in early 1765 while he was still at Oxford. For young bachelors with no particular interest in studying law, the Temple always provided a convenient address and useful connections. Day even talked of taking chambers there when he finished university, but he had no real intent—and certainly no need—to practice law as a career. Searching for a purpose that would govern his future, Day came to the conclusion that the pursuit of virtue should become his life's goal.

Virtue was a noble ideal—and one that had gained totemic status among eighteenth-century writers and thinkers. Samuel Johnson defined virtue as moral goodness, moral excellence or valor in his dictionary published in 1755. Writing nine years later, in his *Philosophical Dictionary,* Voltaire described the noun as "Beneficence towards the fellow-creature." But these dictionary definitions were regarded as a gross oversimplification for many of the era's other great minds. Combining lofty notions of patriotism, bravery against tyranny, fairness in the face of social injustice and charitable acts to those in need with more prosaic ideas of politeness and good breeding, virtue could mean all things to all people.

The philosopher John Locke, whose ideas remained influential throughout the eighteenth century after his death in 1704, argued that social graces were an essential component of virtue; acquiring good manners was therefore a vital part of a young man's education. Virtue was hence the territory of the rich and well-educated male. But Bernard Mandeville, in his satirical poem *The Fable of the Bees: or, Private Vices, Publick Benefits* published in 1705, insisted that good deeds were really motivated by vanity and self-love. Vice, in his view, was therefore an important stimulus to the economy and a benefit to society. Other writers, such as Edward Gibbon, called for a return to the traditional values of the ancient Greeks and early Romans. It was loss of civic virtue—a gradual sliding into decadence and degeneracy—that had led to the downfall of the Roman Empire, he argued. But modernists, like Hume, believed that past ideas of virtue were anachronistic in the present day.

The nature of virtue taxed novelists too. Samuel Richardson, Henry Fielding, Fanny Burney and Charlotte Smith all wrestled with defining it. Through fiction they each explored the apparent contradiction that although virtue was generally held to be the preserve of well-bred, well-educated and wealthy men, in reality it was more often to be found in poor, poorly educated and poorly regarded young women—and occasionally men—from the lowest social orders.

While philosophers and novelists battled with this thorny conundrum, the young Thomas Day was certain that he had the measure of virtue. It was, in his opinion, a simple, definable and unmutable concept. "Surely there is such a Thing as Virtue," he insisted to Bicknell, "it exists in Reality, & only wears different Appearances as it conforms to the different Customs & receiv'd Prejudices of the Times." In a rapidly changing world, where advances in technology, expanding commerce and growing industrialization were combining to plunge ideas of personal liberty and human rights into flux, Day believed "the true Standard of Virtue has been, is, & shall always be the same."

And so before he was even out of his teens, Thomas Day resolved to become the very model of the model virtuous man. Inspired by the heroes of classical history he determined to commit his energies, talents and—most importantly—his fortune to doing good works. Like the Stoics of ancient Greece, he would devote himself to a life of simplicity and self-sacrifice, he would scorn all luxury, fashion and pleasure, and he would practice philanthropy and altruism. Just as Alexander the Great had been "struck with a passion for glory" after visiting the tomb of his warrior hero Achilles in Troy, so Day had been motivated to dedicate his "passions, pleasures, fortune and talents" to the pursuit of virtue through his adoration of classical heroes, according to a close friend. In the midst of the debauchery and decadence at Oxford, the idealistic young Day decided to live his life according to the highest standards of honest, upright and moral behavior— at least as far as he defined these. But it would be no easy option. As one friend put it, Day dedicated himself to "the unremitting practice of the severest virtue." Like a monk committed to penitential devotion, Day regarded virtue in the light of a religion. He would take no personal pleasure in his worship of virtue; he would wear virtue like a hair shirt.

Determined on his true path in life, Thomas Day lacked only one thing: a soulmate to share his life's work. For a single man in possession of a fortune—as Jane Austen would later astutely note—must be in want of a wife. Intelligent, healthy, young and—soon to become—wealthy, Day should have been near the top of Oxford's list of most popular bachelors.

Many young women in search of an ideal husband would probably have been willing to overlook Day's pockmarked face and rounded shoulders, his ungainly gait and his awkwardness in mixed company in favor of his large fortune. Some might even have found his long hair and shabby clothes endearing in a rebellious young student. But his refusal to engage in small talk, to learn the latest dance steps or to acquire the social manners of the day did little to appeal to the opposite sex. Day's contempt for "modern refinements," as one friend put it, meant that he took "no pains whatever to improve his external appearance or manner." In fact he was fully conscious of his lack of grooming and the effect this might have on those he met. In one letter to Bicknell, he referred to his own "Want of Elegance in Table, Dress, Equipage" and admitted: "I have a Kind of natural, rough [way] with my Words, my Actions, my Manner of Life." But he was nevertheless determined not to do anything about it.

At the same time, Day's gloomy, melancholic outlook and dogmatic, overbearing manner did nothing to enhance his allure. Although Day loved to declaim at length, if his views were at all contested he would respond "more deeply and fully than is agreeable to the fashionable tone of conversation," a friend diplomatically explained. In short he had a fiery temper that was liable to erupt whenever his opinions were challenged.

But if these deficiencies were not sufficient to deter interested women, Day had only to describe his anticipated future lifestyle to send them running desperately in the opposite direction. "With his customary frankness he used to declare his intended mode of living," wrote the same friend, "but he did not often meet with marks of approbation from his female hearers." Above all it was Day's peculiar views on women—even by the misogynistic standards of the eighteenth century—that did most to deter any likely candidates for his heart.

In the eyes of the law, women in eighteenth-century Britain enjoyed few independent rights. Essentially they were deemed completely under the control of their fathers until they married and their husbands after marriage. The handing over of a woman by her father to her husband on her wedding day possessed a literal as well as a symbolic meaning. Upon marriage, women also handed over any property and money to their husbands since the law decreed that a wife's existence was entirely subsumed by her husband.

The letter of the law was compounded by society's expectations. Whether they were wives or daughters, sisters or mothers, women in eighteenth-century Britain were required to be demure, passive and deferential to men. Most women had little choice therefore but to comply with their legal and conventional inferior status. Yet for all the law books and conduct guides conspiring to construct complete submission to men, the Georgian era produced some of the most spirited, flamboyant and forthright women of all time who achieved deserved success in the arts, science and politics.

The traveler and writer Mary Wortley Montagu, for example, introduced smallpox inoculation—using live virus—in the teeth of opposition from the all-male medical establishment in Britain after witnessing the practice performed by peasants in Turkey. The portrait artist Angelica

Kauffman was accepted into the predominantly male art world to the extent that she became one of the founders of the Royal Academy. And the classicist Elizabeth Carter was so revered as a linguist that Samuel Johnson believed her Greek translations were superior to those of any male scholar, although he was quick to point out that she could also make a pudding. Inevitably there were some men who grumbled loudly at this apparent overturning of the natural order, yet many others applauded female attainment and supported women's greater role in society.

With his forward-thinking views on liberty and human rights, Thomas Day might have been expected to march in the vanguard of female emancipation. In fact, his views on women were ludicrously old-fashioned even by the norms of his day. Embarked on his crusade to virtue, like a medieval knight in armor, Day saw himself as the protector and defender of weak and helpless women—whether they liked it or not. While still a student at Oxford, Day developed a perverse fixation with the concept of female purity and an intense horror at the idea of female seduction. At one point, as a seventeen-year-old student, he heard of an aristocratic rake—probably a fellow scholar—who seduced a young woman and then abandoned her to penury. Incensed by this behavior, Day dashed off a letter challenging the philanderer to a duel. His gauntlet was evidently ignored. But Day's obsession only increased. In his mind, women could fit one of only two roles: as a pure and taintless virginal maiden or a helpless victim deflowered by a brutish male predator, a stance that no doubt echoed his childhood shock at his mother's apparent seduction by his stepfather.

Setting himself up as a self-appointed champion of fallen women, Day began to develop his very own, and very particular, ideal of female perfection. Borne out of his fascination for classical myth and romantic notions of pastoral innocence, Day conceived his idea of the perfect woman. She would be young and beautiful like a Greek or Roman goddess. She must be pure and virginal like a simple country maiden. Hardy and fearless, she would possess the physical constitution of a Spartan bride. Artless and unaffected, she would have the plain tastes in clothing, food and lifestyle of a humble peasant girl. And above all, she would regard Day as her master, her teacher, her superior. She would be completely subservient to his needs and whims. She would be utterly in thrall to his ideas and beliefs.

Searching for this paragon of female virtue would occupy many of Day's ensuing years.

It did not take him long to realize that he was unlikely to find such a confection of beauty and purity amid the squalid temptations of Oxford—although he tried. Despite his shuffling embarrassment in female company, Day was preoccupied with looking for a potential partner from the moment he arrived at university. His letters to Bicknell from Oxford were peppered with references to women, named or otherwise, who failed to meet his precise specifications. In many cases, their shortcomings seemed chiefly to do with their lack of appreciation of Day.

When he felt himself spurned by a woman he admired, Day reacted with an almost violent temper. "I think I never saw so damn'd conceited a Bitch as Leonora," he stormed in one letter to Bicknell. In another letter he asked: "How does the amiable Miss Charlotte? Salter's Flame—he really I believe fancys himself in Love with her." And then he added: "Were I capable of having any Inclination for a Woman otherwise than in a carnal Way I might perhaps be his Rival." Having concluded that love was an illogical fantasy concocted by novelists for gullible readers he had developed a strangely sexual, yet simultaneously asexual, attitude toward women. "I could never love a wife," he told Bicknell in one revealing aside. Obviously, since the belles of Oxford did not live up to his exalted ideal, he would have to look further afield for the virginal bride of his fantasies.

During the long university holidays, Day set off on solitary walking trips to the West Country and Wales. He had hoped to travel abroad, on the customary Grand Tour of Europe, which was regarded as a rite of passage for moneyed young men. But since his tight-fisted stepfather refused him the funds, he had to content himself with a cheap camping holiday in Britain. Equipped with a rudimentary tent and a few possessions, he followed farm tracks through the agricultural landscape of the Home Counties surrounding London to the rugged hills and heaths of Dorset, Somerset and beyond. Far from broadening his mind, however, Day's travels narrowed his fixed ideas, glorifying his romantic image of peasant life and—especially—peasant women.

Whenever he arrived at a farmhouse or village, Day made a point of talking to the local inhabitants in an attempt to learn about country ways and customs. According to one contemporary, Day judged that by the "manly exercise of walking" he could get to know "that class of men who, as still treading the unimproved paths of nature, might be presumed to have the qualities of the mind pure and unsophisticated by art." Although, of course, it was the class of women in whom he was mainly interested.

With his plain clothes and unkempt hair at odds with his educated voice and evident wealth, Day attracted a mixture of curiosity and mirth when he knocked on cottage doors asking to interview the ragged inhabitants on their philosophical outlook or strode into village inns intent on interrogating the locals over a lunch of bread and water. But the bounty he left behind generally helped to stifle the laughter. He was like a wandering vagrant who gave out alms instead of begging for them.

Alone on these country expeditions, Day confided his romantic anguish in poems he composed in a large, weather-worn journal—which survives still. Written by the light of a windblown candle in a remote cave or under rain-soaked canvas in a field, his melancholy odes and ballads celebrate the primeval power of untamed nature in the turbulent rivers and stormy seas he saw on his hikes. Almost unerringly his scrawled verses tell tales of pent-up passions and unrequited love—which always end badly.

One poem, which he wrote while sheltering in a dripping cave poised perilously above the Severn River, describes a "hopeless Love" for a "heav'nly Maid" against the backdrop of the "raging Passions" of the torrent rushing through the gorge below. He called it, with a literal poignancy, "Sonnet written in a Cavern of dangerous Access near Bristol." As he crossed the Severn into Wales, his anguish only increased. Here he devoted twenty-seven verses to the "hopeless Flame" of a tormented love for a woman who was devoted to a "Hated Rival." The poem climaxes in a violent revenge as the tortured lover swears to "plunge a Dagger in the Heart,/That robs me of my Fair!"

Three of the poems in Day's camping journal invoke the name of Laura. They were probably in homage to the fourteenth-century Italian poet Francesco Petrarca, or Petrarch, who wrote hundreds of poems on the theme of his unrequited love for an unattainable French woman named

Laure. It was common for eighteenth-century poets to invoke Laura as their muse. Perhaps Thomas was also thinking of the Leonora who had snubbed him at Oxford. According to a friend, Day was "wounded by the caprice" of the mysterious Laura but wrote his poems "before her fickleness became indisputable."

Day's poems return repeatedly to her who "alone my constant Breast can fire" and lament the fact that the "lovely Laura" will smile only for someone else. In one of these elegies, even more densely packed with passionate metaphors than the rest, he finally adopts the dark cloak of seducer himself: "This once at least, I clasp thee in my Arms,/The next let Ruin join us in the Grave." For all his protestations about the irrationality of love, young Thomas was plainly as tortured as any other youth by its vagaries. And as he confided his tangled emotions in verse, Laura attained the status of an imaginary ideal.

During his lonely walks and lonelier nights, Day fleshed out his fantasy of a virginal maid who would meet his exacting specifications. In one poem copied into his water-stained journal in the West Country, he described in detail his perfect woman and the perfect life they would lead together. He sought a "gentle Lady of the West" with "Health's rosy bloom upon thy cheek" and "Eyes that with artless lustre roll." This divine maiden would be indifferent to the "eye of Fame" with a "noble mind" not led astray by "false culture." And most importantly, she would happily live "Sequestered in some secret glade" where she would be "heedless of the praise or blame/Of all mankind, of all but me." Seeking his flawless soulmate, he declared, was "my only task."

> *O gentle Lady of the West,*
> *Whose charms on this sequester'd shore,*
> *With love can fire a stranger's breast;*
> *A breast that never lov'd before!*
>
> *O tell me, in what silent vale,*
> *To hail the balmy breath of May,*
> *Thy tresses floating on the gale,*
> *All simply neat thou deign'st to stray!*

So far he had been unable to find the woman of his dreams among the educated, sophisticated, urban women of his own rank. But neither had he found her yet among the red-cheeked, rough-mannered peasant women of the countryside. Even though he was still in his late teens he was rapidly coming to the conclusion that his vision of female perfection might exist only in his fevered imagination. So how in the world could he possibly bring his fantasy woman to life? How could he create his perfect wife?

It was now that Day first began to entertain a new and shocking idea. As he wandered from farm to village his eyes strayed from the buxom, suntanned, strong-armed women laboring in the fields to the flat-chested, thin-legged little girls approaching adolescence who worked alongside their parents. He had been looking for a perfect woman, but perhaps what he needed was a perfect girl whom he could train to meet his needs. If the way that women were educated was the chief reason he could not find his ideal partner, then he could simply educate a girl himself to suit the role. As he would explain to John Bicknell, "the Habits of the Mind are like those of the body; at one Period of Life perhaps they may be totally prevented, at another remedied in Part; & there is doubtless another Stage where they become totally inveterate, & incurable." If only he could teach a girl to absorb his ideas before her mind was prejudiced by other influences then perhaps he could create his perfect woman.

Now his mind turned to the knotty problem of how he might obtain such a girl ripe for grooming. And there were two further difficulties: he needed a trusty collaborator to sort out any troublesome legal problems and a sure method of education to help him attain his goal. As luck would have it, two friends were on hand to provide those vital missing elements.

While Day hiked the hills gloomily moping for a perfect partner, his loyal friend Bicknell was living life to the full. Having studied law at Middle Temple since 1761, Bicknell was well on his way to becoming a barrister. As the second eldest son in one of London's most successful legal dynasties, he was ideally placed to rise quickly once he qualified. But his long student stint in London's prime bachelor abode had provided Bicknell with as much knowledge of the ways of the world as the ways of the law. As the customary training for the bar involved at least three years languidly studying a few books and observing essential rites of passage, there was plenty of time for other pursuits. And since the Inns of Court were at least as decadent as the colleges of Oxford, there was no shortage of opportunities. Far from disdaining the pleasures of the flesh like his friend Day, Bicknell indulged them as much as he could.

Living with his parents in Chancery Lane, Bicknell only had to stroll a few minutes to Fleet Street, then slip through the seventeenth-century gatehouse to enter the legal quarter shared by the Inner and Middle Temples. Originally the base for the Knights Templar, the medieval religious order pledged to protect pilgrims heading for Jerusalem, the area squashed between Fleet Street and the Thames had been appropriated by lawyers in the fourteenth century—and had changed little since then. Like a walled town preserved in Tudor aspic, the huddle of narrow lanes, shady courtyards and teetering brick buildings provided a self-sufficient community for the barristers and students who lived and learned there.

Threading his way down Middle Temple Lane with the Old Post House on his left and the Devil's Tavern on his right, Bicknell would have joined fellow students, barristers and judges in the imposing Middle Temple Hall for the midday meal. Attending dinner at least three times a term for a minimum of twelve terms—there were four terms a year—was one of the few requirements of a legal training that were strictly enforced. Bicknell duly enjoyed his dinners each term from January 1765. But in between these far from onerous demands he was at liberty to pursue less cerebral interests.

With its proximity to the brothels and bagnios of Covent Garden, it is little wonder that Middle Temple proved such a popular retreat for bachelors. James Boswell, the lawyer, diarist and notorious libertine, thought the Temple area "a most agreeable place." Whether Bicknell followed Boswell's example and "picked up a girl in the Strand" and then took sexual liberties with her in an alleyway in return for sixpence or else trod the well-worn path from the Temple to Covent Garden, he certainly adopted similarly lascivious manners judging by later comments.

One female acquaintance would later be shocked to hear of Bicknell's "bachelor voluptuousness" from one of his contemporaries at Middle Temple. Naturally she assumed that Day, with his horror of female seduction, was blissfully in the dark about his friend's proclivities. Bicknell was exactly the kind of predatory male he would ordinarily have challenged to a duel. It seemed that Bicknell tendered no romantic notions about seeking a perfect woman. But he would be more than willing to use his legal expertise to help Day achieve his goal. All Day lacked now was an alternative educational system to put his bold new plan into action.

It was during holidays from Oxford in 1766 that Day met Richard Lovell Edgeworth. Two more incompatible people would be hard to imagine. Although he was only four years older than Day, at twenty-two Edgeworth had already been married three times—in legal terms at least—and was father to the first of many children. But the exuberant and inventive Irishman had no intention of letting family responsibilities diminish his lust for life.

Born in 1744, the second son of an Anglo-Irish family, Edgeworth had been allowed to roam freely around the family's extensive country estate, often in the company of his favorite sibling, his younger sister Margaret. But after his elder brother died, when Edgeworth was six, his parents suddenly became overprotective of their sole remaining heir. Now the boy was muffled from head to toe on the rare occasions he was permitted to leave the house and dosed daily with preventive medicines. From this point, Edgeworth would write in his marvelously candid memoirs, "my feet never brushed the dew, nor was my head ever exposed to the wind or sun." This sudden reversal in his previously carefree upbringing would have a deep impact on his subsequent views on education.

Precociously intelligent, Edgeworth read books voraciously but was far more excited by the prospect of inventing practical solutions to everyday problems. From the age of seven, when he watched his mother being attached to an electrical device in an attempt to cure the paralysis she had suffered during his birth, Edgeworth had been fascinated by all forms of machinery. His childhood interest in mechanics would become a lifelong passion. He discovered his other abiding passion—for women—while still at school.

At fifteen, during celebrations for his elder sister's marriage, Edgeworth playfully pretended to marry the daughter of a local curate using a door key for a ring. His father, a trained lawyer, was so alarmed that the wedding might be deemed legally binding—in an age when it was not uncommon to wake from a drinking bout to find oneself irrevocably married—that he had the mock marriage formally annulled by the church. Edgeworth was already married and divorced, therefore, when he entered Trinity College, Dublin, at sixteen. Uninspired by academic studies, he frittered away the next six months in dissipation. At that point his despairing father promptly removed him from one scene of iniquity and sent him to an even worse one.

So Edgeworth was packed off, at seventeen, to Oxford University under the protection of a family friend, Paul Elers, who lived in the Oxfordshire village of Black Bourton. A lazy man with an expanding family and escalating debts, Elers gamely warned Edgeworth's father that he had four grown-up daughters, all "pretty girls" without a dowry to rub between them. Entering Corpus Christi College in 1761, three years before Day, Edgeworth was diverted from the usual temptations of university life by the even more diverting temptations of the four pretty girls in the Elers household. Within two years he was "insensibly entangled so completely" with the eldest daughter, eighteen-year-old Anna Maria, "that I could not find any honourable means of extrication."

She was pregnant—as perhaps her feckless father had planned. Although his passion had already cooled, Edgeworth felt duty bound to marry the girl. For all his libertine tendencies he was nothing if not honorable. And since they were too young to marry in England without the consent of both sets of parents, the pair eloped to Scotland where they married at the end of 1763. Facing his father's wrath on his return, Edgeworth was made to go through the ceremony again—effectively his third wedding—with his father's grudging consent in the church at Black Bourton in February 1764. The couple's first child, Dick, was born three months later.

With a relatively small allowance, a year later Edgeworth settled his young family in a modest house overlooking the common at Hare Hatch, a hamlet on the main coach road between Reading and Maidenhead, in Berkshire. Already Edgeworth heartily regretted his hasty marriage. His wife was pretty enough—a portrait of Anna Maria shows a dark-haired, slender and graceful woman—even if Edgeworth pronounced her no beauty. But although she was "prudent, domestic and affectionate," she did not possess "a cheerful disposition," he complained. "She lamented about trifles, and the lamenting of a female, with whom we live, does not render home delightful." One family member would remember Anna Maria as "always crying"—but then she probably had much to cry about, since her new husband took every opportunity to escape their unhappy home.

Leaving Anna Maria miserably holding the baby, Edgeworth directed his inexhaustible energies into his passion for invention. He spent much of his time in his workshop, emerging periodically to test bizarre contraptions on the village common with sometimes disastrous results. At one point an experimental carriage powered by sails escaped its moorings and flew across the green with its young inventor in frantic pursuit. Overtaking his "wheel-boat" just as several stagecoaches appeared on the road, he brought it under control and averted disaster. Undeterred, Edgeworth next produced a giant wheel that could be propelled by a man inside walking within a smaller inner wheel. But before he could add the final touch—a set of brakes—the machine was taken for a joy ride by a local ruffian. Rapidly running out of control, the great wheel was dashed to pieces in a chalk pit only seconds after its driver jumped to safety.

Such setbacks only spurred Edgeworth to further inventions. In rapid succession, he turned out of his workshop an eleven-spoked "perambulator" that measured distances, a large umbrella to keep haystacks dry, an articulated wagon, a turnip-cutting machine, a track-laying vehicle and a phaeton with each of its four wheels fixed independently. The last could turn on a tiny circle without overturning and could also be instantly detached from its horses as required—a wise precaution given Edgeworth's earlier mishaps. The tireless inventor bombarded the newly founded Society for the Encouragement of Arts, Manufactures and Commerce with his designs and won the society's silver and gold medals for his efforts. The epithet "ingenious" was applied with liberal abandon to creative figures in the eighteenth century, but few deserved it so much as Edgeworth.

Eager for any excuse to evade domestic duties, Edgeworth frequently lodged in London on the pretext of studying law. Having enrolled in 1762 at Middle Temple, like Day and Bicknell, he began dining in hall from late 1765, although, like Day, he had no intention of practicing law. Instead Edgeworth divided his time between charming London society and staging theatrical displays of his curious inventions. He soon teamed up with Sir Francis Blake Delaval, a gambler, drunkard and libertine notorious for his wild antics, whose idea of a good time included contests to ride horses up a grand marble staircase and party games to bite the heads off sparrows suspended on strings in a macabre version of bobbing for apples. Driven by a mutual taste for mechanics and showmanship, the pair drew crowds to Delaval's town house for mind-boggling exhibitions of conjuring tricks using magnets and pulleys.

Edgeworth's appetite for novelty soon drew him into the orbit of Erasmus Darwin, the genial physician, inventor and part-time poet. Having heard that Darwin shared his interest in carriage design, Edgeworth sent him the blueprint of a prototype phaeton in 1766. A sociable and generous man, Darwin had settled in the prosperous town of Lichfield (some hundred miles from London in the English Midlands) and built up a thriving medical practice. Now in his mid-thirties, though his lumbering figure and full-bottomed wig made him look much older, Darwin invited Edgeworth to visit. Needing no further persuasion, Edgeworth harnessed his horses to his custom-built carriage and sped off for Lichfield that summer.

Darwin was impressed by Edgeworth's sporty chariot and entranced by its designer. With an interest not only in medicine and transport but also in chemistry, geology, mineralogy and mechanics, Darwin opened his home to visitors of a scientific bent. But living too far from London to frequent the capital's numerous clubs and societies for similar enthusiasts, Darwin had begun to build around him in the Midlands an informal circle of like-minded thinkers, inventors and industrialists who exchanged ideas at convivial dinner parties. Meeting for dinner and then discussion on the Sunday (later Monday) nearest to a full moon—for the purposes of traveling safely at night—they took the name the Lunar Society of Birmingham and were sometimes dubbed the "lunaticks." Edgeworth was a natural fit.

During Edgeworth's brief visit that summer, Darwin touted his new friend tirelessly around the Lichfield social scene, pressing him to perform tricks with magnets and mechanical devices like an entertainer at a children's party. Dashing off a letter to urge his industrialist friend Matthew Boulton to join them, Darwin proclaimed: "I have got with me a mechanical Friend, Mr Edgeworth from Oxfordshire—The greatest Conjuror I ever saw." Barely able to contain his excitement, Darwin drummed up enthusiasm for his guest as if he were John the Baptist announcing the Messiah: "He has the principles of Nature in his Palm, and moulds them as He pleases. Can take away Polarity or give it to the Needle by rubbing it thrice on the Palm of his Hand. And can see through two solid Oak Boards without Glasses, wonderful! astonishing! diabolical!!!" With such a fanfare, Boulton could hardly resist.

Into Edgeworth's exhilarating, dazzling, fun-filled world, Thomas Day appeared on a summer's day in 1766 like a looming black rain cloud. Day was home for the holidays at his mother and stepfather's house at Barehill, but being uncomfortable in his stepfather's company he was keen for any excuse to escape. The news that a neighbor had recently attended the same college, and shared the same tutor, provided the ideal opportunity. And so Day ambled the short distance to Edgeworth's home at Hare Hatch to pay his respects.

The tall, stooped, pockmarked youth with his matted black hair and scruffy clothes arrived unannounced. For once, Edgeworth was at home— probably busy in his workshop, his sleeves pushed up to the elbows and his hands covered with grease, constructing his latest invention. Ever ready to welcome a guest, despite appearances, Edgeworth invited his neighbor to stay for refreshments. But the gawky eighteen-year-old did little to improve on first impressions when he spoke in his usual bombastic manner. After conversing together for several hours it was abundantly plain that the pair had almost nothing in common.

Looking back, Edgeworth would later compare himself and Day: he himself was full of "constitutional joy" while Day was "grave and melancholy." While Edgeworth was a man of "strong passions," Day was a sober and misanthropic pedant. And while Edgeworth was "fond of all the happiness" that the company of women could bestow, Day was "suspicious of the female sex, and averse to risking his happiness for their charms or their society." But most of all, Edgeworth was baffled by Day's simultaneous condemnation of "the evils" of love and his remorseless quest for a perfect woman who was divinely intended for him.

Having determined to make the best of his own imperfect marriage, Edgeworth was astounded to learn that Day "expected that, with a person neither formed by nature, nor cultivated by art, to please, he should win some female wiser than the rest of her sex, who should feel for him the most romantic and everlasting attachment—a paragon, who should forget the follies and vanities of her sex for him" and be prepared to "live in a cottage on love." As Edgeworth put it: "Though armed in adamant against the darts of beauty, and totally insensible to the power of accomplishments, he felt, that for an object, which should resemble the image in his fancy, he could give up fortune, fame, life, every thing but virtue."

In short, the only areas on which the pair could agree was "a love of knowledge, and a freedom from that admiration of splendour, that dazzles and enslaves mankind." What is more, Edgeworth was a practical, pragmatic man determined to find workable solutions to problems; Day was a cerebral idealist who seemed hellbent on creating them. Yet despite all their differences, there was something about Day that evidently touched Edgeworth profoundly. Like the handful of disciples, such as Warburton-Lytton and Oriental Jones, Day had attracted at Oxford, Edgeworth found himself in awe of the sober young poet with a childlike belief in noble causes and dogged contempt for luxury.

After no more than a few hours' conversation that first day, the odd couple forged an immediate and lasting friendship that was founded, said Edgeworth, "on mutual esteem, between persons of tastes, habits, pursuits, manners, and connexions totally different." Stopping abruptly as they were walking together along a lane near Hare Hatch, Edgeworth impulsively predicted that they would be lifelong friends. Sure enough, from that first meeting in 1766, through good times and bad, the two would remain loyally devoted.

Whenever Day could escape his studies and Edgeworth could resist the lures of Lichfield or London, the pair would be found holed up in Edgeworth's workshop. As the indefatigable inventor battled to assemble another of his cunning contraptions, his talkative friend would hold forth

on a contentious topic and occasionally lend a helping hand by, for example, in Day's words, "calculating the vibrations of your wooden horse's legs."
So far Edgeworth had dedicated himself to the instant gratification of
impulses—whether seducing the daughter of a family friend or attempting
to build a giant wooden mechanical horse capable of bestriding hedges.
But Day obviously appealed to Edgeworth's latent moral purpose, a desire
to do good. Day was quite simply, Edgeworth stated—and would maintain
until his dying day—"the most virtuous human being I have ever known."

Certainly Edgeworth believed that Day's influence on him was crucial.
Meeting Day marked the beginning of "a new era in my life." Strangely,
perhaps, Mrs. Edgeworth did not share her husband's enthusiasm for his
new friend. Although she apparently felt no unease at her husband's
friendship with the gambling, drinking, lewd Delaval, she took an immediate and fervent dislike to Day. Edgeworth was bewildered. "A more dangerous and seductive companion than the one, or a more moral and
improving companion than the other, could not be found in England," he
protested. Yet perhaps Mrs. Edgeworth had more of an instinct for danger
and immorality than her trusting husband.

The timing of their meeting was critical: it was the beginning of a new
era for Day too. For in between his scientific endeavors and his legal studies, Edgeworth had become enthralled by a radically different approach
to education, which he was eager to share with his latest friend. It was
this experimental new system that would furnish Day with the tool he
needed to solve his search for love.

Although Edgeworth's marriage was far from perfect, he was about to
provide the final piece of the puzzle to help Day create his perfect wife.

THREE

SOPHIE

❧ *Staffordshire, summer 1766* ❧

Enjoying a stroll in the gardens of Wootton Hall, a friend's country house in Staffordshire, Erasmus Darwin stopped outside the entrance to a grotto. With a casual air, which belied his corpulence, the physician stooped down to examine a small flower. Since he had already added botany to the long list of his interests, there was nothing obviously remarkable in Darwin's scrutiny. In fact, however, his seemingly spontaneous action was a carefully contrived ploy. By halting outside the grotto, Darwin was determined to coax out its shy and fearful inhabitant. The trick worked. For out of the gloom loped a thin, frail figure with beady, black eyes. It was the international fugitive Jean-Jacques Rousseau.

Ever since the philosopher had published his controversial views on liberty and education in 1762, Rousseau had been hounded across Europe. Church authorities in his adopted country of France had banned both *The Social Contract*, with its daring views on freedom and equality, and *Émile*, with its progressive ideas on education. Forced to flee France, Rousseau headed for his homeland only to discover that his native city of Geneva had followed suit by publicly burning both books. He spent the next three years lying low in the Swiss mountains until villagers stoned his cottage and Rousseau was on the run again. Finding himself with nowhere left to hide, the fifty-three-year-old exile had reluctantly accepted safe passage

35

to England. Under the protection of David Hume, the Scottish philosopher, who was serving as secretary of the British Embassy in Paris,
Rousseau had crossed the Channel.

Arriving in London in January 1766, Rousseau had been fêted by the
press and mobbed in the streets. "All the world are eager to see this man,
who by his singularity, has drawn himself into much trouble," announced
the *Public Advertiser*. Dressed in the colorful Armenian costume he had
recently adopted, "the celebrated John James Rousseau"—as he was
dubbed by the English newspapers—was deluged by admirers including
the Prince of Wales. Such celebrity status did nothing, however, to improve
Rousseau's temper.

Notoriously cantankerous and neurotic, Europe's most wanted
philosopher detested fame almost as much as he hated obscurity.
Rousseau had no love of England or the English, and he longed for his
companion Thérèse Levasseur until she was escorted across the Channel
a month later by James Boswell, a keen admirer of Rousseau's work. Inevitably, Boswell being Boswell, the job of chaperone entailed several
steamy nights of passion en route. Reunited with his lover, Rousseau accepted the offer of a quiet retreat at Wootton Hall, the country home of
another admirer, Richard Davenport. But the charms of this pastoral idyll
soon wore thin.

Feeling isolated and fed up with the damp English weather, Rousseau
grew miserable and anxious. Always a difficult character, who was as hard
on his friends as he was on his enemies, he began to suspect that Hume
and Davenport were united in a conspiracy against him. He feared that
his food was adulterated by servants, his letters were being intercepted by
spies and the house was surrounded by French assassins. And so when he
was lured out of his hideaway, the grotto beneath the terrace in front of
the house, by Darwin, eager to discuss plants and politics with the foreign
visitor, Rousseau rightly suspected a trick and was duly infuriated. Although Darwin's grandson, the founder of evolutionary theory, Charles
Darwin, would later insist that the pair struck up a friendly correspondence, none of their supposed letters have survived. But his British sym-
pathizers should not have been surprised by such apparent ingratitude.
Stirring up trouble was Rousseau's stock in trade.

In the space of sixteen months, in 1761 and 1762, Rousseau had published three very different but pioneering books that were equally acclaimed and condemned throughout the world. His novel, *Julie, or The New Héloïse*, outraged prudish critics with its sensational and sensuous story. Readers loved it, and the book became the best-selling novel of the eighteenth century. He followed his success as a novelist with two revolutionary books, *The Social Contract*, published in April 1762, and *Émile, or on Education*, which appeared a month later. Both provoked furious debates and sowed profound changes that reverberate still. The founding fathers of American independence would draw inspiration from *The Social Contract* while the leaders of the French Revolution would likewise be fired by its ideals. Arguably, *Émile* would launch even more far-reaching change.

As a child, Rousseau had received no formal education until the age of ten. As a tutor to a wealthy family, while wandering through Europe in his youth, Rousseau had proved a dismal failure. As a father, who gave up all five children he had sired with Thérèse Levasseur to the Paris foundling hospital, he had abdicated all parental responsibility. Yet Rousseau's views on education were both revolutionary and pivotal. *Émile* has been described as the most important work on education since Plato's *Republic*; a modern educationalist has argued that all writing on progressive education since *Émile* is a series of footnotes. Written in the form of a novel, in Rousseau's characteristically direct style, the book outlines an ideal education for the pupil Émile from cradle to adulthood as narrated by his tutor.

In *Émile* Rousseau rejects both the prevailing religious doctrine that children are born with original sin and the more modern view, outlined by John Locke in 1693, that at birth children's minds resemble "white Paper, or Wax, to be moulded and fashioned as one pleases." Instead, Rousseau argues that children are born essentially good but are corrupted by the influences of civilization. In a typically arresting first line, Rousseau announces: "Everything is good as it leaves the hands of the author of things; everything degenerates in the hands of man." Education, Rousseau argues, should be the means of protecting and nurturing those original innocent instincts against society's vices. To achieve such protection,

Rousseau advocates a "natural education" that places the child at the center of the educational process. Entirely at odds with the disciplinarian methods in use in classrooms across Europe at the time—where children learned by rote and by rod—Rousseau proposed a free and unconstrained upbringing in which the child learns at a natural pace through play and discovery.

In accordance with this "back to nature" approach, the infant Émile is breast-fed by his mother, not wet-nursed by strangers; he is left free to kick and squirm, not encased in swaddling bands; and he is tutored by his father rather than hired teachers—although Rousseau accepted that a trusted friend could be substituted since fathers might find themselves rather too busy to become full-time tutors. As a boy—and Rousseau's program was aimed exclusively at boys—Émile grows up in the countryside in the manner of a peasant. He is nurtured lovingly, never scolded and allowed to roam free, but at the same time he is trained to withstand hardships like hunger, cold and fatigue, allowed to fall and hurt himself and taught to fear nothing.

Growing up happy and carefree, despite his bumps and bruises, Émile learns through his mistakes and from his tutor's patient responses to his inevitable questions. There should be no verbal lessons, no attempts to impose ideas through reason and emphatically no books, says Rousseau, insisting: "I hate books." Émile only learns to read when he finds it necessary to do so—and not before the age of twelve. Instead he works out the orbit of the earth by watching the sun rise and set and understands the position of the stars by getting lost in the woods. He grasps geography by making maps of where he lives and physics by playing with magnets. In his teens, Émile learns a useful trade, as an apprentice carpenter, and travels, in order to see the world's vices for himself. Religion should play no part in a child's education, Rousseau says, so Émile should simply be free to adopt whichever religion he chooses based on his own reasoning when he reaches eighteen. Finally, at the age of twenty, Émile is ready to enter society and—crucially—to find a partner to share his worldview. So Émile begins a search for a simple, artless, country maid whom he can educate to suit her allotted role.

Although *Émile* was not the first parenting manual, it has probably proved the most influential. Nobody before—or perhaps since—had gone so far in placing the child at the center of education or advocating a "learning by doing" approach designed to suit a child's natural development. Rousseau had kickstarted a debate between huggers and hard-liners, between carrot and stick, which would ricochet down the centuries. His ideas would change not just educational practice but basic ideas about childhood fundamentally and forever.

Although religious zealots—inflamed by the book's rejection of religious teaching—persecuted Rousseau, many more welcomed his visionary ideas on child care and education with feverish intensity. In nurseries across Europe, mothers embraced breast-feeding, fathers abandoned the birch rod and infants sprung free of their swaddling bands like slaves breaking free from their chains. Some parents even determined to follow Rousseau's child-rearing regime to the letter.

The Prince and Princess of Wurtemberg decided to bring up their baby daughter, Sophie, who was born in 1763, precisely according to the plan outlined for Émile—despite her being a girl. The couple and the author exchanged nearly fifty letters over fine points such as teething. At four months little Sophie was bathed each morning in an ice-cold fountain then left outside naked for much of the day. Although it was then October, her parents boasted that baby Sophie rarely cried. In fact she was probably too weak from cold to cry. Ultimately her toughening regime would prove little use; Sophie died at the age of eleven. Another enthusiast, a Swiss banker named Guillaume-François Roussel, banished his five young daughters to live in the woods, barely clothed, to scavenge for nuts and berries. Eager to pay homage to his idol, the banker visited Rousseau during his mountain exile, but Rousseau was so aghast that he packed Roussel home immediately to end the girls' plight.

When *Émile* was published in English in late 1762, the book attracted even more admirers. Having already adopted Locke's progressive views on education, many upper-class parents in England and Ireland were ahead of their continental counterparts in enjoying more affectionate and liberal relationships with their children. Painters, like Joshua Reynolds and Thomas Gainsborough, reflected this shift in sentimental portraits of mothers dandling cherubic infants and groups of children playing together. Joseph Wright, who was friendly with Erasmus Darwin, went one step further and depicted children watching scientific experiments more or less as equals alongside adults. In one painting, *An Experiment on a Bird in the Air Pump,* he portrayed girls and boys watching a demonstration of a bird, a white cockatoo, being deprived of air in a vacuum flask with a mixture of fascination and horror. There was no shortage, therefore, of followers eager to put Rousseau's ideas into action in Britain.

Richard Davenport, who had placed Wootton Hall at Rousseau's disposal, eagerly adopted his approach in educating his orphaned grandchildren, six-year-old Phoebe and five-year-old Davies. The experiment had mixed results. While Phoebe would exchange friendly letters with Rousseau for many years, Davies regretted his lack of formal education so much that he refused to allow Rousseau's name to be mentioned. Rather more successfully, Emily Kildare, the Duchess of Leinster, set up a little school for her children adjoining the family's seaside villa near Dublin and employed a tutor to teach them à la Rousseau. In this seeming paradise, the Kildare children—eventually numbering seventeen—swam in the sea, grew vegetables in the garden and made hay in the fields.

But nobody in Britain was more enthusiastic about the Rousseau method than Richard Lovell Edgeworth.

While Rousseau was hiding from imagined French assassins in his Staffordshire grotto in 1766, Edgeworth devoured *Émile.* The following year, as Rousseau fled back to France under a false name, Edgeworth resolved to apply the educational system to his three-year-old son, Dick. "His Emile had made a great impression upon my young mind," Edgeworth wrote. "His work had then all the power of novelty, as well as all the charms of eloquence; and when I compared the many plausible ideas it contains, with the obvious deficiencies and absurdities, that I saw in the treatment of children in almost every family with which I was acquainted, I determined to make a fair trial of Rousseau's system."

It took Edgeworth little time to persuade his wife, Anna Maria, to comply with the plan. After four years of marriage to Edgeworth she knew better than to oppose any experimental idea. Having frequently been left alone with the infant Dick while her husband sought adult company in London and Lichfield, Anna Maria had spent much of her time with her sisters at her parents' home in Black Bourton. Now, however, she was forced to give up her only son to his father's bold experiment. For, as

Rousseau specified, the best tutor was the child's father. But if his wife was pushed out of the picture, Edgeworth made sure to involve his new friend Day.

Introduced to Rousseau's ideas by Edgeworth, Day was an instant convert. Here at last was the overarching philosophy that he had been seeking in his studies at Oxford—a modern interpretation of the ancient ideals that he so revered. With his passion for social justice, Day was completely in sympathy with Rousseau's call to liberty and equality—for men at least. At the same time Day agreed wholeheartedly that natural country life was superior to the corrupt trappings of fashionable urban society. Just like the fictional Émile, Day had envisaged living in a rustic haven devoted to doing good. And when Day came to the pages that described Émile's search for a wife to share his retreat, he knew at last he had found what he was looking for. For while Edgeworth seized Rousseau's *Émile* as the sure route to bringing up his young heir, Day now decided that he would use Rousseau's educational system to create his perfect wife.

That year, in the summer of 1767, Day left Oxford without taking his degree. Now nineteen he knew he would soon inherit his fortune and would never need a profession in order to earn a living. And with plenty of time at his disposal, Day threw himself into Edgeworth's project to educate Dick. Taking Dick's education as a template, Day could practice for educating his future spouse.

Since he was already three, young Dick had missed out on the vital early years of Rousseau's natural approach. It is not known whether Dick had been wet-nursed or breast-fed by his mother, but he had obviously learned to crawl, walk and talk without the benefit of Rousseau's guiding hand. Fortunately, the boy had grown up mainly in the countryside—in line with Rousseau's preference—having spent his first year with his parents in Ireland before they settled in Berkshire. But with his father absent from home for much of his childhood to date, Dick had been pampered and indulged by his "soft-hearted mother and tender aunts." Nevertheless, Edgeworth was determined that from now on Dick should grow up like the natural child envisaged in *Émile*. And so for the next five years, from ages three to eight, Dick was to become the subject of an extraordinary educational experiment.

From the beginning Edgeworth embarked on his child-rearing project in precisely the same manner that he launched into creating his sailing carriage or his sporty phaeton or any number of other inventions that emerged from his workshop. He took the materials at hand and set about shaping his new creation with a tireless vigor. With his much-thumbed copy of *Émile* in one hand and his toddler son in the other, and Day watching over his shoulder, Edgeworth followed Rousseau's program with a fiercely literal interpretation.

Having been dressed in petticoats in the manner of all Georgian boys before they were "breeched" at the age of six or seven, Dick was now put into a sleeveless jacket and "trowsers" without stockings or shoes. Having been petted and cosseted indoors by his mother and aunts, now Dick was let loose into the gardens and countryside surrounding his Hare Hatch home. Running barefoot across the common and through the woods and fields of Berkshire, Dick was free to roam and explore at will. With his father's blessing, the boy was encouraged to play outside in all weathers, to splash in puddles and to jump into snowdrifts, to climb trees and to clamber into chalk pits, with never a word of rebuke. There were no restraints, no rules, no routines and no punishments, no matter what Dick did.

It was a child's dream—indeed it was very much the carefree existence that Edgeworth himself had enjoyed in the Irish countryside before his parents changed direction—and a mother's nightmare. As his father encouraged Dick to indulge every whim and brave every peril, his unhappy mother could only stand by and watch helplessly. For, as Edgeworth insisted, "the body and mind of my son were to be left as much as possible to the education of nature and of accident."

It was not all fun and games, of course. There were hardships to bear and hard knocks to withstand. Just as Rousseau recommended that his Émile should enjoy the bounties of nature, so he must endure the miseries nature could unleash too. Dick therefore had to be inured to hunger, thirst and tiredness, to suffer pain and to withstand extremes of climate. Likewise he had to be conditioned to be afraid of nothing. Rousseau proposed that a child must be introduced early to darkness, loud noises and strange creatures, such as spiders. With his practical, no-nonsense manner, this approach appealed to Edgeworth, although he did not record precisely how he accustomed Dick to creepy crawlies and night terrors.

Naturally, of course, books played no part in Dick's educational program, since Rousseau had pronounced reading "the plague of childhood" and books "the instrument of greatest misery." Only if Dick himself picked up a book and demanded to learn how to read should he be taught, the master had decreed. It was this aspect of the Rousseau creed that Edgeworth found hardest to accept. Having himself learned to read by the age of five and enjoyed books avidly all his life, he worried that Dick would suffer by this lack of formal teaching. But Day, Dick's eager assistant tutor, was quick to reassure him. "Never trouble yourself about Dick's reading and writing," he wrote in one letter, "he will learn it sooner or later if you let him alone." Devoid of books, therefore, Dick must learn from observation and experience.

So Dick grew up brave and tough, bright and inquisitive under his father's indulgent eye. "He had all the virtues of a child bred in the hut of a savage," wrote Edgeworth, "and all the knowledge of *things*, which could well be acquired at an early age by a boy bred in civilized society." Dick, of course, had more opportunities to learn about "*things*" than most children. Standing on tiptoe beside his father's elbow at his workbench, Dick could watch wide-eyed as his father constructed his latest magical contraption or performed astounding tricks with magnets. The crowded workshop with its vibrating horse and half-built carriages was a perfect playroom, a small child's paradise. There was always something new to see.

Inspired by conversations with Darwin, who was in correspondence with the Scottish engineer James Watt, Edgeworth was currently engrossed in building a wagon powered by steam, effectively a prototype train, and had fathomed the principles of a tank with caterpillar tracks. In 1768, Darwin told a friend, Edgeworth had "nearly completed a Waggon drawn by Fire—and a Walking Table which will carry 40 Men." Observing these fire-breathing wonders, Dick became fascinated by mechanics and skilled at invention. He would later become one of the youngest-ever recipients of a medal from the Society for the Encouragement of Arts, Manufactures and Commerce, winning a silver medal when he was just fourteen.

And yet, to Edgeworth's bewilderment, young Dick proved totally impervious to authority. Free to do exactly as he pleased, indulged in his toddler tantrums and handed everything he demanded, the "child bred in the hut of a savage" was becoming a perfect monster. There was only one person whom Dick felt any inclination to obey, and that was his father. Having spent barely any time in Edgeworth's presence during his first three years, Dick was now reveling in the full glory of his brilliant father's undivided attention.

Although Edgeworth was surprised that Dick's inborn goodness should express itself in such a rebellious manner, he plowed on regardless with Rousseau's program, with Thomas Day as his chief cheerleader. Just like other parents who were valiantly attempting to apply the Rousseau method with literal exactness, Edgeworth was discovering not only that his son failed to match his particular vision of perfection but that the creature he was bringing to life was proving almost impossible to control.

Rousseau himself was generally bemused when zealous parents tried to apply his educational system to living subjects and professed himself largely indifferent to their success or failure. He did discuss baby Sophie's welfare in letters exchanged with the Wurtembergs, and he would later take pride in Phoebe Davenport's progress. But when other enthusiasts wrote to him for endorsement or advice he responded by saying that *Émile* was simply a philosophical text supporting his doctrine that humans were born naturally good, and not a practical manual for child rearing. "I cannot believe that you took the book which bears this name for a real treatise on education," he exclaimed to one puzzled parent. "You are quite right to say it is impossible to create an Emile." And in truth his response was perfectly just since the book is best understood as a general theory with illustrative examples. Taken as a broad approach toward a child-centered education based on learning through discovery, Rousseau's treatise was—and is—a powerful force for good; taken literally it could become a recipe for producing little savages.

Many of those watching Dick's laissez-faire education from the sidelines did their best to warn his father of impending disaster. Edgeworth met with "opposition" from friends and relatives and "ridicule" from "all quarters," he admitted. But if ever Edgeworth voiced any doubts about the practicality of the system, Day always encouraged him to continue with it. For even as Edgeworth was beginning to perceive some flaws in a literal interpretation of the Rousseau approach, Day was becoming more and more enthusiastic.

The educational program had been progressing for about a year when Edgeworth decided to take Dick on a visit to the family seat in Ireland. Naturally he invited Day, his assistant tutor, to join them. Still thwarted in his desire to travel the Continent by his stepfather, Day readily agreed. He had scoured the West Country and Wales for a suitable candidate for his wife-training scheme—his "gentle Lady of the West"—but perhaps, he considered, he had not been looking far enough to the west. Setting off in early summer 1768, the trio left behind Anna Maria, who had given birth to a daughter, baptized Maria, at Black Bourton, on January 1 that year. There would be no attempt to subvert the education of Maria Edgeworth, the future novelist, to her lasting gratitude. With Edgeworth at the reins of his customized phaeton and Day and four-year-old Dick seated behind, the trio hared off on the main road north for Chester to embark for Ireland.

Eager to provide some light entertainment to break the tedium of the road trip, Edgeworth suggested a practical joke based on the Restoration comedy *The Beaux' Stratagem,* in which two young men attempt to ensnare an heiress by posing as a wealthy gentleman and his servant. Day, it was agreed, would pretend to be "a very *odd* gentleman"—a role that did not demand great acting skills—and Dick—in an equally undemanding role—would play his son, "a most extraordinary child." Edgeworth, meanwhile, would pretend to be a servant who was slimily obsequious to his master's face but rude and arrogant behind his back. In the stage play, the two young rakes enact their deceit when they break their journey at an inn in Lichfield. In Edgeworth's version, the curtain rose on the farce when the three travelers stopped at an inn in the town of Eccleshall in Staffordshire.

Thundering up to the door of the inn, Edgeworth screeched to a halt and employed his innovatory device to release the horses from the carriage with a nonchalant flick of the wrist. As a crowd gathered to ogle the strange vehicle and its equally strange passengers—"sitting composedly in the open carriage without horses"—Edgeworth lifted down the peculiarly attired Dick—in his trousers and bare feet—and then gave his arm to Day. Gleefully entering into the spirit of the jest, the fearless Dick performed several acrobatic feats, such as leaping from the carriage into his father's open arms, as the curious crowd grew.

Strutting into the inn, Edgeworth ordered a meager supper for his master and a lavish spread for himself. But just as Edgeworth was devouring his banquet in the kitchen, the ruse was exposed. A familiar voice hailed him from the dining room, and Edgeworth turned in embarrassment to see Erasmus Darwin, who had arrived at the inn with his friend John Whitehurst, a clockmaker from Derby. The game was up. A sheepish Edgeworth had to confess the whole scam, and the two parties joined company for a more conventional meal in the dining room.

As Edgeworth, Darwin and Whitehurst launched into an animated discussion on the latest developments in mechanics, Day sat silently nursing his water and frugal supper. Making no attempt to join the conversation, since the topic was not to his taste, he remained aloof throughout the meal. Gregarious and effusive as ever, Darwin assumed that Edgeworth's gruff young friend was truly the misanthrope he had played in the drama. It was only when the diners got up to leave and the conversation turned to a more philosophical topic that Day suddenly sprang to life and launched into one of his monologues. Darwin was impressed by the knowledge and eloquence of the nineteen-year-old youth and extended an open invitation to visit him in Lichfield. A new recruit had been drawn into the orbit of the Lunar group.

For now, Edgeworth, Day and Dick pressed on to Ireland. When the three weary travelers finally dismounted from the phaeton in front of Edgeworthstown House, the family's mansion on the edge of the village of Edgeworthstown in County Longford, they created quite a spectacle—certainly in the eyes of Edgeworth's reserved father and sophisticated sister. Having last seen Dick as a one-year-old, they discovered that he had turned into an unruly, spoiled little boy who answered to none but his father. Returning home after more than three years' absence, Edgeworth was evidently as unconventional and rebellious as ever. And then there was the pocked, shy, ungainly and disheveled youth whom Edgeworth brought with him. Of the three odd houseguests it was Day, of course, who would create the most upsets.

Quite why Day came to the conclusion during the course of that summer that Margaret might slip smoothly into the role of his ideal wife is beyond comprehension. With her aristocratic manner, her busy social calendar and her taste for fine clothes and fine food, Margaret was not only the complete opposite of the humble country maiden he had been seeking, she was also utterly different from the meek and simple girl that Rousseau had conjured as a soulmate for Émile. Nonetheless, with Rousseau's *Émile* as his trusty manual, Day came to believe that he could mold Margaret to suit her allotted role.

Rousseau had recognized as he wrote *Émile* that the free-thinking young man he created would need a very special partner to share his life. In typically contradictory style, he warns his readers not to imagine "a model of perfection who cannot exist" and then he tantalizes them by doing just that. "It is not good for man to be alone," he writes, in a direct reference to the story of Adam and Eve in the Book of Genesis, then adds, "We have promised him a companion. She has to be given to him." And with a playful nod to his fellow philosophes, he names his ideal woman Sophie, from the Greek word for wisdom.

In the quest to find Sophie, Rousseau sends Émile into polite urban society, to spend a year amid the despised temptations of Paris, before he airily reveals "we have looked for her where I was quite sure she was not to be found." Instead Émile must scour the countryside to track down Sophie. Tramping over hills and fields on foot, Émile finally finds the girl of his dreams living with her parents in a modest mountainside house in the heart of provincial France. "Let us give Émile his Sophie," announces Rousseau. "Let us bring this sweet girl to life." Four years younger than Émile, sixteen-year-old Sophie belongs to a well-born family living a simple but virtuous pastoral life. Bright but not overly intelligent, Sophie is sweet-natured, hardworking and chaste. Pleasing to look at but not exceptionally beautiful, Sophie dresses modestly, sings sweetly, cooks plainly and dances tolerably well. Émile, of course, falls in love with her immediately. But before she can assume her destined role in life—as a household drudge in a country hovel devoted to her husband's whims—Sophie obviously requires a customized education of her own.

Rousseau has no hesitation in asserting that women are born equal to men. "In everything not connected with sex the woman is man," he declares. "She has the same organs, the same needs, the same faculties." Indeed his own preference for intelligent and forthright women to whom he could kneel in happy subservience suggests he regarded women as superior beings. But in the fictional world that Émile and Sophie inhabit, women are created only to please men. No matter that they might be just as clever and capable as boys, girls must be shaped from infancy to fulfill their subservient role.

So while Rousseau outlines the most radical and progressive education for young Émile, he proposes the most banal and regressive education for Sophie—even by the standards of his most reactionary critics. Instead of being encouraged to run free and indulge her curiosity like Émile, little Sophie plays passively indoors with her dolls, for, according to Rousseau, "the time will come when she will be her own doll." Instead of learning through discovery, Sophie is taught to draw, sew, count and—at a later stage even than Émile—to read, since "almost all little girls learn to read and write with repugnance."

But the most important lesson that girls must learn as they grow up is to submit their will entirely to male figures of authority. Sophie must therefore get used to performing whatever pointless chore her tutor might suggest and then break off in the middle whenever he instructs her to do a different task. "From this habitual constraint comes the docility that women need all their lives," Rousseau explains, since once Sophie is married "she ought to learn early to endure even injustice and to bear a husband's wrongs without complaining."

Not surprisingly, Rousseau's antiquated ideas about women met with fierce opposition from some of the leading women of his day. The poet and socialite Frances Greville praised *Émile*, a friend reported, "but she and several others don't like what he says of women, nor his notions about them." Mary Wollstonecraft would later condemn Rousseau's ideas in her pioneering manifesto *A Vindication of the Rights of Woman* in 1792. Girls

were conditioned to play with dolls—it was nurture not nature—
Wollstonecraft would insist: "As for Rousseau's remarks . . . that they have
naturally, that is from birth, independent of education, a fondness for dolls,
dressing, and talking—they are so puerile as not to merit a serious refuta-
tion. . . . Girls and boys, in short, would play harmlessly together, if the
distinction of sex was not inculcated long before nature makes any difference." Tellingly, most parents who were inspired to educate their daughters
according to Rousseau's ideas chose to emulate the education of Émile
rather than Sophie. But for Day, it all made perfect sense.

As Day pored over Rousseau's words, suddenly everything became clear.
With his contempt for luxury and fashion, his infatuation with peasant
life, his preference for washing in streams and his fondness for roaming
the countryside on foot, Day realized that he was the incarnation of Émile.
And now that he was about to turn twenty, the age that Émile discovers
his Sophie, the time was right for him to meet his ideal woman to share
his planned life of isolated misery. Raising his eyes from the pages, his
gaze alighted on Margaret. All she needed was a little instruction to fulfill
the desired role. Margaret, of course, had quite other ideas.

As the unlikely romance lurched from comedy to melodrama over the
ensuing months, Day bared his feelings in a long letter to John Bicknell.
"I have been disappointed in a Manner to a feeling Heart the most dread-
ful," he wailed when Margaret called the whole thing off in September.
He had been deceived because "I loved an imaginary Being," he wrote
with uncustomary insight. In his trough of despair he even considered remaining a bachelor for life since, he noted, he could father children out of
wedlock—"& their Illegitimacy will have no Effect upon their Rational-
ity"—and satisfy his physical urges elsewhere. As Day put it, "if the whole
female Sex cannot furnish one single rational Woman, I must make use
of them in that Manner for which alone Nature has perhaps intended."

Yet there was a third way. And in his highly revealing letter to Bicknell,
Day first unfolded his startling plan to create the perfect wife. Speaking
of Margaret, Day wrote: "This Lady was brought up in the midst of the
World; early introduc'd to its Customs, attach'd to its Follys; she is disgusted, or believes herself so; yet in all Probability there are some Prejudices which stick so deep as never to be eradicated." Since it seemed,

therefore, impossible to bend a woman brought up within polite society to fit the required role, he now proposed to "try another Experiment" and groom a likely young girl for the task.

That this was not just a rhetorical argument or a flight of fancy, Day made plain. "There is a little Girl of about thirteen, upon whose Mind I shall have it in my Power to make the above mention'd Experiment," he revealed to Bicknell. "Her Understanding is naturally good I believe, her Temper remarkably tender & affectionate; she is yet innocent, & unprejudic'd; she has seen nothing of the World, & is unattach'd to it." Precisely who this girl was, who was so detached from the outside world, and how Day believed he possessed such power over her fate, he did not vouchsafe.

Thinking through the practicalities of his scheme, Day asked Bicknell whether he thought it might be possible "to prevent the Impressions of Prejudice & Folly in a Mind like this?" He added: "Will it be possible to fortify it in such a Manner, that the Pleasures of the World will make no Impressions upon it, because they are irrational." And crucially he wanted to know: "Will it be impossible entirely to exclude the Idea of Love," since "Love I am firmly convinc'd is the Effect of Prejudice & Imagination; a rational Mind is incapable of it, at least in any great Degree." Evidently Day desired Bicknell's opinion not just as a man of the world but as a man of law, for he pressed: "Is my scheme practicable? If practicable by what Means?" Frustrated and impatient, he demanded an answer by the time he returned to England.

Finally, on the last sheet of his eleven-page letter, Day asked Bicknell to perform two mysterious tasks before his return to London. For the first of these "Commissions" he wanted Bicknell to visit his saddler, in Holborn, and arrange for "the Saddle & proper Appendages" to be sent to his home at Barehill. This was evidently a contraption he had already ordered—probably a pillion saddle to enable him to bear away his young girl in the manner of a medieval knight. The second request was to call on Day's tailor, also in Holborn, and order two new suits to be made and sent to Barehill. According to Day's precise instructions these were: "One a Green with light Gold Embroidery, about the Button Holes, as light as possible; the other a plain white or lightish colour'd Suit, Coat, Waistcoat & Breeches, & also an embroider'd Waistcoat adapted to them, as free from tawdriness, & Frippery as possible."

Given Day's scorn for new clothes of any description, especially with such dandified details as embroidery, this was quite an astonishing mission, as Day himself acknowledged. "You are surpriz'd at this, but I do assure you I have no Reason for having laced cloaths, but to convince myself, & other People I have [reasons] which make me wear plain ones." Whether this order was a last-ditch attempt to impress Margaret or a calculated move to impress figures in authority over his teenage nymph, Day did not reveal.

Naturally Day divulged nothing of his bizarre scheme to train a teenage bride to Margaret, or indeed to her brother. When Margaret suddenly decided to hedge her bets and send Day home with an agreement to marry each other unless either found an alternative by the following summer, Day hurriedly buried his plan. Sailing back to England with his expectations high in October he seemed to have forgotten the idea entirely.

Back in London, Day moved into lodgings with Bicknell in the vicinity of Middle Temple and applied himself to his law books through the winter of 1768 to 1769. In his spare time he cemented his new acquaintance with Erasmus Darwin and was welcomed into the circle of Darwin's scintillating Lunar friends.

Day might well have accompanied Edgeworth on one of his excursions to the Midlands in 1769. On one of these visits Edgeworth decided to test-drive his latest mode of transport: a one-wheeled chaise pulled by a single horse in which he perched precariously on a low-slung seat about two feet above the ground with his feet placed either side on wooden boards that collapsed upward whenever they met any obstacle. He had fashioned this latest chariot so that he could speed along the narrow country roads and even through water—with his legs protected by leather attachments shaped like bellows—looking for all the world like a future Hells Angel astride a prototype Harley-Davidson as he startled sheep and scattered ducks.

Stepping into the sparkling spotlight shed by the Lunar circle, Day was its newest, youngest and—without doubt—its oddest member. First formed in the late 1760s, the group was initially a loose network of like-minded men who met to discuss advances and perform experiments in mechanics, chemistry, medicine, geology and a diverse range of other areas grouped under the term "natural philosophy"—or what would later become known as science.

Forming a twin nucleus with Darwin at the center of this circle was Matthew Boulton, the son of a metalworker, who had left school at fourteen and built up a vast manufactory at Soho, near Birmingham, producing luxury silverware and metal trinkets. Both loud, generous, genial characters, Darwin and Boulton gradually drew others into their orbit. An early member was the Staffordshire potter Josiah Wedgwood, who had painstakingly accumulated a small fortune through hard work at his growing business. Yet it was William Small, a quiet, retiring Scottish physician, who had recently set up in medical practice in Birmingham after teaching mathematics in America—including to a young Thomas Jefferson—who formed the linchpin of the group; effectively he became its secretary.

Later this core was joined by James Watt, busy trying to improve the design of steam engines in Glasgow, and James Keir, another Scot and a fellow medical student with Darwin who had just moved to Lichfield after ten years in the army. With their diverse backgrounds, interests and political views, this group of talented and gregarious men would become pioneers in assorted scientific fields and cheerleaders of the Industrial Revolution in the Midlands. A recent recruit into this ingenious community, Edgeworth memorably described the group as "such a society, as few men have had the good fortune to live with; such an assemblage of friends, as fewer still have had the happiness to possess, and keep through life."

The Lunar gatherings provided a lively diversion while Day looked forward confidently to his nuptials with Margaret. His friends shared his grief, but not his surprise, when the wedding plans were called off in spring 1769. Dr. Small, in particular, who was nearly a generation older than Day, sympathized deeply with him and took a fatherly interest in his marital hopes. Margaret, however, had no regrets. A year later she would marry an Anglo-Irish army officer, John Ruxton, who shared her tastes in fine living.

For Day, if nothing else, Margaret's letter, which put an end to his marital hopes, confirmed his opinion that the entire female population was fickle. Now that he was convinced that he would never find the woman that he sought within contemporary society, there was plainly no alternative but to create her for himself. And so as he approached his twenty-first birthday in June he returned to the daring scheme he had sketched out to Bicknell and made arrangements to put his plan into action. Just as Edgeworth was attempting to produce his own version of Émile, so Day would groom his own Sophie.

It was a cold, wet summer with frequent squalls and thundery showers. But the rain did nothing to dampen Day's enthusiasm. On June 22, 1769, when he turned twenty-one, Day gained both his fortune and his independence. He was now master of the house and estate at Barehill, and he took control of a comfortable income of £1,200 a year—today worth nearly £200,000, or $324,000. Out of this fortune, Day had to pay his mother her annual widow's pension of £300. Since she, or more likely his stepfather Phillips, had complained this was insufficient, he increased her allowance to £400 and allowed them both to continue living at Barehill. But more important than his financial independence, Day was now free of any interference from his mother or stepfather. He was the author of his own destiny, and he lost no time in putting his audacious plan into action.

First he needed a collaborator to help him carry out his stratagem. Since the scheme was highly unethical if not downright illegal, he reasoned that a lawyer might prove useful. He dismissed the idea of telling Edgeworth, who was likewise studying law at Middle Temple inn; Edgeworth's status as a married man would later prove vital, but for now he was kept entirely in the dark. Instead Day asked John Bicknell, his closest friend and fellow lodger, to help enact his experiment. Having studied law for a full eight years, Bicknell was finally on the point of qualifying as a barrister. Sworn to secrecy, he readily agreed to the plan. Now all Day needed was to find a suitable young girl.

In licentious Georgian London there was no shortage of pliable young girls in search of a kindly male benefactor. Wide-eyed country maidens stepped down from the coaches at London staging inns every day naïvely seeking their fortunes. Often as young as twelve or thirteen, they made easy pickings for pimps and brothel madams eager to lure them into a career in the buoyant Georgian sex industry. Few people batted an eyelid at the custom of single, or married, men of means maintaining such a teenage mistress in a convenient metropolitan hideaway. But this would not do for Day.

Day, of course, had set his sights on finding a simple, pure, innocent maid unsullied by the vices of urban life and untainted by the ideas of contemporary society. He wanted to be certain of her virginity; it was unthinkable that she might have been seduced by a lascivious rake or a country plowboy before he had the chance to exact his marital privileges. She should be physically healthy and hardy enough to withstand his planned lifestyle in cold, comfortless austerity. She must be young enough to comply with his training without question or resistance, yet old enough so that he would not need to wait too long before they could lawfully wed. With parental consent, girls could marry from the age of twelve; boys from fourteen. Obviously, however, he did not want any meddlesome parents withholding consent or asking awkward questions. Nor did he want to embark on his project in the full glare of gossipy London. It was a tall order to find a girl who would satisfy such an exacting list of specifications. But Day knew exactly where to look.

A few days after his birthday, in the last week of June, Day set out through the driving rain with his trusty friend Bicknell in tow. With the long summer holidays stretching ahead, Bicknell entered into the jaunt with enthusiasm. The pair traveled north on the muddy roads for two or three days, most probably on horseback, stopping overnight on the way. At last they arrived at the little market town of Shrewsbury in Shropshire. Nestling near the border with Wales and almost encircled by the River Severn, the compact walled town provided a pleasant setting for its prosperous residents. Here the two young men crossed the Severn, scaled a winding lane and arrived at the door of a fine three-story, red-brick mansion.

Built as a country branch of the Foundling Hospital in London, the Orphan Hospital at Shrewsbury enjoyed a commanding view of the river as it wound around the town below. The orphanage had opened six years previously to accommodate the overflow of abandoned babies then being deposited at the doors of the charity's London headquarters. Surrounded by fields and orchards, the vast building housed more than 300 children—most of them girls.

Viewed from the town, the imposing mansion presented an elegant façade, but inside the decor was plain and the furnishings simple as befitted its lowly occupants. Yet for all its utilitarian uniformity, the orphanage provided a caring regime where the children were better fed and better treated than many of their young counterparts struggling to survive in the harsh outside world of overcrowded cities and impoverished villages. Taught to read and to do simple sums but not to write, most of the children were being trained in spinning and weaving in the orphanage's own woolen manufactory to prepare them for an apprenticeship in the mills of the nearby Midlands and North. Others learned household skills in the laundries and kitchens in readiness for jobs in domestic service.

At its peak, in 1766, the Shrewsbury orphanage had housed nearly 600 boys and girls, in segregated dormitories and classrooms, looked after by more than forty staff. But since the London charity had closed its doors to abandoned babies in 1760 when its money ran out, and had subsequently increased pressure on its branch hospitals to apprentice those remaining orphans, the numbers had rapidly dwindled. Now only 357 children remained in the Shrewsbury home, and these were being parceled out to apprenticeships as fast as the governors could process them.

Only a few weeks before Day's arrival, the London office had ordered staff at Shrewsbury to send off 100 boys by wagon to apprenticeships in Yorkshire. With nimble boys in constant demand by the woolen manufacturers, girls now outnumbered boys in Shrewsbury by six to one. Acknowledging that the "girls will be harder to be placed out properly" the London office reminded the Shrewsbury governors of "the Care which *should* be taken in the having proper Characters of the Persons to whom Children are placed out."

Drawn from the local gentry and town dignitaries, and all of them volunteers, the Shrewsbury governors took immense pride in the children they had nurtured since they were babies and their various achievements as they grew up. Ordinarily, therefore, they paid meticulous attention to scrutinizing prospective employers before signing over their charges to apprenticeships and maintained a close watch on their welfare after they left the orphanage. Earlier in 1769, the governors had prosecuted an employer who had tied a boy by his neck to a bedpost and beat him so badly that a piece of his ear was torn off. Occasionally there were even instances of sexual abuse, and the governors tackled these just as severely. But given the relentless pressure from London to dispatch the orphans quickly and the voracious demand of the mill owners during the course of 1769, it was scarcely surprising if they were sometimes a little lax in their oversight of their wards.

First impressions spoke volumes in Georgian society. And so when two well-spoken and self-assured young lawyers turned up at the orphanage doors in late June they were warmly welcomed inside. When the men explained that they wanted to take a young girl to be apprenticed as a maid for a friend, the Shrewsbury officials readily agreed. Amid the chaos of packing 100 boys off to Yorkshire, they were naturally eager to find a place for one of their surplus girls. Without hesitation the two men were invited to inspect a lineup of likely candidates.

As he walked up and down the parade of girls standing silently side by side in their identical brown woolen dresses, white cotton aprons and white linen caps, Day was bewildered by the choice. Which of these prepubescent girls could be molded under his careful touch to make a perfect wife? And so it was Bicknell who pointed out the slim and pretty girl with the auburn ringlets and brown eyes. Later acquaintances would describe her as "beautiful" with "chestnut tresses" and dark eyes "expressive of sweetness" fringed with long lashes. Happy to defer to his friend's superior knowledge of the female sex, Day concurred with the choice. Her name was Ann Kingston, and she was twelve.

Abandoned at the gates of the London Foundling Hospital soon after her birth, most probably because of illegitimacy and almost certainly in poverty, Ann had been brought up to accept the disgrace of her past and thank God for her salvation. Like most of the orphans raised on their frugal diet, she had grown up small and slender. But since she had survived a barrage of childhood diseases that had sent weaker individuals to their graves, she was tough and hardy too. Trained in expectation of a life of domestic servitude, she was adept at sewing, cleaning and other household chores and thanks to lessons in the classroom she had learned to read if not to write. Schooled in humility, unsullied by society, she was the perfect subject for Day's experiment.

Satisfied with his choice, Day provided the necessary details to complete the transaction. He informed the orphanage secretary, Samuel Magee, that he wanted to take the girl as a maid to work in the country house of a married friend near London. This last factor was significant since Foundling Hospital regulations stipulated that girls should only be apprenticed into the household of a married man. It was, of course, a lie. Although Magee had no cause to doubt Day's word, it was nevertheless highly irregular to sanction an apprenticeship to an unknown man, particularly one who lived so many miles distant. If a tailor or blacksmith from a nearby village had put forward such a request his credentials would have been thoroughly checked. But faced with two prospective lawyers from London, Magee had no qualms about forgoing the usual vetting process. Without further ado, he agreed to bind the twelve-year-old to a married man he had never met for the next nine years of her life. Naturally she had no say in the matter. Leaving the clerks to finalize the paperwork, Day and Bicknell sped back to London, where Day made preparations for his young pupil's arrival.

A few days later, on June 30, Ann Kingston's apprenticeship was approved, along with that of sixteen others, at a meeting of governors in a Shrewsbury coffeehouse. All the other apprenticeships agreed to that day were for typical local trades—weaver, thatcher, shoemaker, tailor—all within a few miles of Shrewsbury. All bar one included the customary payment—£4 with the girls and £3 with the boys—which was given as incentive to their new masters. And yet without a quibble or a query, the Shrewsbury governors confirmed that Ann Kingston should be apprenticed without a fee until the age of twenty-one or until she married—whichever might come sooner—to Richard Lovell Edgeworth Esq. of Kiln Green, Berkshire.

Printed on parchment and sealed with red wax, the indenture contract—which still survives—pledged that Ann "faithfully shall serve in all lawful Businesses according to her Power, Wit, and Ability; and honestly, orderly, and obediently in all Things demean and behave herself towards her said Master." For his part the absent and unknowing Edgeworth was bound to provide his new apprentice with "meet, competent, and sufficient Meat, Drink, and Apparel, Lodging, Washing, and all other Things necessary and fit for an Apprentice." There was nothing in the document to specify how Edgeworth, and more importantly his two representatives, should "demean and behave" themselves.

Bundled up with apprenticeship papers for ten other children, a copy of Ann's indenture would be sent to London the following month. There it would be ratified on October 4 by the charity's General Committee. Whether it was something about the nature of her selection, or the unusual distance to her place of work, or simply the fact that her supposed master was prepared to accept her without the customary £4 payment, out of the eleven apprenticeships considered by the committee that day only Ann's raised an eyebrow. The following day, the London office wrote to ask Magee: "Pray was any thing remarkable in the Girl Ann Kingston no 4579." Harassed by the press of business, Magee answered no.

Long before then, on August 17, Day and Bicknell retraced their steps to Shrewsbury, probably with the empty pillion saddle at the ready, to sign their names on the approved indenture and claim their prize. Clutching a parcel of new clothes, a Bible, a Book of Common Prayer and a copy of the "Instructions to Apprentices" given to all departing orphans, Ann Kingston walked out of the Shrewsbury orphanage in every expectation that she was about to begin a life of domestic servitude in faraway Berkshire. No doubt she faced the unknown world beyond the orphanage with trepidation. She had no idea how strange that world was about to become. Hoisted up onto the pillion seat behind Thomas Day, she left the orphanage forever. Passing through the orphanage gates the little party headed not for Berkshire, but for London.

FOUR

ANN AND DORCAS

❧ *London, August 1769* ❧

S he had traveled from London to Shrewsbury ten years earlier in a wagon padded with straw, huddled together with seventeen other infants, bawling and sniffling as they jolted over the rough roads. Now she was making the return journey in style in the company of two wealthy young men. With her pretty face and buoyant curls, a twelve-year-old girl on the verge of puberty, she must have attracted some appreciative glances at the stopovers along the way. One look at the two men who were keeping her under intense scrutiny no doubt prompted a few knowing nods.

After the simple formality of institutional life in rural Shropshire, the chaotic clamor of London must have struck Ann Kingston with a resounding shock. With a population of nearly 700,000 the capital boasted more inhabitants than any other city in the world. Although most of its better-off residents would have fled the capital for their summer retreats, the streets were still congested with carriages and farm carts, and the pavements were thronged with pedestrians and vendors. Accustomed to the melodious sounds of the countryside, Ann would have been deafened by the thunder of coach wheels, the yells of men bearing sedan chairs and the bellows of livestock being driven to market. Used to the fresh country air, she must have found the stench of rubbish piled on corners and excrement rotting in the gutters at the height of summer overpowering. Yet infinitely more surprising than the strangeness of the city unfolding before her was the curious young man who appraised her with such close attention.

Arriving in the capital toward the end of August, Day presented Ann to her supposed new master, Richard Lovell Edgeworth. Although Edgeworth was as much in ignorance about her position in his household as she was herself, he did not seem unduly worried by the sudden responsibility for a twelve-year-old orphan: "I had such well merited confidence in Mr. Day, that I felt no repugnance against his being entrusted with the care of a girl, who had been thus put incidentally under my protection." After all, as Edgeworth would have to keep reminding himself, Day was "the most virtuous human being" he had ever known.

Yet although Ann was now legally under Edgeworth's guardianship, she did not move into his Berkshire home to begin work as a maid nor did she remain under his supervision. Instead, Day placed her in some discreet lodgings rented from a widow in the labyrinth of courtyards off Chancery Lane, conveniently at the heart of London's legal district and just a few minutes' walk from the rooms that he shared with Bicknell. Beyond the attentions of the widow, it seems unlikely that Ann had a chaperone. Then even though he had flouted the Foundling Hospital's regulations, Day brazenly attended the next meeting of the charity's general committee—its central management body—on August 30 when he made a generous donation of £50 (about £7,500 or $12,000 today) and was duly elected a governor. Whether he viewed this donation as fair payment for the orphan he had acquired or believed that becoming a governor placed him above suspicion is unknown. Having salved his conscience—or covered his tracks—Day could now begin to groom his future wife.

Lessons started immediately. Neglecting his tedious law studies, Day applied himself with enthusiasm to the far more exciting business of playing tutor to his young captive. They had grown up in completely different worlds. She had been born into poverty, marked with the stain of illegitimacy and schooled to work for her living in austere and lowly surroundings. He had been born into riches, brought up to a life of privilege and taught to expect everything that he desired. Yet he had every confidence that he could transform his illiterate and uncultured orphan into the clever and compliant woman he would one day marry. With his well-worn copy of Rousseau's *Émile* in hand, Day believed that he could teach her to become his equal in intelligence, to bear every physical hardship he could himself endure and to accept unquestioningly his ideological outlook. He would train her to like the same things he liked, to despise the things he despised and even to love his pitted face, straggly hair and rounded shoulders, to give birth to his children and to live with him in perfect harmony in his "secret glade."

Thomas Day was not the first to dream of creating an ideal woman—and he would not be the last. Writers, artists and musicians have always been drawn to the fantasy of bringing to life a supreme being—usually a woman. One of the oldest and certainly the most influential such transformations was described by the Roman poet Ovid in the first decade AD retelling the myth of Pygmalion in his *Metamorphoses*. In Ovid's vivid and erotic tale the sculptor Pygmalion falls in love with the marble statue of a beautiful woman he has carved. Appalled, like Day, by the wicked ways of women, Pygmalion beseeches Venus to bring to life his "ivory girl." The goddess grants his wish, and Pygmalion is overjoyed to find that the cold marble he has sculpted turns to flesh beneath his touch and the statue steps down from her pedestal into his arms. Nine months later their union produces a daughter.

With its simple but timeless theme, the Pygmalion story has been reworked and reimagined again and again over the ensuing centuries. Probably the best-known and best-loved version, George Bernard Shaw's bittersweet comedy *Pygmalion* tells the tale of the phonetics expert Professor Henry Higgins, who accepts a wager to transform the Cockney flower seller Eliza Doolittle into a fashionable woman of the world. By training Eliza to speak with a refined accent, teaching her drawing room manners and dressing her in fine clothes, Higgins wins his bet: Eliza hoodwinks London society into believing that she is a duchess. But Shaw's play, first staged in 1913, subverts the original myth's happy ending. The feisty Eliza ultimately resists the fate of Ovid's statue and refuses to fall in love with her creator. Instead, to Higgins's horror, she rebels against his autocratic arrogance and demands to direct her own destiny; in the final scene she leaves him to marry the lovestruck Freddy. Much to Shaw's disgust, when his play was made into the film *Pygmalion* in 1938, the producers insisted on inventing a romantic conclusion, suggesting that Eliza returns to Higgins. After Shaw's death, the creators of the 1956 musical, *My Fair Lady*, kept that "happy ending," which, of course, was maintained in the 1964 film of the musical.

If the Pygmalion myth has always captivated artists and audiences alike, in the eighteenth century it acquired the status of a cult. More interpretations of the story were produced during the 1700s than in all other periods of history put together. Fired by their fascination for the classical world and fueled by the debate that raged over the balance of nature and nurture in forming personality, the Georgians reveled in the Pygmalion idea. Every schoolboy knew the Ovid myth. The story was re-created in ballet, opera and drama. And the crucial moment when the statue steps down from her pedestal and comes to life was reproduced in paintings, on porcelain and—ironically enough—in statues. Even Rousseau could not resist the lure of the dramatic metamorphosis. In 1762, he composed a poetic drama, *Pygmalion: un scène lyrique*, which took the classical myth to new heights of eroticism. And for the first time, in the Rousseau version, the statue acquired a name—Galatea.

In reality, of course, when it comes to choosing a spouse the vast majority of people have been always content to accept flawed reality over mythical perfection. But not Thomas Day. Nobody—before or since—has tried quite so literally or so systematically to create for themselves their vision of a perfect mate. There is no doubt that Day—with his veneration for classical literature—was well aware of the Pygmalion myth when he embarked on his journey to create the perfect wife. Day was the incarnation of the sculptor Pygmalion intent on bringing to life his ivory girl. He was the original Professor Higgins on a mission to transform an innocent girl plucked out of the gutter into a polished and articulate perfect companion. In a mission as absurd as it was sinister, Day would take the human quest for perfection to its ultimate extreme. If God created woman, Day was determined to go one step further and improve on that divine design.

His young pupil, of course, was completely ignorant of his plans—and Day made no attempt to enlighten her. But if she had no idea of her destiny, Ann Kingston had little knowledge of her true origins either. Beyond the fact that she had been surrendered soon after birth, she knew no details of her arrival at the Foundling Hospital and had no clue to her previous identity.

Day would always seek to bury his pupil's origins in obscurity. His friends would conspire to conceal or obfuscate the events. Ann herself would never discover the full details of her past. And writers down the centuries would assume that her original identity had been lost in the morass of Foundling Hospital records that accumulated over the years; one would even report that there was no trace of a girl being apprenticed from Shrewsbury to Thomas Day, when of course the official guardian was Richard Edgeworth. The story has acquired almost apocryphal status. Was it even true? Like a ghost, Day's orphan pupil has seemed almost impossible to grasp. Yet, in fact, all the time the details of her origins and the key events of her life within the Foundling Hospital had been scrupulously recorded and preserved in the heavy orphanage ledgers—which survive to this day—just as they had for the thousands of babies who had crossed the charity's threshold since it first opened its doors.

Founded in 1741, the Foundling Hospital was the vision of one man: retired sea captain Thomas Coram. Sent to sea at eleven, two years after his mother died, Coram was later apprenticed to a shipwright. After emigrating to America in his twenties, he made and lost a fortune before returning to his homeland. He was appalled by the unemployment, poverty and slum conditions he found in early eighteenth-century London. But most shocking of all, as he walked to London and back each day, was the sight of abandoned babies "sometimes alive, sometimes dead, and sometimes dying," dumped on rubbish heaps by the side of the road.

With no substantial income or significant connections, it took Coram seventeen years to raise sufficient support and funds to build a refuge for orphaned and unwanted babies. But after winning royal backing in 1739 and parliamentary approval the following year, Coram's charity received its first charges on March 25, 1741. By midnight thirty babies had been accepted while others were turned away with an appeal to their mothers not to abandon their infants that night. A clerk recording the event wrote, "the Expressions of Grief of the Women whose Children could not be admitted were Scarcely more observable than those of some of the Women who parted with their Children, so that a more moving Scene can't well be imagined."

From the beginning the charity's governors installed a rigorous system of logging and documenting their charges. While careful to preserve the anonymity of the babies they admitted, and thus erase the stain of their probable illegitimacy, they took meticulous steps to ensure the orphans could be tracked throughout their lives within the charity. On reception, therefore, any distinguishing marks that might later identify a child were carefully noted on billet forms, and mothers were encouraged to leave information about the baby's birth, parentage and other history along with a small memento. Initially the governors hoped that mothers would later reclaim their children on production of relevant identification. In practice few children were ever reunited with their parents.

Carefully stored under lock and key, the billet forms and tokens that accumulated over the ensuing years tell a heart-rending story of desperate parents in desperate times. Some mothers left letters or poems describing the appalling circumstances that had forced them to give up their infants. One mother was under sentence of death at Newgate; another had been raped by two sailors. While most mothers were unmarried, and too poor, too young or too ashamed to support an illegitimate child, a substantial number were married women who had simply fallen on hard times. "This Little Innocent is the Darling Offspring of a Unhappy but truly Virtuous Woman by the fondest Husband," wrote one mother.

The tokens left with their tiny babies by these bereft mothers included coins, buttons, buckles, thimbles and padlocks. Those who had nothing of value left nutshells, bottle tops, scraps of paper or whatever else came to hand. Some mothers left one item of a pair—one earring, one cufflink, one shoe buckle—or tore a playing card in half in the hope of one day joining the two halves when they were reunited with their loved ones. If no token was left, the clerks sometimes snipped a scrap of fabric from the baby's clothes and pinned it to the form.

Upon reception each child was allotted a number, stamped on a lead tag which was tied around the baby's neck, and this was used to track the child throughout its lifetime in the charity. At the same time, immediately upon admission, each child was renamed. The very first babies were named after the charity's benefactors—including Thomas Coram—but when some patrons raised concerns that the little Bedfords and Montagues might grow up to claim familial rights, other names were smartly introduced. Subsequent babies were baptized Julius Caesar, Walter Raleigh and Elizabeth Tudor after dead heroes, and when these ran out, children were named after places, flowers or virtues they might aspire to, such as Patience, Prudence and Faith. But as these too were used up, babies were named simply Jane or John as befitted their lowly station in life. With a new name, new clothes and new surroundings, the first day of admission marked day one of a brand-new life.

As the charity moved in 1745 into a permanent home, a grand building with two wings north of Holborn, support grew. Paintings donated by William Hogarth adorned the walls, and music composed by George Frideric Handel filled the chapel at the benefit concerts popular with fashionable society. Opulently dressed visitors flocked to hear the orphans singing or to watch the boys making fishing nets in the ropewalk. Although Captain Coram was later ostracized from meetings for his outspoken contributions, he continued to attend baptisms, standing godfather to twenty children. Reduced to poverty again in his old age, he remained a familiar figure in the orphanage gardens, red-coated and red-cheeked, sharing gingerbread among the children with tears spilling down his face. When he died in 1751 the captain's body was escorted by orphans to its burial in the chapel.

Yet for all its support and fashionable cachet the charity could not keep pace with the flow of babies arriving at its door. After a while a ballot was introduced to determine which children were accepted on reception days. Hopeful mothers picked a ball from a bag to decide whether their baby could be admitted: white meant acceptance, red put the child on a reserve list and black signaled rejection. But as babies continued to exceed beds, the governors appealed to Parliament for aid. In 1756 the House of Commons awarded a generous £10,000 (£1.78 million; $2.9 million today) grant but with one crucial catch: no more babies could be turned away.

The General Reception, as it became known, began on June 2, 1756, and continued until March 25, 1760, at which point—with government funds and the patience of Members of Parliament exhausted—the governors wryly named the last child Kitty Finis. In all a staggering total of 14,934 babies were admitted during a period of less than four years. While previously babies had been selected through a careful process to weed out those least likely to thrive, now any unwanted baby was brought to the hospital gatehouse or left outside in a basket at any time of day or night. Many were in dire health. One child was described as "a Mear Skirlinton Covered with Rags with a hole in the Roofe of the Mouth," while another was simply "The most miserable object Ever Received." Mortality rates leapt from an already tragic 45 percent to more than 70 percent—although even this figure was better than in some London parishes where every one of the pauper babies farmed out to wet nurses died.

As the charity struggled to find sufficient wet nurses to suckle the rising tide of infants, entire villages were transformed into nursing outposts. When these youngsters grew up, ready to leave their foster mothers for schooling at the age of five or six, the governors had to build six country branches—like that at Shrewsbury—in areas where the orphans might find future employment. It was during this period of misery and mayhem that Ann Kingston had been admitted to the Foundling Hospital.

Thursday, May 24, 1757, dawned a gray, sunless day, which grew progressively gloomier as rain swept in on a chilly northwest wind in the afternoon. After a harsh winter of soaring food prices, the spring had so far failed to nurture any green shoots of recovery. Weaving through the crowds on that bleak day an unknown person headed northwest in the teeth of the wind, from the squalid slums of Clerkenwell to the black iron gates of the Foundling Hospital, bearing a small bundle.

Business was brisk at the lodge that day. Already five babies had been admitted; a seventh was still to come. Only the sixth baby, carried from Clerkenwell, came from London. According to the hospital regulations, immediately after the baby was brought into the lodge the clerk would have locked the door to detain its bearer and rung a bell to alert a nurse in the adjacent room. Clerks were under strict orders on pain of dismissal not to attempt to discover the identity of mothers, or anyone else, who brought babies for admission, but they were expected to extract vital details of the baby's origins including the parish of birth. After questioning the anonymous bearer of this sixth baby, the clerk began to fill in the printed form.

The billet form, which survives to this day in the charity's archives, records simply that a "female child," numbered 4579, was brought to the hospital on May 24. Unlike other foundlings, there was no token left in expectation of a later reunion or any record of the clothing the baby wore, if indeed she had any. Under distinguishing marks, the clerk noted that the little girl was "marked on the Left Ear greatly," though whether this was a birthmark or an injury sustained subsequently was left unsaid. And although she was obviously under six months old—the age limit for admission at that stage—no date of birth was given. The parish of origin, volunteered by the person who brought the baby to the lodge, was recorded in the clerk's phonetic spelling style as "St Jons Clarkenwell."

One further piece of information was provided. A note, which must have been handed over with the baby by her bearer, was left with the child. Pinned to the billet form for posterity, this scrap of paper declares that the infant had already been baptized, in St. James's Church, Clerkenwell—the neighboring parish to St. John's—and given the name, recorded as the clerk heard it, Manima Butler. Having provided the clerks with the requisite information, the anonymous bearer—her mother, her father or a parish official—reemerged into the street, empty-handed, to disappear forever into the London crowds.

Despite the assertion on the billet form, no record exists in the St. James's Church register of a baby baptized Manima Butler or any similar name. But whether she was really baptized or not, the name was undoubtedly a misspelling of Monimia. Meaning "the lonely girl" in Greek, the name Monimia was first coined by the playwright Thomas Otway for the orphan heroine of his 1680 tragedy *The Orphan: or, The Unhappy Marriage*. Hugely popular during the eighteenth century, the play was regularly performed on the London stage. In Georgian parlance, therefore, the name Monimia was synonymous with orphanhood. Ann had originally been named for an archetypal orphan—although whether she would act out the play's subtitle and make an unhappy marriage would remain to be seen.

No details of Ann's mother were recorded beyond the fact that she gave birth in Clerkenwell. Sandwiched between the thriving financial center of the city's square mile and the fashionable quarter of the West End, Clerkenwell was home to some of London's poorest and most desperate people. Its maze of dead-end alleys and dark courtyards, where ramshackle tenement buildings blocked out the sun, housed thousands of families in attics and cellars devoid of sanitation or ventilation. Nearly half the population, including children from the age of six, were dependent on the area's renowned clock- and watchmaking trade. It was here, to the constant thrum of hammering and grinding echoing in the narrow streets, that Ann's heart first began to beat. Whether her mother was a maidservant seduced by her master or an heiress involved in an illicit liaison, the likelihood is that she was illegitimate; certainly that would remain the assumption throughout her life.

Illegitimacy rose throughout the eighteenth century in Britain as in Europe; the Georgian era has been dubbed "the century of illegitimacy." But far from proving an upsurge in lax moral behavior, the rise was probably due chiefly to planned marriages being abandoned through unforeseen disasters. Traditionally it was common practice, especially in the countryside, for couples to enjoy intimate relations that were only legalized in church if and when the woman fell pregnant. But high living costs and wartime conscription, along with the Marriage Act of 1753 making weddings more complicated to arrange, deterred or prevented many well-intentioned couples from proceeding up the aisle.

All these factors reached a climax in spring 1757—around the time of Ann's birth—when a peak in bread prices, an increase in adult mortality and the continuation of the Seven Years War combined to produce a sharp spike in illegitimate births. Deserted or bereaved by her seducer or her lover, therefore, Ann's mother may have thrown herself on the mercy of the parish and given birth in the Clerkenwell workhouse. There she may have died in childbirth or given up her newborn baby reluctantly to parish officials or even taken the baby herself to the Foundling Hospital in the hope that she was thereby assuring her a better future.

The enigma mattered little to the staff of the Foundling Hospital who had long since surrendered curiosity for pragmatism. With six other infants to register that day, the clerk promptly stamped the baby's number, 4579, on a lead tag and tied this around her neck with a piece of silk.

Bathed clean by the nurse and dressed in a regulation white smock, she was handed to a wet nurse and whisked away to the nursing ward. Meanwhile the clerk completed the billet form and entered the new arrival's details in the General Register along with her new name: Ann Kingston. Plucked at random from a list of approved names, this was how she would be known during her life within the charity. Only three of the seven babies admitted that day lived beyond infancy; Ann was one of the lucky ones.

Unknown to Thomas Day, therefore, his chosen child bride had been born just a few miles from his own birthplace. She had been deposited at the gates of the Foundling Hospital in the same year that he walked through the gates of Charterhouse School a few minutes' walk away.

Her stay in the hospital was short. On the same day that she arrived, Ann was handed over with a parcel of baby clothes, including three shirts, three caps and a gray woolen coat, to a new wet nurse, called Mary Penfold, who had traveled in from the countryside earlier that day. A receipt details the clothes provided along with the nurse's weekly wage of 2s and 6d. Unable to write, Mary Penfold signed for the goods received—both baby and clothing—with a cross. And along with four other foundlings and their respective nurses, Ann set out on a slow twenty-seven-mile journey by horse-drawn cart to her new home in pastoral Surrey.

Although the charity's legion of wet nurses was paid basically to suckle their charges, essentially they were foster mothers to the babies committed to their care. Cartoons and novels frequently depict eighteenth-century wet nurses as ignorant, drunken and neglectful. Yet most of the women who nursed the Foundling Hospital orphans were loving surrogate mothers to the children they brought up until the age of five, six or older. Like Mary Penfold, most were the wives of poor farm laborers and country artisans with several children of their own who viewed the monthly 10s fee as a lifeline in times of widespread hardship. Although this generous wage was plainly the main motivation for some, many became so emotionally attached to their foster children that they appealed to keep them permanently or simply refused to give them up. Occasionally such requests were granted and foundlings were apprenticed to their foster families; usually they were refused.

Whether Mary Penfold had been spurred to volunteer from altruism or poverty, from the moment she accepted Ann and her bundle of clothing she became the central figure in her young life, effectively becoming the mother she had never known. The fact that Ann was breast-fed—in accordance with the charity's enlightened policy—inevitably deepened that bond. Until the mid-1700s, newborn babies were often fed, or "dry-nursed," with bread, cake or biscuit mixed with cow's milk, butter and sugar—known as "pap"—supplemented by brandy, rum or wine. But the Foundling Hospital's physician, William Cadogan, had convinced the charity's governors—and later popularized the idea—that breast was best. Benefiting from this progressive nursing regime, breathing the fresh country air and nurtured by Mary Penfold, Ann thrived. Like the country maiden of Thomas Day's fantasies—like the Sophie created by Rousseau for his Émile—Ann grew up among peasant folk according to simple country ways. But it was no rural idyll.

Living in the hamlet of Wotton, three miles outside the market town of Dorking, Mary Penfold already had her hands full when she took in her foundling. Her family comprised James, sixteen, Mary, fifteen, Betty, six, John, two and Thomas, who was just four months old. His nose abruptly pushed out, baby Thomas must have been promptly weaned or had to share his mother's milk with the little stranger. Rising at dawn and going to bed at dusk, the Penfold children would have spent much of their day helping in the fields and around the house. There was no cosseting and few cuddles for children in the laboring classes. But when the chores were done, there was freedom to play on the village green or scramble over the chalk hills, to whirl around the maypole in spring and tumble in the haystacks at harvest. For Ann, trading the noxious squalor of overcrowded Clerkenwell for the pure Surrey air, it was a clear change for the better.

On her first birthday, her foster mother's care was acknowledged with a ten shilling bonus—equivalent to an unskilled laborer's weekly wage—the reward given to all wet nurses if the baby survived twelve months. This was no mean achievement. Of all babies sent to wet nurses during the General Reception, more than half never returned. Ann's survival, in the face of such odds, was due in no small measure to the diligence of the charity's local inspector, Hugh Kerr. A busy surgeon based in Dorking, and a volunteer like all the inspectors, Kerr took responsibility for seventy-six orphan babies in the surrounding villages from June 1756 to June 1757 alone; of these only fifteen died.

Yet just over two years after Ann's arrival in Wotton, in August 1759, the Foundling Hospital officials suddenly announced that they wanted to transfer the oldest children in the Dorking area to new country hospitals to make way for the torrent of babies still arriving at the hospital gates in London. Forced to surrender their orphans after two years—instead of the usual five or six—the wet nurses protested loudly. "The poor Women think it Extreamly hard to come up in Harvest & to leave their Children so Young," complained Kerr. "If these Children could be left here untill next Spring the poor Women after all their trouble would have some small comfort of them this Winter," he begged. Unusually, the governors acceded to appeals from two families near Dorking who had grown so fond of their foundlings they could not bear to part with them. No such request came from Mary Penfold.

At two-and-a-quarter years old, her bright coppery curls about level with the ears of wheat waiting to be harvested in the fields, Ann was brought by Mary Penfold back to the London Foundling Hospital on August 14, 1759, and separated from her foster mother forever. One Foundling Hospital clerk, who supervised a band of orphans being parted from their foster mothers the previous month, recorded that the nurses "shewed the most lively sorrow in parting with them" and the children "cried very much after their Mammys." Himself a former foundling, he spoke from the heart.

No sooner had she said goodbye to her "Mammy" than Ann was taken to one of the hospital's huge dormitories where she spent the next two nights. Two days later she was placed in a horse-drawn wagon padded with straw with eleven other girls and six boys for a grueling eight-day journey to Shrewsbury. Accompanied by nine nurses sent from Shropshire for the purpose, the sizable party stopped overnight at inns on the long and bumpy journey.

With the Shrewsbury Orphan Hospital still only a blueprint, the wagon pulled up outside a converted warehouse, where Ann and her fellow infants were lifted down. Institutional life would wait. Inside the temporary orphanage Ann was presented to a new nurse, Ann Casewell, along with another foundling who had also been transferred from Dorking at the same time, named Deborah Verner, who was a year younger. Like Mary Penfold, Ann Casewell was illiterate; she signed the receipts for her two foundlings and their respective clothing with a cross. Like Mary Penfold, she was married with young children—a four-year-old daughter, Mary, and a son, Robert, who was nearly two.

Growing up with her new foster family and her foundling "sister" Deborah in the Shropshire countryside, Ann remained for the next six years, as the Shrewsbury Orphan Hospital rose slowly on the distant horizon. She was almost eight years old, in April 1765, when she and Deborah were brought to live in the orphanage for the first time. After nearly six years with the Casewell family, it must have been another wrenching separation.

Brought up in their small foster family within a tightly knit rural community, the two girls no doubt felt overwhelmed by the vast orphanage with its tall windows, high ceilings and great oak staircase, alive with the sound of whirring looms and spinning wheels, along with the hubbub of more than 500 children. At first they were probably inoculated against smallpox and isolated for several weeks in a nearby house—as were all the new arrivals—before being introduced into the girls' dormitory. But if it all seemed strange and new there was no time to stop and stare.

Between chores in the kitchens and laundry, lessons in the schoolroom and work in the weaving and spinning rooms—where the children produced the woolen cloth for which the orphanage was renowned—there were few opportunities for leisure. In common with its London headquarters and five other country branches, the Shrewsbury orphanage kept to a rigid timetable for meals, lessons, work, prayers and bedtime in its efforts to inculcate habits of order and discipline in its young wards.

The Shrewsbury governors, who had been responsible for hundreds of orphans since their first arrival from London in 1759, supervised their upbringing with a mixture of paternalistic affection and pragmatic realism. Volunteers who were recruited from the ranks of the local gentry and aristocracy, they watched over the "nurslings" growing up in their foster families and took turns to visit the orphanage to check on the children's welfare. According to hospital rules, staff had "to behave with Tenderness" toward the orphans and see that "all Regulations concerning the Children are observed." One governor, making a spot check on the orphanage on a Sunday morning, recorded indignantly in the Visitors Book that the children were about to leave for church "with large holes in their stockings their Cloaths dirty & likewise their faces."

Pressed by the board in London, the governors pared costs and trained the children for work in the mills. Not only did the orphans produce their own uniforms in their manufactory, they sold surplus cloth in the Shrewsbury market and even made bespoke livery for the local sheriff's men and greatcoats for the governors. But careful not to overtax their charges, unlike the mill owners who worked child laborers to death in the nearby factories, the governors never managed to turn a profit from this hive of industry since "The Days are short & the Children Novices."

However well intentioned the regime, it was impossible—in an age before effective medical care—to stem the onslaught of disease and the steady roll call of deaths. When one of the girls, named Sweet Rose, recovered from smallpox there was evident rejoicing—"she is a very Good Girl, and one of our best Spinners," the secretary informed London. But when another died of convulsions he deemed her death a blessing "as it was the Greatest Cripple that I ever saw." The unfortunately titled Waste Book, which recorded daily events, notes without comment the names of farm animals giving birth or being butchered, staff being appointed or sacked and children arriving from their nurses, being apprenticed or dying.

As she grew accustomed to this stark but caring regime, Ann learned her lessons and performed her chores in every expectation of her lowly station in life. She seems to have been selected to perform housework rather than being trained for a job in the woolen trade; a register of children's occupations lists her as "in the house" between 1765 and 1768 rather than in the spinning or weaving rooms. When she was not doing housework, she took her seat in the schoolroom. Like all Georgian children who were fortunate enough to enjoy an education, whether rich or poor, the Shrewsbury orphans were taught in large classes to read from improving books—mainly the Bible—and to learn by rote religious texts. At its peak in 1766, when Ann was nine, the orphanage boasted four schoolmasters and six schoolmistresses. It was a point of pride that all the foundlings could perform simple sums and read, if not write, by the time they left for their apprenticeships.

The children rose at six in the morning in summer and seven in winter, and each day passed with little variation. There was meat three times a week, church on Sundays and plum pudding every Christmas. Growing up, Ann mastered her alphabet, learned to count, practiced her catechism and labored over her chores. Although the orphans worked long hours, they were sent outdoors to play after lunch and before bedtime. The only significant change came in the ebb and flow of children arriving from their nurses or leaving for apprenticeships and dying from disease. In April 1768, when Ann was eleven, a measles epidemic swept through the orphanage and affected more than 200 children although—remarkably—only four died.

Yet as she thrived and grew tall, Ann was moving relentlessly closer to the moment when she would leave her friends forever for an apprenticeship in an unknown place of work. In 1768, the orphanage was being pressed to apprentice children so fast that it ran out of the Bibles it gave them as parting gifts. The following year, when she turned twelve, the London office sent instructions to the branch hospitals that all children who had been admitted as babies before December 31, 1758—like Ann—should be placed out as apprentices "as soon as conveniently may be."

So when Ann had been called in June 1769 to take her place in a parade of girls for the perusal of two young gentlemen, she knew that she might be leaving. As she was plucked from the line by one of the two men, she was probably relieved to find that she would become a maid in a country house instead of working the spinning machines in one of the woolen mills. When the men had returned in August to take her to London, she had meekly accepted that she was about to begin a life of domestic service. And even now that she found herself living alone in an apartment in the heart of London and visited daily by this wild-haired, disheveled young man who seemed determined to devote himself patiently to her education, she had no reason to raise questions.

All her life she had been trained to bow to authority and to meekly accept her fate. If she turned for reassurance to the charity's "Instructions to Apprentices," which she had been given as she left the orphanage, she found the same message. "You are placed out Apprentice by the Govrs. of this Hospital," the text began. "You were taken into it very young, quite helpless, forsaken & deserted by your Parents & Friends. Out of Charity have you been fed, clothed, and instructed; which many have wanted." She should not feel ashamed of having been brought up in the Foundling Hospital, the guidance told her. "Own it; and say that it was thro' the good Providence of Almighty God that you were taken care of." All she needed to do was to remember her religious teaching, work hard, speak truthfully, behave honestly and avoid "Temptations to do wickedly," the instructions urged. She likely had no idea what form those temptations might take.

Day had chosen well. Ann was a quick and enthusiastic pupil, eager to please her teacher and responsive to his praise. Oblivious to his plans for her future, she flourished under his attentions and absorbed his teachings like a sponge. And he lost no time in beginning his young orphan's transformation. Inspired by the sight of the turbulent river that he had crossed to claim his future bride, Day renamed her Sabrina, Latin for the Severn. Doubtless Day was aware of the Celtic legend that the river had gained its name from the illegitimate granddaughter of an ancient British king, a virginal maiden called Habrena in Welsh, Sabrina in Latinized English, who was put to death there by drowning. The tale had been evoked by Edmund Spenser in *The Faerie Queene* and later by John Milton in his play *Comus* in celebration of chastity. Day added the surname Sidney, after a childhood hero, the Elizabethan courtier, soldier and poet Sir Philip Sidney. It was her third new name in twelve years. The girl who had been first named Monimia Butler, and then Ann Kingston, number 4579, was gone forever; in her place Day had created Sabrina Sidney, his future wife.

Changing his pupil's name was a smart move on Day's part. Even though she was now living within a mile of the Foundling Hospital headquarters in Holborn, she would prove impossible for the governors to trace. Yet for all her pretty looks, her readiness to learn and her promising talents, Day was still unsure whether he would succeed in moulding Sabrina Sidney into his ivory girl. His deep-rooted suspicion of the opposite sex still niggled. He had secured the perfect pupil—of that he felt sure—but how could he be certain that she would bend sufficiently under his training to blossom into the perfect wife? He wanted, therefore, to be doubly sure of success. And so just a few weeks after he had begun Sabrina's education, on September 20, Day set out for the Foundling Hospital headquarters in Holborn again.

Once again Day told the charity's officials that he wished to select a young girl to work as a maid in his married friend's home. Now that he was a generous benefactor and an elected governor of the charity he had no trouble convincing the clerks of his honest intentions. Once again he walked up and down a row of adolescent girls lined up for his perusal in their identical brown uniforms. And once again Day gave his friend Edgeworth's name as the girl's proposed employer. Indeed, it seems likely that Edgeworth accompanied Day on this second visit since he signed the chosen orphan's apprenticeship indentures. But this time—by way of contrast—Day picked out of the line an eleven-year-old girl with blond hair and blue eyes. Like Sabrina she was described as "beautiful," but unlike Day's first choice she was "fair, with flaxen locks, and light eyes." Her name, within the orphanage at least, was Dorcas Car. Shepherded through the gates of the hospital by Day, she was whisked back to the lodgings near Chancery Lane to meet her fellow pupil.

Like Sabrina, Dorcas had been abandoned at the gates of the London Foundling Hospital as a baby and promptly renamed by the governors. Like Sabrina, she was immediately renamed by Day. This time he chose the name Lucretia, presumably in homage to the legendary heroine of classical history whose rape and subsequent suicide sparked the rebellion that led to the creation of the Roman republic, rather than the infamous daughter of the Borgia Pope who was reputed to have helped murder her husband and given birth to a child by her brother. A fitting complement to Sabrina, Lucretia was said to be equally alluring yet opposite in looks and personality. Each possessed an "extraordinary beauty but each with a beauty in contrast to the other," wrote one acquaintance. "One of them, Sabrina, had the air of a sensitive nature coupled with delicate features, a slim waist, eyes suggestive of spirit and engaging manners" while Lucretia "was more classically beautiful with a radiant complexion, plump face, smiling eyes and the look of a joyful soul."

They were opposite sides of the same coin; they were two of a kind. Day was not taking any chances on his future marital happiness; he was hedging his bets. Much in the way that the heads of aristocratic families aimed to father two sons—"an heir and a spare"—so Day had obtained a second orphan in case his first choice failed to match his exalted expectations. In the past he had been humiliated and spurned by the "bitch" Leonora and the "toad" Margaret, but now that he had two young girls at his command, who were free of womanly wiles, he could feel sure he would never be rejected by a woman again. He planned to educate them both according to the Rousseau system, pick the winning candidate for his future wife, and then simply discard her failed companion. Lucretia, of course, had no more idea than Sabrina of the future that lay in wait. But, just as with Sabrina, orphanage records reveal her past.

A year younger than Sabrina, Lucretia had been born within the same parish, Clerkenwell, on May 11, 1758, just a few streets away from her new playmate's place of birth, and she was baptized in the same church with the name Ann Grig, probably in the presence of one or both of her parents. For most of that year she had thrived. But as winter approached, some kind of calamity must have hit the family and she was surrendered to the Foundling Hospital, a chubby, well-nourished, breast-fed, blond-haired baby of nearly six months, during the General Reception on November 9. As with Sabrina, no token was left with the child, but this time two tiny scraps of material—a square of blue and cream striped cotton and another of gray and cream striped silk—were snipped from her clothes by the clerks as an identifying clue in the event of a future reunion with her family. They would remain to this day pinned to the billet form that was filled out on her admission day, mysterious remnants of a buried past.

Like Sabrina, Ann Grig was given a number, 10,413, and her new name, Dorcas Car. Unlike Sabrina, Dorcas had been allowed to stay with the same foster mother, in the village of Brentwood, just north of London, until she was nearly eight. At that point, in January 1766, she had been returned to the Foundling Hospital in London and there she remained for the next three years while she learned her alphabet, read from the Bible and became proficient in sewing and spinning until the moment that she had caught the eye of Thomas Day on his second wife-hunting expedition in September 1769.

Over the next few weeks, Day visited the two girls on a regular basis to conduct their lessons while his friends looked on with a mixture of disbelief and mirth. "They were eleven and twelve years old, good humoured, and well disposed," wrote Edgeworth. "Mr. Day's kindness soon made them willing to conduct themselves according to his directions." Cooped up with only each other for company for much of the time, the two children grew close. They had much in common, of course, and there was much to talk about—not least their curious situation left alone with only their widowed landlady as an occasional chaperone. But although the girls were eager to please their attentive teacher, Day made sure they remained in total ignorance of his true motives. His friends, however, were well aware of his intentions from the start, and even if they had some misgivings, none made any efforts to halt the experiment.

Day's plan was spelled out from the first in clear terms in a legal document that was apparently drawn up at the time by the ever obliging Bicknell, who stood as its guarantor. In this remarkable contract, Day pledged that within twelve months he would decide which of the two girls showed most potential to become his wife. He would then surrender the other and bind her as an apprentice to a "reputable tradeswoman" with £100 (£15,000 or $24,000 today) for her maintenance. He would continue to provide her with financial support "if she behaved well" until she married or began trading herself, at which point he would advance a further £400. The remaining girl would continue under his control to be educated by Day "with a view to making her his future wife." Careful to leave nothing to the imagination, Day swore "never to violate her innocence." And if he should at any point renounce his plan of marriage he would support her in the home of a "creditable family" until she married, at which point he would provide a handsome wedding dowry of £500.

According to an acquaintance who described the contract, the document was presented to the Foundling Hospital along with credentials proving Day's age and moral probity in exchange for the requisite two orphans. Perhaps Day himself promoted this explanation. But nothing of the sort was ever seen by the charity's staff or governors. Even supposing that the governors or clerks could have been persuaded to consent to such a morally repugnant idea, which was completely at odds with their usually vigilant care of the orphans' welfare, the charity's rules strictly forbade single men from taking apprentices. And in any case it was Edgeworth, not Day, who was formally named in the charity's records as the girls' apprenticeship master. The contract, therefore, must have been a private undertaking secretly agreed to between Day and Bicknell. But however much the arrangement was couched in legal language, there is no doubt that Day's actions were highly irregular and completely illegal.

Even in the laissez-faire world of Georgian morals, Day's scheme was outrageous and scandalous. He had abducted two innocent and helpless young girls through an elaborate deceit and changed both their names to conceal his plans. When Edgeworth's licentious friend, Francis Delaval, lured a young actress into living with him earlier in the 1760s, her father pursued him through the court of King's Bench and won her release—though once freed she walked away arm in arm with charming Frank. In France, just a year before Day's escapade, when the Marquis de Sade imprisoned a young woman in his chateau, his mother-in-law had obtained a royal arrest warrant. At a time when stealing a handkerchief was a capital offense in Britain, a man with lower social standing might have expected little mercy for such an act. Yet Day knew that he was protected by his rank, wealth and status. He was a rich landowner with influence and connections living in a man's world; they were powerless girls, born into poverty and branded with the shame of illegitimacy, without friends, family or rights.

At a time when women were commodities, to be exchanged in marriage for vast fortunes and land or bought in a dark alley for sixpence, Day had purchased two girls as easily as he might buy two shoe buckles. As obsessed as he was with the idea of virtue and feminine purity, he had not the slightest compunction about jeopardizing the reputations of the two girls now in his control. But now he came to the obvious conclusion that the busy, gossipy metropolis was not the ideal place for a respectable bachelor to attempt a controversial experiment on two young girls. As the weather cooled, the hordes of fashionable society were flooding back to the capital from their summer retreats in the country. In the first week of November, therefore, Day abandoned his legal studies, collected his two pupils and set sail for France.

FIVE

SABRINA AND LUCRETIA

❧ *Paris, November 1769* ❧

Life with Thomas Day was certainly an education. For most of their short lives, Sabrina and Lucretia—as they were now known—had been accustomed to the repetition and routine that marked out their dreary hours at the Foundling Hospital. Now each day brought something new. Having barely had time to marvel at the crush and chaos of London, by early November the two girls were immersed in the sights and sounds of Paris.

Like fugitives evaporating into the London fog, Day had smuggled his orphans across the Channel during the first week of November, most probably in the sturdy little packet ship that plied its way between Dover and Calais carrying the mail. A popular route with British travelers embarking on continental tours through France and Italy, the twenty-two-mile voyage could take as little as three hours in favorable conditions or as many as fifteen if contrary winds blew the ship off course or, worse, dropped and left it helplessly marooned mid-Channel. Passengers unerringly complained of feeling seasick as the tiny vessel pitched and rolled. And by the time they had been conveyed to and from the ship in open boats in both Dover and Calais harbors, many were drenched as well as nauseous. While nearly all around them retched and groaned, Sabrina and Lucretia proved robust travelers, Day would later boast, and they made not a murmur of complaint.

From Calais the little party headed for Paris, rattling along the well-paved, straight roads of northern France, most probably in a regular stagecoach, or *diligence*. The 188-mile journey commonly took three days including overnight stops at inns. But the steady stream of carriages and hired post chaises trundling along the main route between coast and capital could sometimes prove so dense that travelers were obliged to share rooms with complete strangers at the wayside inns. In his comic novel *A Sentimental Journey Through France and Italy*, published a year before Day's trip, Laurence Sterne told the true story of a friend who had to surrender one of the two beds in his room to a Frenchwoman who had arrived late at night. The roommates negotiated their sleeping arrangements, which stipulated that the curtains around the woman's bed must be pinned firmly shut and the Englishman must wear his breeches all night. Given the high demand for beds on the busy tourist trail, chances are that Day and his two wards were likewise obliged to share a room, although Day would always, figuratively, draw a curtain over their particular sleeping arrangements.

When they entered through the gates of Paris after days on the open road, the girls would have been assailed by the uproar of carriages and pedestrians jostling for space in the narrow streets. The city's population was half a million by the second half of the eighteenth century—about half that of London—but its streets were at least as congested and rowdy. The lack of pavements made them hazardous for pedestrians while the traffic din was increased by the echoes reverberating around the apartment buildings that towered up to seven stories high. As they took in the foreign shops, the foreign clothes and—not least—the foreign language, there was much for the girls to see and hear.

The trio arrived in the city during the second week of November. Jubilant at his first taste of continental travel, now that he was twenty-one and free from his stepfather's purse strings at last, Day was looking forward to touring the city sights. But his encounter with French food and hospitality in Paris largely confirmed his bias for the English way of life.

No doubt the sight of the greasy-haired and scruffily dressed Englishman with two wide-eyed girls in tow reinforced a few French stereotypes about English eccentricity along the way.

The idea of taking his pupils to France, and particularly to Paris—Europe's capital of culture and center of fashion—seems an odd choice for Day given his avowed horror of urban polite society. He could easily have found a suitably remote country retreat in England or Ireland. And being as much a Francophobe as his hero Rousseau was an Anglophobe, Day would automatically have wanted to protect the two girls from everything he knew, or thought he knew, about France. Like many Englishmen, Day associated the French lifestyle with a slavishness to fashion and foppish effeminacy, which he naturally abhorred. Certainly the move surprised his friends. "Mr. Day had as large a portion of the national prejudice in favor of the people of England, and against the French, as any man of sense could have," observed Richard Lovell Edgeworth, adding that it was "therefore something strange, that he should take two young girls to that country, one of whom he destined to be his wife."

Day would later attribute his move to France to a recommendation from his new friend, Dr. William Small, to seek a change of climate to improve his health. But the major benefit of the move was to safeguard his wife-training project rather than his own well-being. In France, the girls were not only beyond the legal dominion of the Foundling Hospital's governors, they were out of sight and earshot of chattering London society. The two foundlings, the girls named Ann and Dorcas, had vanished into thin air. And there was a further reason—which was even more pertinent in the context of Day's plan. Without a word of French between them, the two orphans were completely divorced from any source of aid and every outside influence except for that of Day himself. To make doubly sure that the girls were cut off from any other contact, Day took no English servants, so that, as one friend noted, "They might receive no ideas, except those which himself might choose to impart."

Even Rousseau, in stipulating that Émile should be educated in the countryside to protect him from external vices, had not dreamed up quite so foolproof a shield against unwanted influences. Day's belief that the flaws inherent in the female sex were largely owing to the foolish, faddish world in which girls were brought up had convinced him that the orphan destined to become his future wife should be educated inside a virtual bubble. In France, he knew, he could control his experiment just as effectively as the philosopher turning on and off the oxygen to the imprisoned cockatoo in Joseph Wright's painting.

Having settled himself and the girls in a Paris hotel, Day devoted the week to exploring the French capital. He had been pleasantly surprised by the welcoming inns, the well-cultivated countryside and the "well cloth'd and healthy" peasants on the journey from Calais—so different from the "Wretchedness and Misery" he had been led to expect. But his prejudices now reasserted themselves with a vengeance as he trod the capital's crowded streets. Paris, he was delighted to report to his mother in a dutiful letter sent on November 18, was no match for London. "Its streets are narrow, always dirty, without foot-ways, and the houses high—nothing can be more inconvenient than walking in this most elegant and polite City, for you are in continual Danger of being run over by the Carriages." Furthermore, the Parisian shops were inferior to those in London and the French food less palatable.

Like many an English traveler visiting France, Day yearned for hearty roast beef instead of fancy dishes smothered in rich sauces. He marveled that the French could "cook up a dish out of any thing," and reported: "I have had one Dish almost every day I have been in Paris, which is compos'd of nothing but the Pinions of Fowls, fricasied." But he told his mother, "I own I am yet so little Frenchified, that I prefer, or should prefer if I could get it, one good joint of Meat, to all their Fricasies." There was nothing like home cooking.

Naturally Day did not mention the single most interesting aspect of his travels: the two young companions who shared his journey, nor their thoughts on Parisian street life or French cuisine. Not surprisingly, he had divulged nothing of his experiment to his mother or stepfather. So whether the two girls were enjoying chicken wings every day, or even spreading their own wings in the Paris air, was left unsaid. But Day had obviously not lost sight of the main motive for his trip since he was paying close attention to the women he saw with his usual eye for detail. His scorn for the female sex was plainly undiminished. The women of Paris exhibited "the most fantastic Mixture of Slovenliness and Finery," he spluttered. On the one hand they wore their hair "drest to the highest Extravigance of the Mode"—following the contemporary fashion for lavishly piled up hairstyles—and yet their clothes were "dirty, splash'd and sluttish beyond Conception."

Day, of course, was not alone in denigrating his French neighbors. As soon as the Seven Years War with England's oldest enemy had ended in 1764, English travelers had flocked to France chiefly to reassure themselves of their national superiority. Samuel Johnson's friend Hester Thrale was shocked by the contradictions of French fashions when she noticed a countess who sported diamond earrings yet wore a "dirty black handkerchief" around her neck. Another seasoned traveler, Robert Wharton, turned his nose up at the French habit, among both men and women, of urinating in public—even though this was not uncommon in London streets. Others pined for clean beds, decent roads and plain cooking yet their complaints did nothing to deter most English visitors from merrily extending their French leave. Day, likewise, pronounced Paris "altogether very disagreeable" and immediately resolved to explore France further.

Just as disagreeable to Day as the city of Paris itself was no doubt the sizable community of British living in or visiting the capital. With large numbers of well-to-do families passing through on their holidays and young men fresh out of university making their first stop on their grand tours, along with assorted businessmen, diplomats, tutors, servants and hangers-on, the French capital positively bustled with English visitors— and buzzed with English gossip almost as much as London did. There was even an English coffeehouse where customers could read the English papers and circulate the latest rumors. If he stayed in the city for long, Day could be sure to run into somebody he knew, or worse, who knew his mother. And so after just one week of sightseeing, he decided to press on south toward Lyon. On November 19 he paid his hotel bills, gathered his two girls and set off in search of more convenient surroundings and warmer climes.

It is possible, in making for Lyon, that Day was hoping to track down his hero Rousseau and seek advice on training his orphans just as other disciples pestered the writer for guidance on educating their children. After fleeing England in 1767, the philosopher had laid low in various refuges in northern France under a false name, Jean-Joseph Renou—he was no master of disguise—with Thérèse masquerading as his sister, until friends persuaded him it was unsafe to remain. With his books still banned and the arrest warrant still in force throughout most of France, there was a real risk that Rousseau might end up in the Bastille, where his publisher, Pierre Guy, had already been incarcerated. Just because he was paranoid does not mean that Rousseau was free of danger.

By 1769, when Day arrived in France, Rousseau had settled in a village less than thirty miles from Lyon but in a district outside the jurisdiction of the Parisian Parlement. Feeling as tormented as ever, he devoted his days to writing his saucy and candid *Confessions*. Since Day had made sure to pack his trusty copy of the banned *Émile* as child-care guidance when leaving England, he too risked prosecution if he stayed within the environs of Paris. And so he followed in his idol's footsteps on the road south.

The route from Paris to Lyon was a major thoroughfare for continental travelers meandering through France toward Italy. Most took the *diligence* or alternatively hired a chaise as far as Chalon-sur-Saône from where they could continue to Lyon by boat—the *diligence par eau*—on a picturesque two-day voyage down the Saône. Most made the trip in spring or summer. To undertake the journey at the onset of winter, when heavy rains transformed the rivers into swollen torrents that washed away the bridges and flooded the roads or made them impassable with mud, was courageous if not downright foolish. For a man with little knowledge of the language and no experience of the terrain to take two young girls on such a journey might be regarded as reckless.

One British traveler who had braved the same route in November 1742, twenty-seven years before Day, complained that in places the road was so flooded that his coach was forced to make a detour through fields and vineyards. At other points the rushing floodwaters coursed down the ruts in the roadway so fast that they threatened to overturn his carriage meaning that the only safe course was to walk.

Taking the two-day boat trip was plainly far too dangerous with the Saône in full spate. So Day and his wards traveled by the *diligence* where possible and hired post chaises and drivers where not. By day they negotiated flooded roads and crossed surging torrents on flimsy wooden bridges at risk of being swept away, stopping every twelve miles or so to change their exhausted horses. At each posting stage Day had to cajole the postmasters to supply fresh horses and attempt the next stage of the journey. French postilions, whose job was to ride one of the leading horses, had a reputation for obstinacy among British visitors. One exasperated traveler exclaimed: "I might just as effectually argue with a horse as with a French postilion." By night, Day found refuge for himself and his two girls in cold country inns with lumpy beds and lumpier suppers. At Lyon, where most travelers veered east toward the classical ruins of Italy, Day continued due south for a further 140 miles. Finally they arrived at the towering medieval walls of Avignon.

It was here, in the Church of Sainte-Claire d'Avignon, at mass on Good Friday, April 6, 1327, that the Italian poet Petrarch had first seen the mysterious and unattainable Laura who would unleash his lifelong infatuation and inspire more than 300 sonnets. She may have been Laure de Noves, the seventeen-year-old daughter of a local nobleman, who had already been married for two years to a French count—an ancestor of the Marquis de Sade. Exiled in Avignon with his parents, Petrarch, in his early twenties, followed her obsessively. By all accounts she spurned Petrarch's devotion, for she gave her husband eleven children before she died, aged thirty-eight. She was buried in the city's Franciscan Church. Day was not the first Englishman to make a pilgrimage to the tomb of Petrarch's elusive perfect woman; in Avignon he hoped to succeed where Petrarch had famously failed.

Day, at least, survived the rigors of the journey unscathed, as he informed Edgeworth in an uncharacteristically exuberant letter written soon after arrival at the end of November. "Behold me at Avignon, full six hundred and fifty miles, three quarters, and one furlong, from Barehill," he announced jubilantly, "and yet, by heavens! I am alive! And what is more, tolerably well." Travel—or at least the attentions of two spellbound girls hanging on his every word—plainly agreed with him. Edgeworth would later say that Day's letters from Avignon were "almost the only instances of gaiety of manner, which ever appeared in his correspondence."

With boyish exhilaration, Day continued: "Were I to relate the stage-coaches I have travelled in, the post-boys I have talked big to, (nay, I have gone so far as to say *sacre Dieu!*) the inns I have lain at, the rivers I have passed with no more than a three-quarters of an inch plank between me and destruction, I should make you shudder!" Visualizing Edgeworth working on his latest invention "in a warm comfortable room" back in Berkshire, Day extolled "the toils, the dangers, of us who travel to see the wonders of the world." But whether the two orphans who were the chief object of the entire journey were likewise alive and well was left entirely to Edgeworth's imagination. Day made no direct reference to the girls beyond an enigmatic "Everything belonging to me goes on well."

Perched on a rocky outcrop above the Rhône, the ancient city of Avignon provided an ideal winter refuge. Having served as the seat of seven popes for nearly seventy years during the fourteenth century—when it was the center of the medieval Western world—Avignon still fell under papal control as capital of the enclave, the Comtat Venaissin. The heavily fortified citadel was therefore conveniently beyond the reach not only of English but of French laws, making the city a favorite destination for political, religious and tax exiles of all nationalities as well as a natural hideout for smugglers and other criminals.

Several British aristocrats who had supported the failed Jacobite uprisings in 1715 and 1745 fled to Avignon to lick their wounds. They were followed in later years by fellow Britons seeking sun and scenery for a year or two in Provence so that, according to one source, more than a hundred English people made Avignon their home. Sterne poked fun at the city's profusion of titled British and French residents in his novel *The Life and Opinions of Tristram Shandy, Gentleman*: "for they are all Dukes, Marquisses, and Counts, there." Lively, cultured and prosperous, the city owed its economic well-being as much to its vigorous black market in contraband goods, like tobacco, gunpowder and playing cards, which it sold to its surrounding French neighbors at competitive prices, as to its vibrant silk and calico industry.

Far enough off the tourist trail to provide a degree of anonymity for a young man traveling with two young girls, Avignon was still a sufficiently popular residence with French and British upper-class society to assure Day of intellectual adult company. With its shady squares and cool court-

yards encircled by three miles of solid ramparts, Avignon provided a pleasant haven where he could pursue his educational experiment without fear
of disturbance. Day ushered Sabrina and Lucretia through one of the city's
seven gates and rented a house in Avignon's most desirable district, the
Quartier des Fusteries.

Close to the great papal fortress, the Popes' Palace, the fusteries district
owed its name to the wood sellers, the *fustiers*, who once lived there alongside other poor artisans, but now it was dominated by grand town houses,
called *hôtels*, belonging to the idle rich. Having rented his house from a
certain Monsieur Fréderic, Day employed native-speaking servants so that
he could continue to exclude any outside influences on the two girls. Here
Thomas Day began the difficult task of choosing which of his two pupils
should become his perfect wife. But first he planned to go out and ingra-
tiate himself with Avignon society.

Discarding his usual drab garb, he sailed out into the Avignon streets
in a new laced coat, which he had probably bought in one of the fashionable shops of Paris, or in Lyon, which was famous for its silk and embroidered cloth. When in Avignon, Day presumably reasoned, he should
dress like the locals. The novelist Tobias Smollett scorned extravagant
French fashions at least as much as Day, but he explained that in France
English travelers either had to adopt flamboyant French clothes or make
themselves look even more foolish by comparison: "When an Englishman comes to Paris, he cannot appear until he has undergone a total
metamorphosis."

For men this metamorphosis meant a shopping spree for new clothes, a
new wig, a new hat, new shoes and even new buckles and ruffles. The costume varied according to the season. French fashion decreed that in spring
or autumn men should wear a suit made of "camblet," a blend of goat or
camel hair with silk. In summer, they should wear a suit of silk, and in winter a suit made of "cloth laced with gold, or velvet." Decked out in his laced
coat, perfectly in vogue for the winter season, Day was ready to enter the
best Avignon society. Even if he had only just begun the process of trans-
forming his two girls, he had easily mastered his own metamorphosis.

Looking the very picture of the perfect fop, Day spent a dizzying first
week visiting Avignon's abundant coffeehouses, concert halls and soirées.
Adopting French couture, French manners and even testing his schoolboy's

French conversation, he was warmly welcomed into French society and impressed his hosts as "the traveller, the polite scholar and the fine gentleman," he told Edgeworth in this new spirit of effervescence. "I have been introduced into all the polite assemblies. I know something of their manner of life, at least the outward and visible signs." Although he was shocked by the capacity of the local bourgeoisie for squandering their days in idle leisure—gambling, drinking and gossiping—Day was delighted at the ease with which he had infiltrated French society:

> There is indubitably among the French a greater spirit of dissipation than among the English: they are accustomed to no kind of employment, to no kind of attention; their mornings are spent in dress and in sauntering about, and their afternoons in visits. . . . In their visiting rooms, you see a number of beings lolling, walking, standing, yawning, talking of the same trifling subjects, which you would hear discussed in England with the same indifference, till the happy moment arrives, which sets them down to the gaming table. . . . If you go into their coffee-houses you find a number of idle people playing at dice, sitting round a stove doing nothing, gaping, yawning, getting up, and sitting down again.

Yet it was "so much easier for a stranger to get into society here" than in England, he continued, while there was also a "more generous spirit of politeness among the French." In France, "a man runs less hazard of being affronted, or meeting with any kind of incivility or positive rudeness," and with good reason, he noted, since the rules of etiquette laid down that a genuine insult or argument could only be settled on the dueling ground— and usually in death.

As to how his young companions were spending their time, Day maintained an infuriating silence. With a careful eye on his future reputation, he was obviously concerned that his letters might fall into the wrong hands. So just as with his letter to his mother from Paris, Day's first letter to Edgeworth from Avignon covered everything except the most interesting aspect of his trip. He seemed delirious with the excitement of his first continental travel or perhaps drunk on the thrill of his daring experiment. Yet his role as teacher was evidently on his mind. He ended his let-

ter by asking for news about Dick and his ongoing program of education—"let me hear of nothing but your boy, your wooden horse, and other
domestic occurrences"—and signed off with a battery of questions: "Have
you got a house yet?—have you got a patent?—a title?—a fortune?—a
child?—a medal?—a new chaise?"

At home in wintry Berkshire, a frustrated Edgeworth wrote back to
press his friend for news of the girls. Although he was busy enough jug-
gling all of the issues that Day had listed—another child was on the way,
his father was seriously ailing in Ireland and he was hunting for a new
house—Edgeworth knew that, in England, at least, he was legally responsible for his young apprentices' welfare. Furthermore, as he struggled to
apply the Rousseau regime to the truculent Dick, Edgeworth was feeling
increasingly doubtful as to the practicalities of the educational theory. Now
that he was five, Dick showed no inclination for either reading or writing.
While Rousseau's *Émile* insisted this was perfectly acceptable even until
the age of twelve, Edgeworth naturally worried that his son would not acquire his own love of books.

By the time Day replied a few weeks later, toward the end of 1769, he
was already tiring of France and French society—or perhaps the denizens
of Avignon's salons were tiring of him. The jaunty, jovial Day who had
bounded through the gates of Avignon in November had returned to form
as the gloomy and embittered young man who harbored a grudge against
everyone and everything. "That gaiety, my friend, which you remark in
my letter, is neither an effect of French, nor of the recovery of my health,"
he explained. "It is an effect of either a constitutional philosophy, or of
habit to make a jest, at least to others, of what is most disagreeable to me."
It was irony, he now insisted. And in a complete change of mood from
his previous enthusiasm, he continued: "For be assured no one circumstance of life was ever half so [disagreeable], as my residence in France."

Now he lamented that the French had no interest in discussing politics,
agriculture or science and no reason to discuss the weather since it was
"constantly serene." Bored and snubbed, he spent much of his time reading
and thinking. But even though he missed the "fogs and showers of Old
England," he was determined to last out the winter and continued to grace
the concert parties and assemblies he despised decked out in the comical

finery he detested. "Oh, my dear friend, you'd be quite surprised to see me now," he told Edgeworth. "Oh Lord! I am quite another thing to what I was—I *talks* French like any thing; I wears a velvet coat, and a fine waist-coat, all over gold, and dresses quite *comme il faut*: and trips about with my hat under my arm, and *'Serviteur Monsieur!'* and *'J'ai l'honneur Madame,'* &c. O dear, it's charming upon my soul!"

When he was not attempting French small talk, Day skulked moodily in a corner and fumed over his hosts' lifestyles and, in particular, their attitudes toward women. "Nothing can be more ignorant than those of the French Nobility whom I have seen," he told Edgeworth. "Attached entirely to exteriors," they were "enslaved by their king" and—a far more serious charge in Day's book—by "their women." French girls were generally educated in convents or brought up at home by governesses, Day told Edgeworth. When they were old enough to enter society, they "bring prejudice, extravagance and coquetry to their husbands: no laws, nor the force of the religion they are bigoted to, can restrain them; the feeble ties of modesty, decorum, or shame, are unknown."

Appalled at the tolerance within the French upper classes for what he termed "universal infidelity," he stormed, "the men can feel nothing but indifference for their nominal wives; hence all the ties of nature are broken through, all the sweet connexions of domestic life unknown." Naturally, it did not occur to him that his own behavior toward the opposite sex might be deemed immoral. And rising to his climax Day spluttered, "But the most disgusting sight of all is to see that sex, whose weakness of body, and imbecility of mind, can only entitle them to our compassion and indulgence, assuming an unnatural dominance, and regulating the customs, the manners, the lives and the opinions of the other sex, by their own caprices, weakness, and ignorance." This nightmare vision, a topsy-turvy world in which women dominated men, completely reinforced Day's faith in his educational project. It must have been a relief to return from these wild parties where women ruled the roost to his peaceful house where his two young girls waited meekly for their master.

More convinced than ever that adult upper-class society would never furnish him with a suitable spouse, Day threw himself into his educational project with relish. "You inquire after my pupils," he at last volunteered in his letter to Edgeworth. "I am not disappointed in any one respect. I am more attached to, and more convinced of the truths of my principles than ever." The girls' company had preserved him from "many melancholy hours," he wrote. "I have made them, in respect to temper, two such girls as, I may perhaps say with vanity, you have never seen at the same age. They have never given me a moment's trouble throughout the voyage, are always contented, and think nothing so agreeable as waiting upon me (no moderate convenience for a lazy man)."

Stoical, patient and submissive, the two girls were proving themselves perfect examples of the transformative powers of education—their education within the Foundling Hospital at least. More than a decade spent under the charity's guiding influence had produced models of subservience; their last few months in the company of Day could have had little impact as yet. Day was sure, however, that Rousseau's educational program would prove perfect for his needs. As he told Edgeworth, if all the books in the world were to be destroyed, the second book that he would save, after the Bible, would be *Émile*. "It is indeed an extraordinary work—the more I read, the more I admire," he enthused. "Every page is big with important truth. . . . 'Excellent Rousseau!' first of humankind! Behold a system which, preserving to man all the faculties, and the excellences, and the liberty of his nature, preserves a *medium* between the brutality and ignorance of the savage, and the corruptions of society!"

Batting away Edgeworth's own growing doubts about the Rousseau method, Day advised him not to worry about Dick's slowness to read and write, only to take care not to advance his education too quickly: "In respect to your child, I know of only one danger, which is you may enlarge his ideas too fast," he urged. It would never be too late to add to Dick's understanding, but "a single error, like a drop of poison" might contaminate him forever. "Never trouble yourself about Dick's reading and writing, he will learn it, sooner or later, if you let him alone; and there is no danger, except that the people of Henley may call him a dunce." Evidently Day had no concern about how the taunts of the residents of Henley, the nearest town to Edgeworth's home, might affect poor Dick.

Confident that he could stand, godlike, between his two foundlings in their brutal and ignorant natural state and the appalling destiny that

awaited them if they were left to the mercy of society's corrupting influences, Day embarked on their syllabus with gusto. While he had obviously
lost much time in starting the girls' education at the ages of eleven and
twelve, he was undeterred, for Rousseau himself had remarked: "Give me
a child of twelve who knows nothing at all; I should return him at fifteen
as knowledgeable as the child you have instructed from the earliest age."
And of course while Rousseau had detailed an educational program for
boys from babyhood to manhood in minute detail, he had made plain that
the education of girls needed far less attention and labor.

In fact, the method Day hit upon to train his two foundlings in Avignon was a hybrid of his own making, which combined Rousseau's approach for Émile and Sophie. Like the fictional Sophie, the girls were
taught to read and perform simple arithmetic—skills they had already
begun in their schoolrooms at the Foundling Hospital, and for the first
time were taught to write. And since Day was adamant that his future
wife should serve his every domestic need, the girls were encouraged to
cook, clean and wait upon their teacher as willing little helpmates just like
Sophie. With little if any help from servants, and certainly none speaking
English, the girls were therefore responsible for the bulk of the housework:
sweeping, mopping, swilling, cleaning grates, making fires, fetching water,
cooking, washing dishes, laundering, mending clothes and countless other
menial tasks. But since Day detested the usual social graces that were
prized in young girls within well-heeled families, unlike Sophie the orphans did not study a musical instrument or dance the latest steps or take
any interest in clothes. Unlike Sophie, they would not be moulded into
life-size versions of little dolls.

At the same time, Day was eager that his future wife—whichever of
the two girls she might be—should be able to converse with him on
weighty matters with intellectual interest. And so he adopted the curriculum that Rousseau laid down for Émile in order to teach the girls the basic
principles of geography, physics and astronomy through the pioneering
method of practical demonstration and experiment. The girls were therefore encouraged to work out the movement of the earth by observing the
rising and setting of the sun over the Avignon rooftops and to discern the
pattern of the seasons by studying the moon and stars in the dense black
Provençal night sky.

Both of the girls proved obliging pupils. With their heads bent over their letters and numbers, their chestnut curls and blond locks falling respectively over their books, Sabrina and Lucretia worked hard at their lessons. Their eyes widening in amazement as Day revealed the marvels of the natural world in homespun experiments on the dining table or field trips around the walled city, they progressed in their studies as the days shortened. But at the same time Day's lessons also included lectures on all the corrupt vices of society—especially appertaining to women—that he most despised.

"He taught them by slow degrees to read and write," wrote Edgeworth, "by continually talking to them, by reasoning, which appeared to me to be above their comprehension, and by ridicule, the taste for which might afterwards be turned against himself, he endeavoured to imbue them with a deep hatred for dress, and luxury, and fine people, and fashion, and titles." And before the end of the year, as evidence of his pupils' achievements, Day proudly included in his correspondence with Edgeworth an extraordinary letter, written in his own hand but "word for word" dictated by twelve-year-old Sabrina.

"Dear Mr. Edgeworth," the letter began, "I am glad to hear you are well, and your little boy—I love Mr. Day dearly, and Lucretia—I am learning to write—I do not like France as well as England—the people are very brown, they dress very oddly—the climate is very good here." Having dutifully imbibed her teacher's disdain for all things French, Sabrina continued: "I hope I shall have more sense *against* [by the time that] I come to England—I know how to make a circle and an *equilateral* triangle—I know the cause of night and day, winter and summer." And if any doubts of her appreciation for her teacher lingered, the letter ended: "I love Mr. Day best in the world, Mr. Bicknell next, and you next." The letter, Day assured his friend, was a "faithful display of her heart and head." Despite Day's efforts, Sabrina was not yet able to write herself, but it was the first expression of her own voice. There was no accompanying letter from Lucretia, however, to display her end-of-term progress.

Throughout the mild Mediterranean winter, the girls were kept diligently to their lessons, emerging periodically from the house to trail after their tutor on excursions around the town when Day would point out objects of scholarly interest or denounce the Gallic vices they passed along the way. Not surprisingly, the two English beauties with their blond and chestnut hair caused quite a stir as they trooped through the stepped streets and around the ramparts behind their gawky young teacher. According to Edgeworth, Day "excited much surprise by his mode of life, and by his opinions" in Avignon—although it was perhaps his ménage-à-trois that really excited the surprise. Just like his indulgent English friends, however, Day's French hosts displayed a remarkable tolerance for his strange mission. Their initial shock was "soon removed," wrote Edgeworth, by Day's "simplicity of conduct, uncommon generosity, and excellent understanding" so that "both he and his pupils were treated with kindness and civility by the principal people in Avignon." As before, on his hikes around England, Day's liberal dispensing of alms soon suppressed any questioning looks or ribald comments.

Although there is no evidence that Day went beyond the customary duties of a schoolteacher in grooming his two young girls, he did not present himself as the most responsible guardian for them, either. On one excursion beyond the city walls, he hired a boat to take himself and the girls across the Rhône. Since the famed nineteen-arch bridge of the old French folk song, "Sur le pont d'Avignon," had long since collapsed into the turbulent river, the only way to cross was by ferry. During winter, when the Rhône flowed notoriously fast and furious, even experienced boatmen would rarely attempt the perilous crossing. Day, however, was undeterred, but soon after he pushed off from the Avignon bank, his boat was caught in the current and capsized midstream so that the three were thrown into the torrent. Since neither girl could swim, both flailed helplessly as they were swept downriver. Luckily, Day was a strong swimmer, and he managed to drag both of the girls to the bank though not without "difficulty and danger to himself."

In an almost equally reckless escapade, Day took umbrage when he heard that a French army officer had spoken to his pupils "with too great freedom" one day when they were out for a stroll on their own. It was fine for Day to assume proprietorial rights over the girls but not for a stranger to make advances toward them. Storming out of the house, he confronted the officer with a pair of pistols, declaring that "he was ready to defend their minds, as he would their persons, from insult, at the hazard of his life." Challenging a seasoned soldier to a duel was foolhardy to say the least, especially since French rules of etiquette dictated that honor could only be satisfied with the death of one of the duelists. Evidently Day did not stop to think what would happen to the orphans if their protector was killed. Fortunately for Day, and his charges, the officer gallantly backed down and assured the Englishman that he had had no intention of offending.

As he tutored the girls throughout the winter of 1769 to 1770, Day silently monitored their progress. Every day as Sabrina and Lucretia labored over their lessons, carried out their chores and listened to their teacher's monologues on politics or fashion, Day assessed their intelligence, their readiness to learn and—especially—their willingness to bend to his command. With his particular views on dress, comportment and demeanor, Day noted how each of the girls spoke, moved, drank, ate and behaved as measured against his desired ideal. Alert to any signs of coquetry, vigilant for any hint of defiance, all the time he was making up his mind which of the two would best fulfill the role of his future wife. Naturally, he was weighing up their different appearances too; no matter how unworldly Day might appear he could hardly ignore their contrasting attributes. He had pledged, in the contract with Bicknell made in the summer of 1769, to decide within twelve months which of the orphans he would marry and discard her companion. He knew that before long he would have to make this choice. Would he choose auburn-haired and brown-eyed Sabrina or blond and blue-eyed Lucretia? Who would be the lucky winner of the undeclared contest to become Mrs. Day?

Like Pygmalion sculpting his ivory girl, Day naturally desired a woman who fitted the ideals of feminine beauty of the time. With the Georgians' reverence for the ancient Greeks and Romans, the perfect eighteenth-century woman looked remarkably similar to the classical ideal. Perfectly proportioned, like a statue of a Greek or Roman goddess, the sublime eighteenth-century woman possessed ivory-white skin—any hint of suntan suggested an unseemly life of labor—with rounded arms, a shapely figure, a slender waist, a long, graceful neck and an oval face. Her hair should be luxuriant and flowing, her nose fine and aquiline, her eyebrows delicately arched, her lips full and her eyes large, shining and expressive.

Eighteenth-century artists and sculptors who depicted Galatea at the moment she descends from her pedestal toward a waiting Pygmalion strove to reproduce this image of feminine perfection. In most representations Galatea is simultaneously girlish and innocent, with long, loose hair and a slim, hairless body, and yet sexually arousing at a time when most respectable women were covered from head to toe. Almost naked, like Eve in the Garden of Eden, she stretches out her hands in innocent invitation and smiles in sinful compliance. She is both chaste—with her eyes downcast and her lower half discreetly veiled—and completely available.

When in 1763 the French sculptor Étienne Maurice Falconet unveiled his marble sculpture of a kneeling Pygmalion enraptured at the moment that Galatea leans down from her pedestal toward him, visitors were overawed. Denis Diderot—one of the era's three great Francophone philosophers, along with Voltaire and Rousseau—declared the sculpture to be so lifelike that he urged spectators to touch the marble and feel it "yield to your pressure." Indeed, the cult of the living statue had an impact on a friend of Day's: her sister's suitor suddenly lost interest in her when he met a woman who resembled a statue of Venus. Upon marrying the woman, said the friend, he obtained his *"breathing* Statue."

Day's specifications for his paragon of womanhood had much in common with the idealized Galatea. He favored ivory skin and round, white arms as much as the next man. But in addition, his "breathing statue" must wear plain and simple dress, with her hair left long and natural, her face devoid of makeup and her body unadorned by jewels or ribbons, just like the country girl of his romantic poetry. Edgeworth summed up his friend's singular recipe for the perfect wife with typical aplomb: "Mr. Day had an unconquerable horror of the empire of fashion over the minds of women; simplicity, perfect innocence, and attachment to himself, were at that time the only qualifications which he desired in a wife."

But at the ages of eleven and twelve, still growing and developing daily, hardly out of childhood and only just approaching puberty, Lucretia and Sabrina presented a conundrum. It was no easy task to predict which of them might mature into the beautiful woman of his dreams or develop the ideal characteristics of his lifelong companion. As he turned from one girl to the other, Day felt helpless to decide.

Day's friends and acquaintances would make much of the fact that Sabrina and Lucretia possessed equally alluring but contrasting styles of beauty. To make Day's dilemma worse, the girls had equally pleasing but completely opposite characters too. So although he found himself drawn toward plump, fair-haired Lucretia with her sunny, jolly personality, he was also attracted to slender, chestnut-haired Sabrina with her quieter, more reserved nature and her eagerness to learn. What was a man to do? As the orange trees began to blossom in the surrounding fields in spring 1770, Day knew that he had to make a decision.

Slowly, gradually but decisively, one of the girls edged steadily ahead of the other in Day's secret talent contest. Since there was nothing to distinguish between the two pupils on looks, the contest hinged on their application to Day's lessons and their willingness to bow to his whims. As might have been predicted from her eager and obedient letter, which she had dictated to Day for Edgeworth, it was twelve-year-old Sabrina who showed the greater aptitude for learning. Her days laboring over her alphabet and numbers in the Shrewsbury schoolroom had not been wasted. Naturally bright and eager to advance, Sabrina blossomed under the care of her personal tutor.

With Sabrina, said one acquaintance, Day found "all of his projects were completely successful" while Lucretia demonstrated "not a single bit of progress in any study or any perseverance." Or as Edgeworth put it, no doubt repeating Day's own blunt assessment, Lucretia proved "invincibly stupid." According to Edgeworth, Day found that she was "at the best not disposed to follow his regimen." No matter how hard or carefully he chiseled, Lucretia remained a cold, dull block of marble.

Whether blond Lucretia was really quite so dumb as her tutor had concluded—or was simply rebelling against her teacher's methods and demands—remains open to question. Far away from familiar surroundings, fed up with foreigners gawping and gossiping about her and traumatized by her drenching in the Rhône, she had probably had quite enough of her irregular schooling arrangements. Yet if Lucretia was apparently impervious to his educational skills, her eyes wandering around the makeshift schoolroom in boredom, Sabrina plainly had eyes only for him. After all, she had already exclaimed: "I love Mr. Day best in the world." It was Sabrina, therefore, whom Day selected to become his child bride. Neither of the girls had any knowledge of their teacher's agonizing choice, of course, but whether they were entirely innocent of the competition for his attention is another question.

Accounts differ wildly on the state of domestic harmony in the little household in Avignon. One writer, who knew Sabrina in later life, painted a poignant picture of a happy trio. According to this view, Day could not look upon his "two charming foundlings" without "a mixture of admiration and pity" in the knowledge that he had plucked them from a life of hardship and now held their fates in his hands. Day, apparently, "could never see these two young girls without melting into tenderness; and this sensibility towards them brought out in him a softness of voice, a tenderness of manner, when he spoke to them that touched them so much that they, in return, could never reply to him without eyes full of tears in recognition of his kindness." Edgeworth, too, went to great pains to emphasize that Day treated the orphans with unremitting kindness so that both of them were always eager to do his bidding.

Another contemporary, however, who knew both Day and Sabrina at a later period, told quite a different story. According to this account, both girls quickly became fed up with their tutor and with each other. "They teized and perplexed him; they quarrelled, and fought incessantly; they sickened of the small-pox; they chained him to their bed-side by crying, and screaming if they were ever left a moment with any person who could not speak to them in English. . . . He was obliged to sit up with them many nights; to perform for them the lowest offices of assistance." Finally, according to this version, Day was "heartily glad to separate the little squabblers."

Yet while there may well have been times when the two girls bickered or grew petulant as they vied for the attentions of their teacher, as Day favored one pupil and then the other, the latter account is probably exaggerated. Sabrina and Lucretia were far too well trained by their Foundling Hospital upbringing to rebel quite so forcefully. And it is extremely unlikely that they came down with smallpox, the disease that had disfigured Thomas Day. Lucretia had been inoculated against the disease immediately on returning from her foster mother to the London Foundling Hospital, in 1766, when she was seven, according to the charity's records, and Sabrina had almost certainly undergone the same procedure in Shrewsbury.

By the spring of 1770, at any rate, Day—if not his pupils—had had enough of their French vacation. Homesick for English company and cooking, and even missing the country's seasonal fogs and showers, Day escorted his wards back through France and across the Channel to London. Thoughtfully he brought back a gold-embroidered waistcoat for Edgeworth. He confessed that he was anxious that it might be "seized" at customs; the more likely prospect that his two wards might be seized by suspicious customs officials had apparently not entered his head.

Arriving back in London, Day immediately set about discarding the unwanted Lucretia. Sticking to the terms of the contract he and Bicknell had agreed to, he placed her as an apprentice in a milliner's shop in Ludgate Hill and left her with a £400 farewell gift, which was a third of Day's annual income. Worth nearly £60,000 ($96,000) today, it was a small fortune for a humble milliner's apprentice and would certainly buy her a suitable husband. Lucretia would eventually make a happy marriage to a draper; she had not been so stupid after all. "In this situation," Edgeworth would later write, "she went on contentedly, was happy, and made her husband happy, and is, perhaps, at this moment, comfortably seated with some of her grandchildren on her knees." For Sabrina, however, the trials would continue.

Certain now that he had found the girl he could groom to become his perfect wife, Day determined to resume her education in earnest. Since he was still eager to shield his prize pupil from the vices of the metropolis and from prying eyes, he placed her in temporary accommodation with Bicknell's mother, at a house in the countryside not far from London. In the meantime he set about finding a convenient home where they could live together discreetly while he continued the experiment. At last, in late spring 1770, Day took a twelve-month lease on a delightful house in a perfect location where he could devote himself to molding the teenage Sabrina to fulfill his future dreams.

SIX

ANNA AND HONORA

❧ Lichfield, spring 1770 ❧

G rowing up in the plush Bishop's Palace in its prime position beside Lichfield Cathedral, Anna Seward had naturally come to dominate the social and intellectual life of the prosperous town. Her mother, Elizabeth, was the daughter of the Reverend John Hunter, the tyrannical headmaster of Lichfield grammar school, who had beaten an education into Samuel Johnson. Although he had since escaped Lichfield for London, Dr. Johnson would always say that his knees quaked at the sight of his headmaster's granddaughter with her striking resemblance to his former torturer. Educated at home, in a rather gentler fashion, by her own father, the Reverend Thomas Seward, Anna had grown up an intelligent and precocious child who at the age of three could recite Shakespeare and Milton. Since her father considered himself something of a poet, and had once declared his support for women's education in a poem entitled "The Female Right to Literature," the Reverend Seward taught Anna and her younger sister Sarah to appreciate the arts. After the family moved from Derbyshire to Lichfield when Anna was seven, on her father's appointment as Canon Residentiary of the cathedral, she immersed herself in literary pursuits. The family's home in the Bishop's Palace—which the bishop himself had vacated for even more salubrious accommodation else-where—had become the focus of learned Lichfield society.

Encouraged by her father, at nine Anna recited her early efforts at po-etry for admiring guests at soirées in the drawing room. She found that she enjoyed writing poems almost as much as she liked being the center of attention. She was just thirteen when she came to the notice of Eras-mus Darwin, who, on his arrival in Lichfield in 1756, moved into a house in the west end of The Close, which encircled the cathedral. As impressed by the confident teenager as she was by the exuberant physician, the two exchanged verses. Two years later, when Darwin announced that Anna's poetry was even superior to her father's, Canon Seward briskly decided that his daughter's literary ambitions had gone far enough. A "female's right to literature" was not, it seemed, to be taken quite so literally. Anna's mother, meanwhile, fretted that too much education might jeopardize her strident daughter's chances of marriage. Anna was promptly ordered to abandon her poems. Undaunted either by her parents' qualms or the city's veneration for its celebrated literary son Johnson, Anna refused to give up writing, in the conviction that her talents easily equaled those of any man.

Anna's youth in the happy company of her sister Sarah was an "Edenic scene," she would later say, made complete by the arrival in 1757, when Anna was fourteen, of five-year-old Honora Sneyd. The daughter of a prominent Lichfield family, Honora was adopted by the Sewards when her mother died and left her father unable to cope with eight young chil-dren. A pretty but fragile child, Honora grew close to Sarah, the quieter and gentler of the Seward sisters, and looked up rather in awe at the tall and forthright Anna. Spending their days in constant companionship, living more intimately than many Georgian husbands and wives, the three girls shared a suite of rooms at the rear of the palace, strolled arm in arm in the palace gardens and read aloud to each other on the palace terrace.

When Sarah died suddenly at the age of nineteen, Anna was distraught but compensated with bracing speed by anointing twelve-year-old Honora as her sister-substitute. Within days of her sister's burial, Anna assured a friend that Honora "more than supplied my Sally's place." Setting aside her grief, Anna plowed her considerable energies into polishing the teenage Honora's learning and finessing her charms. Half afraid that Honora might be snatched away in death like her sister Sarah, Anna told a friend: "This child seems angel before she is woman; how consummate shall she be if she should be woman before she is actually angel!"

Through her twenties Anna attracted several proposals of marriage, but none of them met her exalted ideas of romantic love. Swatting them aside like troublesome flies, she poured her passions into poems and letters extolling the virtues of her "sweet Honora." One poem, written in June 1769 to mark the twelfth anniversary of the arrival of the "lovely infant-girl," celebrated their "Angelic Friendship"; a typical letter praised "the oval elegance of those delicate and beauteous contours." As Honora blossomed into a beautiful, willowy and accomplished young woman, whose dainty features were framed by sleek dark hair, she too became a magnet for ardent young men beating a path to the palace door. Jealously guarding her protégée, Anna vetted them all with scrupulous care.

In eighteenth-century Britain, many female friends enjoyed intense relationships, which they celebrated in romantic terms. Some probably compensated for stiff and formal relations with parents by forging close bonds with same-sex friends. In one case, Eleanor Butler and Sarah Ponsonby ran away from their families in Ireland to set up home together in Wales, where they would live in mutual harmony for more than fifty years. Known as the Ladies of Llangollen, they attracted visitors from far and wide who venerated their romantic story with never a hint that the friendship might be anything other than platonic. Anna Seward would become one of their greatest devotees, and she established close friendships with other women too. But Anna's love—as she always described it—for Honora was by far the most intense.

Now twenty-seven, Anna presided over palace soirées with eighteen-year-old Honora at her side and reveled in her position as undisputed queen of Lichfield social life. With her acute eye for change and sharp ear for gossip, there was little that happened in Lichfield that escaped her notice. And so when two new arrivals slipped quietly into the neighborhood in the spring of 1770, Anna was the first to know. Always on the lookout for a consummate man who would equal the "consummate" woman she had skillfully crafted, Seward surveyed the new residents with interest. An invitation to the palace soon followed.

Taking a year's lease on a substantial villa called Stowe House, a discreet mile outside the city, Thomas Day brought Sabrina to Lichfield in late spring of 1770. With Edgeworth having dashed back to Ireland, as his father's failing health took a turn for the worse, Day had decided to settle in Lichfield to live near his new friend Erasmus Darwin and his invigorating circle of freethinkers. It was a bold step. Until now he had kept his wife-training experiment under wraps, concealing Sabrina in London and then France with Lucretia and later, on her own, with John Bicknell's mother in the countryside. Now, for the first time, he decided to live openly with his prize pupil in the full glare of gossipy Georgian society.

Lichfield was a shrewd choice. On his return from France Day had first gone to visit his mother and stepfather at Barehill. Although by rights he could have taken control of the property, his estate by inheritance, he could hardly bring his pretty young orphan to live in the family home to continue her wifely education. Lichfield, however, was far enough from his parental home to evade unwanted interest and far enough from London to remain outside the orbit of the scandal-obsessed newspapers, yet it was sufficiently lively to afford him all the pleasures of cultivated society.

Situated at the crossroads of the main coaching road from London to Chester and surrounded by the mills and potteries of the fast-encroaching industrial Midlands, the peaceful city in its fertile valley still retained an air of country charm and refined gentility. The two lakes, known as Minster Pool and Stowe Pool, which spanned the valley from east to west and cut the city in half, offered tranquil walks and green meadows. The crowded social calendar of concerts and plays, card parties and musical evenings, promised congenial company. And Stowe House provided a perfect haven.

Standing on its own in a secluded spot on the far side of Stowe Pool, Stowe House was only a fifteen-minute stroll from the heart of Lichfield. A tall and symmetrical villa, perched on a mound near the edge of the lake, the house had been built about twenty years earlier. Seen from the town, the redbrick house seemed almost to float above the water; at dusk the white edging to its windows and corners glowed ethereally. It was a view much loved by Anna Seward, who could see Stowe House from the windows of her dressing room at the rear of the palace. In fine weather she liked to sit on the palace terrace, sipping tea with Honora and looking out over the "watry mirror" of Stowe Pool with its reflections of "the Trees upon the bank, & the Villa near the edge." The "villa, rising near the lake" would figure often in her poems—especially once she discovered the events that were about to unfold within.

In Shaw's play *Pygmalion*, Professor Higgins bets that he can transform the coarse-spoken, rough-edged Eliza from "a draggletailed guttersnipe" into a duchess within six months. His honorable friend Colonel Pickering insists that Higgins should inform Eliza of his plan. "If this girl is to put herself in your hands for six months for an experiment in teaching, she must understand thoroughly what she's doing." Grudgingly Higgins agrees. "Eliza: you are to live here for the next six months, learning how to speak beautifully, like a lady in a florist's shop," he tells her. "At the end of six months you shall go to Buckingham Palace in a carriage, beautifully dressed." When Eliza moves into Higgins's house she is taken under the wing of the capable housekeeper Mrs. Pearce, who does her best to ensure that the professor comports himself with decorum in the flower girl's presence. Even so, Pickering cross-examines Higgins on the propriety of allowing a young woman to share his roof. "I hope it's understood that no advantage is to be taken of her position," presses Pickering. Higgins answers: "What! That thing! Sacred, I assure you. You see she'll be a pupil; and teaching would be impossible unless pupils were sacred."

Generous to a fault, Thomas Day was resolved to commit twelve months to train Sabrina for her role—double the time the fictional Higgins would spend on Eliza. But unlike Higgins, Day remained as determined as ever to keep her in the dark about his plans. If he gave her any information at all, it was to say that she was apprenticed to him as a servant; certainly this was the fiction he would later maintain. And unlike Eliza, now that Day had cast off Lucretia, Sabrina would be living with him alone. As Edgeworth made plain, Sabrina lived with Day in Lichfield "without a protectress." With no experience of the outside world, this was of no consequence to Sabrina; she was completely trusting in her kindly teacher. As she climbed the stone steps to the front door of Stowe House she had no idea that her trust would be tested to the limits over the coming months.

Inside Stowe House a wide entrance hall opened on to three handsome reception rooms. To the left, a cozy library contained a delicately carved chimney piece. At the far end of the library a door led into a spacious dining room that looked out onto the stables and gardens at the back. And completing the circuit of the ground floor, a door opened at the other end of the dining room into an elegant drawing room overlooking Stowe Pool. From the library a hidden staircase descended to the kitchen and laundry room in the basement. From the entrance hall, a grand oak staircase ascended past a stained-glass window depicting the Judgment of Solomon—an apt scene for a foundling's home—and proceeded up to two more floors containing six bedrooms.

Exploring her new home, Sabrina would have seen her reflection—a slim, pretty, auburn-haired girl on the verge of puberty—in the vast arched mirror set into the dining room wall. Standing in the drawing room looking out over the lake she would have seen the three spires of the distant cathedral perfectly framed in the central sash window. In the morning, when the sun rose behind the house, she could watch the fishing boats sliding across the sparkling water. In the evening, when the sun set behind the cathedral, she could see the wild ducks flying in to land on the dark still pool. But there was precious little time to admire the view.

As before, in Avignon, Day employed few, if any, servants. He may have hired men to tend the grounds and look after the horses, but there were no domestic staff living in the house. He was determined to live as frugally as possible, without fancy food or comforts, and his personal needs were few. But since Day anticipated that his wife would perform the bulk of the household chores in their country hideaway, he regarded housework as a vital part of Sabrina's training. So with Lucretia now gone, the task of managing the large four-story house fell squarely on Sabrina's slender shoulders. It was a long, tiring climb up those dark stairs from the basement to answer Day's calls in the library and to carry his plain meals to the dining room. It was even more exhausting to trudge up the two flights of stairs to clean and air the bedrooms. Day was determined to get his money's worth from his £50 donation to the Foundling Hospital.

On top of her increased housework, Sabrina's lessons continued unabated. Now that she had mastered the basics of reading, writing and arithmetic, Day concentrated on explaining the mysteries of the natural world and sharing his knowledge of the arts. So far he was still following the regime laid down by Rousseau in *Émile*. For as Rousseau recommended, once Émile found his Sophie he should teach her "everything he knows, regardless of whether she wants to learn or whether it is suitable for her." This curriculum spanned philosophy, physics, mathematics and history—"everything in fact," said Rousseau—although he conceded that women needed only "a nodding acquaintance with logic and metaphysics." Flourishing in her one-to-one tutorials, Sabrina progressed well.

With her chores and her lessons, life in Stowe House was scarcely less arduous than Sabrina's former regime in the Foundling Hospital. But even when these duties were fulfilled there was no time for rest or play since Day was impatient to introduce his promising pupil to old friends and new acquaintances. Eager to gain approval for his chosen bride, he escorted Sabrina on a giddy round of social visits to Lichfield's most affluent and influential residents. Before they left the house Day took care to ensure that his little novice was turned out in the modest and maidenly style that he favored. Her dress must be simple and unadorned, her arms and neck modestly covered, her face scrubbed clean without cosmetics and her auburn ringlets left loose and free. Her appearance adjusted to his satisfaction, Day set off on the path that skirted Stowe Pool with Sabrina at his heels.

The arrival of the wealthy young bachelor, who turned twenty-two that summer, with a girl of thirteen in tow might be expected to raise eyebrows in even the most liberal of neighborhoods. According to the unwritten code of conduct that constrained Georgian society like a corset it was strictly taboo for a respectable woman to be left alone with a man under any circumstances unless they were formally engaged; and even then a chaperone was usually mandatory. Even exchanging letters between a single man and a single woman was frowned upon. The entire plot of Fanny

Burney's novel, *Evelina*, hinges upon the heroine's horror at her (mistaken) belief that her hero asks her to collude in a private correspondence.

An unmarried man openly setting up home with an adolescent girl without servants or other chaperones would usually result in his being branded a despicable rake and her being shunned as his kept mistress. Yet far from attempting to conceal his dubious domestic arrangements, Day went out of his way to parade Sabrina around Lichfield's best-appointed drawing rooms. What was even more bizarre was that Day's conduct was apparently condoned without a murmur of dissent.

Even Edgeworth thought that this relaxed reception was "something singular." But ever eager to laud Day's "virtues" he reasoned: "His superior abilities, lofty sentiments, and singularity of manners, made him appear at Lichfield as a phenomenon"—Day was certainly that—while his "unbounded charity to the poor, and his munificence to those of a higher class, who were in distress, won the esteem of all ranks." Consequently "his breeding up a young girl in his house, without any female to take care of her, created no scandal, and appeared quite natural and free from impropriety." Before long, wrote Edgeworth, "all the ladies of the place kindly took notice of the girl, and attributed to Mr. Day none but the real motives of his conduct." Although, of course, Day's real motives were kept to himself.

In fact, Day's easy assimilation into Lichfield society is no mystery. In Georgian Britain money and status opened doors and closed eyes. Just as Day had bamboozled officials at the Foundling Hospital with his well-spoken accent and educated air, so he inveigled himself into Lichfield parlors. And if his imperious manner failed to silence chattering mouths, his generous donations to worthy causes sealed lips.

Acceptance at the Bishop's Palace was crucial to Day's entry into Lichfield polite society. Even for those with little or no religious belief, the Church of England played a central role in English country life. "Every stranger, who came well recommended to Lichfield, brought letters to the palace," explained Edgeworth, since the Reverend Seward's home was "the resort of every person in that neighbourhood, who had any taste for letters." Day certainly came well recommended, both by Darwin, Lichfield's most popular doctor, and by Edgeworth, who was already established as a favorite guest at the palace.

Edgeworth had met Anna Seward on his first visit to Lichfield, when he had dazzled Darwin with his electrical marvels in 1766. He had electrified Seward too. When Edgeworth last visited, a month or so before Day's arrival, Seward had written feverishly that the palace was graced by a "whole cluster of Beaux, one of them no *common* Beau, the lively, the sentimental, the entertaining, the accomplish'd, the learn'd, the scientific, the gallant, the celebrated Mr Edgeworth." His path smoothed by Edgeworth and Darwin, Day strode confidently up to the palace gates with his little orphan at his side.

Initial introductions went well. Day was welcomed with open arms by Canon Seward, who was regarded as something of a social climber, and his wife, Elizabeth, who may have sized up Day as a potential suitor for her wayward daughter, Anna. Although Day was no religious enthusiast, his literary pretensions along with his handouts to the city's poor and needy helped to ease his entry into church circles. Before long, said Edgeworth, Day was "intimate at the palace."

At the same time, the Sewards were enchanted by Sabrina. Quite how Day introduced the thirteen-year-old orphan, who was rather intimate in his household, remains unclear. He may have lied and described her as his apprentice maid—as he told Sabrina—though that did not explain her inclusion on social visits or excuse her lack of chaperone. Whatever story he spun, Sabrina was "received at the palace with tenderness and regard." According to Edgeworth: "She became a link between Mr. Day and Mr. Seward's family, that united them very strongly." Day had successfully stormed the palace, but his acceptance was not worth the paper his letters of introduction were written on without the approbation of Lichfield's acknowledged social queen.

From the start Anna Seward was fascinated by the "eventful story" that she soon divined was taking place in the house on the other side of Stowe Pool. As an avid reader of romantic novels, she could hardly resist the unlikely tale of the unworldly young man and his devoted little orphan. She would later write "it would be inexcusable to introduce any thing fabulous;

to embellish truth by the slightest colouring of fiction, even by exaggerating singularity, or heightening what is extraordinary" in describing those events. But then the "circumstances of Mr. Day's disposition, habits, and destiny were so peculiar," as she had to admit, that she had no need for any exaggeration.

Meeting Sabrina, Seward was entranced. She was a "beauteous girl" with a "glowing bloom," dark eyes and chestnut tresses, she wrote. Quick to recognize the sentimental value of an orphan, she had already described her beloved Honora as "a little orphan child," even though her father was alive and well. How much more exciting was it to embrace a genuine foundling, with all the mysteries of her birth to conjure with. She immediately took Sabrina under her wing. Thomas Day was equally intriguing.

First impressions were not promising, however. "Mr. Day looked the philosopher. Powder and fine clothes were, at that time, the appendages of gentlemen. Mr. Day wore not either," she wrote. But while others were repulsed by Day's slovenly appearance and eccentric manners, Seward regarded these rather as signs of a free and untamed spirit. Although she could be as vain as the next woman about her appearance, Seward had no patience with changing trends; contrary to the fashion for women to wear extravagant wigs or to cover their hair with thick gray powder, she took pride in wearing her luxuriant, auburn hair naturally loose. She could even forgive Day's loping, ungainly figure.

"He was tall and stooped in the shoulders, full made but not corpulent, and in his meditative and melancholy air a degree of awkwardness and dignity were blended," Seward observed approvingly. Despite his heavy eyelids and the marks on his face of the "severe small-pox" that he had suffered as a child, Anna admired Day's "sable hair, which, Adam-like, curled about his brows" and was beguiled by his "large hazle eyes," which flashed expressively when he delivered his impassioned monologues.

A portrait of Day, painted by Joseph Wright while Day was staying in Stowe House in 1770, is an accurate likeness, according to Seward. Wearing a gold satin jacket, which he had presumably brought back from his travels, now rather straining at the buttons after his reunion with English cuisine, Day leans casually against a pillar, his shoulders wrapped in a scarlet mantle, staring soulfully into the distance. Although he is only twenty-two, his fleshy features betray the beginnings of a double chin, but Wright has tactfully masked the signs of smallpox on Day's pink cheeks. Lost in philosophical contemplation, he holds an open book in his left hand; it was almost certainly Rousseau's *Émile*.

Living in Liverpool at the time, Wright was still struggling to establish himself as a portrait painter. His remarkable group portraits, *A Philosopher giving that Lecture on the Orrery, in which a lamp is put in place of the Sun*, and *An Experiment on a Bird in the Air Pump*, showing children enthralled by home science lessons, had been exhibited in 1766 and 1768. Wright had probably been lured to Lichfield by Darwin, his friend and doctor; he painted a portrait of Darwin at about the same time as that of Day. It was probably through Darwin that Wright obtained the commission to paint Day.

In fact Wright produced two large, almost life-sized, oils of Day for a fee of twenty guineas each (today about £3,000, or $5,000). Although almost identical they are two different pictures—not copied one from the other. One was probably painted to order for Edgeworth—he later placed the portrait of his friend above the sofa in the sitting room of his home in Ireland; the other was presumably for another friend. But in contrast to Wright's portrait of Darwin, who is seated at a desk with his arms folded in business-like fashion to denote the professional man of the age, Day stands in the open air against a dark sky in a meditative pose to suggest his communion with nature and poetical sensibility. With his outdated costume—the open-necked shirt evokes the seventeenth rather than the eighteenth century—and his dreamy gaze, Day appears to be a man from a past age lost in another world. Observing the "tempestuous, lurid, and dark" sky of Wright's portrait, Seward typically let her imagination run away with her when she added that "a flash of lightning plays in Mr. Day's hair, and illuminates the contents of the volume." There is no lightning in Wright's painting. But the stormy skies would certainly prove ominous for their relationship.

Day's renowned aversion to mixed company and undisguised contempt for the female mind did not augur well considering Seward's keen literary ambitions and her faith in sexual equality, if not female superiority. His religious skepticism and frugal lifestyle were not obvious ways to impress the vicar's daughter who liked to host convivial tea parties. As Seward noted, Day was "a rigid moralist, who proudly imposed on himself cold abstinence, even from the most innocent pleasures" who was marked by a "tincture of misanthropic gloom" and displayed "a proud contempt for common-life society." Yet in other ways they were kindred spirits. They were both afflicted by difficult relations with their parents; they had both suffered unfulfilling romantic experiences; and they both poured these frustrations into poetry. And so Seward was drawn to the "youth of genius," and she pronounced Day to be "less graceful, less amusing, less brilliant than Mr. E. but more highly imaginative, more classical, and a deeper reasoner."

Since Honora, the usual target for her affections and audience for her secrets, had been sent to Bath that summer in the hope the spa waters would restore her precarious health, Seward and Day became close friends and confidants. Before long Seward was divulging the secrets of her various romantic trials, and Day was describing the details of his eccentric marital project. Initially, at least, Seward was captivated rather than shocked when she heard about the astonishing educational experiment that was taking place on her very doorstep. Had she not, after all, been engaged in her own educational program in helping to tutor Honora Sneyd? Although their ideas about the desired attributes of womanhood were distinctly different, Seward and Day were both committed to grooming their particular vision of a perfect woman.

Seward, too, was an admirer of Rousseau. When Rousseau's novel *Julie, or The New Héloïse* was first published, she had asked Honora to translate the book into English for her. Having learned French at a local day school run by a French couple, ten-year-old Honora had read the steamy passages aloud while Anna listened with breathless appreciation; the reading sessions must certainly have proved educational. When *Émile* appeared, Anna read the English translation and declared the writing "exquisitely ingenious." She probably already knew of Edgeworth's efforts to apply the educational theory on young Dick. It was only later that she would describe the idea of putting Rousseau's system into practice as "wild, impracticable, and absurd."

On Day's repeated trips to the palace over the summer, Seward listened with rapt attention as he described his "aversion" to contemporary women's education, which he blamed for "the fickleness which had stung him." Day was still smarting from his rejection by Margaret; Seward realized the young poet was scarred by love as well as smallpox. Although Seward believed that it was better to be ditched at the church door than to "plight at its altar the vow of non-existing love," she found that Day was still determined to marry. And as she encouraged him to reveal all, she marveled at his recipe for the perfect spouse. She would later describe his plan with relish: "He resolved, if possible, that his wife should have a taste for literature and science, for moral and patriotic philosophy. So might she be his companion in that retirement, to which he had destined himself; and assist him in forming the minds of his children to stubborn virtue and high exertion. He resolved also, that she should be simple as a mountain girl, in her dress, her diet, and her manners; fearless and intrepid as the Spartan wives and Roman heroines."

Of course, as Day had concluded, there was "no finding such a creature ready made; philosophical romance could not hope it." And so, as Seward reported: "He must mould some infant into the being his fancy had imaged." Unwisely, perhaps, Day now divulged the whole story of how he had procured Sabrina from the Shrewsbury Foundling Hospital and then embarked on her training "with a view to making her his future wife." Recounting the tale much later, Seward described the contract Day signed with Bicknell pledging him "never to violate" his orphan's innocence. Enthralled by Day's scheme, Seward surveyed his "bachelor mansion" from her dressing room window with interest to see what would happen next.

His acceptance at the palace secured, Day made haste to introduce his pupil to Darwin at the other end of The Close that encircled the cathedral. Escorted by Day across the little Chinese-style bridge that spanned the moat in front of the doctor's house, Sabrina was warmly welcomed and became a favorite guest with the whole family. But there was little gaiety in the Darwins' house that summer. Darwin's wife, Mary, or Polly as he called her, had been ill for several years and despite her husband's ministrations—and liberal quantities of opium and brandy—died on June 30, 1770.

Darwin was devastated. He had married Polly, the daughter of a Lichfield lawyer, when she was seventeen and he twenty-six, in 1757. In one love letter, urging her to marry him quickly, he had jokingly claimed to have found a book of recipes. One recipe, he wrote, was entitled "To make Love." Darwin copied it out: "Take of Sweet-William and of Rose-Mary, of each as much as is sufficient. To the former of these add Honesty and Herb-of-grace; and to the latter of Eye-bright and Motherwort of each a large handful: mix them separately, and then, chopping them altogether, add one Plumb, two springs of Heart's Ease and a little Tyme." But when he came to a recipe called "To make a good Wife," Darwin told Polly: "Pshaw, an acquaintance of mine, a young lady of Lichfield, knows how to make this Dish better than any other Person in the World." Darwin had successfully mixed the ingredients for his perfect wife. Now he wept over Polly's corpse before tearing himself away to visit patients in an effort to "abstract my mind."

The following morning he returned for a last look at her, and wept again as he reread their love letters and compared her lively portrait with "the palid Hue of her dead Features." Left a widower at the age of thirty-eight, with three sons aged four, ten and eleven, Darwin invited his sister Susannah to take charge of his household. But there was little time for grieving. With his young family, his busy practice and his relentless scientific research, the doctor soon filled his hours—and his bed.

Although both Seward and Darwin had been let into the secret of Day's plans regarding Sabrina, neither made any attempt to enlighten her. Both were effectively complicit in his scheme. But their willingness to turn a blind eye to Day's errant conduct perhaps owed less to complacency and more to the need to suppress the inconvenient truths in their own lives. For behind the elegant doors of Darwin's house and the Bishop's Palace scandal skulked. That summer, just as Day and Sabrina settled into Stowe House, rumors were beginning to percolate around The Close concerning the overly friendly relationship between Anna and one of the cathedral's lay vicars.

John Saville had arrived in Lichfield from Ely in 1755, a shy but good-looking youth of nineteen, who took up a post as one of the vicars choral. A lay position with no religious duties or clerical outfit, the job entailed singing in cathedral services. Since he was already married, Saville had moved into one of the medieval cottages in the Vicars' Close, near the cathedral, with his wife, Mary, who was a year younger. The young new-lyweds soon produced two daughters; indeed they may have married because Mary was already pregnant. An intelligent young man, with a keen appreciation of music and a melodic tenor voice, Saville was naturally invited to gatherings at the palace where he was often called upon to sing or play. He may even have given young Anna music lessons. But the intimate friendship that gradually evolved between Seward and Saville was regarded as going beyond the normal duties of a musical tutor by his furious wife.

After her disappointment with earlier suitors, Anna drew close to Saville in her early twenties and before long she was deeply in love. Following one musical soirée in 1764 she enthused: "The ingenious Mr S-, whose fine voice and perfect expression do so much justice to the vocal music of Handel, was at my side in warmly defending the claims of that great master." Whether Saville was equally smitten, or simply felt powerless to resist Anna's unstoppable dynamism, would never be clear. With Anna it was always all or nothing: unbounded loyalty and all-encompassing friendship or venomous enmity and utter rejection. Certainly she was not going to let a wife and two daughters stand in the way of her desires; she would later describe Mary Saville as "the vilest of Women & the most brutally despicable."

Not surprisingly, by 1770 Mrs. Saville had become fed up with the amount of time her husband was spending at the palace and suspicious about the activities that detained him there. Rumors suggesting that the friendship between Anna and the tenor had gone beyond a mutual love of music began to spread. An anonymous letter to the Reverend Seward—which may have been written by Mrs. Saville herself—alleged that Anna and Saville shared an unseemly intimacy. In short, Anna was being accused of adultery.

Anna Seward knew that she could never marry Saville, unless, of course, he became a widower. For the vast majority of people in Georgian England marriage meant literally "till death us do part." A legal divorce, allowing remarriage, was impossible to obtain without a private Act of Parliament that required vast amounts of money and powerful connections and would prompt unthinkable scandal—most especially for a lay vicar and a vicar's daughter. Yet she would not give him up either. Furiously denying any suggestion of improper conduct to her parents, Seward insisted that Saville—or Giovanni, as she liked to call him—should remain a guest at the palace. It was the beginning of a love affair that would last thirty years—until death did indeed them part—in defiance of opprobrium from parents, friends, neighbors and even Church of England authorities. In her inimitable style, Seward would always refuse to acknowledge any hint of wrongdoing and imperiously insist on her right to pursue her desires. "He cannot be my husband," she would tell one disapproving friend, "but no law of earth or heaven forbids that he shou'd be my friend." She would always maintain that the relationship was purely platonic—and it is entirely possible that it was—yet she would celebrate the undying devotion between herself and Saville in fifteen love poems in which she changed their names to Evander and Emillia. In alternating voices, the poems describe the jealousy and anguish of two lovers who are separated by circumstances beyond their control yet pledged eternally to stay faithful to their "long-disastrous love." Forever forbidden from consummating their love, the pair will only be "Clasp'd in each other's arms" in the "bed of death."

For the moment, however, Saville continued as guest at musical evenings at the palace, where he was duly introduced to Day and Sabrina in 1770. Sabrina struck up a lasting friendship with Saville's eldest daughter, Elizabeth, who at nearly fourteen was just a few months older than her. And glad of a new confidant with a secret at least as explosive as her own, Anna confessed her love for Saville to Day. Both of them kicking against the conventions of contemporary society, they provided mutual sympathy.

It was not long before rumors began to circulate at the other end of The Close. Just a few weeks after the death of his beloved Polly, Darwin employed a young woman, seventeen-year-old Mary Parker, as a live-in nanny for four-year-old Robert. And while helping the young boy to cope with his grief, she was soon helping his father to recover from his. Within a year Mary Parker was Darwin's mistress. While living in the doctor's house she would give birth to two daughters by Darwin, Susan born in 1772 and Mary in 1774, who were both brought up as part of the family. Indeed, Darwin's grandson, the future naturalist Charles Darwin, would even suggest that the physician fathered an earlier illegitimate daughter, with a different mother, born in summer 1771 and who was conceived, therefore, in autumn 1770. Day's friends in Lichfield were clearly in no position to condemn his questionable domestic setup at Stowe House, even if they had wanted to, in 1770.

With the summer season of garden parties and concerts getting into full swing, Day and Sabrina became a familiar sight as they shuttled along the poolside path—or took the longer, drier route via Stowe Street— between Stowe House and the town's attractions. It was another wet summer. When Samuel Johnson made his "annual ramble" to Lichfield in July he complained that "this rainy weather confines us all in the house." Since his friend Elizabeth Aston, the landlady of Stowe House, was away from her home higher up the hill that summer, there was no reason for Johnson to brave the rain for his usual stroll around Stowe Pool, where he had learned to swim as a boy, and past Stowe House. Grumbling that "nothing extraordinary" was happening in Lichfield that summer, he cut his visit short and left for Derbyshire.

Johnson was wrong. For as the rain beat against the windows of Stowe House that summer some very extraordinary developments were taking place within. Pleased with the progress Sabrina was making in her lessons and chores, Day was eager to take her education to the next level. Having so far focused his attentions on shaping Sabrina's mind, now he devoted himself to grooming her body. Since he had determined that he and his future wife would live in primitive isolation—"Sequestered in some secret glade"—Day wanted to be sure that Sabrina was sufficiently strong to withstand all the privations and hardships of their planned life together in mutual misery. Indeed, as there would be no servants in this spartan household, Day's wife would probably need even greater stamina than he in order to perform her domestic drudgery. So Day devised some bizarre challenges. Inside the villa by the lake and within its secluded grounds, Day set out to test Sabrina's strength, courage and endurance to the very limits.

Drawing his inspiration partly from the program set down by Rousseau designed to steel the young Émile against hardship, but largely from his own fertile imagination, Day embarked on a series of trials designed to accustom Sabrina to extremes of cold, pain and terror. Rousseau, of course, had stipulated that children should be taught to withstand adversity by exposing them as infants to cold baths, to hunger and thirst, and to terrors such as spiders and thunder. "Harden their bodies against the intemperance of season, the climates, the elements. Inure them to hunger, thirst and fatigue. Dip them in the waters of Styx," exhorted Rousseau. "When reason begins to frighten them, make habit reassure them. With slow and carefully arranged gradation man and child alike are made intrepid in everything."

Day was not the only Rousseau fanatic to subject his pupil to physical ordeals. Edgeworth, of course, had followed the same regime in turning young Dick out of doors in all weathers—and with much success. It was for the same reason that the Wurtembergs doused baby Sophie in freezing fountains and the Swiss banker Roussel abandoned his five babes in the wood. Richard Warburton-Lytton, Day's friend at Oxford, who was another Rousseau disciple, would send his infant daughter Elizabeth out in winter to roll in the snow. And many more Georgian parents inspired by Rousseau adopted a similar approach in "hardening" their children by exposing them to cold temperatures and wet weather. Indeed, the idea became so fashionable that the surgeon John Hunter curtly demanded of one father, whose five children had all died as babies through exposure, whether he intended to kill his sixth child as he had "killed the rest." It was the other side of the nurturing Rousseau method—the school of hard knocks in conjunction with the classroom of soft cushions.

But Rousseau's tough love was intended to turn boys into men—not girls into women. According to his scheme, girls should undergo a gentler, kinder and more domesticated upbringing with its own particular privations; it was mind-numbing tedium, rather than finger-numbing cold, that girls were expected to bear. Day's attempt to impose a rigorous physical training on Sabrina was therefore a perverse striving for sexual equality.

Growing up with her foster families in the countryside Sabrina had been used to meager meals and bitter cold. Living in the Foundling Hospital she had endured long days of hard labor. And even over the last year living with Day, she had grown used to his plain diet and domestic servitude. But nothing could have prepared her for the trials he was about to unleash. If Day's actions had appeared essentially benign so far, now they began to smack of sadism. Across the Channel in France, the Marquis de Sade had progressed from subjecting occasional young women to his brutal fetishes to committing wholesale sexual violence upon a stream of men and women he abducted or hired. Day's behavior could not be described as sadistic—he took no particular pleasure in his torments—yet he plainly felt that he too possessed a right to inflict pain upon an unwitting young girl.

Behind the closed doors of Stowe House, Day ordered Sabrina to roll up her sleeves and bare her shoulders. He then took a stick of sealing wax and began to heat it in the flame of a candle. Ordering her not to move or to cry out, he dropped globules of molten wax onto her bare back and arms. Not surprisingly, Sabrina jumped up and screamed as the hot wax burned her skin—at least at first. As a variation on the ordeal by sealing wax, Day sometimes stuck pins into Sabrina's flesh and commanded her not to move or cry. The pain endurance tests were repeated on a regular basis. But this was only the beginning of her trials.

As well as learning to withstand pain, Sabrina had to be conditioned to extremes of temperature. For this challenge Day led her down to the banks of Stowe Pool in front of the house. There he forced her to wade into the lake fully dressed until the water reached her chin; according to one report he even threw her in. Unlike Samuel Johnson who had learned to swim in the lake, Sabrina was unable to swim, as Day knew, having had to save her from the Rhône the previous year. After nearly drowning in the French torrent, she was no doubt petrified in the murky waters of Stowe Pool.

Once he had satisfied himself that she was thoroughly soaked, Day allowed Sabrina to scramble onto the bank. Then he took her to the nearby meadows—marshy from the summer's downpour—and made her lie down in the grass. There she had to stay while her clinging garments and wet ringlets dried slowly in the sun. If she had not already been so well hardened to the battery of infectious diseases that had seen off weaker foundlings, she might have succumbed to pneumonia. Sabrina had survived the waters of Stowe if not Rousseau's "waters of Styx," and now Day wanted to test her resistance to fear. Rousseau had recommended that tutors subject their little pupils to thunderclaps or hairy spiders to wean them away from unfounded terrors by gradual degrees. He had even suggested accustoming children to loud noises by firing pistols. Typically pistols of the period were loaded with a single ball, which was rammed down the barrel after the main charge of gunpowder. A smaller charge of powder was packed into the cavity called a "pan" and ignited by striking a flint. This sent a "flash" through a small hole into the barrel to ignite the main powder charge and propel the ball. Rousseau recommended firing a pistol initially merely by putting powder in the pan to produce a flash, then placing increasing amounts of powder in the barrel to sound louder and louder bangs. Day decided he would apply Rousseau's test with a literal precision.

With no prior warning Day marched Sabrina to a secluded spot—probably in the enclosed gardens behind Stowe House. Then he took a pistol out of its box—probably one of the two dueling weapons with which he had threatened the lascivious officer in France—and instructed Sabrina to stand still and not utter a sound. He walked some distance away, cocked the weapon, took aim and fired directly at her skirts. Whether the pistol had been charged with gunpowder and loaded with ball Sabrina had no idea, and Day had no intention of enlightening her. She was expected to react with perfect calmness as he repeated the firearms test on a regular basis.

How well and how often Sabrina withstood these bizarre tests of strength was described with varying reports by various sources. "His experiments had not the success he wished and expected," Anna Seward would later write. "Her spirit could not be armed against the dread of pain, and the appearance of danger. . . . When he dropped melted sealing-wax upon her arms she did not endure it heroically, nor when he fired pistols at her petticoats, which she believed to be charged with balls, could she help starting aside, or suppress her screams." But another acquaintance, living in Lichfield at the same time, told a different story.

Richard George Robinson, who was chancellor vicar in Lichfield cathedral in 1770, wrote: "What Miss Seward says respecting Sabrina's not bearing pain heroically is not true. I have seen her drop melted sealing wax voluntarily on her arm, and bear it heroically without flinching."

Whether the Reverend Robinson was a guest at some event where Day demonstrated Sabrina's stoicism to prove the success of his training or for some reason Sabrina felt the need herself to prove her ability to withstand the hot wax to doubters, Robinson declined to say.

Another contemporary supported Robinson's version of events. Mary Anne Schimmelpenninck, who was the daughter of the Lunar club member Samuel Galton, was transfixed by the stories of Sabrina's ordeals, which she heard from a mutual acquaintance. "We heard how she stood unmoved when, every morning, he fired a pistol close to her ear, and how she bore melting sealing-wax being dropped on her back and arms." And another anonymous writer suggested that Day's pistol was definitely loaded with a potentially lethal ball. This source stated that when Day fired his pistol at Sabrina's skirts "the ball went through her cloaths but without injury."

There were further challenges ahead as Day invented ingenious methods and went to ludicrous lengths to measure his future bride against his ideal. To test her resistance to luxury and vanity, Day presented her one day with a large box. When Sabrina lifted the lid she found it full of beautifully handmade clothes. She had spent the majority of her life in her drab brown orphanage uniform, which she had exchanged for the plain gowns of Day's preference, so it is not hard to imagine her brown eyes widening with delight. What teenager would not have been impressed by the present of stylish new clothes? Then Day commanded her to throw the entire box onto the fire and watch as the flames reduced the expensive silk and lace to ashes. Mary Anne Schimmelpenninck recorded that "we were told of her throwing a box of finery into the fire at his request," and she could not help adding wistfully: "Sometimes I wished I were a philosopher."

Just in case Sabrina might be tempted by some choice foods or pretty adornment offered by a kindly soul when she was out of Day's sight, he made sure to forbid any of their acquaintances to indulge her. "I always discouraged every appearance of indolence & finery with the greatest vehemence," he would later tell her, "& I particularly desired every person who approached you to regulate his behaviour by these principles: of this there are many living witnesses at Lichfield." He maintained strict control of every aspect of her life at every moment.

Other trials were aimed at testing Sabrina's loyalty and obedience. For one assignment, Day invented some secrets concerning a supposed danger to himself which he confided to Sabrina under strict instructions that she must not reveal the details to anyone else. To his fury Sabrina blurted out the stories to others. As Anna Seward reported, "When he tried her fidelity in secret-keeping, by telling her of well-invented dangers to himself, in which greater danger would result from its being discovered that he was aware of them, he once or twice detected her having imparted them to the servants, and to her play-fellows." Since there were no servants within Day's household, she presumably meant the palace or elsewhere. Sabrina's indiscretion was hardly surprising; she was probably worried about the perceived danger to her protector—although there were obviously lots of secrets that Sabrina could have divulged concerning Day's treatment of herself had she so wished.

Yet there was one terror that, no matter how hard Day tried, Sabrina was unable to conquer: she was petrified of horses. To be afraid of horses was a most inconvenient phobia in the eighteenth century, when horses provided the chief mode of transport, the main vehicles for communication and the most important source of power. Horses were the driving force of the Georgian world. Yet Sabrina steadfastly refused to approach any horse no matter what inducement Day tried—and naturally he tried his damnedest. "Mr. Day told me he could not conquer her dread of a horse," wrote the Reverend Robinson, "and that no persuasion or bribe could prevail upon her to stroke its neck, though it was held by the bridle." She would rather suffer molten wax on her arms than stroke a horse. Robinson did not know the origin of Sabrina's terror, if indeed she knew it herself.

Even harder to explain is the fact that Day felt fully entitled to impose his torments on Sabrina, and those who knew about his actions did nothing to prevent him. The Georgians were not noted for their kindness to animals and children. Many children were forced to work in the mills, scale chimneys, beg on the streets or live by prostitution from the age of ten or less. Yet premeditated, pointless and repeated violence such as Day imposed on Sabrina was rarely condoned. Was Day simply impervious to the pain and terror he inflicted? Or did he just believe he had every right—as a wealthy, upper-class, educated man—to enact whatever cruelty he could dream up in his quest to create the perfect wife?

Although Day would later be praised for his kindness to animals—he refused to break in horses through the usual method and even opposed hunting for a time—he evidently felt no compunction about subjecting a thirteen-year-old girl to repeated physical and psychological abuse. As he would later explain in a letter to Sabrina, "I never thought I had a right to sacrifice another being to my own good or pleasure; but I thought myself sufficiently entitled to make an experiment where, whatever else ensued you would be placed in circumstances infinitely more favourable to happiness than before." Since he had rescued her from the Foundling Hospital and saved her from a life of hard labor, Day believed he was entitled to do what he pleased. Of course, he felt no need to ask Sabrina for her views. Like Professor Higgins, he presumed she did not have "any feelings that we need bother about." Yet as Sabrina's trials by water, sealing wax, pistols and horses proceeded over the summer months his friends in the Lunar Society viewed his project with growing alarm—for Day, if not for Sabrina.

Dates and details of early Lunar Society meetings are sketchy; indeed there would never be a formal constitution or a fixed membership. In the early 1770s, gatherings were usually held in Darwin's family home in Lichfield or Boulton's mansion at Soho, near Birmingham. As the prime movers, Boulton and Darwin tended to invite whoever they could reach at short notice to assemble for dinner and scientific debate on the Sunday nearest a full moon.

Quite why Day was invited to these lively, practical, gregarious get-togethers remains baffling. While the other members were all actively involved in some aspect of scientific progress—Darwin and Small testing advances in medicine; Keir manufacturing glass and experimenting with chemicals; Wedgwood improving ceramics; and Boulton collaborating with James Watt to improve steam power—Day took not the slightest interest in such marvels. At one point he would reject an offer from Boulton of some rocks and fossils with the blunt reply that he was far too engrossed in the "study of man" to be bothered with the study of science. While most of the Lunar men were driven by an entrepreneurial spirit to make their names and their fortunes, Day had nothing but disdain for the kind of luxury items that Boulton and Wedgwood were turning out of their factories

to embellish the homes of the rich. At the same time his puritanical outlook, his wearying propensity for long monologues and his intolerance of
contradiction were entirely at odds with his friends' warm, bubbling enthusiasm for each other's company and ideas. Day was not what Samuel
Johnson would term "clubbable." Or as Boulton would delicately put it,
he was "rather inclinable a little to the Misanthrope." Day was the dark,
cold, hidden side of the lunar surface, the wobble in its orbit.

Yet while Day's involvement in the Lunar group would always be spo-
radic, it would also be enduring. He did share the other members' largely
skeptical, sometimes atheistic, view of religion and their radical, occasionally revolutionary, politics. He also shared his money. Day lent significant
sums to Small, Keir and Boulton to help finance their business ventures.
Just as money smoothed Day's path into Lichfield so it oiled the wheels
of the Lunar circle.

But one aspect above all made Day uniquely interesting to his Lunar
friends: his marital obsession. For Day was conducting an experiment that
was far more astonishing than anything the rest of the group could conjure
with their chemical apparatus and their electrical machines. While they
mixed explosive chemicals, drew sparks from electrical charges and forged
steam engines, Day was meddling with the human mind. Even in the so-
called age of experiments, this was an experiment to top the lot.

Although in 1770 most of the group had only very young children or
were yet to marry, they all took a close interest in the subject of education
and were broadly enthusiastic about Rousseau's ideas. The Lunar men
would exchange views on education as their children grew—and sometimes exchanged their children too. In line with the Rousseau philosophy,
they encouraged their children to take part in scientific debates and sometimes involved them in Lunar meetings. Darwin liked to include his three
boys in educational demonstrations—the two boys depicted by Wright in
his air pump picture were Darwin's eldest sons—and Edgeworth would
shock visitors by passing valuable scientific instruments around his
youngest children. In later years, Darwin and Wedgwood would send their
children to stay in each other's homes and consulted each other on their
schooling.

Mary Anne Schimmelpenninck would certainly be encouraged to
watch events at Lunar meetings later held at her father Samuel Galton's

house. She would remember with delight one particular evening when she was allowed to catch and keep a snake that escaped from a guest's pocket. Whether Sabrina was brought along to any gatherings held on moonlit nights is unknown, but Day certainly introduced her to his Lunar friends and they followed her fortunes with interest. In particular, Keir and Small paid close attention to Day's wife-rearing experiment and took a paternalistic concern in its progress—for Day's sake at least.

A huge corpulent figure, with flabby jowls and a double chin, James Keir was a brash, hearty man with a sharp wit and keen business acumen. He had just bought a lease on a glassmaking workshop at Amblecote, near Stourbridge, not far from Birmingham, and lived in a house behind. Turning thirty-five in 1770, Keir had recently retired from the army partly in order to find a wife—perhaps, as he told Darwin, "some Lichfield *fair* that has more money and love than wit." Yet he certainly planned to find her through more conventional means than Day. It was grounded facts and fixed formulas that stirred Keir, not wild dreams of imaginary women.

Practical and rational, Keir regarded Rousseau's ideas on education as ridiculous and Day's plan to put the scheme into action as laughable. "Nothing surely can be more absurd than the principle of this plan of education, or more impracticable in execution," Keir argued. He blamed Day's cracked idea on youthful naïveté, which drew him into "delusions created by heated imagination" so that while others were merely amused by Rousseau's ideas, they sank "deep into Mr. Day's young and sensible mind." As Keir explained: "It is no wonder then, that at this period he was led, like many others, by the seductive eloquence of *Rousseau*, into worlds of fancy respecting education." Quick to laugh off his young friend's eccentric behavior, Keir would always be ready to excuse Day's errant conduct and conceal any inconvenient problems that arose. If Keir watched Day's project unfold with bemusement, William Small would do his utmost to bring it to an end.

True to his name, Dr. Small was a thin, wiry man. Although shy and withdrawn, he possessed a knack of bringing friends together, which made him dearly loved by those closest to him. Generous and compassionate, he had built a medical practice in Derby where he treated the rich for large sums and the poor for free. In his spare time he helped to found the city's first hospital as a permanent service to those who could not afford private treatment. Something of a father figure for Day, whose own father died before he was two, the doctor held "paramount" influence over Day, friends said. Prone to introspection and melancholy, just like Day, Small would never marry—and yet he took an intense interest in Day's mission to create a suitable wife.

Gently but doggedly, Small tried to persuade Day to abandon his Pygmalion project and adopt a more conventional approach to seeking a marriage partner. Convinced that an adolescent foundling—no matter how well educated—could never become the perfect wife for the bright young philosopher, Small tried to convince Day to discard Sabrina, and he even produced what he thought were more suitable candidates. As Edgeworth wrote, "He never saw any woman, whose character and situation in life appeared suitable to Mr. Day, without mentioning her to him, and endeavouring to give him an opportunity of judging for himself." With Small set on changing Day's direction and Keir determined to guard his reputation, nobody was paying much attention to Sabrina's fortunes. But just as Keir and Small were trying to subvert Day's Pygmalion project, the subject of his experiment was getting heartily fed up.

At first, when she had arrived in Lichfield that spring, Sabrina submitted meekly to Day's demands. Since he had plucked her from poverty, fed, clothed and educated her, and treated her for the best part with kindness, she was understandably devoted to him. But as the months passed she began to resent the boring lessons and question the cruel torments. According to Seward: "She betrayed an averseness to the study of books, and of the rudiments of science, which gave little promise of ability." Toward the end of the year she even had the audacity to complain about her onerous chores. As Day would later put it, in a letter to Sabrina summarizing her perceived flaws, "the dislike you soon discovered for every species of domestic application was one of the first causes of dispute which occurred between us." Shocked at this challenge to his authority, Day complained that "I found it out of my power to make you apply as I would wish." Sabrina, he later told her, "grew tired of living with me, & consequently negligent in your behaviour to me." The ivory girl had stepped down from her pedestal and stamped her foot. The foundling had found her voice.

The problem, as Seward acutely observed, was that Day offered neither incentive nor explanation for the bewildering demands and perverse trials. "The difficulty seemed to lie in giving her motive to exertion, self-denial and heroism," she wrote. Sabrina's "only inducement" was her "desire of pleasing her protector, though she knew not how, or why he became such." In that desire, Seward wrote, "fear had greatly the ascendant of affection, and fear is a cold and indolent feeling." Sabrina herself would later tell a friend that Day had "made her miserable—a slave &c!"

She was growing up. As an innocent twelve-year-old who knew only the world inside the orphanage walls, she had unthinkingly accepted Day's interest as the kindness of a benevolent gentleman like those who served the foundling charity. Now that she was heading toward fourteen and spent each day immersed in fashionable society, alert to the playful comments and meaningful looks of the adults who flirted around her—and perhaps even with her—she began to question her puzzling situation in Day's household. She occupied a strange position without parallel in the families she had come to know, a curious hybrid of privileged daughter and unpaid skivvy, hovering precariously between the upper echelons of the gentry and the lowest rungs of society. Her visits to Darwin's home, where seventeen-year-old Mary Parker was absorbing the doctor's attentions, may have prompted some questions about her position; her friendship with Elizabeth Saville, in the midst of her father's intimate relationship with Seward, may have suggested some answers. Her body most likely had begun changing too, but there was no motherly figure or chaperone to explain the onset of puberty.

Day refused to explain her role in his scheme. Although he made no secret of his marital intentions to friends, he kept Sabrina in total ignorance of this rather important detail. Indeed, he would always maintain the deliberate fiction that she was apprenticed to him as a domestic servant. He would later tell Sabrina: "When I originally took you, you were articled to me as a servant; it was in that capacity I received you, & talked to you; my whole behaviour was in unison with that idea, excepting the admitting you to sit with me, & raising you above the common drudgery of a family." As to her future, Day told her that she could earn a position as his housekeeper if she passed her peculiar probation tests, but if she failed to meet his exacting standards he would dispatch her to learn a trade like the unfortunate (or perhaps in fact fortunate) Lucretia. Yet from the looks that she was receiving from Lichfield's residents, if not from some of Day's associates, Sabrina was rapidly becoming conscious of her dubious social position. Whether Day's physical training went even further than singeing her shoulders with burning wax would remain concealed forever behind the wooden shutters of Stowe House.

Day's friends would always be at pains to emphasize his moral probity—Keir tirelessly praising his "virtue" and Edgeworth hymning his "strict morality"—almost to the point of protesting too much. He had, of course, undertaken to Bicknell "never to violate her innocence." Certainly there was no direct evidence that Day took sexual advantage of Sabrina. At a time when contraception was haphazard at best, an unwanted pregnancy was usually the result of a prolonged sexual liaison—though the Georgians were highly adept at concealed pregnancies and secret births. Equally at times there was something perversely asexual about Day's awkwardness in mixed company and his obsession with fighting female seduction. Even if Day's conduct toward Sabrina was spotlessly honorable, however, he had certainly placed her in a perilous position that would inevitably tarnish her future reputation.

The ambiguity of Sabrina's situation would absorb Henry James more than a century later when writing his first novel, *Watch and Ward*, published in 1871. Although James transplanted the drama from eighteenth-century England to nineteenth-century America, he plainly based his seemingly far-fetched plot on the true story of Sabrina Sidney and Thomas Day. In the novel, the wealthy Roger Lawrence unofficially adopts a twelve-year-old orphan, Nora Lambert, and educates her with a view to making her his "perfect wife." Yet while Roger confides his plan to friends he refuses to answer Nora's frustrated questions about her role in his life. "What are you?" Nora asks. "Neither my brother, nor my father, nor my uncle, nor my cousin,—nor even, by law, my guardian."

Later James would all but disown his early novel, not least for its clumsy sexual imagery such as the moment when Roger "caught himself wondering whether, at the worst, a little precursory love-making would do any harm. The ground might be gently tickled to receive his own sowing; the petals of the young girl's nature, playfully forced apart, would leave the golden heart of the flower but the more accessible to his own vertical rays." In the novel, in accordance with the Pygmalion myth, Roger and Nora ultimately marry. In reality, just like Shaw's Eliza Doolittle, Sabrina was refusing to fall in with Day's plans. By the time the autumn mists over Stowe Pool turned to ice at the end of 1770, the teenage orphan was on the point of rebellion.

It was Richard Lovell Edgeworth, bringing some rare cheer to the house when he visited over Christmas, who brought Sabrina's ordeal to an end. After a long illness, his father had died in August, leaving Edgeworth the family estate and a sizable fortune. He now enjoyed an annual income of £1,500 (£225,000, or $363,000 in today's currency). Returning to England in the autumn, with another addition to his growing family, a second daughter, Emmeline, Edgeworth was still straining at the reins of his unhappy marriage. With relief he escaped to Lichfield in December "curious to see how my friend's philosophic romance would end."

Riding up to the front door of Stowe House in one of his sporty carriages Edgeworth was impressed by his friend's "pleasant house" near the town. But he was troubled by the situation he found within. Surveying Day's young apprentice after a gap of more than a year, Edgeworth discovered that the shy little girl he remembered had blossomed into an attractive and accomplished young woman: She had "a beauty, which was then more striking, because other people wore enormous quantities of powder and pomatum. Her long eyelashes, and eyes expressive of sweetness, interested all who saw her, and the uncommon melody of her voice made a favourable impression upon every person to whom she spoke."

It was immediately plain to Edgeworth what everybody in Lichfield apart from Day had already concluded: that Sabrina was "now too old to remain in my friend's house without a protectress." Joining Keir and Small in their efforts to subvert Day's quest for the perfect woman, Edgeworth sought to persuade Day to find more suitable arrangements for his thirteen-year-old lodger. Little did Edgeworth guess that he would find his own perfect woman first.

Drawn into the Christmas revels that centered on the palace, Edgeworth renewed his acquaintance with Anna Seward—and with her beloved Honora, who was now nineteen. On previous visits he had barely cast Honora a glance, as the vivacious Anna eclipsed her quiet protégée. But that Christmas, Edgeworth suddenly saw Honora emerge from the shadow of her mentor, and he was dazzled by her classical beauty and unassuming grace. To his amazement Edgeworth discovered that this radiant creature shared his fascination for mathematics and mechanics. Desperately miserable in his loveless marriage, for the first time in his life he had found "a woman that equalled the picture of perfection, which existed in my imagination." Edgeworth, for one, had found his ideal partner.

The attraction was entirely mutual. If Edgeworth had taken his time in perceiving the charms of Honora, she had plainly been enamored of Edgeworth for some while. Back in April, when Seward had gushed to a friend about her scintillating evening with the "celebrated Mr Edgeworth," Honora had been too overcome to add a postscript. While she had been away with her father and sisters in Bath, Honora had written secretly to Mrs. Seward—behind Anna's back—imploring her to persuade her father to send her back to Lichfield. The moment that the summons arrived, Honora had battled through autumn floods and arrived breathless in Lichfield to "bound into the dining-room" with "tears of joy" in her eyes.

As far as Anna Seward was concerned, this intrepid flight was motivated solely by Honora's desire to be reunited with her "books and conversations with me, and with a few dozen friends!" But it happened at exactly the time that Edgeworth arrived back in England; it was obviously Edgeworth with whom she was desperate to be reunited. Now that he had finally noticed her shy glances and blushing smiles, she told him he was the "first person, who had seen the full value of her character."

Rather forgetting the inconvenient fact that he was already married, that Christmas season Edgeworth wore down the footpath between Stowe House and the palace to spend all his leisure hours in company with Honora. When he was not at the palace discussing mechanics with Honora, he was pestering his friends to affirm the superiority of Honora's looks and talents. Good-humoredly, Darwin, Keir and Small agreed "unanimously" with his verdict—though privately they may have despaired that neither of their two young friends could manage their matrimonial affairs very wisely. Only Day dissented. Since she failed to match his particular vision of female perfection, Day sniffily pointed out that Honora danced too well, that she was too swayed by fashion and that her arms were not sufficiently plump and white. As he laughingly dismissed his friend's foibles, Edgeworth blamed this insensibility to the attractions of his ideal woman on the fact that "Sabrina Sydney had, perhaps, preoccupied his mind."

Somewhat foolishly Edgeworth confessed his passions to Seward. To his delight he found that she listened sympathetically and even claimed to have guessed his interest before he had realized it himself. Indeed, she seemed "gratified" by the praises he heaped on her clever pupil and eager to place Honora's attainments in the "most advantageous point of view." Or so Edgeworth believed. In reality, Seward was appalled to learn that Edgeworth had now taken her own place in Honora's affections. Determined that if anyone was going to mastermind Honora's love life it would be she, Seward was not prepared to see her "lovely Honora" wasting her attentions on a married man. She had her own experience of that bitter sorrow. The vicar's daughter moved in mysterious ways. Even as she encouraged Edgeworth to unburden his heart, she was plotting to undermine his interests. Casting about for a more suitable suitor, she alighted on the obvious candidate: the stoic philanthropist of Stowe House.

The New Year brought new challenges. Early in 1771, as Sabrina approached the age of fourteen, Day conceded that it was no longer respectable for her to remain in his "bachelor mansion." After nearly twelve months of lessons and ordeals in Lichfield, Day concluded that his daring educational experiment had been a failure. At that point, he promptly "renounced all hope of moulding Sabrina into the being his imagination had formed," according to Seward, and ceased "to behold her as his future wife." As Day bluntly informed Sabrina and told his friends, she had failed to meet his expectations. In reality, it seems, he had begun to focus his expectations elsewhere.

As the ice thawed on Stowe Pool, Sabrina packed her plain dresses and few possessions and said goodbye to her benefactor and newfound friends. With no explanation for her abrupt dismissal apart from Day's complaints about her inattention to her lessons and her chores, Sabrina was dispatched to a boarding school eight miles away in Sutton Coldfield. If she worked hard, Day told her, she might later be apprenticed into a suitable female trade. Coldly taking his leave, he instructed the schoolmistress to concentrate on teaching his failed pupil to improve her reading, writing and arithmetic but—maintaining his iron grip on her future—on no account to allow her to learn either music or dancing. There would be no revels in Sabrina's new life. Abandoned by her guardian of the past two years at the school door, just as she had been abandoned at the gates of the Foundling Hospital fourteen years earlier, Sabrina would spend the next three lonely years bent over her books in the little school.

Men, it seemed, could be every bit as fickle as women.

SEVEN

ELIZABETH

⇜ Sutton Coldfield, spring 1771 ⇝

Although it was just eight miles from Lichfield, Sutton Coldfield might as well have been on the other side of the world. Banished to boarding school in early 1771, Sabrina had exchanged her friends for strangers, her progressive and intimate tutorials for traditional rote learning in a classroom full of girls and the vibrant social life of Lichfield for dreary seclusion. For although it stood just two miles from the busy coaching road between London and Chester, the quiet little town could only be reached by a narrow, winding and lonely track across barren wilderness.

Named Sutton (Old English for South Settlement) because it was the town directly south of its bigger neighbor, Lichfield, and Coldfield for the bleak and inhospitable heath that lay between the two, Sutton Coldfield had acquired a reputation for hard drinking and lawlessness. The expanse of open common that bordered the town was notorious for robberies; travelers who did not meet a highwayman on horseback demanding their money were as likely to meet a dead one hanging from a gibbet. Those who dared to cross the moors on foot ran the risk of disappearing forever into a bog or into an inn. One traveler, a woman peddler laden with jewelry, paused for refreshment at a remote tavern and never reemerged; her bones were discovered years later beneath an enclosed wooden bench. So while many of the local people worked hard in the district's mills, producing knives, ax blades and gun barrels for the traders of Birmingham, others made less honest use of those products to earn their living.

It was little wonder that the townsfolk kept mainly within town boundaries. Certainly Sutton Coldfield itself boasted a number of fine houses, a handsome church, a reputable boys' grammar school and even a book club. But the dearth of other diversions—there were no concerts, plays or assemblies—left the inhabitants with little sport beyond drinking. One resident, writing to *The Gentleman's Magazine* in 1762, boasted that the town's citizens were such "strangers to gaming and whoring" that there had been only "one kept mistress in the place these forty years." But he was quickly contradicted by another inhabitant who replied that far from there being a lack of kept mistresses, "I hardly ever knew the town without one." The controversy was plainly the most exciting occurrence there for decades for the dialogue was published as a pamphlet with a title page containing the wry motto: "Here Dullness, Universal Dullness Reigns, / O'er brainless Heads and desolated Plains."

For the town's newest resident, unpacking her clothes in her boarding school, the next three years promised little variation. Since she was sleeping in a dormitory once again, and in all likelihood sharing a bed, with her few possessions stored inside a box, her days would be little different from her former life in the Foundling Hospital. Except that now the routine of lessons, meals and visits to church was not even alleviated by singing or dancing.

Edgeworth described Sabrina's school as "very reputable." No doubt her fellow scholars were daughters of the local gentry sent to perfect their skills in writing, arithmetic, needlework, music and dancing. There was a wide choice of such schools, usually run by a schoolmistress and a few assistants, devoted chiefly to preparing young girls for a suitable marriage. They offered precisely the kind of female education that Day professed to despise.

With few opportunities for pleasure, and the specter of the town's workhouse to remind her of her fate if she did not succeed, Sabrina had little alternative but to work hard at her studies. The monotony of her humdrum days would be enlivened only by letters and visits from Day on the rare occasions when he broke his journeys between Lichfield and Birmingham or London to cross the forbidding heath and check on the progress of his pupil. Since he paid her school fees and promised her advancement if she progressed, he remained the most significant force in her life. Spending her weekends and holidays incarcerated inside the school, watching out of a window for a glimpse of a tall, stoop-shouldered, lank-haired visitor, she must have felt herself all but forgotten.

Meanwhile, life in Lichfield was anything but dull. Once Day had placed Sabrina out of sight in Sutton Coldfield, he found no trouble in simultaneously putting her out of mind. His trust in the power of education had "faltered," according to Anna Seward. His trials had all proved "fruitless." But if he could not fashion an ideal wife through careful tutoring, then he would simply have to fall back on finding one ready-made. As luck would have it, his friend Edgeworth had already found the supreme candidate: Honora Sneyd.

As with all Day's romantic interests, the relationship began badly. Despite visiting the palace almost daily for the best part of a year, Day had proved impervious to Honora's fabled beauty and lauded talents. When Anna Seward had eulogized her pupil's aptitude for learning and graceful elegance, Day had yawned politely. When Edgeworth had poured out his longings for the clever, beautiful woman of his dreams, Day had pompously reminded him of his domestic duties. But after months of listening to Seward and Edgeworth lavishly praising Honora's accomplishments, Day finally began to perceive her attributes for himself.

For all her slender and bronzed arms, her disconcerting skill at dancing, her troubling pleasure in fashionable clothes and her polished manners, Day now grudgingly admitted that nineteen-year-old Honora might just possess the necessary qualifications to become his preferred partner—provided she underwent a rigorous retraining in the Rousseau manner and subject to passing the usual trials. It was, the lovesick Edgeworth observed, the strangest romance. Utterly confounded by his friend's indifference to his loved one's charms, Edgeworth wrote, "few courtships ever began between such young people with so little appearance of romance."

Edgeworth's exasperation was understandable. Coming from a family of renowned good looks and substantial means, Honora had already won a string of admirers. A powerful dynasty, the Sneyd family had been established in Staffordshire since medieval times. Honora's father, Edward Sneyd, was the third son of one branch of the family that owned an estate at Bishton, a village in Staffordshire, near the border with Wales. Since he was unlikely to inherit the family fortune, he had enlisted in the Royal Horse Guards, married the daughter of an Essex vicar, Susanna Cooke, and set up home in Lichfield. Over the next twelve years Mrs. Sneyd gave birth to ten daughters who arrived in unvaried succession followed, finally, by two sons—the rather belated heir and a spare—named Edward and William. Four of the girls died in infancy, but their six sisters—Anne, Lucy, Mary, Honora, Elizabeth and Charlotte—all thrived. Mrs. Sneyd did not. Shortly after William's birth, in 1757, she died—exhausted—leaving her husband beside himself with grief and surrounded by eight motherless children under the age of eleven.

Just as Honora had been welcomed into the Seward family, her siblings were parceled out among family and friends in the manner of foundling babies being dispersed to foster mothers—albeit into rather more comfortable circumstances. Growing up in their scattered families, the Sneyd sisters attracted widespread sympathy and uniform admiration. Three of the girls—Lucy, Honora and Elizabeth—were acclaimed as "celebrated beauties." Some—not least Anna Seward—considered Honora to be the most beautiful of them all.

Initially, Honora had basked in Seward's possessive affection, sharing her love of reading and her ideas on life with slavish enthusiasm. Over time, Honora struggled to escape this suffocating adoration and developed her own ideas of how she wanted to live her life—and with whom. Although she would always maintain a calm and demure exterior, Honora could be just as determined in her quiet, cool manner to get whatever she wanted as Anna with her fiery declamations. Just as Day had discovered with Sabrina, when the beautifully crafted woman came to life on her pedestal, she began to view the world with her own eyes.

Courted by a succession of admirers, Honora had been pursued by a young clerk, John André, a few months her junior, during a summer trip to Buxton in 1769. André charmed Honora and—more importantly—

won the approval of Anna, her ever-present chaperone. The couple became engaged. On his return to London, André struck up a regular correspondence with the palace. In accordance with the usual protocol, his impassioned letters were addressed to Anna, and it was she who replied, rather than his modest fiancée who occasionally scribbled a hurried postscript. As André and Seward competed to extol the virtues of their darling Honora—fashioning together a perfect romance—the object of their enthusiasm barely noticed. Having filled page after page with devoted praises, André lamented that "very short indeed, Honora, was thy last postscript!" Indeed, when Edgeworth returned to Lichfield at the end of 1770 and met André at a palace party, he thought André was paying court to Anna. Obviously Edgeworth and Honora only had eyes for each other. It was plainly a relief—to Honora at least—when the couple's lackluster engagement was summarily ended by Mrs. André and Mrs. Seward at the beginning of 1771.

Poor André would never recover; in desolation, he enlisted in the army. Given charge of British secret services during the American war of independence, he would in 1780 be hanged as a spy, on George Washington's orders. Equally devastated by the end of this perfect romance, Seward would publish a dramatic elegy, *Monody on Major André*, in 1781, which celebrated his doomed love and heroic death and incorporated the love letters exchanged between André and herself on behalf of Honora in 1769. The poem would make André a national hero and Seward a household name.

Shedding no tears over her broken engagement, Honora was freed to concentrate on a more compelling romance. During his Christmas break with Day, Edgeworth had spent every possible moment in Honora's company and found that "the more I saw, the more I admired her." His unhappy domestic circumstances only made his anguish worse. "I had long suffered from the want of that cheerfulness in a wife, without which marriage could not be agreeable to a man of such a temper as mine," he wrote. "I had borne this evil, I believe, with patience; but my not being happy at home exposed me to the danger of being too happy elsewhere."

Determined, nonetheless, to stay faithful to his wife, Edgeworth forced himself to stifle his desires. Although he was a man of impulse who lived in the moment, he would always stick solidly to his honorable principles;

he was a rare blend in Georgian times. And so once he had persuaded Day to relinquish Sabrina to her boarding school and noticed his friend's halfhearted interest in Honora, Edgeworth backed discreetly out of the scene. Leaving behind a pining Honora, Edgeworth returned reluctantly to his melancholy wife and young family at Hare Hatch in early 1771.

Now that the field was clear, with both Sabrina and Edgeworth safely out of the way, Seward seized the moment. Although she would later note that "marriage is often the grave of love," she could never resist an opportunity for matchmaking. Inviting Day more and more often to the palace, Seward took every opportunity to bring together her favorite philosopher and her adored pupil. In a letter to a friend, Seward divulged her scheme. Day, she proclaimed, was "the only man I ever saw, except one, who I think *quite* worthy my Honora."

Describing him as her version of the ideal male, she enthused: "Mr Day's character rises ev'ry hour—he puts on Virtue & it clothes him, his goodness is more than a robe or a diadem. I must take a quire of paper was I to set about enumerating particular instances of his active benevolence. With a fortune of which a Dunce wd be proud—talents which wd make a beggar look down upon the world & dispise it—with ev'ry virtue under Heaven—he knows not what pride is, & values nothing less than Titles or Dress or Figure." Granted Day had his "singularities" for which "the Envious, ridicule & dislike him." Yet Seward was sure that these eccentricities made him all the more suited to Honora since she too, in Seward's view, detested ambition, vanity and luxury and "would be happier in stooping to the lowest duty of humanity than to glitter in a ball room with all the splendor & elegance of dress & equipage."

But did the pair like each other? Seward was convinced that Day was enamored of Honora even if he showed scant evidence of this interest. "He admires, he esteems, he praises her. I think he feels passion for her & if he does I think it will be mutual," she wrote, then allowing her imagination to run on she added, "& if it shd [be] they will marry—to be sure it is an event which promises me much happiness." The truth was that Seward believed that a match between Honora and Day would be perfect chiefly because it would mean that she would not altogether lose her beloved girl. Since many of Day's friends lived in Lichfield and thereabouts, the couple would more than likely live nearby. She admitted as much to her friend Po: "Remember dear Po that all I have said upon this subject arises only from my own wishes & dont imagine that they are *Lovers* for they are yet only friends."

Slowly, haltingly, as the spring flowers opened along the banks of Stowe Pool, the friendship between Day and Honora blossomed belatedly into romance—with much careful nurturing on the part of their chaperone Anna. Tramping the path to the palace with increasing regularity, Day escorted Honora to plays and concerts in his usual aloof manner and monopolized her with didactic monologues explaining his worldview at assemblies and soirées. In protracted conversations on chaperoned walks, he outlined his plans to live apart from society in rural isolation with neither comforts nor diversions and described the exact requirements of the woman with whom he wished to share this domestic idyll.

Since Honora was already acquainted with Sabrina and aware of Day's experimental efforts, she could have been in no doubt as to the spartan existence he had in mind or the stoical qualities he expected in a wife. It went without saying that the candidate for this privileged position would also need to undergo stringent training of the type he had already imposed on Sabrina. How could she resist? Seward held her breath in eager anticipation as she egged each of them on to acknowledge the other's virtues in her favorite position at the apex of the love triangle.

Finally, Day wrote to Edgeworth to confess his new love interest and ask his friend whether he could subdue his own feelings for Honora sufficiently to brook the prospect of her marrying Day. It was "one of the most eloquent letters" Edgeworth had ever received. It would need to be. Insisting that he did not want to harm their friendship, Day helpfully pointed out the folly of Edgeworth pursuing a "hopeless passion" and asked: "Tell me, have you sufficient strength of mind, totally to subdue love, that cannot be indulged compatibly with peace, or honour, or virtue." Edgeworth could hardly disagree with his friend's assessment. And so to test his forbearance in seeing his darling Honora on the arm of his best friend, he gamely undertook to move his family to Lichfield.

In late spring of 1771, therefore, Edgeworth brought his wife, Anna Maria, and three children to live in Stowe House with Day. Quite how

Edgeworth explained this sudden uprooting to Anna Maria can only be guessed at. While Dick, now seven, ran amok in the grounds of the house, closely followed by his devoted sister Maria, who was three, poor Mrs. Edgeworth tended baby Emmeline. Determined to test his resilience to "the dangerous object" to the limits, Edgeworth took over the lease on the house while Day stayed on as a guest—and tested the resilience of Mrs. Edgeworth, who disliked Day as much as ever.

Introducing the sorrowful Anna Maria into the Lichfield social circle for the first time, Edgeworth forced himself to smile benignly as Day courted Honora. Everywhere they went, Edgeworth saw Day and Honora together, and when the pair were apart, Day bent his ear by describing his feelings in exacting detail. "I saw him continually in company with Honora Sneyd," wrote Edgeworth, adding wearily: "I was the depositary of every thought, that passed in the mind of Mr. Day." With Edgeworth's patience stretched to breaking point, Day blathering about the daily ups and downs of his courtship and Mrs. Edgeworth growing increasingly exasperated by the whole scenario—while Dick tore around the house barefoot—the tensions must have been palpable in the tranquil-looking villa.

Finally steeling himself for the event that he now viewed as inevitable, the wretched Edgeworth assured Day that he not only approved of his marriage to Honora but firmly believed he would feel pleasure in the couple's happiness. Nothing now stood between Day and marital bliss but "a declaration on his part, and compliance on the part of the lady," observed Edgeworth ruefully. Yet with the engagement expected daily, Day still dithered.

A few days later, while strolling under the flowering limes in The Close one evening in early summer with a party of friends, Edgeworth managed to sneak a few private words with Honora. One of the group had airily referred to the long-expected engagement between Honora and Day as a foregone conclusion, but Honora then made a comment that cast doubt upon the plan. Assuming that she must be referring to some perceived uncertainty in Day's mind, Edgeworth warmly assured her that his friend was indeed eager to marry. Honora simply shook her head.

The very next morning Edgeworth left his family in Stowe House and trod the well-worn path to the Bishop's Palace bearing a parcel of papers that contained a proposal of marriage. Sadly, for poor Edgeworth, the proposal was not from himself but from Day. Having finally taken the plunge to ask Honora to marry him, Day had drawn up a long and detailed summary of his precise expectations of marriage, his particular requirements in a wife and his proposed mode of living according to the outline he had already discussed at length with Honora. Written out laboriously over several sheets of paper, the parcel contained "the sum of many conversations that have passed between us," Day informed Edgeworth. "I am satisfied, that, if the plan of life I have here laid down meets her approbation, we shall be perfectly happy," he added. Day told a skeptical Edgeworth that he felt sure that "if once she resolves to live a calm, secluded life she will never wish to return to more gay or splendid scenes." And then, like a true romantic, he had asked the tormented Edgeworth to deliver his bizarre proposal to the palace. Solemnly accepting the parcel Honora promised to respond by the following morning, and Edgeworth trudged glumly back to his wife and family for a miserable twenty-four-hour wait. The following day Edgeworth retraced his steps and accepted Honora's written reply, which he dutifully presented to Day.

To Day's horror—and Edgeworth's heartfelt relief—Honora rejected the marriage proposal outright. In an impeccably argued response, which Edgeworth later reported, Honora declared that she "would not admit the unqualified control of a husband over all her actions; she did not feel, that seclusion from society was indispensably necessary to preserve female virtue, or to secure domestic happiness," and furthermore, she refused to believe that marital happiness could ever exist without "terms of reasonable equality." Honora was certainly equal to Day's imperious demands. In summary, Honora informed Day that as he had "decidedly declared his determination to live in perfect seclusion from what is usually called the world, it was fit she should decidedly declare, that she would not change her present mode of life, with which she had no reason to be dissatisfied, for any dark and untried scheme."

Seward had taught her pupil well—perhaps just a little too well for her own liking. Explaining her decision to Anna, Honora said that she admired Day's talents and virtues, but no matter how hard she had tried to "school her heart into softer sentiments in his favour," she had failed. There was just something about Day's vision of married bliss in a remote hovel in complete subservience to his whim that apparently did not appeal. Now more in awe of the feisty Honora than ever, Edgeworth considered her response "an excellent answer," which met Day's arguments in favor of the rights of men with "a clear dispassionate view of the rights of women."

Day, however, was so shocked by the rejection that he fell immediately into a fever and took to his bed for several days. Only the tender care of Dr. Erasmus Darwin, who bustled round to Stowe House to siphon several ounces of blood from Day's veins and apply some stern words of advice, managed to revive the jilted lover's spirits.

A few weeks later Major Sneyd marched into Lichfield, commandeered a large townhouse in St. John's Street, rounded up his four unmarried daughters and promptly installed them in his new quarters. As Honora was recalled from the palace and eighteen-year-old Elizabeth was brought back from Shrewsbury, so their two sisters, Mary, twenty, and Charlotte, seventeen, were returned from their foster families elsewhere. The major had evidently decided that he needed to keep his eligible young daughters under more careful vigilance. Having retired from active service, Major Sneyd settled down in genteel comfort and threw himself into Lichfield social circles. A stern father and a wily businessman, Mr. Sneyd began to accumulate a tidy sum by investing his army savings in shares in the canals being cut throughout the region. Over the next two years he would accrue nearly £10,000 (£17.8 million or $2.9 million today), and his earnings thereafter would continue to soar. With four daughters each requiring handsome dowries to make successful marriages he knew that he would need the funds.

Naturally Anna Seward was distraught at Honora's departure for her father's home. She had lived in intimate companionship with Honora for fourteen years, and she felt as if she was losing a second sister. "The domestic separation proved very grievous," she told a friend although she consoled herself with the fact that Honora was "in the same town; we were often together, and her heart was unchanged." In a poem, "Time Past," written eighteen months later, Seward would look back sadly on the cozy domestic evenings when she and "My loved Honora" had formerly gathered before a cheerful winter fire. Now the center of her domestic world—the symbolic hearth of her home—was gone, and "many a dark, long eve I sigh alone." For Honora, however, reunited with her three sisters after more than a decade under the stifling attentions of Anna Seward, the change was probably a relief. Indeed, it is not impossible that she had written another secret letter asking to be summoned back into the family fold.

As Seward lamented Honora's loss and Day nursed his wounded pride, Edgeworth threw himself into organizing a suitable diversion: a summer archery contest with a silver arrow as a prize. The day proved idyllic. With butts set up on a bowling green, all Lichfield society turned out to enjoy the event. While the gentlemen limbered up to compete in the archery tournament, the ladies of the town gathered along the sidelines to cheer on their chosen beaux. As well as archery, the indefatigable Edgeworth had organized music, dancing, fencing and athletics so that there was plenty to occupy both adults and children.

Anna Seward arrived arm in arm with Honora. Thomas Day was sufficiently recovered from his fever to shamble over from Stowe House, although he had no intention of joining in the music or dancing. John Saville had almost certainly helped to arrange the music and may well have sung a solo or two. And it is easy to imagine a portly Erasmus Darwin sporting with his three boys and perhaps their young nanny, Mrs. Edgeworth prompting her children to join in the fun as she managed a weak smile and a host of clerics in black wool stockings, black breeches and flowing black gowns leaping and dancing like a flock of rooks.

As master of ceremonies Edgeworth was in his element. Not only was there nothing he loved better than a party, he was also a nimble dancer and a sprightly athlete. He had drawn swooning debutantes to admire his dancing skills as a student on vacations in Bath; years later at the age of sixty he would still be able to jump clear over a dining table. And, of course, he had good reason for high spirits. For since Day had been rejected by Honora, Edgeworth felt that "the restraint, that had acted long and steadily upon my feelings, was now removed." He could admire the woman of his fantasies with "unabated ardour"—although again he was forgetting the rather more awkward restraint of his marriage. Nonetheless, as the shadows lengthened at the end of a glorious day, it was easy to understand Edgeworth's pleasure in watching his closest friends enjoy "a summer's evening [that] was spent with as much innocent cheerfulness, as any evening I can remember."

It was as the air of a country dance faded away that Major Sneyd strode up to inspect the revels with his second youngest daughter Elizabeth on his arm. Pretty, lively and lighthearted, with large brown eyes, a rosy complexion and a ready laugh, Elizabeth presented a charming contrast to her elegant and reserved older sister Honora. In effect, she was Lucretia to Honora's Sabrina. As all eyes turned to survey the newcomer, stepping out in Lichfield for the first time, Honora quickly took her arm and steered her toward Edgeworth. Concerned that Elizabeth would become prey to unwanted attentions, Honora asked Edgeworth to partner her sister for the first dance.

Observers were divided as to which of the two sisters was the more desirable, Edgeworth later noted—though, of course, there was no doubt in his mind. Elizabeth was better educated, more knowledgeable, more sophisticated, more vivacious and wittier than her older sister and yet—Edgeworth observed as he spun her around the dance area—she was less graceful, less skilled at dancing, and did not possess the strength or agility of mind that he so valued in his adored Honora. Anna Seward naturally agreed. Elizabeth was "very pretty, very sprightly, very artless, very engaging," she admitted, yet "countless degrees inferior to the endowed and adorned Honora." If Edgeworth and Seward were not overly impressed then somebody else certainly was. Watching the dancers gloomily from the wings Thomas Day suddenly took notice of the attractive newcomer with the charming smile.

As his eyes followed Elizabeth being spun expertly across the grass by his friend Edgeworth, Day noted with approval that she tended rather to plumpness and danced a little clumsily. Quickly rousing himself to make the newcomer's acquaintance, he discovered to his delight that Elizabeth listened meekly when he expounded his views and concurred politely when he described his more outlandish ideas. For all her fashionable attire and sophisticated education, Elizabeth seemed admirably impressed by Day's scorn for money and titles and his philanthropic ideals. Whoever won the silver arrow in the archery contest that day went unrecorded, but Cupid's arrow had certainly found its mark.

Having grown up with cousins, in a well-connected family living in Shrewsbury, Elizabeth—or Bessy, as she was known—had undergone a distinctly more worldly upbringing than her sister Honora. Elizabeth had enjoyed the typical education of a country gentleman's daughter, endowing her with the refined manners and courteous conversation that were common currency in upper-class salons. As she grew older, Elizabeth had spent winter seasons in London and Bath, mixing in elite social circles, and summer vacations hobnobbing with the Shropshire gentry. Well dressed, well mannered and well bred, she had been formally presented at the London assemblies that served as marriage markets for single girls and eligible bachelors. In short, Elizabeth was the absolute opposite of the simple, natural, peasant girl of Day's fantasies.

Yet regardless of her apparent unsuitability for the vacant position in his life, over the next few weeks, Thomas Day courted Elizabeth Sneyd with a zeal that astounded his friends. During the long summer days and fine evenings, the pair conversed intently on walks around The Close and sat together at supper parties on the palace terrace. Anna Seward captured one such gathering in late July when the "dear Quartetto" of Darwin, Edgeworth, Saville and Day entertained their female admirers. "Our rambles upon the Terrace have been *very* animated these last 7 or 8 evenings," she told a friend, with "Mr Edgeworth enlivening us by a wit extensive as the light of the Sun . . . Doctor Darwin laughing with us . . . Il Penseroso Saville sighing & singing to us" and, last but not least, "Mr Day *improving* our minds while he delights our imagination."

Watching his friend fall under Elizabeth's spell with astonishing speed, a dumbfounded Edgeworth reported, "Everybody perceived, that Miss Elizabeth Sneyd had made a greater impression in three weeks upon Mr. Day, than her superior sister had made in twelve months." Day was plainly captivated. Not only did Elizabeth listen demurely when he launched into one of his long lectures, she was entranced by his novel ideas on education, philanthropy and even marriage.

Far from being shocked when Day described his quest to find a perfect wife and his sorry efforts to train a young orphan for this role, Elizabeth was fascinated by the tortured poet who "appeared to her young mind the most extraordinary and romantic person in the world," according to Edgeworth. She was even enthralled by Day's vision of living apart from society with a devoted wife so much in love that "the rest of the world vanished, and lovers became all in all to each other," wrote Edgeworth. Elizabeth began to fancy that "if such a man loved her with truth and violence," she would be willing to make the necessary sacrifices to fit that role. Of course, if she believed that Day thought love belonged in marriage, she had obviously not been listening quite attentively enough. Buoyed along by this rapidly escalating romance in the sultry summer days, within weeks of their first meeting Day asked Elizabeth to marry him. At last, he was sure, he had found a woman ideally suited to become his wife. It was his third marriage proposal in three years, not including his plans for Sabrina.

There was only one obstacle to a potentially perfect match. Surveying her gauche, unkempt and ill-dressed suitor with a well-practiced eye, Elizabeth replied that she would consent to marry Day if he would just spruce up his appearance and polish his manners. Although she assured him that she considered such airs and graces to be just as frivolous and ridiculous as he did, she argued coyly that Day could not in all fairness criticize the typical accomplishments of a refined gentleman unless he could prove that he was capable of acquiring them for himself.

Besotted by his new love and persuaded by her perverse logic, Day now thought that perhaps it was his lack of elegance and social graces that had led first Margaret Edgeworth and then Honora to reject him. For, obviously, it could hardly be his personality or his singular outlook on life. And so he agreed that he would dedicate himself for the next year or so to learning the requisite talents of a polite gentleman. Just as Day had tried to mould Sabrina to fit his vision of pastoral simplicity, now he submitted to being groomed to suit his prospective spouse's idea of fashionable urbane manhood.

In the same way that artists, writers and philosophers hotly debated their preferred model of the perfect eighteenth-century woman, so opinion leaders agonized over the ideal Georgian gentleman. All agreed that the swaggering, staggering, full-blooded libertine of the seventeenth century had had his day just as surely as had the formal courtly behavior expected of high-ranking men in Restoration Britain. At the dawn of the eighteenth century, periodicals like *The Spectator* and *The Tatler* led the way in calling for changes in male behavior and appearance to suit the rational, reasonable, egalitarian modern age. Just as advances in science and technology were expected to improve the lot of society, so the Enlightenment demanded a more civilized man.

Equally at ease in town or country, in male or mixed company, with dukes and duchesses or dairy maids and drovers, this new breed of "polite gentleman" combined inner virtues of honesty, altruism and benevolence with outward elegance and gentility. But as the piles of articles, guide books and sermons devoted to outlining acceptable behavior might suggest, achieving this ideal was easier said than done. For although the emphasis was placed on demonstrating a more natural and sincere style of behavior, in practice this meant having to follow a fiendishly complex code of conduct.

In essence, the perfect Georgian man was expected to be well read without parading his knowledge, benevolent without exhibiting his generosity and courteous without being showy, and all his outward behavior— whether in dress, movement or conversation—should reflect this modest and discreet persona. Elaborate rules governed every aspect of public conduct, whether at the dinner table, on the dance floor, in the drawing room or in the street, in order to achieve this apparently effortless elegance. In conversation, the polite man should be witty and inclusive, should never dispute another's viewpoint and should certainly never introduce lewd or offensive topics. In dress, the polite man should be neat, clean and elegant without excessive adornment or fuss in order to obtain the desired medium "between a Fop and a Sloven."

Negotiating this tricky tightrope walk usually required years of study. Georgian boys from well-heeled families learned the basics of gentlemanly conduct in school, supplemented their lessons by reading essays and conduct books and smoothed off any rough edges by taking dancing lessons. Typical conduct guides described how to stand (with feet turned out and one hand inside the waistcoat), to bow (with hat in hand, one knee bent and eyes downcast) and to walk (with head high and arms free) along with helpful pictures of the ideal poses, as well as detailed instructions on table manners and how to dance the minuet. Dance masters not only taught young men the steps to fashionable ballroom routines but also how to walk, stand, sit and bow with grace and poise. "It is the graceful Motion of the Body in Walking, reaching out the Hand, Bowing, or performing other common Actions of Life, in a free, easy, and genteel Manner, that distinguishes the well bred Person from the Clown," one dance tutor explained.

Inevitably there were men who openly flouted these written and unwritten rules. At one extreme groups like the "macaronis" flaunted foppish manners and dress. Others, inspired by Rousseau, argued that men should express their natural feelings with open displays of emotion even to the point of trembling and weeping. But as this "culture of sensibility" gathered pace, it too attracted critics who ridiculed men for bursting into tears at the sight of a limping dog.

By the second half of the eighteenth century the debate over proper manliness had reached a crescendo with writers falling over each other to celebrate or satirize "sentimental" heroes in tear-jerking novels. As novelists took their art to absurd levels, readers were often unsure whether to laugh or cry. Laurence Sterne had fun depicting a French peasant who is inconsolable over the death of his donkey in *A Sentimental Journey Through France and Italy* in 1768. The Scottish writer Henry Mackenzie enjoyed a similar romp through the emotions in his 1771 novel *The Man of Feeling* in which his luckless hero Harley weeps repeatedly at his endless misfortunes. But the Irish writer Henry Brooke took the sentimental novel to new levels in *The Fool of Quality*, which crammed as many affecting scenes and melancholy mishaps as humanly possible into five volumes published between 1765 and 1770. Brooke's odyssey tells the story of Henry Clinton, the younger son of an earl, who is banished to live among peasants for a natural education à la Rousseau. Rejecting fashionable fripperies and false etiquette he wins hearts and minds through a series of selfless acts and heroic deeds. It was Day's favorite novel.

Most of Day's friends readily accepted his argument that he despised artificial rules of etiquette and contrived appearances in favor of finer feelings. But this did not wash with Elizabeth Sneyd. She might be willing to support Day's liberal views and subscribe to the idea of his romantic retreat, but she did not want to be seen on the arm of a dirty and disheveled misfit who stumbled clumsily into drawing rooms, slurped from his soup bowl at the dinner table and offended polite conversation. And so to satisfy his new fiancée Day agreed to return to France, the acknowledged finishing school for the fashionable man about town, to learn the airs and graces he so patently lacked. Elizabeth, however, was not to escape without some sacrifice herself. As her part of the bargain, she solemnly promised not to visit the heinous capitals of fashion, London and Bath, or indulge in any other society events and to apply herself to a course of reading prescribed by Day.

Leaving Elizabeth to her books and her thoughts, Day left Lichfield on August 17, 1771—exactly two years after he had removed Sabrina from the Foundling Hospital—and set sail for France with his trusty companion Edgeworth. Helplessly in love with Honora, Edgeworth had convinced himself that a long holiday abroad was the only way to subdue his passion. Rather than be tempted into an illicit liaison that would subject Honora to scandal and immerse his already faltering marriage in further turmoil, he chose to flee. He had become "insensibly entangled" once before—the outcome then had been Dick and an unhappy marriage—and he could not risk it happening again.

In a snatched conversation before he left, Edgeworth urged Honora to marry even if she could not obtain her perfect husband. Sending his disgruntled wife back to live with her parents and sisters at Black Bourton, Edgeworth took with him the unruly Dick, now seven, and an English tutor, in order to continue the boy's progressive education. And arriving in Paris for a brief stopover, the travelers decided to call on their idol Rousseau.

Having returned to Paris the previous year, in defiance of his exile for the banned books *Émile* and *The Social Contract*, Rousseau had gradually assimilated himself back into French intellectual society. Now fifty-nine, he lived quietly and simply in a few cramped rooms on the fifth floor of an apartment building in an unfashionable quarter of the city near the Louvre with his lifelong companion, Thérèse Levasseur. Although he was widely revered across Europe and America for his radical views, Rousseau scratched out a meager living by copying music and accepted few visitors while he worked on finishing his *Confessions*.

Growing increasingly introverted as he delved into his own past and psyche, Rousseau had become disillusioned with his published works. He now argued that anyone who understood *The Social Contract* was cleverer than he was and said he regretted ever writing *Émile* because it had stirred up too much trouble. Even so, the opportunity to meet one of the products of his celebrated educational doctrine proved too hard to resist.

Climbing the steep, dark stairs to the fifth floor, Day and Edgeworth called on Rousseau toward the end of August and were admitted into his attic apartment. As thin as ever from his frugal diet, Rousseau still retained the piercing black eyes that could transfix friends and enemies alike. His rooms were furnished sparely with two single beds, a table and a few chairs. Hanging from the ceiling were several cages containing canaries. Inviting nature in to share his city retreat, Rousseau fed crumbs to sparrows, which clustered daily on his windowsill. One visitor who was struck by this picture of the frail philosopher surrounded by birds in his city eyrie, likened Rousseau to "an inhabitant of the air." Dodging the bird cages as they crowded into the cramped apartment, Day and Edgeworth ushered Dick forward to meet his maker.

Rousseau had, of course, exchanged letters with the Prince and Princess of Wurtemberg on bringing up baby Sophie and remonstrated with Guillaume-François Roussel over his five feral daughters, but he had never before come face-to-face with the fruit of his teachings—his fictional Émile made flesh. Fixing Dick with his beady black eyes, Rousseau was fascinated. He invited the boy to accompany him on his customary morning walk around Paris, in a poignant reconstruction of the educational excursions by the imaginary teacher and pupil in his book, leaving Edgeworth and Day to wait nervously behind. Tramping the Parisian parks and streets for the next two hours, Rousseau quizzed the boy closely on his understanding and outlook.

Brought up to speak his mind in the manner of the fictional Émile, Dick answered Rousseau's questions with neither fear nor tact, proudly flaunting his knowledge of science and history and imperiously insisting on the superiority of all things English. If Rousseau pointed out a handsome horse or stylish carriage or even a smart pair of shoe buckles, Dick insisted that they must be English. Dick's patriotism was hardly surprising. Devoted to his Anglo-Irish father, the brilliant inventor of carriages, who was friends with Boulton, the world's most popular maker of silverware, Dick naturally assumed that all the best coaches and buckles must be English.

Rousseau returned to his visitors with a grave face. He was impressed by the boy's intelligence and knowledge, he reported, but appalled by Dick's outspoken jingoism. Rousseau warned Edgeworth sternly, "I remark in your son a propensity to party prejudice, which will be a great blemish in his character." Already harboring deep misgivings about Dick's liberal education, Edgeworth was mortified at the verdict. Day kept strategically silent about the disappointing outcome of his own educational experiment.

Moving rapidly on, the party headed south to spend the winter in Lyon, where, Edgeworth noted, "excellent masters of all sorts were to be found." On arrival Day set about hiring suitable tutors in fencing, dancing and horsemanship, and Edgeworth devoted himself to overcoming his infatuation for Honora in the only way he knew how: by throwing himself into work. Offering his services to the city authorities for free, Edgeworth took charge of an ambitious engineering project aimed at altering the direction of the mighty Rhône in order to reclaim land. For the next two years Edgeworth would attempt to suppress his passion for Honora by battling to divert the surging river from its natural course. Day and Dick, meanwhile, began their respective lessons.

Since his father was busy directing teams of French laborers all day, Dick was left in the hands of his English tutor and assorted local teachers who were supervised by Day. Although Day's efforts at educating Sabrina had failed so dismally, he would always be regarded as an oracle on bringing up children by Edgeworth and other friends. Finding himself trapped in a schoolroom with a stack of Latin primers for hours on end after four years of glorious liberty and indulgence, Dick rebelled furiously. Quick-witted but implacably stubborn, he flung his books aside and treated his English tutor with contempt. When Dick and his tutor both took French lessons from a native teacher, Dick quickly mastered conversational French while his tutor stumbled and floundered over the grammar. Gleeful at his superiority, Dick now refused to learn Latin altogether and would not listen to his tutor or anyone else.

His father despaired over his wayward son. "It was difficult to urge him to any thing that did not suit his fancy, and more difficult to restrain him from what he wished to follow," Edgeworth confessed in bafflement. Finally Edgeworth concluded that his Rousseau experiment had utterly failed—just like Day's—although in truth it had succeeded only too well. Having been encouraged from an early age to run wild and please himself, to endure extreme hardship and fear nothing, Dick had inevitably grown up fiercely independent and unwilling to bow to authority. Now that he found himself handed over by his father to a variety of strangers and a pile of books in a foreign country, it was only natural that he should rebel. The little boy who had stood at his father's elbow while he created marvelous inventions and accompanied him on madcap road trips to Ireland and France had grown up in his father's image: bold, fearless, determined—and fascinated by mechanics. Poor Dick simply wanted to stay at his father's side as he conjured ingenious bridges and cranes on the banks of the Rhône, not to be shut in a classroom with his fumbling tutor and a scowling Day.

Reproaching himself for ever being "dazzled by the eloquence of Rousseau," Edgeworth was now convinced that the Rousseau system was founded on "mistaken principles." Physically, the system had transformed Dick into a fine, strong, stoical boy, but in character, Dick was obstinate and wild. Was it nature or nurture? Edgeworth was convinced it was the latter. "In short, he was self-willed, from a spirit of independence, which had been inculcated by his early education," he wrote. He would later issue a stark warning to other parents not to follow Rousseau's advice, and he would devote himself to devising a more practical program of education. Edgeworth blamed himself for neglecting Dick in favor of his work after their arrival in France, but still he could not tear himself away from his great engineering project. Finally he resolved to abandon the educational experiment—and Dick.

Dismissing the various tutors, Edgeworth placed Dick in a Catholic seminary near Lyon. Attracted to the school for its discipline, order and neatness—in total contrast to the liberal education he had previously espoused—Edgeworth solemnly instructed the father to make no attempts to convert Dick to Catholicism. Although Edgeworth visited from time to time to check on Dick's progress, effectively he had given up on his son for good. For Dick, accustomed to unbounded freedom and liberal home schooling by his beloved father, the change was miserable indeed. Just like Sabrina, packed off to boarding school in Sutton Coldfield after her progressive education had supposedly failed, Dick was reduced to waiting and watching at windows for the familiar figure he missed.

Meanwhile, lessons were proving equally challenging for Day. While Edgeworth dirtied his clothes and his hands on the muddy banks of the Rhône, Day devoted up to eight hours a day attempting to polish his manners, refine his deportment and improve his wardrobe sense. Straining and sweating, Day tried to coax his limbs into unnatural positions under the instructions of the city's best teachers of fencing, dancing and dressage. Humiliated and bad-tempered, he stood for hours at a time with his legs clamped between two wooden boards in an effort to straighten his gait or with his torso screwed into a frame designed to push back his shoulders.

Apart from the equestrian coaching, which suited his ideas of classical manhood, Day detested every minute of his French education. One acquaintance later said that Day "despised the French for their effeminacy and affectation" but a delicate Englishman he regarded as "doubly contemptible." Yet for the sake of his new fiancée, he forced himself to learn the latest dance steps, to thrust and parry with the small sword and to visit tailors, barbers and wig-makers. Filled with bitterness and self-loathing, he practiced his newly acquired skills in genteel manners and polite conversation on members of the French aristocracy at card parties and salons.

A bemused Edgeworth, perhaps recalling the torments that Day had inflicted on Sabrina, watched in amazement as his friend suffered "every species of torture." He wrote: "It was astonishing to behold the energy, with which he persevered in these pursuits. . . . I could not help pitying my philosophical friend, pent in durance vile for hours together, and his feet in the stocks, a book in his hand, and contempt in his heart." Little by little, inch by painful inch, Day's training bore fruit. In letters brimming with cynicism and self-mockery, he sent progress reports to Anna Seward in Lichfield. Slipping back easily into her favorite role as go-between, she passed on details of Day's gradual transformation to his bride-to-be.

By November his education was well under way. Writing from Lyon, he complained sardonically of "the fatigue of deciding the Embroidery of my new Coat" and declared "I am grown the politest creature imaginable." His letter ended with a mock proclamation forbidding any residents of Lichfield from referring to him in the future as a "philosopher." He had persuaded several of his newfound French friends to sign the letter testifying that "Monsieur Day, Gentilhomme Anglais" was "every thing to be admir'd, esteem'd, & lov'd."

By December his transformation was nearing completion. In a letter heavy with sarcasm, Day told Seward that he had given up philosophy altogether and whatever intellectual faculties he had once possessed were now all "melted down" as he pursued his goal of becoming a gentleman. "I am a lac'd coat, a bag, a sword, and nothing else," he wrote. "I am become a Type, a parable, a Symbol. Eyes have I which see nothing but Absurdity, ears which hear nothing but nonsense, a Mind which thinks not." Thanks to his lessons he could now "speak French very prettily" and had become "what a Gentleman should be."

Day was fully aware of the irony of allowing himself to be molded into an idealized creature, just as Pygmalion had sculpted Galatea—and just as he had tried to change Sabrina. He told Seward that he would define the ideal gentleman "so exactly, that he shall seem to live and breath before you." His recipe for this concoction followed:

> *Imprimis, let him have birth, Riches, & Education Enough to make him value himself, and despise the rest of the world. Let him have learning enough, to be able to ridicule religion, principle, & humanity, & to spell out a Billet-doux, or even to write one himself, if his footman is out of the way. Let him modernize the celebrated antient maxim, of know thyself, let him know his own Accomplishments and be very vain of them. Let him have from nature, Insolence, Frivolity, Unfeelingness; from Education, the Politeness of the world, which is affectation, the Gallantry, of the world which is Hypocrisy; from his dancing master grimace; from his Travels Impertinence; & from his Taylor fine Cloaths upon credit.*

Thus adorn'd, with all of nature & all of art, hang the Constellation up on high, & the world shall worship him, whatever hemisphere he chuses to enlighten: his own Sex shall envy him; & the Ladies shall adore him.

Yet for all his efforts, Day seemed almost to have forgotten the purpose of his travails. In response to a note written in another, anonymous, hand in a corner of Seward's last letter—which Day evidently took to be an inquiry from Elizabeth Sneyd as to his future intentions—he replied: "I have no schemes; I am too much convinc'd of the uncertainty of human affairs to have any certain Expectation of the future." Far from having no plans, however, Day proceeded to reel off a list of exotic locations—Naples, Barcelona, Copenhagen, Amsterdam and even St. Helena—which he proposed to visit in an extended Grand Tour over the next three years. He was perhaps toying with Elizabeth's emotions, goading her even into telling him to stop the ridiculous charade. "Tell me Miss Seward have I made you cry?" he demanded and declared that he could not bear causing "a moment's Sorrow to those lovely Eyes!" although it was no doubt Elizabeth's large brown eyes he pictured filling with tears.

By the end of 1771, Day's metamorphosis was all but complete—and his mortification absolute. He brushed off invitations to join the New Year's Eve revels at a masked ball thrown for "the Quality of Lyons" and sat down instead to write Seward a masterpiece of self-parody. In a rambling, almost incoherent letter that veered from melancholia to mania—he may have been drunk—Day argued that to a man of the world friendship was a "stale Pretext, by which two fools cheat themselves or two knaves each other." Virtue, he wrote, was a "Masque to hide an ugly Face." He was now so skilled in hypocrisy, he said, that he could prove Frenchwomen were in a state of innocence that made them "perfectly indifferent whether their conversation is dirty, or clean, chaste, or obscure, whether they are dress'd or naked, whether they sleep with their Husbands, or their Gallants."

Day told Seward that he believed "my Education" would be finished when he could conceal any last remaining opinion of common sense or honesty and could "praise a woman's Sentiments when they shock me; admire them when they disgust me, and say tender Things to her when I hate her." Most of these, he admitted, "I can do already," but his transformation would be complete, he wrote, when he attended a masked ball and danced with "The Shepherdess in the Blue Dress & dirty Gloves." He ended his letter the following day, January 1, 1772, with a New Year's resolution to attend that evening's ball—and with a bizarre postscript inviting Honora Sneyd to meet him in Lyon. He was perhaps so drunk or befuddled that he transposed Honora's name for Elizabeth's. Yet despite his transformation, the self-imposed torture continued into the New Year.

The correspondence at least brought some much-needed cheer to Seward, who was so taken with the wit of "Monsieur Le jour" that she copied long passages into letters to her friend Po. Anna's fortunes had taken a tumble since the idyllic summer's evening of the previous year when she had entertained her "dear Quartetto'"on the palace terrace. Having lost Day and Edgeworth to their French sojourn and Honora to her father's home, she had been forced to give up her beloved Saville too. A furious Mrs. Saville, exasperated at Seward's continuing intimacy with her husband, had banned Anna from her home in the Vicars' Close in late 1771. When this did nothing to curtail the pair's relationship, Mrs. Saville complained first to the Reverend and Mrs. Seward, and then to the dean of Lichfield, John Addenbrooke.

Anna's protestations that she was innocent of any sexual misconduct were accepted by her parents—and were quite possibly true—but that did not quell the rumors. In a casual aside during a dinner party at the palace in March 1772, Darwin suggested that he believed there was more to the complaints than idle gossip. Seward would never forgive him. Horrified by these revelations, the Sewards banished Saville from the palace and threatened to disinherit Anna if she ever saw him again.

For the moment Seward had little alternative but to comply with her parents' commands, although she complained bitterly about their "deaf and inexorable cruelty" and the social stigma they inflicted on her "by the prohibition so disgraceful to my character." Putting his loyalty to Anna before his marriage vows, Saville refused to accept the dean's offer of a new post on the same remuneration away from Lichfield in the knowledge, Anna later said, that "I cou'd not bear a total separation." Nearly thirty yet still financially dependent on her parents and forced therefore to bow to their commands, Anna confided her desperation to Day. While other friends urged her to forget Saville for the sake of social decency and parental obedience, she knew that Day could be relied upon to offer non-judgmental sympathy.

Meanwhile, Edgeworth, at least, seemed ready to mend the fractures in his difficult marriage. Confident now that he was beginning to attain mastery over the powerful Rhône, he invited Anna Maria to join him in Lyon in early 1772. She made the long journey reluctantly with one of her sisters, leaving little Maria and baby Emmeline with their great-aunts in London. It was not a happy holiday. Edgeworth was still preoccupied with his plans and his constructions for most of the time, and his wife disliked French society and customs. But at least she would be spared the society of Day.

After nearly a year of being groomed, coached and bullied by his despised French tutors, Day felt sufficiently confident to return to England and, in Edgeworth's words, "to claim, as the reward of his labours, the hand of Miss Elizabeth Sneyd." Packing his bags to leave Lyon, he was besieged by beggars and poor peasants who were mortified to find their chief source of charity was about to depart. A large crowd gathered outside his door. Some of them merely "lamented, very pathetically, the grievous losses both of him and his bounty" while others made the wily suggestion that Day should leave behind a large sum "as a prudent supply for their future wants."

Rushing back to England in early 1772, he hurried around to present himself at the Sneyd residence in Lichfield. When she saw Day after nearly a year's absence, Elizabeth Sneyd could hardly believe her eyes. The scruffy young poet who had intrigued her during the balmy days of the previous summer had changed beyond recognition. Dressed in the height of French fashion, in colorful silk breeches, flamboyantly embroidered waistcoat and shapely long jacket, his wild black hair shorn and covered by a neat gray wig and his feet shod in silver-buckled shoes, Day bowed low in the customary manner and addressed his fiancée in the mannered style of a town dandy.

The effect was ridiculous. For all his efforts and lessons, Day looked even more awkward than before. "The studied bow on entrance, the suddenly recollected assumption of attitude, prompted a risible instead of the admiring sensation," laughed Anna Seward. "The endeavour, made at intervals, and by visible effort, was more really ungraceful than the natural stoop, and unfashionable air." Day's "showy dress" was "not a jot more becoming," she wrote. All in all, the sight of "Thomas Day, fine gentleman" was infinitely more unattractive than the plain, unkempt Thomas Day of old, Seward noted.

The ladies of Lichfield sniggered behind their handkerchiefs; Elizabeth Sneyd was aghast. Her efforts to fashion the ideal husband had proved no more successful than Day's attempts to create his ideal wife. She had sent him away to become the perfect gentleman, and he had come back a perfect fool. Recoiling in horror at the strange creature that she had summoned to life, Elizabeth swiftly broke the engagement. A furious and tearful row ensued before Day stormed off in a rage. With relief, Elizabeth threw away her books on metaphysics, and by March she was dancing merrily at an assembly in Shrewsbury.

Rejected once again, Day fell into another deep gloom. For all his serious stances on politics and manners, he was now a laughingstock among friends and associates far and wide. Even Darwin's son, also named Erasmus, who was only thirteen at the time, would capture Day's humiliation in a mischievous poem written secretly to his younger brother Robert a few years later.

> Mr Day too was there, who was reckon'd you know
> A Man who had travel'd & rather a beau
> The very first moment we enter'd the Town
> Good Lord! I discovered he was but a Clown;
> Though he powders his Hair, & strives to look gay
> But I charge you don't tell him a word that I say.

Casting aside his stylish new clothes and his curled wig, Thomas Day resumed his plain dress and let his hair grow long and tangled again. He would later write a bitter defense of his slovenly ways in the form of a mock court case entitled "The Trial of A. B. in the High Court of Fashion." The charges read: "That he the said Defendant, A. B. had at sundry times, been guilty of the highest, and most enormous, offence against the dignity and majesty of the Court then assembled." The defendant's "crimes" included "That in dress he went remarkably plain" and "That in the management of his house he was notoriously guilty, keeping no more servants than were just necessary, and arbitrarily forbidding, upon pain of dismission, the use of curling irons, powder, and pomatum." But he recovered swiftly enough.

Retreating back to Paris, in March 1772 Day wrote to tell Seward that he had never been "much in Love" and did not believe he ever would be again. Commiserating with Anna over her painful separation from Saville, he assured her that he knew from experience that time healed all wounds. "In respect to my fair Lichfield Friend, I have forgotten the very feelings of Passion. It is in my mind as a thing which never has existed." He did not doubt that Elizabeth would have made him happy if they had married, he wrote, but "that I am disengaged with honour to myself, & without prejudice to her Happiness, I rejoice." Unlike Margaret Edgeworth, the "toad" whom he said he still regarded with "abhorrence," he bore no hard feelings toward Elizabeth. And he wanted Seward to tell her so. "Tell her if you see her that I am not at all in love with her, but that I have an higher opinion of her, & more affection for her than ever."

At age twenty-four, Day was now totally convinced of the fickle nature of women. He told Anna that he had befriended "some fair female Acquaintances at Paris, with whom I talk of nothing but Sensibility" and who "continually exhort me to marry because it is a great pity so much sensibility should be lost." Yet his wealth of experience in love made him realize, he said, that "when a woman fancies herself in love with me, tells me she shall love me eternally" and "would suffer death or torture, or poverty for me" he was "seldom deceiv'd." He ended the letter with a poem to "Celia"—plainly Elizabeth—which recounted his "despair" when "with weeping eyes, you bid your swain adieu." The poem did not explain whether the tears were due to sorrow or laughter.

Nevertheless, for all his bad luck with women, he had still not given up his romantic ideals entirely. Mixing in Parisian intellectual circles, Day met Amélie Suard, the liberated and intelligent sister of the writer and publisher Charles-Joseph Panckoucke, at about this time. Mme Suard, who was married to the French journalist Jean-Baptiste Suard, was perhaps one of the "fair Female acquaintances" so eager to talk about sensibility with Day while exhorting him to marry. Although Mme Suard, who was twenty-nine in 1772, was already married, Day apparently "paid his court to her"; one source would say that he was "in love" with her. Evidently Day had decided to adopt the contemporary French approach to marital fidelity. But however much Mme Suard was taken with Day's sentimental ideas, she gave his advances short shrift.

Despite his brave words to Seward, Day was still smarting from his rejection by Elizabeth when he visited Sutton Coldfield at the end of July. He must have been paying one of his rare visits to check on the progress of Sabrina's education at her boarding school. Now fifteen, she had spent the past eighteen months poring over her books and being excluded from singing and dancing lessons while her guardian pranced and bowed as he practiced the minuet in France. But Day paid her little attention.

Stopping at an inn in the town he scratched a poem on the window lamenting his rejection by Elizabeth Sneyd and signed it T. D., July 24, 1772. Regarded rather as a mark of romantic sensibility than as a mindless act of vandalism, scrawling odes on windows, walls and doors in public places was not an uncommon practice for aspiring writers. Rousseau, for one, had scribbled a proclamation condemning the conspiracy he believed was working against him on the bedroom door of an inn near Lyon in 1769. In his usual passionate and declamatory style, Day's poem envisages fleeing the sorry scene of his recent humiliation for Italy and Switzerland. "On, on ye coursers! roll ye rapid wheels!" he begins, as he urges his horses to bear him speedily away from the "friendless grove" and "dull diminished spires" of Lichfield where he has been rebuffed by the "cold Nymph." Anticipating visits to Etna and the Alps on his travels, he ends the ode: "Full many a Nymph the wandering swain shall find / In other realms, as faithless and as fair." The quest continued.

Returning to France—Italy and Switzerland would have to wait—Day rejoined the Edgeworths in Lyon. For once, Mrs. Edgeworth was pleased to see him. Having found herself pregnant not long after the reunion with her husband, she was now thoroughly fed up with French society—and with her husband's obsession with mastering the Rhône. Now that he had succeeded in carving out a channel for the anticipated new route of the river, and the approach of winter threatened a surge of water, Edgeworth was busier than ever. Terrified of giving birth in a foreign country, Mrs. Edgeworth wanted to return home and Day gallantly volunteered to escort her back. A distracted Edgeworth waved them off.

Soon afterward, Edgeworth was warned by one of the boatmen he had befriended that a "tremendous flood" was on its way. Desperate not to lose all his hard-won labors, he begged the river company to employ more men to work day and night in order to complete the fortifications. The company refused. A few days later Edgeworth was woken at dawn by a deafening roar and the bustle of crowds rushing to the banks of the river. He got there in time to see all his ingenious engineering work, along with piles, barrows, tools and timber, "carried down the torrent, and thrown in broken pieces upon the banks." To forget Honora, he had thrown himself into taming the Rhône, but the Rhône had beaten him. He consoled himself by designing experimental windmills to while away the winter months.

In the New Year Edgeworth made one last desperate effort to repair his battered marriage. In an earnest letter to his wife on January 12, 1773, he promised that she could choose where they would live in the coming summer and offered to renew their marriage vows.

> *Will you agree to be unmarried again?—I mean as to the contract made between ourselves—and shall we make a new one?—If you will give it under your hand I will seriously—You become more agreable to me every day—and I hope the reason is that you become more deserving—Your character really and truly is mended and is I think a very desirable one—let the past be past—And I will return to England with a real desire to be pleased and to please.*

It was probably the last letter that Anna Maria received from him. In March she gave birth at her aunts' house in London to a fourth child, a daughter named Anna, and then died ten days later. Maria, now five, would remember being led to her mother's bed for a last kiss. Edgeworth received the news later that month and immediately abandoned his work, then wended his way, pensively, back through France with Dick to arrive in London in May. Poor little Maria, bereft at the loss of her mother, had thrown tea in someone's face, and as a punishment her great-aunts had shut her in a gap between two doors to consider her sins. From her dark prison she suddenly heard a voice that struck her as being "quite different" from any she had previously heard. When the doors opened she saw a man dressed in black whom she immediately decided was "sublimely superior to all she ever saw before." It was her father.

A letter from Day awaited him. After a winter in Paris, he had returned to Lichfield and ascertained the answer to the question his friend most wanted to hear. They arranged to meet in the village of Woodstock near Oxford. Edgeworth had probably been visiting his wife's grave at Black Bourton nearby. Immediately Day informed his friend that Honora was still single—and what was more she was "in perfect health and beauty; improved in person and in mind, and, though surrounded by lovers, still her own mistress." Edgeworth needed no more encouragement. He had failed to stem the force of the Rhône; he had tilted at windmills in vain.

Heading straight for Lichfield, he rushed to the Sneyds' house where he found the drawing room crowded with friends and acquaintances. In a trance of mixed fear and excitement, Edgeworth threaded his way through the room. Later he would say that friends told him that the very last person he came to was Honora. "This I do not remember," he wrote, "but I am perfectly sure, that, when I did see her, she appeared to me most lovely, even more lovely than when we parted." When Edgeworth asked Honora to marry him, she, of course, agreed.

Scandalizing many of their friends and relations, the couple refused to wait the conventional year of mourning. They were married a few weeks later, on July 17, 1773, by the Reverend Seward in Lichfield Cathedral. A glowering Major Sneyd, fuming over the hasty marriage and furious with the brash Edgeworth, reluctantly gave his daughter away. His son-in-law William Grove, the husband of Honora's eldest sister Lucy, was equally horrified by the surprise match and made his views well known. Honora's sisters, Mary and Elizabeth, sat glumly unsmiling throughout the ceremony; indeed Elizabeth had fallen into a "strange gloom" immediately after the marriage had been announced. By refusing to bow to her father's views, Honora had incurred the wrath of most of Lichfield society. "They call her behaviour undutiful, & spare her not for presuming to judge for her self & for being too wise to sacrifice her felicity to her Father's, & Mr. Groves, & the World's idle prejudices," wrote Anna. But Seward, as chief bridesmaid, and Day, joined in the celebrations with enthusiasm.

After the ceremony the party adjourned to Major Sneyd's house for a wedding breakfast, and at noon a beaming Edgeworth helped his bride into his sporty phaeton and dashed away. Edgeworth, at least, had secured his ideal wife; perfect in his eyes, she needed no changes or improvements. Honora, for her part, was equally confident that she had found her ideal husband—the perfect gentleman—and she now enjoyed "the utmost happiness." Eager to escape the disapproving sneers in Lichfield, the newly-weds headed immediately for Edgeworth's estate in Ireland, taking his three young girls with them—Dick being sent to another boarding school—and proceeded to live in blissful harmony in their country retreat. Having abandoned Rousseau's educational dogma but still attached to the philosopher's natural approach to learning, Edgeworth now devoted his spare hours to educating his daughters—and many future children—with his special brand of tolerance, insight and verve.

Left behind, their friends waved them off with mixed emotions. Both Seward and Day had lost their closest friends and confidants. Although Anna professed herself delighted that "the two fond Lovers" had found happiness, she was well aware that she was unlikely ever to enjoy such bliss for herself. Her beloved Saville had now left his family home and moved into the house next door to it. Although he had reignited his relationship with Anna they would never be free to marry; indeed his wife continued to shop for him and launder his clothes. Destined therefore to live a single life, Seward was inconsolable at the loss of "my Honora" as she admitted to a friend: "she is happy. I bless Heaven that she is—but she is *absent*, & *I must mourn*." From now on Honora was effectively lost to her.

All her life Anna would invoke Honora in poetry; Honora's name appears on almost every page of her published poems. Seward regarded Honora's marriage as the ultimate betrayal. She would never forgive her for breaking the "vows" they had made and abandoning her for a mere man. In future poems she would lament that Honora's "plighted love is changed to cold disdain" and addressed her former soulmate as "false Friend!"

But Seward was disappointed with Day too. He had abruptly ended her matchmaking plans by failing to measure up to Honora's aspirations and had made himself a laughingstock in his efforts to woo Elizabeth. There would be no more jovial correspondence with "Monsieur Le jour." Her strongest ire, of course, was reserved for Edgeworth, who had stolen the "matchless prize" from under her eyes. She would accuse him of scandalously stealing Honora from the heroic John André and—when Honora's health began to fail—of coldly neglecting his wife.

Day suffered more stoically. He went to stay with his Lunar friend Dr. Small in Birmingham, from where he wrote a melancholy letter of congratulations to Edgeworth in August. Although he sent the "sincerest wishes" for Edgeworth's happiness, Day glumly observed that his intimate relationship with his old traveling chum was now likely to fade. Previously they had shared all their confidences, Day reminisced. "When you experienced vexations, you sought a comforter in me, and I hope sometimes succeeded: to me you entrusted your uneasiness, your hopes, your fears, your passions." Likewise Day had confided in Edgeworth all his romantic trials—with Margaret, Honora, Elizabeth and, of course, Sabrina. "To you, when my hopes were more active, and life a novelty, I entrusted all the fantastic emotions of my own heart—schemes of happiness, which a young man conceives with enthusiasm, pursues with ardor, and sees dissipated for ever, as he advances." But Edgeworth's marriage and move to Ireland "must necessarily make us of less active importance to each other," he reasoned.

While Edgeworth would now find companionship with his "amiable friend in a wife," Day expected to spend his time "roving about the habitable earth, not in pursuit of happiness, but to avoid ennui." His pride wounded from his failed romances and his ludicrous attempts to transform himself, Day proclaimed that he felt "an indifference to all human affairs, an aversion to restraint, and engagement, and embarrassment, continue to increase in my mind." Day was happy that his friend had finally achieved his perfect marriage. There were no hard feelings, he assured Edgeworth. "With what pleasure shall I, when I meet you again, contemplate that happiness, which you say you so fully possess!" And with a dramatic flour-ish he now declared that fate had marked him out for "an old bachelor."

It seemed that Day had abandoned his marital aspirations forever. And yet, he knew, there was still one person who had been carefully molded to suit his rare and particular expectations who waited in anxious anticipation for his visits.

Stormy weather. Thomas Day by Joseph Wright in 1770, portrayed in gold waistcoat and red mantle against gathering clouds while living at Stowe House in Lichfield. The book in his hand is probably Rousseau's *Émile*.

Core members of the Lunar Society (clockwise from top left) Richard Lovell Edgeworth, Dr. Erasmus Darwin and James Keir. Jean-Jacques Rousseau (bottom left) provided the inspiration for Day's educational experiment.

Day's women. The poet Anna
Seward (top left) was an early ally
and confidante of Day. Beautiful
Honora Sneyd (top right) captivated
both Seward and Day. Novelist
Maria Edgeworth (bottom right) was
deterred from writing by Day but later
used his wife-training project in her
fiction. Esther Milnes (bottom left)
thought Day her ideal man.

Georgian philanthropy. The London Foundling Hospital (above), built amid fields to the north of London, opened in 17... The charity was founded by se... captain Thomas Coram (left) v... was shocked to see abandoned babies on London roadsides. Mothers left whatever they had hand as tokens (below) when t... gave up their babies.

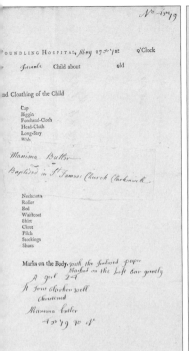

FOUNDLING HOSPITAL, *May* 17* 57 *at* 9'Clock

Female Child about old

nd Cloathing of the Child

Cap
Biggin
Forehead-Cloth
Head-Cloth
Long-Stay
Bibb

Manima Butler

Baptised in St James's Church Clarkenwell

Neckcloth
Roller
Bed
Waistcoat
Shirt
Clout
Pilch
Stockings
Shoes

Marks on the Body. *with the inclosed paper*
Marked on the Left Ear greatly

A gul. 24

A Tom Clarken well
Christened
Manima Butler

15719 N' A'

ina's billet form (under the name Monimia Butler), filled out when she was abandoned as a
in 1757, and her apprenticeship form from 1769 survive still.

Shrewsbury House of Industry.

Published by C. Hulbert.

Shrewsbury Foundling Hospital, where Sabrina grew up, was perched on a hill overlooking
River Severn. After it closed in 1771, it became a "house of industry" or workhouse. Today it
s part of Shrewsbury School.

3.ᵈ *The Bow.*

Cannot sculp

6.ᵗʰ *Dancing the Minuett.*

Cannot sculp

**How to crea[te]
the perfect [gentleman]**
Books on ma[nners and]
grooming we[re]
bestsellers in[ ]
Georgian Br[itain.]
These pictur[es]
from *The Pol[ite]
Academy* (176[ ])
demonstrate[ ]
to bow and [dance]
the minuet.

**The Inner a[nd]
Middle Tem[ple]
Inns** (below)[were]
popular addr[esses]
for the Geor[gian]
man about to[wn.]

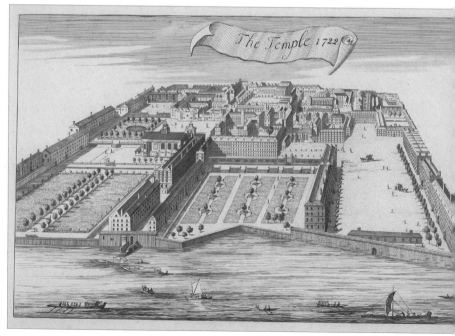

The Temple 1722

bountiful **...eys**. Charles ...ey (right) took ...na under his wing ...she was widowed ...two young sons. ...was embraced ...e Burney clan, ...ding Charles's ...the novelist ...y Burney (far ...).

Burney School ...ned Charles ...ey's house (below) ...eenwich.

from a sketch taken 4th May 1839. by P.B.

Sabrina and her sons. The only known portrait of Sabrina Bicknell, this engraving shows her at 75 with her copper curls as buoyant as ever. Her younger son, Henry Edgeworth Bicknell (below left), was a happy-go-lucky, high-flying lawyer who lived to 91 while her elder son, John Laurens Bicknell (below right), was a status-conscious worrier who died at 59.

EIGHT

SABRINA

~ London, July 1773 ~

The mystery over the author of the impassioned poem against slavery had all literary London guessing. Published as an anonymous pamphlet at the end of June 1773, *The Dying Negro* related the true story of a slave who had escaped the previous month from the London house of his master, a certain Captain Ordington, and been baptized in order to marry a fellow servant, an English maid, with whom he had fallen in love. Marriage to an Englishwoman would automatically have made the African a free man. But before the couple had time to say their vows, the slave was seized on the London streets and taken on board the captain's ship moored in the Thames and bound for the West Indies. Desperate to avoid being sent back to a life of bondage, the slave shot himself in the head with a pistol.

Although the story had merited only a single paragraph buried in the news columns at the end of May, which did not even record the couple's names, the poem, which described the slave's ordeal and tragic fate, became an instant best seller and drew widespread attention to the issue of slavery. Both eloquent and powerful, the poem was written in the form of the slave's last letter to his lover before he committed suicide. By July Thomas Day was privately letting it be known that he was the chief creator of the nineteen-page polemic. In truth it was a joint production between Day and his old schoolfriend John Bicknell. The literary duo "Knife and Fork" was back in action.

Having settled in London earlier in 1773, Day had resumed his desultory study of law at Middle Temple while devoting his plentiful leisure hours to debating politics in the local taverns and coffeehouses with Bicknell and other radical young lawyers. Now twenty-seven and a well-established barrister, Bicknell had just become a commissioner of bankrupts. Appointed by the Lord Chancellor, the bankruptcy commissioners were notorious for charging lucrative fees and expenses; sometimes their charges were so exorbitant that they left nothing for the creditors, thereby ensuring a constant supply of new bankrupts. With this steady source of income, Bicknell had exchanged his previous poky chambers in Garden Court, close to the noxious kitchens of Middle Temple Hall, for more salubrious premises in New Court within earshot of the tinkling notes of the Temple fountain. But since Bicknell preferred to spend his time gambling for high stakes at cards to scrutinizing his law briefs, he was almost as likely to be in debt as his hapless clients. Reunited with his old literary collaborator, Bicknell introduced Day to fellow firebrands including many of the Inn's American students.

Middle Temple had been a magnet for settlers from the American colonies wanting to make their name in the legal profession since the 1600s. Over the ensuing centuries, those Middle Templars who returned to the colonies with the foundations of English law etched deeply in their hearts had assumed prominent roles in American public life, and they in turn sent their sons to study law at Middle Temple. The Inn's popularity with the colonists peaked in the eighteenth century when as many as 150 Americans were admitted. So when fury erupted in the colonies at Britain's imposition of direct taxes in 1765, those Americans who had imbibed the principles of citizens' rights as young students at Middle Temple were among the most vociferous opponents. It was a Middle Templar, John Dickinson, who coined the rallying cry "No taxation without representation." As resentment against British authority simmered to the boiling point in the early 1770s, so Middle Temple had become a bubbling cauldron of angry young Americans whipping up support for greater independence. Mingling with these campaigners for liberty and equality over dinner at Middle Temple Hall, Bicknell and Day found common cause. The fact that many of these agitators came from families who relied on slavery for their wealth had not escaped their notice.

When Day and Bicknell read the short news article in the *Morning Chronicle* at the end of May describing the slave's last desperate act, they were appalled. It was Bicknell who suggested they should write a poem to publicize the scandal, and he led the way by drafting the first eight lines. Working by candlelight, most probably in one of the drinking haunts near the Temple, they passed the quill from one to the other to compose succeeding lines. With its graphic depiction of the man's abduction from Africa and his brutal treatment in the sugar plantations of the West Indies, the poem evoked Rousseau's idealization of "natural man" and the popular sentimental image of the "noble savage" while also echoing Rousseau's rallying calls for social equality and liberty. By the time they laid down the quill, as the poem reached its climax with the narrator's dying cry of "remember me!" Bicknell and Day could be proud of their shocking and moving condemnation of slavery.

Rumors immediately began circulating that attributed the verses to Day—although Bicknell had written almost half of the poem. While Day made no public claims to authorship, he did little in private to contradict assumptions—or to share credit with Bicknell. In July Anna Seward could not resist informing a friend: "Pray have you read the dying Negro, which I know is chiefly Mr Day's, tho' he avoids owning himself the Author." Although the next two editions, in 1774 and 1775, would remain anonymous—it would be 1787 before the two authors were finally named on the title page—the poem would be popularly acclaimed as Day's. When the writers' individual contributions were later revealed, even Edgeworth was surprised that nearly half of the poem had originated from Bicknell's pen.

As one of the first literary contributions to the fledgling antislavery movement and the first major poem to attack slavery, *The Dying Negro* was timely and influential. Already the British justice system and popular opinion were beginning to turn against the slave trade. A vociferous campaign had been launched in the 1760s by Granville Sharp, a government clerk who published the first anti-slavery tract in 1767. Sharp went on to champion the cause of an escaped slave, James Somerset, who won his freedom in a landmark court case in 1772 when Lord Mansfield ruled that no slave on British soil could be forcibly returned to his master or deported. Although the ruling was widely regarded at the time as a complete ban on slavery in Britain, in fact it only meant that enslavement could not be enforced by law; it would be 1833 before the Abolition Act finally made the slave trade illegal.

In *The Dying Negro*, Day and Bicknell used their legal skills to expose the limitations of the Mansfield ruling. More important they drew on popular notions of sensibility to evoke sympathy for the enslaved African. By narrating the poem in the African's dignified voice and using his English lover to channel empathy for his story of life on the plantations—"The trick'ling drops of liquid chrystal stole / Down thy fair cheek, and mark'd thy pitying soul"—the two writers made an emotional case against slavery. In short, they made the political personal. As a critic in the *Monthly Review* remarked, when praising the poem's "author" in July: "He expresses the highest sense of human liberty and rigorously asserts the natural and universal rights of mankind." The poem would inspire many more writers to use the power of verse in the campaign to end the slave trade.

Day's part in writing *The Dying Negro* helped to launch him on a successful literary and political career. The kudos he won through his laudable contribution to the antislavery movement established his reputation for progressive and visionary ideals on the world stage. Yet as they applauded the forceful arguments against slavery and wept with the tragic hero of *The Dying Negro*, few readers would have suspected that its chief author secretly maintained a teenage girl who was completely subordinate to his commands and whims.

Obediently applying herself to her studies at the Sutton Coldfield boarding school, Sabrina heard from Day infrequently and saw him even less. For two years, she had been isolated from the friends she had made in Lichfield; she had no contact with the outside world except through Day. Banished with no word of explanation, she had been told only to work at her lessons in readiness for an apprenticeship. Since she continued to believe Day's story that she was apprenticed to him—even though she was legally still bound to Edgeworth—she had little choice but to comply with his strictures. Moreover, the stern letters that Day sent appraising her academic progress, his payments for her school fees and the few occasions when he deigned to visit kept Sabrina in thrall. She was living in relative comfort, with adequate food, shelter and clothing, so her situation plainly did not equal enslavement, but the chains existed nonetheless.

Now that she was sixteen, Sabrina looked toward the end of her schooldays with uncertainty. She had no relations, no friends and no guardian figure except for Day; he remained the most important person in her life. On the rare occasions when he wrote or visited, his manner varied between warm praise on her progress and cool words of reproach on her failings, according to his perceptions of her conduct and his mood. Although Day had sent her away for failing to meet his exact ideals of perfect womanhood, he continued to exert control of every detail of her life. Having insisted that her schoolteachers exclude her from music and dance lessons, he ordered them to ensure that she was kept hard to her studies and denied any rich food or fancy clothes. If women like Margaret Edgeworth, Honora and Elizabeth Sneyd had spurned him, he could, at least, still maintain control over his teenage captive. Although he kept Sabrina on a long leash, he could not quite give up his project to groom her toward his pinnacle of female perfection. She would always be there—in case she was needed. For her part, Sabrina, in the manner of many child hostages, viewed her captor with devotion; yet—as Seward had noted—it was a devotion born largely of fear.

Oblivious to any whiff of hypocrisy, Day threw himself into defending human rights with gusto. Over the next few years, he would dedicate himself to campaigns to secure liberty and independence for slaves, for Americans, for working men and for religious skeptics. But since his commitment to civil rights frequently did not extend to being civil to his fellow campaigners, he would end up in conflict with many of his compatriots—and even with his greatest idol.

Now that Day had cemented links with the Lunar circle in the Midlands, he began forging new friendships among radical political groups in

London. Needing a base in the capital, he took lodgings with his old university chum William Jones, the expert linguist, who had chambers in Pump Court in Middle Temple. Even if he showed little regard for the rights of women, Day used his legal learning in support of human rights and even the broader cause of animal rights.

In keeping with his frugal approach to meals, Day had always disliked eating meat. He told friends he would happily abstain from eating all animal products were it not that his philosophy—in accordance with the Rousseau veneration for nature—suggested that humans were naturally intended to eat meat; indeed he concluded that "the practice of rearing and killing animals for food was productive of more happiness than of pain to them." But wanton cruelty to animals, which was a common enough sight in Georgian Britain, "used to give him uneasiness," according to Keir. He was so sensitive to animal feelings that he even refused to kill a spider when it scuttled out from some dusty books in his lodgings. Addressing his fellow lodger Jones as he might do a jury, Day declared: "I will not kill that spider, Jones. I do not know that I have a right to kill that spider!" In typically sentimental terms he urged Jones to imagine how he would feel if a "superior being" suddenly demanded that a companion "kill that lawyer," reminding his friend that "to most people, a lawyer is a more noxious animal than a spider." It was a rare glimpse of Day's comic side.

When he was not defending spiders and other animals, Day enjoyed mixing with American radicals. He had met Benjamin Franklin, the American diplomat and science enthusiast, in Lichfield in 1771. Introduced by Darwin, Franklin had been impressed by the earnest young man who shared his liberal ideas on citizens' rights and his skeptical views on organized religion. Since Day had so far laid the blame for the slave trade squarely on European shoulders, he could overlook the fact that Franklin had originally arrived in England with two slaves in tow. And so when Franklin asked Day to join an elite dining club of religious skeptics that he had just established, Day was more than happy to accept.

Meeting at Franklin's lodgings in Craven Street, off the Strand, or at Old Slaughter's coffeehouse nearby in St. Martin's Lane, the group included Wedgwood, Thomas Bentley, who was Wedgwood's business partner in London and an ardent antislavery campaigner, and a flamboyant

Welshman, David Williams. Originally a dissenting minister, Williams had been stripped of his clerical post because of his growing religious doubts and was now a confirmed deist, believing in the existence of a single creator but disavowing any need for organized religion. Like Day, Williams was a disciple of Rousseau's educational ideas. He had set up a boys' school in Chelsea where pupils learned through experience and conducted their own court to determine matters of discipline. Franklin called his group the Club of Thirteen—probably in reference to the thirteen colonies fighting for independence—and its membership remained fixed at that unlucky number.

Meetings focused on Franklin's idea for a multidenominational church where all who accepted "the existence of a supreme intelligence" could come together in celebration of common ideas of morality rather than fixed religious doctrines. In an era when the activities of Catholics, Jews, Quakers and anyone else outside the Church of England were heavily restricted, this was a bold humanitarian move. The chapel would eventually open in Margaret Street near Cavendish Square on April 7, 1776—Easter Sunday—when Williams welcomed more than a hundred people to celebrate "a being infinite and immense" in a spirit of religious tolerance remarkably rare to the eighteenth century. But by then the amicable club that first spawned the project had been splintered by religious, political and personal differences into almost thirteen parts.

Arguments between deists like Williams and Bentley and materialists or atheists like Day caused the first fractures in the convivial club. When Williams was accused of heresy in the press, Day leaped to defend him by sending long, hyperbolic, anonymous letters to the *Morning Chronicle*, which only reinforced the accusations and exposed Williams to further scandal. "Those letters were undoubtedly of service," Williams wrote wearily, "but they diffused a suspicion and alarm concerning me which I was not disposed to counter." When Williams tactfully broached his concerns, Day turned on the Welshman and accused him of being jealous of his literary merits. A shrewd and charitable man—he would later set up the Royal Literary Fund to help cash-strapped authors—Williams said that while Day affected "to be spotless," he was in fact driven by "insatiable ambition."

It was the growing rift between Britain and its American colonies that next created conflicts for Day. Mounting anger at Britain's determination to tax its colonists, this time on their tea, boiled over when protesters tipped £9,000—roughly £1.1 million or $1.8 million today—of the best East India Company brew into Boston harbor in December 1773. Franklin, who was so shocked by the destruction of private property at the Boston Tea Party that he offered to pay for the ruined tea, suddenly found himself cast in the role of chief negotiator for the colonies. Hauled before the Privy Council in January 1774, he was castigated for his compatriots' actions. Fearful of being arrested or attacked by a mob, Franklin took refuge with Williams in Chelsea. Yet while Franklin could always count on support for American independence from Williams and other members of his club, including Wedgwood and Bentley, the same could not be said of Day.

Discussing the vexed question of independence with American friends in rowdy debates in Middle Temple Hall or the smoky taverns nearby, Day announced that he could not support the Americans' cries for liberty while they denied that same right to thousands of slaves. He had acknowledged, in *The Dying Negro*, that European traders first initiated the slave trade and Britain had later established a monopoly in the triangular transatlantic business. Yet by the 1770s hundreds of thousands of slaves were working cotton, tobacco and rice plantations in the southern colonies of America—there were 60,000 black slaves in South Carolina and 140,000 in Virginia alone—as well as in the West Indies. Many of the most prominent Americans lobbying for independence were slave owners. George Washington inherited ten slaves when he was eleven years old and cultivated his farm on the labor of 100 slaves; Thomas Jefferson inherited fifty-two slaves when he turned twenty-one and had a "slave family" numbering more than 170 on his plantation. But even in London, it was hard to ignore the issue of double standards.

The sight of American businessmen, and plantation owners from the West Indies who styled themselves Americans, walking the streets of Georgian London with black slaves was familiar to all. Indeed it was not uncommon to see American law students strolling through the courts and lanes of the Temple with a slave at their heels. So as British troops moved to confront the rioting protesters in Boston in the summer of 1774, Day decided to make a courageous stand.

William Flexney, the publisher of *The Dying Negro*, had been clamoring for a reprint of the popular poem. As the appetite for battle between Britain and its rebellious colonists intensified, so Day and Bicknell sharpened their quills to fortify their verses. The first word set the tone. Instead of the passive "Blest with thy last sad gift—the power to dye," the poem now began: "Arm'd with thy last sad gift—the power to die." The resigned lament in the fourth line, "The world and I are enemies no more," became an explicit rallying cry: "Where all is peace, and men are slaves no more." And working through the poem the pair augmented the language to create a more strident, militant and confrontational stance, which culminated in an extra two pages containing a shocking warning. The first edition had ended with the shackled slave calling on heaven to sink the ship on which he is about to die as he utters his pitiful lament "remember me!" But now Bicknell and Day added fifty-four more lines—forty-four of them were Day's—in which the slave foresees a bloody vengeance being exacted on his tormentors. There was no ambiguity in the message to their American friends in the words: "I see your warriors gasping on the ground; / I hear your flaming cities crash around." But just in case there were any lingering doubts, Day added a long dedication to precede the poem, which spelled out his views on American calls for liberty in no uncertain terms.

Day addressed this eight-page dedication to his enduring hero Rousseau, who had begun his *Social Contract* with the transcendent words: "Man is born free, and everywhere he is in chains." Day acknowledged in his dedication that he had not actually asked the philosopher's permission to make his homage, an oversight he would come to regret. In a blistering attack on the American campaigners Day proclaimed: "For them the Negro is dragged from his cottage and his plantane shade; by them the fury of African tyrants is stimulated by pernicious gold; the rights of nature are invaded; and European faith becomes infamous throughout the world. Yet such is the inconsistency of mankind, that these are the men whose clamours for LIBERTY are heard across the Atlantic Ocean!" He ended his assault with a stark challenge: "Let the clamours of America prevail, when they shall be unmixt with the clank of chains, and the groans of anguish: let her aim a dagger at the breast of her milder parent, if she can advance a step without trampling on the dead and dying carcases of her slaves."

Day had leveled an unequivocal charge of hypocrisy against the American revolutionaries fighting for their liberty. Having delivered the explosive second edition of *The Dying Negro* to the printers just as his law studies ended for the summer, Day packed his bags to head off for a sight-seeing holiday on the Continent. But first, he had to visit his own little hostage in Sutton Coldfield.

Coming to the end of three years at boarding school in the summer of 1774, Sabrina had grown into a popular, charming and accomplished young woman of seventeen whose slender figure, chestnut ringlets and lively brown eyes turned heads. Having applied herself diligently to her lessons, she had "gained the esteem" of her teachers. So when she saw the familiar stooped figure loping through the school gates, she may have thought her long program of improvement was finally over. She may even have harbored hopes that she would be taken back into Day's heart and home. She was wrong. Instead Day brusquely informed her that she was being bound in a new apprenticeship to a couple, the Parkinsons, who were mantua-makers, that is, dressmakers. Day had selected this occupation on the grounds that dressmaking was, as he later told her, "a trade which I thought exposed you to no temptation, while it would teach you habits of industry & frugality more than you could learn in any other situation." It was a curious choice to say the least.

While originally a "mantua" denoted a formal woman's gown usually worn over hoops and split at the front to reveal petticoats underneath, by the second half of the eighteenth century "mantua-making" had come to mean dressmaking in general. Mantua-makers were usually commissioned by wealthy and middle-class clients to produce bespoke clothes from patterns often copied from the latest designs in London or Paris. Since needlework was a staple lesson in most girls' education, working as a mantua-maker was regarded as a respectable job for daughters of the rising middle classes and certainly one step up from becoming a domestic servant.

Yet given Day's averred hatred for fashion and declared determination to protect Sabrina from all frivolity and vanity, his decision seems bizarre. The idea that the teenage Sabrina should faithfully copy the extravagant designs of French couture in exotic silks and printed cottons while inwardly despising any interest in fashion seems irrational—even for Day. She would be producing precisely the kind of garment he had earlier instructed her to throw on the fire. But, of course, she had no say in the matter. She was effectively his chattel to be passed on as he pleased.

Day delivered Sabrina to the Parkinsons at some point in 1774. It is unlikely that there was a formal apprenticeship agreement, for Day made plain both to Sabrina and to the Parkinsons that she remained "under my protection." Day paid the Parkinsons for Sabrina's board, gave them explicit instructions that she should work hard at her chores and—as usual—she should be denied any indulgences or comforts. Sporadically keeping in contact with the couple and with Sabrina, Day maintained his command and continued to appraise her conduct. Naturally this was a thankless task. "During this time I always had a disposition to like you," Day told her later, "which was always checked by my opinion, that you would not take the trouble of acquiring the qualities I could wish & therefore my ideas & behaviour were various; I sometimes taking some pains to improve you & correspond with you, at other times totally giving up the idea and paying you no attention whatever." He had no intention of loosening those invisible chains.

It is probable that the Parkinsons ran a dressmaking shop in or near Lichfield, since Sabrina now renewed her links with friends there including Anna Seward, Erasmus Darwin and the Savilles. Happily returning to familiar territory, she retraced her steps to The Close. At the Bishop's Palace, she was welcomed back by Anna Seward for teas on the terrace and musical evenings provided by her ever loyal John Saville. According to Seward, Sabrina had matured considerably since she had first arrived in Lichfield. The gauche little orphan who had hidden shyly behind her "protector" at social events four years earlier had turned into a "feminine, elegant, and amiable" young woman who comported herself with grace and could hold her own in conversation. Sabrina was "beautiful and admired" and "made friends wherever she went," wrote Seward.

The fact that this metamorphosis had been effected largely during her last three years' attendance at an orthodox girls' school rather than her eighteen months being coached and tormented by Day did not escape Seward's notice. "This young woman proved one of many instances that those modes of education, which have been sanctioned by long experience, are seldom abandoned to advantage by ingenious system-mongers," she remarked. Despite Day's best intentions, Sabrina had emerged from school as a polished young woman at ease in polite society.

At the other end of The Close, Sabrina revived her visits to the growing Darwin household. Mary Parker, the nanny to eight-year-old Robert, had just given birth to her second daughter by the doctor. Despite their illegitimacy the two little girls were brought up within the house—in defiance of Lichfield gossips—where they were doted on by their father. Around the corner, in the Vicars' Close, Sabrina renewed her friendship with Elizabeth Saville, who was nearly eighteen. Known as Eliza to her friends, she was still living with her embittered mother but trooped next door for singing lessons with her father.

Keeping Sabrina in the Midlands was both prudent and convenient for Day. He could maintain his supervision over her progress when visiting his Lunar friends, as before, and they could keep him informed of her conduct whenever he was away. James Keir, in particular, performed this function. Now happily married, to Susannah Harvey—"a beauty" in the words of Dr. Small—and living behind his glass factory near Stourbridge, Keir maintained a vigilant watch on Day's young apprentice. It is likely that Keir handled the payments to the Parkinsons; certainly he managed any awkward questions. At the same time, Small continued his paternalistic interest in Day's romantic fortunes and continued to recommend suitable candidates for marriage. The fact that Keir and Small were both financially indebted to Day did no harm in ensuring their discretion over his connections with Sabrina.

Working with her needle beside a window during the long summer hours, and by candlelight as the days shortened toward winter, Sabrina learned to craft lavish silk gowns, cotton petticoats and flimsy muslin caps to designs supplied by well-heeled customers. Often the rich silks and printed cottons with which the dressmakers worked, imported from

France and Belgium or sent from mills in the Midlands, cost far more than the fees they could charge for making up the clothes. As an apprentice Sabrina was unpaid for her labors. Yet her working conditions were certainly better than those of many of her fellow foundlings who were even now enduring long hours in overheated, deafening and dangerous mills nearby. In fact, her apprenticeship proved significantly easier than for many young girls in similar trades.

From the first, the Parkinsons treated Sabrina with kindly indulgence. Perhaps out of deference to Sabrina's well-spoken and wealthy patron, or conceivably out of confusion over the true nature of his relationship with their pretty young apprentice, the couple ensured that her sewing duties were relatively light and frequently excused her from the domestic chores that she was expected to perform. Day would later reprimand the Parkinsons for failing to induce "industry & frugality" in their charge. Indeed they appear to have acted like the fond parents of a favorite daughter, or foster parents doting on an adopted orphan. Since Sabrina was very probably better educated and certainly better connected than they were, this was hardly surprising. It must have been difficult to insist that Sabrina perform menial chores on her knees in the scullery between her social outings to the palace and the doctor's house. It would have been awkward to force her to labor over dresses for customers with whom Sabrina was on tea-drinking terms. Living in comfort and harmony with the kindly Parkinsons and resuming her close friendships in Lichfield, Sabrina was probably happier than she had been for many years.

All the same she remained in a dubious position. Although she was ostensibly working toward independence as a dressmaker in her own right, she was still financially dependent on Day. And while she now enjoyed the liberty to manage her own social life and friendships, everyone in her social circle knew that she was invisibly connected with her absentee guardian. He still pulled the strings. She remained effectively Day's property, and he directed her fate just as surely as any master his slave.

Showing no regard for the Lichfield gossips, Day left Sabrina and crossed the Channel in July 1774 for a three-week tour of Holland. Sending letters back to Bicknell and his mother, he revealed no better liking for the Dutch and their lifestyle than he had for the French. The drinking water was "bad," the landscape "disagreeable," the country houses "detestable" and the women, as ever, not to his liking. "The Dutch ladies are, to my taste, not a little disagreeable," he solemnly informed his mother. "They are so intolerably nasty and gluttonous, stuffing themselves all day with bread and butter and tea, then retiring to discharge their superfluities at the little house, without any decency, or even taking the trouble to shut the door." There was no chance of finding his flawless female there then. Equally the Dutch women may have wondered why the scowling Englishman was skulking around the "necessary house" when they wanted a little privacy.

To Bicknell, Day wrote a typically high-handed letter insisting that they should retain editorial control of *The Dying Negro* rather than sell the rights to Flexney for a sum that Day hinted was as much as a hundred guineas, a little more than a hundred pounds. If true, this was a colossal sum for a single poem—worth about £13,000 ($20,000) today; Fanny Burney would receive £20 (£2,600 today) for her novel *Evelina* in 1778. Bicknell, who was frequently short of cash, had evidently accused him of being "too scrupulous" about profiting from their literary success. Day replied by describing two men, one a "man of real genius" and the other a "man of inferior talents" who "mistakes his part, and endeavours to sustain a character he was not born to fill." There was little doubt which of these characters Day believed he was. But for form's sake he continued: "Among which ever of the two the authors of the Dying Negro may find a place, I cannot now determine: but I own I could not easily reconcile my mind, after having talked of stoicism and J. J. Rousseau, the dignity of human nature and disinteredness in public, to thank any set of persons for presenting, truth, virtue, humanity, and J. J. Rousseau, with an hundred guineas."

Despite his pomposity, Day was engaged on a rather less noble collaboration with Bicknell in the summer of 1774. While Day was in Holland, Bicknell was putting the finishing touches to another anonymous pamphlet. It seems that Bicknell was the instigator and probably wrote the bulk of the work, but the resulting text contains all the hallmarks of Day. With breathtaking arrogance, they published a satirical attack on plans to provide music lessons at the London Foundling Hospital.

The idea to create a music school within the orphanage was put forward by Dr. Charles Burney, a musician who eked out a living by teaching music to the sons and daughters of wealthy families. Inspired by similar initiatives on the Continent, Burney proposed that he and a friend should be employed to give music lessons at the Foundling Hospital. The foundlings had long been renowned for their stirring singing performances, and Burney believed that some of the most talented singers could be trained to earn a living by their voices. But less than a week after the music school opened on July 28, the governors abruptly closed the venture on the grounds that it did not comply with the charity's legal remit. Deeply humiliated by this sudden reversal, Dr. Burney was further mortified when a jeering pamphlet appeared the following month.

Published under the pseudonym Joel Collier and dedicated to the governors of the Foundling Hospital, *Musical Travels Through England* was a brazen parody of Dr. Burney's acclaimed book on the history of music based on his travels throughout Europe, *The Present State of Music in France and Italy*, which had been published three years earlier. In the best Georgian bawdy manner the narrator reveals that he changed his name to Coglioni—Italian for testicles—to pursue a career in music. Traveling through England he meets Dr. Dilettanti, who cuts his meat, eats and has sex to the rhythm of a metronome, and spies on Signor Manselli having sex with two young women when, at the point of climax, an "immediate explosion of the most musical intonation I ever heard, issued from behind." While the tract poked fun at the emasculation of British values by continental influences—a favorite Day theme—it heaped scorn on the idea of a music school where orphans could be trained to "sing and play *Italian airs.*" Appealing to the Georgian lust for spiteful satire, it sold so well that two new editions would be published over the next twelve months.

After the usual mystery over the identity of the author, it would be many more years before Bicknell was named as the chief writer, but it was almost certainly written in collaboration with Day. With its reprise of the arguments espoused by the pair under their previous guise as "Knife and Fork" in their juvenile poem on politeness and its attack on Day's pet hatred of music lessons for children, which he believed a frivolous luxury, the pamphlet bore the telltale signs of a joint venture. Yet since Day was formally still a Foundling Hospital governor, and had furthermore illicitly abducted two foundlings, the work was hypocritical indeed.

Poor Dr. Burney was so humiliated by the attack that he almost gave up writing his latest book on music, *A General History of Music*. According to one acquaintance, he spent £200 buying every copy of the pamphlet he could find—although another source suggested it was actually Bicknell, in remorse, who later attempted to buy and burn every copy. Certainly today they are rare indeed.

By the time Day returned to London for the autumn term at Middle Temple in October 1774, the second edition of *The Dying Negro*, with its fierce assault on Americans fighting for liberty, was selling fast. Although it was still anonymous, there was now no secret as to who the authors were. As the quarrel between Britain and its thirteen colonies grew increasingly fraught, so the question of American independence divided families and friends.

Within the Lunar club, Wedgwood, Keir and Darwin wholeheartedly supported American independence while Boulton sided with the British government, albeit largely for commercial reasons. Still they continued their convivial scientific dinners. The Club of Thirteen, however, was terminally split. David Williams recorded sadly that "a spirit of discord pervading the country affected the little society formed at Dr. Franklins." One of the main sources of that discord was the controversy sown by Day over slavery. Although Wedgwood and Bentley were among the most vociferous battlers against slavery, they put aside their concerns in order to support the independence cause. Only Day stuck firmly to his principles—on America at least—and refused point-blank to back American independence while Americans still depended on slaves.

Arguing his case with the young American revolutionaries at Middle Temple, Day won a powerful convert to the abolition cause. John Laurens enrolled as a student at Middle Temple in October and moved into lodgings with John Bicknell's brother, Charles, also a lawyer, in Chancery Lane. The eldest son of a wealthy family from South Carolina, nineteen-year-old Laurens lost no time in joining with his compatriots in demanding independence. Like many of his friends, Laurens owed his comfortable lifestyle to his family's connections with slavery. His father, Henry Laurens, had sold thousands of Africans in his slave-importing business in

Charlestown and plowed the profits into plantations in South Carolina and Georgia, which were all worked by slaves. But through his developing friendship with John Bicknell and through him with Day, John Laurens began to question not just his family's but his country's reliance on the slave trade.

Convinced to take up the abolition standard, Laurens now urged fellow Americans, including his father, that while demanding their liberty, they should also free their slaves. He even persuaded Day to petition his father on the issue. In an eloquent and forceful letter to Henry Laurens, which was later published as a pamphlet, Day insisted that since America had taken up arms against "the nation to which it owes its establishment" so Laurens must admit that "there are such things as right and justice, to which the whole human species have an indefensible claim." It was plain that these rights did not derive their legitimacy from might, otherwise Laurens's slaves would one day be justified in forcing him "to labour naked in the sun to the music of whips and chains." But in case Henry Laurens remained to be convinced, Day declared that slavery was "a crime so monstrous against the human species that all those who practice it deserve to be extirpated from the earth." He added: "If there be an object truly ridiculous in nature, it is an American patriot, signing resolutions of independency with one hand, and with the other brandishing a whip over his affrighted slaves." John Laurens would eventually drop his law studies to take up arms with the American troops fighting for liberty, but he would never give up lobbying to free American slaves.

On both sides of the Atlantic, whatever their views on independence, people were contemplating the ending of the 150-year relationship with all the tangled emotions of the separation between a child and its parent. Having given birth to, nurtured and protected the colonies, many Britons saw America as an ungrateful teenager storming impetuously out of the parental home. "America is our child," wrote the literary hostess and writer Elizabeth Montagu, "and a very perverse one." Like the unruly offspring of parents inspired by Rousseau, America was turning from a benign and malleable creature into something uncontrollable and threatening.

During the Christmas break from legal studies over the winter of 1774–75, Day resumed his continental travels. But his visit was cut short suddenly in February 1775 when he received the devastating news that his old friend Dr. Small, who was only forty years old, was seriously ill. Day left Brussels immediately to be with his friend. Darwin and Boulton sat helplessly at their friend's bedside at Boulton's home, Soho House. Small died on February 25, probably from malaria contracted when he was living in America. Day arrived a few hours too late to say goodbye to his friend. He was bereft. He had never known his father; he had never much liked his stepfather. The shy and sympathetic doctor had come closest to a father figure for him. According to Keir, Day would grieve for Small for the next two years. There is no doubt that Day lamented the doctor sincerely although, in his usual matter-of-fact tone, only a month after Small's death, Day told Boulton to "give a sigh to the dead, but think not too often about it" and added: "Our life is too short, & too miserable, to permit a long indulgence of sorrow."

The loss of the doctor, who had provided the still calm hub at the center of the whirling Lunar wheel, threatened to send all of their lives out of kilter. Writing to convey the news to James Watt, Boulton was so distraught he could hardly put one word after another: "My loss is as inexpressable as it is irrepareable. I am ready to burst." Boulton confided that if he had not had his own family, he would consider following Small to the "Mansions of the Dead."

Yet Small's death also seemed perversely to galvanize the Lunar fraternity. It was Small who had urged Boulton and Watt to join forces to perfect the steam engine. Now the pair threw all their energies into the project. It was Small who had encouraged Day's quest to find a wife, even introducing Day to potential candidates he met along the way. Since his rejection by Elizabeth Sneyd, Day had told himself and friends that he was a confirmed bachelor. But the death of the doctor now concentrated his mind on his own mortality—and posterity. Life was indeed too short to wallow in misery. He had failed to find the woman of his dreams in Lichfield, London or the Continent. Finding himself dazed and adrift in Lichfield, after Small's funeral, Day called on his forgotten apprentice. And now he saw Sabrina with fresh eyes.

After nearly a year learning her trade as a dressmaker, Sabrina had grown close to the Parkinsons; Day would refer to them when writing to Sabrina as "your friends." But at some point, in late 1774 or early 1775, her happy apprenticeship had come to an abrupt end. It seems that the dressmaking business had gone bankrupt; Day described it as having "failed." Far from sympathizing or providing a timely loan as he had to Boulton and others, when Day had met the Parkinsons for the last time he had castigated them for defying his instructions to induce "industry & frugality" in their young apprentice.

Although the couple had previously assured him that Sabrina was completing her chores whenever he quizzed them, Mr. Parkinson then "very ingeniously confessed"—in Day's words to Sabrina—"that you had never done any thing but what was perfectly agreeable to yourself." Disappointed in his teenage pupil, once again, Day had sent Sabrina away—although where she stayed is unknown. But when Day met Sabrina in Lichfield soon after Small's death in early 1775 he was pleasantly surprised by the changes he perceived in her.

Now that she was on the brink of eighteen, Sabrina was an attractive, self-assured and refined young woman. The admiring glances she had grown accustomed to receiving on her outings in Lichfield must have made her aware of her physical attributes. During her time at the Parkinsons' dress shop she would have come to know the most flattering cuts and the most attractive hairstyles. With her slender figure, pretty features and auburn curls, she may even have modeled new designs for customers. Taking tea on the palace terrace or in Dr. Darwin's drawing room, she would have put into practice the polished manners she had acquired at boarding school.

Day had cast Sabrina aside four years earlier when she was thirteen, a slip of a girl who regarded him with a mixture of fear and affection, and he had scarcely seen her since. But now that he appraised the attractive and demure young woman before him—a butterfly who had hatched from her cocoon—Day admitted that "I thought you improved, & felt my former dispositions recur." The fact that this improvement had taken place under other teachers and in his absence gave him no pause for thought. After all his failed romances and his tireless travels, Day was more convinced than ever that he would never find the woman of his fantasies among his own ranks. But suddenly it occurred to him that he had missed the obvious solution.

He had chosen Sabrina—or at least acceded to Bicknell's choice—and had tried his best to shape her to meet his ideals; even though he had sent her away he had retained rigid control over her life. Perhaps all she needed were a few finishing touches—a little more careful sculpting—to complete her transformation. Day now dared to imagine that his experiment might work after all. Flinging aside his determination to remain a bachelor, he decided that the girl he had taken from the Foundling Hospital might still become his perfect wife. His mission to educate Sabrina was back on track. "I therefore determined," wrote Day, "to behave with less caution than I had hitherto done & to make one decisive trial." Naturally, of course, he did not communicate his real motives to Sabrina.

His hopes resurrected, Day conveyed Sabrina to his friend Keir's house, behind his glassmaking factory near Stourbridge about twelve miles from Birmingham. Here he sat Sabrina down and spoke to her "more explicitly" than ever before. "I told you if you would now behave to please me, I would finally take you to live with me," Day later said. "I explicitly told you I had no confidence in your behaviour & therefore was determined to make a full and sufficient trial whether you were capable of conforming to my ideas." Still he made no mention of his true purpose.

Later he would vehemently insist, "I solemnly & positively assert that I never gave you the least hint that I thought of making you my wife." Quite what Day expected Sabrina to think of his proposal that she could come to live with him was left unclear. She was presumably meant to believe that this was simply his usual prescriptive application procedure for the position of housekeeper. But even if he did not enlighten her about his real intentions, he did make plain that she was now embarking on a final test that would decide her future once and for all. In his usual cold and clinical manner, Day warned Sabrina that if once she violated his commands then "I would make no further experiments upon you, or ever see you again."

Sabrina consented immediately to undertake Day's trial. Even if she now possessed the body and poise of a young woman, she retained a childlike trust in Day and a childlike innocence about his motives. Since he had been the most significant adult figure in her life since the age of twelve—her teacher, her guardian and her benefactor—this was scarcely surprising. Even now, as she existed in a state of limbo after her dress-making job had come to an end, he was maintaining her financially. For all his aloof and imperious ways, Sabrina remained devoted to him and was delighted to be granted another chance to win back his esteem and praise.

Where Sabrina lived during this final stage of her training and ultimate test is unknown. It is most likely that she stayed with the Keirs in Stourbridge, where Day could visit her on his frequent trips to the Midlands and be certain that in the intervening periods his pupil remained under constant surveillance. At the time Keir was busy fashioning intricate glass articles—including scientific instruments for his friends' experiments—and attempting to produce synthetic alkalis for industrial use; it made perfect sense that the "mighty chemist," as Watt described him, should oversee this most singular of experiments. Edgeworth would reveal only that Sabrina was staying with a mutual "friend" while Seward noted that Day now saw Sabrina only when witnesses were present. Day would later advise Sabrina to "consult & be guided by" Keir "& your worthy friend Mrs. K." And the fact that Sabrina would later regard the Keirs "with great resentment" suggests they certainly played an important role in her destiny.

Now nearly forty, the former army captain had been married for four years and was devoted to his beautiful wife, Susannah. She was either pregnant with or had recently given birth to a son, baptized Francis, in 1775. The arrival of an eighteen-year-old with proven domestic skills would have been a welcome addition to the Keir household. Equally, it is not known how long Sabrina's final trial lasted; it may have been only a few months or as long as a year. But what is clear is that this time Day was grimly determined to succeed in his efforts and that Sabrina was equally desperate to comply.

If Day's tests and strictures had seemed exacting and pedantic the first time, now they were positively perverse. Previously he had taught her to read and write, to add and subtract, to understand the solar system and to appreciate the laws of nature in accordance with Rousseau's ideas. She had learned to consider the poor, to put her own needs after those of others and to value plain and simple living. All these were lessons that had stayed with her. Then she had been a child, readily absorbing information and ideas, and eager to please her teacher. It was only when he had forced her to labor long hours at domestic chores that she had begun to rebel. Now Day made no attempt to enlarge Sabrina's education or inspire her with new ideas; she had gleaned all she needed from books and lessons. He was quite simply hell-bent on remolding her character to fit his exact and specific idea of the perfect wife.

This was no longer a naïve youthful experiment to educate a young girl according to the progressive teachings of Rousseau. This was now a systematic program of indoctrination designed to subvert completely another human's will to his own; it was a battle of wills bent on breaking her spirit as surely as a rider might break in a horse, or a slave-master his slave. The philanthropist who could not pass a beggar without parting with his money, the nature lover who felt he did not have the right to stamp on a spider let alone mistreat a horse, the humanitarian who opposed slavery because it was the "absolute dependence of one man upon another," was utterly convinced he had every right to keep a young woman subject to his total command and groom her to meet his desires. As Eliza miserably told Professor Higgins after her transformation in Shaw's *Pygmalion:* "I'm a slave now, for all my fine clothes."

As before, Sabrina proved an enthusiastic and obedient pupil. She was quick to embrace Day's radical views, to abhor slavery, to despise luxury and vanity, to condemn music and dancing and to ridicule polite manners and fashionable airs. Equally she was keen to conform to his expectations of the perfect woman, to wear whatever clothes he suggested in the manner of his choosing and to style her hair in his preferred way without adornment. Having devoted the past few months to copying the latest Parisian fashions, now Sabrina submissively dressed according to Day's puritanical tastes. She even assured him that she would be content to live a bleak, comfortless existence with Day as her sole companion and his improving lectures as her only diversion.

Over the weeks and months Sabrina evidently excelled in her progress. "She surpassed all his ideas," wrote one acquaintance, "she even surpassed all his hopes." His instincts had been right all along. The only sure way to find the perfect wife was to create her for himself. Delighted with his protégée on his frequent visits from London, Day filled voluminous letters extolling Sabrina's virtues to Edgeworth in Ireland.

When Edgeworth heard that Day had become "attached" to Sabrina once again he was at first surprised, and then perturbed and, before long, deeply troubled. Day's prediction that he would rarely see his friend after his marriage to Honora had proved wholly accurate. Although it was Day who longed to live in humble isolation and marital bliss, it was Edgeworth who had now achieved that dream. Living in his rambling ancestral home amid the flat and featureless County Longford landscape, Edgeworth was gloriously happy with his adored Honora and ever-expanding family. Since there were few neighbors and fewer diversions they were "much alone," wrote Edgeworth, but did not "feel the want of society" because they were so absorbed in their "great and *untired* felicity." The happiness was entirely mutual. Supervising improvements to the house and estate, Honora said that they did not disagree over the planting of a single shrub. "If it is happy for us, which it certainly is, to agree in such trifles as these," she told a friend, "how much more happy is our agreement in sentiments, opinions & tastes of the greatest consequences."

The Edgeworths had created a completely equal, harmonious and loving relationship, utterly different from the rational, one-sided arrangement Day had once proposed to Honora. At one point, when Honora realized she had dropped her wedding ring in the fields, she ordered forty laborers to sieve the newly raked earth until it was found. Normally so cool and collected, she swore she would not lose the ring again except with her life. The only blot on the couple's horizon was Honora's recurrent ill health and ominous cough. While she suffered stoically, Edgeworth maintained his characteristic optimism.

Life was not quite so joyful for everyone in the family. Dick, now eleven, had been packed off to a new boarding school where his fearless determination endeared him to his schoolmates but infuriated his teachers. He was still a prodigy of the Rousseau system. Maria, now six, had accompanied the family to Ireland but was miserable and defiant with a father she barely knew and a stepmother who was beautiful but aloof. Maria tried in vain to shatter the newlyweds' joy by trampling in fury on some newly glazed hotbed frames and impishly cutting out squares from an aunt's sofa. Although she was soon won over by her father—always bubbling with life—she looked with terrified awe on her stepmother, whose retribution for perceived misdemeanors, from the children at least, was always swift and severe.

The laissez-faire system advised by Rousseau and previously championed by Edgeworth had been abruptly dropped in favor of a new tough love regime. Instead of running carefree through the grounds, the children were now subjected to a regime of discipline and order; they were expected to make their own beds from the age of three. Although Maria was sent to boarding school when she reached seven there were still Emmeline, four, and Anna Maria, two, from Edgeworth's first marriage, at home, and they were quickly joined by two more children—Honora and Lovell—in 1774 and 1775. Gloriously happy in his wife, his home and his young family, Edgeworth fervently wished that Day could find equal joy. He was just not convinced he would find it with Sabrina.

When first Day had presented Sabrina as a twelve-year-old orphan, Edgeworth had seriously doubted she could ever become "sufficiently cultivated" or gain "a sufficiently vigorous understanding" to become his friend's wife. Even if Day managed to give her a basic education, Edgeworth believed that Sabrina could never be trained to sacrifice her own needs and desires to Day's commands. So when Day had sent Sabrina to boarding school—at Edgeworth's insistence, of course—the end of the first experiment had come as something of a relief. Now, however, as Edgeworth read the barrage of letters in which Day boasted of Sabrina's daily progress toward accepting his ideas and conforming to his rules, Edgeworth had to concede that Day might after all be right. Perhaps Sabrina really was the woman his friend had been searching for.

"Mr. Day took great pains to cultivate her understanding, and still more to mould her mind and disposition to his own views and pursuits," wrote Edgeworth. "His letters to me at this period were full of little anecdotes of her progress, temper and conduct." Indeed Day's letters describing his revived experiment on Sabrina in minute detail were apparently so effusive—and so revealing—that Edgeworth would later burn the lot. At length, after "much time and labour," Day wrote jubilantly to announce that his project was complete. According to Edgeworth, Day had succeeded at last in shaping Sabrina into "a companion peculiarly pleasing to him in her person, devoted to him by gratitude and habit, and, I believe, by affection. . . . He certainly was never more loved by any woman, than he was by Sabrina; and I do not think, that he was insensible to the preference, with which she treated him; nor do I believe, that any woman was to him ever personally more agreeable." Sabrina loved him just as he was, with all his flaws. The young girl who had once dictated the words "I love Mr. Day best in the world" still felt that he was the most important person in her life.

So certain did it seem that Day had finally found his ideal wife that Edgeworth now expected any day to receive a letter announcing his friend's engagement. Since Sabrina was under the age of twenty-one, Edgeworth, as her legal guardian, would be required to give consent. There was only one problem: Day had yet to inform Sabrina of this forthcoming happy event. It simply never occurred to him that she needed to know, or that she might have any relevant views on the matter. Yet although he kept her in the dark, he naïvely declared his intentions to their friends. As he later told her, "I studiously avoided the word marriage to you, though I used it to your friends." Whether this was the Parkinsons, or the Savilles, or even the Sewards, Day failed to reveal, but inevitably at some point Sabrina's friends felt the need to inform her of her benefactor's marital plans.

When Sabrina confronted Day about the rumors she had heard, he at last admitted that he wanted to marry her—though not, crucially, that this had been his original plan all along. One acquaintance, who later heard the story from Sabrina herself, reported: "He finally explained to Sabrina, in full confidence of seeing the happy recognition that she had shown him until then, developing into a gentle love based on friendship and esteem." Even now Day expected her to celebrate her luck at being selected for this choice role. He was baffled and perturbed by her reaction.

To Sabrina the discovery that Day was intent on marrying her came as a devastating shock, which threw her emotions into turmoil. According to a friend of hers, "immediately, she became serious, silent, and sad." Sabrina had looked on Day as her guardian, her teacher and her employer, as a benevolent father figure and a well-meaning philanthropist—but never as her husband or lover. She knew, of course, that she owed Day everything. He had looked after her, educated her, and maintained her since she was twelve. But the idea of sharing his bed and bearing his children seemed monstrous—at least at first.

Sabrina wrestled with her conscience. Many women in Georgian times consented to far less suitable marriages on the basis of economic prudence; the notion of marrying for love was still a relatively modern concept. Girls younger than Sabrina were commonly betrothed to men they had never even met who were significantly older—and less attractive—than Day by parents arranging advantageous matches. To marry Day was not, therefore, completely implausible. He was rich, clever and influential, a landowner, a lawyer and a poet, with a rising literary reputation and a lively political flair, and he was largely well-meaning even if he was utterly self-absorbed and arrogant. And whereas the idea of a man of twenty-one marrying a girl of twelve might seem distasteful—even in Georgian times—the gap between a woman of eighteen and a man of twenty-seven seemed perfectly reasonable. Yet at the same time Sabrina knew that marriage to Day would entail constant and enduring adherence to his petty scruples and stringent rules. And since marriage was virtually impossible to end, except through the death of one or other spouse, it would be a life sentence.

Baffled by her confusion, Day now tried to persuade Sabrina to consent to marriage by stressing that his own happiness "was dependent uniquely on her," but this only served to make her more troubled still. "As soon as she seemed convinced of this truth, the more sensitive she appeared and even to be softening, the less happy she seemed to him," her friend would later say. Day continued regardless to make plans for the wedding in the confidence that their "mutual esteem" would lead to "conjugal bliss." At last Sabrina seemed resigned to the marriage. Day was poised to set the wedding date; Edgeworth waited in anticipation. And then suddenly Day's plans went horribly awry.

Leaving Sabrina with his friends—probably still at the Keirs' house— while he proceeded with the preparations, Day disappeared for a few days. But before departing he gave Sabrina, as usual, some precise instructions over the manner of her dress, and she, as usual, solemnly promised to comply. When Day returned, he walked into the room, took one look at Sa-

brina and recoiled in horror. She had dressed herself contrary to his directions. Day flew into a rage.

Precisely how Sabrina had violated Day's dress code on her final judgment day would never be adequately explained; indeed it may have been
a smokescreen. It was a "trifling" consideration, wrote Edgeworth, who
heard the story from the "gentleman" at whose house the drama took place.
"She neglected, forgot, or undervalued something, which was not, I believe,
clearly defined," he wrote somewhat evasively. "She did, or she did not,
wear certain long sleeves, or some handkerchief, which had been the subject of his dislike or of his liking." Sabrina, Edgeworth reasoned, was just
"too young and too artless, to feel the extent of that importance, which
my friend annexed to trifling concessions or resistance to fashion, particularly with respect to female dress." But whatever rules she had supposedly
transgressed, Day took her omission as proof of her "want of strength of
mind," said Edgeworth. Sabrina had failed her ultimate obedience test.

Even Day would later have trouble recalling the exact particulars that
Sabrina had supposedly contravened, or else he was equally eager to obfuscate the facts. "I gave you particular injunctions," he later told her,
"whether these injunctions were mild or harsh, proper or ridiculous, it is
now unnecessary to inquire; you undertook to comply with them." The
"accusations" against her were "neither great or many," he would later concede, but were "rather faults in respect to my particular modes of thinking
than any crimes in you." But he added: "That you did violate them, you
well remember, and my behaviour has been exactly as was then predicted."

Keir, who almost certainly knew, and probably witnessed, the final
showdown chose to remain steadfastly mute. But another contemporary,
who knew Sabrina in later life, suggested that rather than waiting placidly
for Day to return and bear her down the aisle, Sabrina had in fact run
away in panic at the planned wedding. "She completely disappeared for a
few hours, astonishing him with dismay at this unprecedented turn of
events," she wrote. Day was both distraught and disturbed that Sabrina
had run off without his permission, she said.

Whatever the actual cause of the rift, the outcome was the same. Sabrina had flouted Day's rules, she had thrown off her chains and declared
her independence. Just at the moment that America rose up in defiance

against its mother country, as battle commenced in Massachusetts, so Day found that the creature of his own invention had turned against him. The perfect woman he had created in his own image was no longer under his control. Galatea had rejected Pygmalion's embrace. Faced with this insubordination, Day acted precisely as he had warned that he would. He coldly informed Sabrina that since she had violated his instructions, the trial was over and he would never see her again.

Day was true to his word. He dispatched Sabrina immediately to a boardinghouse on the outskirts of Birmingham with an annual pension of £50. While this sum was more than five times the annual wage of a housemaid, it was far from sufficient for her to live in the manner that would assure her access to the social circles she had so far enjoyed. Furthermore, since her apprenticeship had ended prematurely and she had no means of earning her living, she was still financially dependent on Day. More significantly, since her name had been so closely linked to Day's for so many years—and most of their friends believed they were about to get married—she now had little chance of making a respectable marriage elsewhere. According to the double standards of eighteenth-century Britain, a man could cavort with any number of women and still be sure of making a successful marriage, but if a woman was regarded as being romantically linked to any man—no matter how innocently—her chances of marriage were damaged irrevocably.

Sabrina would never describe in her own words her treatment by Thomas Day during his long and bizarre wife-training experiment. On the contrary, she would beg friends not to refer to what she called "my checker'd & adventurous history." Over the ensuing years, Day's payments would arrive reliably, his stern letters would continue to come and their lives would always be inextricably linked. But he would never see her again.

Most of Day's friends were relieved when they heard that his wife-training experiment was at last over. Edgeworth, however, was shocked at his friend's behavior. To abandon his marriage plans over "such a trifling motive" seemed not only absurd but deeply troubling. The letter that arrived from Day describing his actions did nothing to relieve his uneasiness. Although Edgeworth realized that with Day's "peculiarities" he had "judged well for his own happiness," he added gravely that "in the same situation, I could not have acted as he had done." Edgeworth, of course, had only married his first wife on the grounds that they were so "insensibly entangled" that he could not walk away with honor.

Looking back in later life on his descriptions of Day and his extraordinary experiment, Edgeworth would feel concerned that he had somehow "betrayed" his friend. He never intended to "throw ridicule" on Day, he would protest, and he continued to insist that Day was "the man of the most perfect morality I have ever known." Yet, as he burned Day's letters, he wanted to make clear in depicting Day's extreme behavior that "too much of one thing is good for nothing."

Edgeworth's bewilderment was understandable. Day's explanation defied all logic. Even for Day, Sabrina's errors seemed ridiculously petty motives on which to decide his matrimonial future once and for all. He had teetered on the brink of marrying the woman he had devoted so many years to crafting just when she appeared to have reached the point of perfection. The truth was obviously much more complicated; in reality other factors were at play. The judgment was driven not only by Day's exacting expectations and Sabrina's ultimate rebellion but also by his warring emotions.

Day had chosen, created and crafted the woman of his fantasies. But at the very moment when he was poised to consummate his dreams and embrace his ivory girl, he had suffered a crisis of confidence. Should he carry through his daring scheme and marry his foundling? Having created his ideal woman, did he really want the creature of his own making? Day had taken the human quest for perfection to the ultimate extreme—and found perfection wanting.

For even if he had not yet admitted the fact, just as Day was about to announce his engagement to Sabrina, he had already met the woman who would fulfill his dreams. Like Sabrina she was an orphan, but there the resemblance ended.

NINE

ESTHER

~ *Wakefield, Yorkshire, 1775* ~

C lever, amiable and wealthy, at twenty-three, Esther Milnes was popular with girlhood friends and male admirers alike. Having lost both
her parents within a few months of each other when she was four, a not
uncommon experience for children in Georgian times, Esther had been
brought up by her older sister, Elizabeth, and assorted aunts and uncles
in homes scattered across Derbyshire and Yorkshire. On her sister's death
in 1769, Esther had become the sole heiress at sixteen to her family's mines,
land and property worth a total £23,000—more than £3m ($5.6 million)
in modern terms—and immediately she found herself prey to fortune
hunters, not least her brother-in-law. With her expressive dark brown eyes
and plump red mouth in a pretty face, Esther could have her choice. Yet
while friends and family pressed her to marry, Esther had remained deter-
minedly unattached. Making her home with two aging uncles in prosperous Wakefield, Esther was simply waiting for the right man to propose.

Born in Chesterfield in 1752, Esther was descended from a long line
of merchants who had accumulated wealth through astute dealings in the
wool industry across Derbyshire and Yorkshire. Two great-uncles had cor-
nered the wool market in Wakefield by exporting manufactured goods to
Russia in return for timber. Her father, Richard Milnes, had accrued a tidy
sum from lead mines in Derbyshire and advanced his prospects further

by marrying an heiress, Elizabeth Hawkesworth, who added the Palterton Hall estate, near Chesterfield, to the family fortune. Of the couple's nine children, only Esther, the youngest, and Elizabeth, twenty years her senior, survived childhood. Despite being orphaned, Esther grew up happily with her sister in Palterton Hall under the watchful care of their numerous relatives living nearby. When Elizabeth married an ambitious young lawyer named Robert Lowndes in 1761, Esther continued to live in the family home with the newlyweds. But as Esther grew fond of her charming brother-in-law, she found herself suddenly packed off by her sister to a London boarding school at the age of eleven.

At school in Queen's Square, Esther had impressed her teachers with her application to study, her skill at languages and her dexterity at the harpsichord. Her superlative knowledge of classical history and literature earned her the nickname Minerva after the Roman goddess of wisdom while her teenage efforts at poetry were roundly acclaimed. Esther addressed flattering odes to her best friends, her favorite teacher and even her books—"Dear instructive constant friends"—and wrote hymns that reflected her late parents' dissenting faith and her dedication to charity. As compassionate as she was loyal, Esther won lasting friends, who fondly called her Hetty or Essy.

During the school holidays, friends deluged Esther with letters entreating her advice on problems with parents, brothers or suitors, and Esther responded with mature counsel, which they ignored at their peril. Writing to one friend, who was about to travel to India to join her parents, fourteen-year-old Esther wrote: "You will shortly, my Friend, commence a new Life, & enter upon a Scene, where all those innate Seeds of Worth and Excellence, which you have hitherto cultivated, will be either brought to Light, or destroyed by the Contagion of Vice & Folly." Urging her friend not to deviate "from the Laws of Virtue," Esther concluded with a few edifying lines of her own verse. To another friend, who sent gushing letters dithering between one suitor and another, Esther urged "be cautious how you form the indissoluble Tie" and added sagely: "When an Agreement of Sentiment & Sympathy of Soul are wanting in the conjugal state Felicity cannot be found."

As Esther parted with her friends on leaving school at fifteen, she stepped up the steady flow of prim but sincere letters advising them to remain virtuous as they entered urban society with all its temptations. Exhorting one friend to avoid the "giddy, fantastick whirl of amusements," she added: "How melancholy is it, my friend, to consider that so many of our sex should think of nothing but the embellishment of a body, which must soon or late moulder in its original dust." While her friends practiced their dance steps and flirted with beaux at bustling assemblies, Esther preferred to stay "far remov'd from the hurry, crowd, and noise" reading her books and writing poems in contented solitude.

In a juvenile essay, on "Politeness," Esther scorned the "unmeaning flattery and troublesome ceremony" that had lately become fashionable as "a false gloss." True politeness could only come "from the heart and understanding," she insisted. In another essay, on marriage, she criticized the trend for marrying for money with the words: "When two congenial minds possessed of virtue, understanding, and sensibility, are united in Hymen's bands, by the gentle tie of love, strengthened with the golden cord of Friendship, I can conceive no happiness equal to what the conjugal state must afford." And she even outlined her vision of the ideal woman, who wore her learning lightly, spoke with "pure, delicate and unaffected" language and expressed sentiments "'beautiful, sublime, and just." Yet while she freely advised friends on their conduct Esther was not quite so clear-headed when it came to handling her own life.

Esther's innocent world had been turned upside down when her sister died in 1769, leaving husband Robert with two boys, Milnes and Thomas, aged four and two, to bring up alone. Immediately Esther found herself the hostage in a battle of wits between her guardians, Ann and Richard Wilkinson, who were cousins of her late father, seeking to protect her fortune and reputation, and wily Robert, who was determined to hang on to his dead wife's money by any means. The Wilkinsons endeavored to keep Esther safe in Wakefield, but Robert implored her to come and comfort him and her motherless nephews in empty Palterton Hall. In her grief and confusion, Esther sent Robert a tender poem in which she promised to "cheer / Thy upright mind, and wipe the dewy tear." With dutiful concern for her nephews she added innocently: "May I each kind, parental office share, / And guard thy offspring with maternal care."

But Robert's mind was less than upright, and he had other parental offices in mind than chastely bringing up his sons. Esther's Aunt Ann urged her to tell Robert it would be "improper" to live with him for reasons that might seem "mysterious" to her for the moment. When her aunt learned that Robert had professed "a regard" for Esther "of a more tender nature than what ought to subsist betwixt such relations," she begged Esther to treat him with "great reserve" and wished that she was happily married to someone else as "the best shelter from the artifices of a designing Man."

Steadfastly resisting the appeals of her brother-in-law, Esther found herself shuffled between friends and relatives from one end of the country to the other like a parcel of priceless but cursed gems. At one point, while staying in Manchester in 1773, she had almost consented to marry a certain Mr. Lees. Yet just as friends expected her to name the wedding day, Esther confessed to another aunt, also named Esther, her qualms as to whether her fiancé met her romantic notions of a husband or whether she was even suited to marriage at all. Eager to reassure her niece, Aunt Esther admitted it was "a very difficult question to answer you whether you would be happier in a married, or a Single state, as it depends on your own Inclination & opinion." The aunt could not help adding some rumors that Mr. Lees was "fond of Liquor" and "rather profane in his conversation." The wedding was promptly canceled.

Rejecting one disappointing suitor after another, Esther despaired that she would ever meet her ideal man. She told friends that she was probably best suited to "the Single State." Repulsed by ostentatious wealth and shallow frivolity, Esther feared she would never find a man who shared her distaste of greed, vanity and fashion. While her friends seemed interested only in snaring a rich husband and stocking their wardrobes, Esther wanted to live a simple, frugal life surrounded by her books and devoted to charitable works. She would demonstrate her philanthropic ideals by promising a bequest for a young girl, a foundling, who lived in Aunt Esther's home in Wakefield. In a world of shallow diversions and rampant consumerism, it was certainly a challenge to imagine a suitor who would appreciate Esther's devotion to a traditional notion of virtue, her reverence for classical history and her passion for poetry. Who could possibly fit the bill?

From the moment that Esther cast eyes on Thomas Day she knew she had found her perfect partner for life. The only problem was convincing him. Esther had first met Day in 1774 through an introduction engineered by William Small. The doctor had chanced upon Esther, most probably on one of her visits to Birmingham, in the early 1770s. She sometimes stayed with relatives in Temple Row, a few doors from Dr. Small's home, and may even have consulted the doctor about her health. When the matchmaking doctor encountered the delightful Esther he could scarcely contain his excitement.

Cautiously Small had made inquiries about her character through friends in the north and even surreptitiously obtained some copies of her letters. His findings confirmed his wildest hopes. Esther's benevolence was widely celebrated in Yorkshire while her letters revealed a mind of superior intelligence. With the excitement of a chemist who had just isolated a new element or a doctor discovering the elixir of life, Small wrote to Edgeworth to announce his discovery. He told Edgeworth "he believed he had at last found the lady perfectly suited to Mr. Day; a woman, who was capable of appreciating his merit, and of treating the small defects in his appearance and manners as trifles beneath her serious consideration."

Tentatively Small mentioned his discovery to Day. According to Edgeworth, the doctor waited until Day had finally severed his attachment to Sabrina. But since Day only reignited his interest in Sabrina after the doctor's death—according to Day's own account—that would have been impossible. It was therefore before Day had embarked on his second trial of Sabrina that Small had first broached the subject of Esther. With characteristic suspicion, Day had quizzed the doctor closely over the young heiress's attributes.

First Day demanded to know whether the talented Miss Milnes possessed the plump, white arms he so admired. Small, with his professional eye for female physique, affirmed that she did. Did she then wear the long petticoats required by Day's stringent dress code? Uncommonly long, Small agreed. But was she also sufficiently tall, strong and healthy to endure Day's anticipated retirement to a humble country cottage? In exasperation, the physician retorted that Esther was actually quite short and not particularly robust. But how could Day, the doctor demanded, expect that an attractive, cultivated and charming woman with a large fortune and views that matched his own be formed "exactly according to a picture that exists in your imagination?" But this, of course, was precisely what Day expected.

With a keen awareness of time running out, Small persisted: "This lady is two or three and twenty, has had twenty admirers; some of them admirers of herself, some, perhaps, of her fortune; yet in spite of all these admirers and lovers, she is disengaged." There was still, however, one overriding objection: Esther's fortune. Determined that he would never allow financial considerations to taint his choice of a bride, Day argued that he could not marry an heiress. But the astute Small had an answer there too. "What prevents you from despising the fortune, and taking the lady?" he asked coyly. Beaten into submission Day grudgingly agreed that he would meet the inestimable Miss Milnes. And so at some point in 1774 he had ventured into Yorkshire to make her acquaintance.

Besieged by bachelors baying for her money and lovesick admirers swooning over her hand, Esther had almost given up hope of finding a suitable suitor. When Thomas Day walked into her life she could hardly believe her eyes. She was immediately entranced by the wild-haired and unworldly young poet. Pleasantly impressed by his disdain for her fortune, she was delighted by his devotion to the pursuit of virtue, his progressive ideas on human rights and his benevolence to charity. Having read his antislavery poem, *The Dying Negro*, she wholeheartedly embraced his political ideals and his literary passions. She was even beguiled by his determination to live in romantic isolation with only books and a wife for company. Esther knew beyond any doubt that she had found her ideal partner. "My affection for you was the spontaneous effusion of my heart," she would later tell him. She added, "you alone realised all my ideas of Perfection, became the Universe to me, & in you, I found an Object capable of filling my whole soul."

Anyone but the most obtuse perfectionist could see that they were ideally matched. Day, of course, remained to be convinced. He had to concede that, but for her diminutive stature and occasional ill health, Esther fulfilled all the physical requirements, intellectual abilities and personal characteristics of the sublime woman for whom he had hunted halfway across Europe. Yet still he hung back. He had been betrayed before by the caprice of women who offered him their hearts only to humiliate him by rejection. It must have seemed scarcely possible that after all his efforts at education he would find his ideal woman waiting patiently on his doorstep. It had to be a trap. In the meantime, he had embarked on his second attempt to train Sabrina.

Caught in a quandary, Day wavered between Sabrina, his ivory girl, his Galatea, whom he had painstakingly molded to meet his precise requirements, and this vision, this Minerva, who gazed on him with adoration and fulfilled very nearly every one of his criteria as if by magic. Stunned into indecision, Day was cordial but cool whenever he met Esther; he treated her with "no more than esteem & friendship," she would later say. But once he had finally given up Sabrina as a lost cause, at some point in 1775, Day felt ready to pay Esther a little more attention. And now that she knew that the field was clear, Esther was keen to respond.

Friends watched with bated breath. On the rare occasions when Day had reason to travel north he made the diversion to Esther's home with her uncles in Yorkshire to pay court to the heiress. Among Wakefield's distinguished residents in the villas lining the town's broad streets, the Milnes family was known as merchant princes and their mansions as palaces. But since Day spent most of his time in London, still languidly toying with his legal studies, Esther took pains to throw herself into his company whenever she could visit the capital.

They met sporadically for conversations on literature and philosophy over tea in chaperoned drawing rooms. In between these brief encounters they exchanged poems. At one point Esther sent Day some verses she had written on female seduction—a theme always guaranteed to command his attention—inspired by a reportedly true story of a woman who died "of a broken heart" after being debauched by a libertine. In response, Day wrote a poem to Esther addressed "To the Authoress of 'Verses to be Inscribed on Delia's Tomb,'" which began "Sweet Poetess" and went on to bewail "ruined innocence" and laud "virtuous love." In one verse Day earnestly inquired, "Lives there a virgin in the secret shade, / Not yet to shame by perjur'd man betray'd?" to which Esther must have silently screamed yes, yes, there is! But stubbornly skeptical that Esther could meet his high standards, Day refused to make any further commitment.

Remaining selflessly devoted, Esther counted out the years in teaspoons while Day kept his options open. He still sent paternalistic letters and annual payments to Sabrina, secreted in her Birmingham boardinghouse. In the meantime he scanned the horizon for other potential partners. At some point in 1775 he wrote another of his many poems on unrequited love addressed to a woman he called "Hannah," whom he was destined to "love in vain." Keeping Esther on a long rein, therefore, Day continued his law studies and threw himself into politics with renewed gusto.

Mixing with American firebrands at Middle Temple, Day staunchly maintained his antislavery stance. The third edition of *The Dying Negro*, published in 1775, reiterated Day's dedication to Rousseau with its excoriating attack on American slave owners. But caught up in the revolutionary zeal as American students celebrated their homeland's first military victories in the second half of 1775, Day abruptly changed sides and backed independence. Just as George III sent a huge invasion force to quell the uprising at the end of 1775, Day declared his unequivocal support for the American cause. The campaign against slavery would have to wait.

Day greeted the dawn of 1776 by publishing a fiercely pro-American poem, *Ode for the New Year*, which depicted Britain as an unnatural mother who had turned on her offspring and "drinks her Children's gore!" He followed with an even more combative poem, *The Devoted Legions*, in support of the colonists. But timing was never Day's strong point. Unfortunately, his spirited defense of the American cause in his two new poems and his blistering attack on the revolutionaries who owned slaves in the dedication in *The Dying Negro* were now circulating at the very same time.

As the British fleet anchored off New York and Americans stiffened their resolve by issuing the Declaration of Independence in July 1776, Day sauntered along to a meeting of the Club of Thirteen. Although the club's original number had dwindled since Franklin had fled back to America the previous year, a solid core still gathered on Sunday evenings at Thomas

Bentley's house in Chelsea. On this particular evening Bentley was bubbling with excitement. When the group was duly assembled, Bentley announced that he was planning a trip to Paris where he hoped to meet his hero Rousseau. Bentley wanted to present the liturgy that David Williams had written for his multidenominational services in the Margaret Street chapel, which had recently opened. But knowing that Rousseau was notoriously reclusive, Bentley was worried he might be turned away. Day came up with a brilliant solution. He gave Bentley a copy of *The Dying Negro* with its passionate dedication to Rousseau as a sure passport into the writer's refuge.

A few weeks later Bentley climbed the stairs to Rousseau's garret with his precious cargo of books and pamphlets. When the door was opened by Thérèse Levasseur, Bentley was turned away, just as he had expected, but was allowed to leave his parcel. Two days later Bentley returned and was overjoyed when he was welcomed in to meet the venerated philosopher. But his delight quickly turned to horror as Rousseau launched into a tirade over one of the publications that Bentley had left. It was not Williams's controversial liturgy that had stoked the writer's ire but Day's antislavery poem with its eight-page dedication to Rousseau.

Rousseau was livid that Day had taken the "improper liberty" of writing the dedication to him without his permission and even more incensed that the homage attacked the American fight for independence, which Rousseau fully espoused. A flustered Bentley defended Day by arguing that the poet had written the tribute before he had realized the justice of the American cause but was now an enthusiastic supporter of the rebels. Rousseau replied crisply: "He should not write upon subjects that he does not understand then." When Bentley left, Rousseau sent his "*most respectful* compliments" to Williams and added pointedly "and my compliments to Mr Day."

Back in London, Williams heard of the encounter in a letter read by Mrs. Bentley and begged her not to tell Day. Williams was convinced, he explained, that if Day heard Rousseau's derogatory comments it would end their friendship because "my poetical friend will not bear the apparent preference." At the next meeting of the Club of Thirteen, Williams arrived to see Bentley already deep in conversation with Day. One look from Day told Williams the worst. Day shunned his company and never spoke to Williams again. Furious and humiliated, Day was mortified that Rousseau, the inspiration for his controversial educational experiment and the fount of all his political ideas, had scorned his adoring words. But if Day had been spurned by Rousseau, he was ready now to turn his mind once more to his matrimonial destiny.

There was still time for one more diversion. Leaving Esther to wait in vain in Wakefield and Sabrina to languish in solitude in Birmingham, Day continued to play the field. On one of his visits to the Midlands, Day encountered Darwin's niece Elizabeth Hall, who was the daughter of the physician's eldest sister, Elizabeth, and her late husband, the Reverend Thomas Hall. Elizabeth, who turned twenty-two in 1776, lived in Westborough, Lincolnshire, where her father had been rector until his death in 1775 at which point her brother, also Thomas, had taken over the rectorship. Day may have met Elizabeth while she was visiting her Uncle Erasmus some time after her father's death. A silver paper tray, which Day ordered from Boulton's factory to be sent to the doctor's house in Lichfield for "Miss Darwin" in December 1776, was perhaps intended for Elizabeth—even though her surname was Hall. Enamored by the vicar's daughter, Day proposed to Elizabeth before the end of summer 1777. Once again, however, his petty restrictions on female conduct scuppered his romantic chances.

The story of Day's fourth engagement (not counting Sabrina) would only be revealed more than a century later in a letter from Erasmus Darwin's granddaughter, Emma Galton, to her cousin, the naturalist, Charles Darwin. "Mr. Day was at one time engaged to our cousin Miss Hall," Emma confided to Charles, who was then writing a biography of their grandfather. But Day objected to Elizabeth wearing a pair of diamond earrings that had been a gift from her grandmother, Emma explained. Although Elizabeth was particularly fond of the earrings because of their sentimental attachment she faithfully promised she would never wear them again. This, however, was not good enough for Day. "No wife must ever have earrings in their possession," Day sternly commanded his fiancée to which she indignantly replied: "Then our intended marriage must never take place."

The sudden breach bounced Elizabeth into making a hasty marriage with Roger Vaughton, a landowner living at Ashfurlong House near Sutton Coldfield, who was sixteen years her senior. The couple married on September 17, 1777. According to Emma Galton, Elizabeth accepted Vaughton "in a hurry," which might be taken to imply that she was actually pregnant by Day; her first child was baptized ten months after the wedding although baptisms could easily be delayed to hide inconvenient details. But it is more likely that the haste was necessary to protect Elizabeth's reputation after being betrothed to Day. It was "not a brilliant marriage," Emma Galton claimed, although it was certainly a fruitful one; the Vaughtons had thirteen children.

The actual date when Elizabeth broke off her engagement to Day is hard to pinpoint. It must have been shortly before September 1777, when she made her hurried marriage. Day was pressing Matthew Boulton to pay the interest on the loans he had made—perhaps to finance his anticipated wedding—in early 1777. He later complained of feeling ill—his usual response to being rejected—during most of that summer. Day told Boulton that sciatica "added to an old sprain" had been "near crippling me all the summer" in a letter in December 1777 by which time he was "perhaps nearly recovering."

Reeling from yet another rejection, Day surfaced in the new year of 1778 to give serious consideration to his future. He was not getting any younger—he would turn thirty that summer and his assorted ailments were a reminder of mortality—so if he wanted to marry and father an heir there was little time to lose. At last it occurred to him that after all his years of searching for the perfect companion, perhaps after all she was waiting patiently for him in Yorkshire. When next he met Esther—by chance, according to Keir—Day finally asked her whether she would be willing to renounce all her comforts and company to live with him in isolated penury devoting her life to doing good works.

Esther, of course, ecstatically agreed. She had waited four years for him to appreciate her virtues. Yet even now, Day being Day, he hesitated. After all his disappointments Day was determined that there would be no going back and no rejections this time. He therefore subjected Esther to the most rigorous examination and detailed inquisition in long interviews and lengthy letters to test her mettle for her future position.

As Day dallied, his friends were confounded. "With Mr. Day there were a thousand small preliminaries to be adjusted," wrote Edgeworth—back in England now with Honora and his young family—"there was no subject of opinion or speculation, which he did not, previously to his marriage, discuss with his intended bride." Any other man, said Edgeworth, would have concluded the courtship in a few months. "In fact, I believe, that few lovers ever conversed or corresponded more than did my friend and Miss Milnes," he wrote. According to Keir, Day was "very explicit on the subject of his future mode of life" during "frequent opportunities of conversation." It was a grueling interrogation designed to test Esther's resolve to the limits.

As Day stubbornly laid down his demands and outlined his plans for the future Esther seemed desperate to please him. During their courtship she wrote: "what made you so dejected last night. . . . Was I all all [sic] concerned? Why was I not wth you to raise yr drooping spirits? Is there upon Earth a power so delightful as that of soothing the eases & alleviating the sorrows of those who are dearer than ourselves?" Her own spirits had also "been rather in a low key," she confessed.

Esther proposed a secret tryst away from the usually vigilant eyes of her guardians, the Wilkinsons. "I think, I cd like to have yr Company tomorrow to myself on several accounts," she wrote while also suggesting a rather more conventional meeting for tea with her guardians "above stairs" at a later date. In case Day should have any doubt about her meaning she added a postscript: "I do not know whether I have expressed it quite clearly that you are to drink tea wth me below." Most likely Esther simply wanted a private parlor conversation to persuade Day of her genuine commitment and perhaps encourage him to make a formal proposal. Or she may have had rather more intimate ideas in mind; the term "below stairs" was a well-known sexual euphemism. The letter was signed "yr most affectionate and faithful Friend." And in reply to that or a similar note, Day wrote: "It is utterly impossible you should be troublesome, or that I should think you so—In either case I was ready to wait upon you, but it will be more convenient to do it at the hour you have now fixed between six & seven." His response was signed "eternally & unchangeably yours."

Finally Day was ready to make a formal proposal via Esther's guardians. Although she was now twenty-five it was still common practice to ask a parent's or guardian's permission before marriage. Writing to the Wilkinsons in the first half of 1778, Day sought approval to marry Esther with the intention of "making her happiness the great business of my life." Well aware that the Wilkinsons had probably heard stories of his unorthodox conduct—and in particular his prior plans to marry a foundling—Day assured them that "in what you have hitherto known of me, there is no part of my past conduct, which is capable of giving you just apprehensions for the future."

It can be no coincidence that Sabrina turned twenty-one in May 1778 and could therefore no longer be considered his moral responsibility, although he would continue to support her financially. There only remained the persistent problem of Esther's fortune. Insisting that he had no interest in it, and had even "rejected the idea of marrying any woman of fortune," Day proposed a marriage settlement—a prenuptial agreement—which assured Esther's fortune remained in her own hands. At a time when the law dictated that a woman's property was automatically transferred to her husband upon marriage, this was a highly unusual suggestion. Even if the Wilkinsons had reservations about their ward's eccentric suitor and unconventional past, they could hardly object to his terms.

In early summer of 1778, Day moved to Bath to seek some relief for his continuing ailments from the celebrated spa waters. The most popular spa resort in Britain, particularly in the busy "season" through spring and summer, Bath was renowned as the Georgian capital of fashionable excess and scandalous dissipation. Members of the gentry and nobility migrated to Bath each summer to stroll along the Grand Parade, drive around the Royal Crescent, cavort at crowded balls and gossip over tea about whom they had seen and with whom; taking the waters for real or imagined complaints was an optional extra.

The novelist Tobias Smollett described the mixed bathing, with women clothed demurely from head to toe in long linen costumes and frilled bonnets and the men almost as completely covered, in his novel *Humphrey Clinker*, published in 1771. Gingerly stepping into one of the four baths, Smollett's country squire Matthew Bramble bridles at sharing the murky water with patients covered in sores and ulcers from scurvy or syphilis and then wonders whether the guests imbibing the glasses of cloudy water in the Pump Room are swallowing "the scourings of the bathers." Smollett, however, personally commended the healing powers of the waters. Day did too.

Arriving in Bath in June, Day took lodgings in Kingston Buildings, a few minutes' stroll from the Roman baths and the Royal Parade. He must have looked an incongruous figure in his plain clothes and usual wild hair as he plunged into the pools among the belles and beaux of elegant society and swigged the water in the fashionable Pump Room. Day would later tell his old chum Bicknell that he had consulted "half the physicians and surgeons in London" and even tried electrical therapy for three months without the least benefit to the aches and pains in his legs, yet the spa waters at Bath had brought him "very great medicinal virtues."

The hot waters certainly revived his spirits. For it was in Bath, in St. James's Church, on August 7, 1778, that Thomas Day finally married Esther Milnes. He was thirty and she twenty-five. The search to which he had devoted almost half his life was at last over. Day had married his perfect wife, or so he hoped.

The sound of champagne corks popping must have reverberated through the houses of all their long-suffering friends and acquaintances. Thomas Bentley wrote jubilantly to tell Wedgwood the happy news. Wedgwood replied: "I hope he will contrive to be happy & make his lady so. They are good people & I hope will not sacrifice real solid happiness to whim & caprice." When Boulton heard the news, he generously offered Day his mansion, Soho House, as a honeymoon retreat while he was away in Cornwall drumming up business for his and Watt's steam engine.

A month later, Keir, who was valiantly trying to sort out Boulton's chaotic business, sent a jaunty note to Boulton in Cornwall reporting that Day and Esther, with her cousin, Miss Walker, had arrived at Soho House "& strut about the Gardens as if all Soho belongs to them." Visiting friends in Lichfield on their honeymoon tour, the Days called at the palace for tea with Anna Seward. She pronounced Esther "extremely engaging" although Day was "just what he us'd to be," Seward told a friend, without needing further explanation. She added: "Of the degree of his attachment to her I cou'd form no judgment, but never did I see a Woman, whose ev'ry word & look bore greater testimony of infinite tenderness, mix'd with no small degree of awe." While friends certainly celebrated Day's marriage, Sabrina's reaction to the news is unknown. There is no record of when or how or even if Day informed her of his marriage.

All their friends at least were in no doubt that Day and Esther made a peerless match. In Keir's words, "the tastes of two persons could not be more in unison than theirs." Edgeworth thought the couple "peculiarly suited." And Esther's nephew, Thomas Lowndes, would later talk of the "extraordinary similarity in their taste, disposition, and understanding" and "their hearts and minds being so extraordinarily in unison."

Day had finally found his perfect wife in the most unexpected of guises—in a conventionally educated and independently wealthy woman who possessed all the means, manners and accomplishments of high-ranking Georgian society. Esther had been born into privilege, brought up amid the dissipation and luxury of urban life and educated at one of the top girls' schools to acquire the standard attributes of a debutante. By nature and by nurture she amounted to everything that Day had despised. Yet everyone could see that Esther was Day's consummate woman. In intellect, interests and ideas they were ideally suited; prim, philanthropic and passionate about poetry, Esther was a mirror image of her husband. It was the perfect marriage of hearts and minds, and they should have been perfectly happy. There was only one dissenter who believed that Esther needed any change—and that was Thomas Day. In his view, Esther would require continual checks and corrections in order to fine-tune her character and conduct to approach his unattainable ideal. Her marriage would be one long program of improvement.

By the beginning of November the honeymoon was well and truly over. Leaving behind the sumptuous furnishings and delightful pleasure gardens of Soho, Day took Esther to Hampstead, at the time a village one hour's coach ride north of London, where he had rented a small furnished house.

Here he began the arduous process of breaking Esther in for her future life of deprivation. Or as Edgeworth put it, "by living in inconvenient lodgings, where he was not known, and consequently not visited by any body except his chosen few, he should accustom his bride to those modes of life, which he conceived to be essential to his happiness."

The Edgeworths, who had settled in nearby Hertfordshire, came to visit the newlyweds in the midst of winter. They were astonished to find the diminutive Mrs. Day, who had always had a reputation for delicate health, trudging through thick snow on Hampstead Heath at her husband's side wrapped in a cloak and wearing thick shoes. The hardening exercises had begun. But even more astonishing to the love-struck Edgeworths was Esther's complete submission to her husband.

In conversation, Esther could hold forth on any subject with equal knowledge and articulacy as Day possessed, Edgeworth noted, and by calm reasoning she frequently won listeners over to her view while Day alienated people with his long, dogmatic speeches. She was "really mistress of the English language, and she spoke with great eloquence," he said. Yet although the couple conversed and argued constantly, Esther always ultimately deferred to Day. "I never saw any woman so entirely intent upon accommodating herself to the sentiments, and wishes, and will of her husband," a dumbfounded Edgeworth wrote. In every situation, Esther always showed the "most complete matrimonial obedience."

Eager to revive their days of youthful companionship, Edgeworth tried to persuade Day to make his home near his own house so that they could get together often. But Day was implacably opposed to living anywhere near his friends. According to Edgeworth this was in order to protect Esther from coming into contact with "any opinions contrary to his system of connubial happiness," though it may also have been to protect her from coming into contact with Edgeworth; after all, his charming friend had already stolen one former lover.

Steering clear of Hertfordshire, then, the Days stayed in Hampstead through the bitter winter. Day was busy viewing houses and buying furniture in January, he told Darwin's son Erasmus Junior in January 1779. In March he took delivery of a silver coffeepot and steak dish he had ordered from Boulton; there would be a few comforts at least. In the spring

Day found the ideal home. It was a small, drafty, dilapidated house on a rough piece of land near the village of Stapleford Abbotts in Essex. "The house was indifferent and the land worse," wrote Edgeworth, who was used to the boggy landscape of County Longford.

Reached at the end of a long drive, the redbrick house was shielded from view until the last minute by a dip in the lane and thick trees. It contained only one decent room and "was ill adapted" to the needs of a family, according to Edgeworth. Although it was only five miles from the nearest town of Ongar and less than twenty miles from London, the hidden house was ideal for Day's purposes. While Day was within easy reach of the capital so that he could continue his pursuits as he wished, he could rest assured that Esther was sufficiently removed from her family and friends in Yorkshire and secluded from inquisitive neighbours to protect her from any corrupting ideas. Sequestered in this "secret glade," Day embarked on the puritanical life he had so long envisaged with his chosen helpmeet at his side.

Dispensing alms, food and medicine among the poor in the vicinity, the couple led a life with scarcely more comforts than those they sought to relieve. Day employed local laborers to dig his poor soil and continued to pay them during the winter when most farmers laid off their workers. One laborer would later remember that Day helped him financially and that Mrs. Day sent wine to his wife when she was in labor. In his efforts to extend the house and improve the land, Day studied architectural and agricultural manuals. He found one book on architecture at a market stall and determined that he would attempt the building work himself. But he soon tired of this manual labor because it disrupted his long conversations with Esther on their daily walks, so he employed stonemasons and carpenters to complete the work.

Not long afterward, Edgeworth was paying his friend a visit when a mason interrupted to ask Day where he wanted a window placed in the first floor extension. Engrossed in a book, Day curtly told the mason to build the walls first and cut out the windows later. Mrs. Day's dressing room would always be windowless; she would have to put on her long petticoats and plain gowns by candlelight. But that was the least of her hardships.

Since music was banned from the house, Esther no longer practiced the harpsichord. Since Day believed that women should not be allowed to write, Esther no longer wrote poetry. And since all other pleasures and luxuries were banished, she was permitted no carriage or any other means to escape her solitude and no maid to help with personal chores. Day proudly boasted to Bicknell that he drank "nothing but water" and ate "scarcely any meat," and there is no doubt that Esther had to follow the same regime. At the same time, Day insisted on taking daily exercise in all weathers so that he rode across the countryside for two or three hours every day and escorted Esther on long walks in rain, sleet or snow. "I know no medicine which is worth a farthing," he told Bicknell, "but spare living and much riding produces the great and most certain effects."

It was probably an exaggeration when Anna Seward later suggested that Esther's life was entirely devoid of comforts or friends. There were certainly one or two servants: Esther's relative Mrs. Walker served as the couple's housekeeper, and a laborer, George Bristow, stayed with the family for several years. There were also visitors. Esther's nephews, Thomas and Milnes, who were now in their teens, sometimes came to stay, and an old school friend visited once or twice. But Seward was probably correct when she stated that Esther "often wept" as Day made frequent tests on her temper and her loyalty. And it was certainly no exaggeration when Seward said: "No wife, bound in the strictest fetters, as to the incapacity of claiming separate maintenance, ever made more absolute sacrifices to the most imperious husband." At a time when married women, even in the highest ranks of the aristocracy, had little if any independent income, Esther was virtually unique in maintaining full control of her sizable fortune; but in submitting her will entirely to her husband's command she made herself as dependent as the poorest waif.

Yet the Days were devoted. When Day described Esther as "the dearest object to me, which this world affords" he was plainly speaking the truth. When Esther told Day that "my whole soul" is "wrapped up in you" she spoke with sincerity. Day had found his perfect soulmate, his Sophie, the innocent, docile virgin willing to share his spartan life. They were living the Rousseau dream—and it should have been paradise. But such a romantic idyll could easily turn into a nightmare, as Rousseau himself belatedly suggested.

When Rousseau died in July 1778, just a few weeks before Day and Esther married, several unfinished works were found among his papers. There was an addition to his racy 1761 novel *Julie, or The New Héloïse*. There were the shocking *Confessions*, detailing Rousseau's juvenile sexual exploits and subjugation to women, which would appall even his most avid supporters when published, the first half in 1782 and the second in 1789. And there was a sequel to *Émile*. When it was later published in English, under the title *Emilius and Sophia; or, The Solitaries*, the book's editor felt the need to add an apology for its "repugnance." Thousands of admiring readers of *Émile* had rejoiced at the moment when Émile had married Sophie and anticipated their marital happiness. Now they were horrified to read the fate of the perfect couple in the sequel that Rousseau had been working on when he died.

Perhaps as a correction to all those parents and other readers who had taken his ideas so literally, or perhaps as a cautionary tale born of his own romantic disappointment, Rousseau had painted a hellish picture of Émile and Sophie's perfect marriage foundering on the rocks. After one of their two children dies, the couple grow bored and scornful of each other. Sophie takes a lover and becomes pregnant with his child, then Émile flees in disgust and descends into a demented despair. The story peters out as Émile wanders the world and is sold into slavery.

For Thomas and Esther marital bliss would prove almost as elusive. Their wedded life was blighted by stormy rows and bitter recriminations as Day repeatedly found fault with Esther's conduct, accused her of disloyalty and chided her about her treatment of previous suitors, while she protested at his coldness and bridled at his severity. There would be no marital infidelity or children born out of wedlock (or in wedlock, for that matter), but the Days' married life would be nearly as stormy as that of their idols. On at least two occasions, and possibly many more, their arguments were so fierce that Esther walked out, and she even contemplated separating from Day forever.

One of these quarrels, four years into their marriage, was prompted by Day accusing Esther of fickleness—his pet hate in women, of course—toward her former fiancé Mr. Lees and another past suitor, Mr. R. It was no excuse that these supposed indiscretions had occurred long before Esther knew Day or that but for her "'fickleness'" she would never have been able to marry him. Esther responded, with justification, by criticizing Day's treatment of Sabrina as equally fickle. At that Day erupted in fury, and Esther left him with the threat that she would stay away permanently. But only a few days after leaving, when she was probably staying at his mother's house in Berkshire—for she had nowhere else to go—Esther wrote a poignant eight-page letter begging his forgiveness and insisting that the faults were entirely on her side.

"I have not for a long time, experienced such a dejection of spirits, as I have done since I parted from my dearest Love," she wrote. "How melancholy is the condition of human things when two people so formed in many respects to contribute to each others happiness, so often inflict mutual uneasiness. In the moments of calm deliberate reflection, when I contemplate my own conduct, with an unprejudiced eye, I feel, & now acknowledge, with conscious shame, that I have too great a share in producing our unhappy dissensions."

Now Esther blamed all their past quarrels on her own "weakness & timidity" and her failure to guard "my own temper," which, she said, was seeded in the "wounded Vanity" and "Self Love" of her youth. "As to what passed on wednesday evening, in the comparison I drew between your Conduct & mine, nothing but the blindest passion could have prompted me to say, what certainly betrayed the most contemptible folly as well as palpable injustice," she wrote. "For I assure you in the most solemn manner, that I think your behaviour to Sabrina, was that of a man of sense & honour; mine to Mr Lxxx, such as from its indiscretion & inconsistency, would have disgraced the weakest of my sex." As to her affection for her other suitor, Mr. R., she now realized this had only been "founded upon Gratitude." But her love for Day, she assured him, was superior to that for either of these previous lovers. "I have always maintained & still continue to assert, that my ideas of you, & feelings for you, have been far beyond what I have experienced before."

Esther blamed her disappointing behavior on "the errors of my youth," which she could only excuse by pointing out that she had not been lucky enough to have a father or brother, like Day, "capable of instructing me in the severe duties of female decorum." And she added: "All that I proposed in leaving you, was to pass the rest of my days in gloomy Solitude, cherishing the same tender mournful esteem & affection for you which I should do for the memory of a beloved, departed Husband." Although she admitted that she sometimes felt "anger & resentment" at his "severity," she assured Day of "my perfect Love & Veneration for you."

After another argument and separation, a year later, when Esther repaired again to her mother-in-law's to contemplate her failings, she wrote another letter seeking his forgiveness. She apologized for the "foolish and inadvertent things" she had said in "moments of anger" and fully accepted that her lapse was due once again to her "caprice and unsteadiness." Promising to try harder in the future, she wrote: "I flatter myself I am already improved in some parts of my character since my connection with you; & therefore, may reasonably hope to make still farther improvements in the regulation of my mind & character." She added: "If I had before contemplated myself in that faithful mirror, which my dear Love has held up to me, I should have found the task more easily accomplished." For all her "thousand inconsistencies" she pledged that "in one thing I am uniform; in feeling for you, all that one human Being can feel for another." Little by little, Day chipped away at Esther's self-esteem, making minute corrections as he tirelessly strove to perfect his imaginary being. He could never be happy; as an obsessive perfectionist, perfection would always stay tantalizingly out of reach.

If the Days led a hard, spartan life, there was little comfort for the Edgeworths either when they came to stay in early 1780. As the telltale symptoms of consumption weakened Honora's health, Edgeworth had taken her to Lichfield the previous summer to consult Darwin. The physician gave Edgeworth little hope that she would live much longer. More devoted than ever, Edgeworth was distraught. He had felt the "violence of love" before his marriage, he said, but six years later he felt it even "more strongly." In a desperate attempt to prove Darwin wrong, he consulted "every physician of eminence in England." Having given up their Hertfordshire home, the couple came to stay with the Days so that they could visit the best doctors in London. To his dismay Edgeworth found that the capital's physicians offered no better prognosis while the Days did little to relieve his despair. "They were very kind to Mrs. Edgeworth," he wrote, "but they did not see her danger in as strong a light as I did."

Taking their leave of the Days' cold comfortless farm, Edgeworth took a house in Shifnal, Shropshire, to be close enough to Lichfield for regular medical visits. He nursed his wife until the end. In her last letter, Honora wrote: "I have every blessing & I am happy. The conversation of my beloved Husband, when my breath will let me have it, is my greatest delight. He procures me every comfort, & as he always said he thought he should, contrives for me every thing that can ease & assist my weakness." She ended with an excerpt from a popular poem: "Like a kind Angel whispers peace & smooths the bed of Death." At the moment she died, in her husband's arms, on May 1, 1780, Edgeworth heard the sound of something falling on the floor. It was Honora's wedding ring, which she had gripped on her wasted finger, until her last breath. She was twenty-eight years old.

Edgeworth was devastated. Lying on the bed beside his wife's corpse all night, he wrote to tell twelve-year-old Maria, at school in Derby, of her stepmother's death. "She now lies dead beside me, and I know, I am doing, what would give her pleasure if she were capable of feeling any thing, by writing to you at this time to fix her excellent image in your Mind." The following day he personally prepared his wife's body for burial as she had requested. And even as she lay in the coffin, Edgeworth could barely tear himself away. He attended the funeral in a trance. "I followed the coffin," he wrote, "I heard the service." But when the earth was shoveled into the grave he stumbled away and found himself back at his house with no idea how he had got there.

Clearly deranged by grief, Edgeworth thought he might find solace in conversation with Day. He took his youngest daughters, Anna and Honora, with him to stay at the Days' farm. But somehow neither Day's long diatribes nor his bleak house alleviated Edgeworth's sorrow, for he found that "even divine philosophy was in vain" and confessed: "I merely existed, and I felt indifferent about every thing and every place." Writing nearly thirty years later, Edgeworth would describe Honora as "The most beloved as a wife, a sister, and a friend, of any person I have ever known." No woman, for Edgeworth, would ever match his second wife.

Almost as bereft as Edgeworth to hear of her adored Honora's death, Anna Seward mourned her surrogate sister with a passion that had been distinctly lacking in real life in recent years. When the Edgeworths had called at the palace a few years after their marriage, in 1776, Seward had collapsed in hysterics and refused to see them for a full hour until prevailed upon by an aunt. Later, when Honora was plainly dying, Edgeworth brought a portrait of her he had commissioned to show Seward. But Seward had recoiled in horror at what she regarded as Edgeworth's "vanity" in possessing "the original." She told a friend that had the picture not been such a poor likeness she would have obtained a copy for "when she is no more." In truth, Honora had been dead to Seward ever since she had married Edgeworth; no likeness painted for Edgeworth could ever approach the idea of Honora in her distorted memory.

After Honora's death almost every letter Seward wrote would include a reference to "my lost Honora." The phantom of her idealized woman—the "loveliest of the maids" with her "peerless face" who possessed "every excellence, that e'r combined / To breathe perfection on the female mind"—would haunt all her poems. Determined to wreak revenge on her perceived rival, Seward accused Edgeworth of neglecting and mistreating his wife—a travesty of the truth—in both private and public. In her *Monody on Major André*, published the year after Honora's death, she callously and erroneously depicted the dead soldier as Honora's true love. Writing to a friend even ten years later she would describe Edgeworth as "the specious, the false, the cruel, the murderous Edgeworth, who cankered first and then crushed to Earth, the finest of all human flowers."

While Edgeworth would mourn Honora all his life, he knew that—for the sake of his six children at least—he could not remain alone. Returning to Lichfield he resolved to carry out Honora's dying wish: to marry her sister Elizabeth. Edgeworth joined Elizabeth Sneyd on a seaside expedition with her siblings to Scarborough, where he found that the bracing air and bracing company gradually restored his spirits. Elizabeth had previously described Edgeworth as "the last man of her acquaintance" she would have considered as a husband, and Edgeworth believed Elizabeth was "as little suited to me." But by the time they returned from the seaside they were both determined to marry.

Major Sneyd was aghast at the news and blankly refused his approval. The gossiping neighbors of Lichfield were horrified. Not only was it widely considered immoral to marry a brother-in-law, but some critics believed such a marriage was actually illegal. Edgeworth wrote to Boulton, who had married his sister-in-law after his first wife's death, for advice; Boulton assured him, if necessary, they would brave hell together. Then Elizabeth took matters into her own hands. She fled her father's house on October 24 and took refuge with friends in Cheshire. Her father would never forgive her; to lose one daughter to the irrepressible Edgeworth was bad luck, to lose a second was unspeakable. Barely able to hold a pen in anger he wrote in his diary: "To my inexpressible concern my Daugr. Elizabeth left me & went off with her Bror. in Law." He promptly changed his will to disinherit Elizabeth and bind all his children never to speak to Edgeworth again.

When Edgeworth's sister Margaret expressed similar shock at his marriage plans, Edgeworth wrote in an uncharacteristic fury "perhaps I shall send all my little children to you for I cannot bear their present orphan state." On the point of getting married in Staffordshire, the couple were left standing at the altar when the vicar got cold feet and canceled their wedding. Undeterred, Elizabeth and Edgeworth headed for London where they were finally married, on Christmas Day 1780, at St. Andrew's Church, Holborn, with Day as one of the witnesses. Elizabeth could never replace her sister in Edgeworth's eyes, but their marriage would prove happy and successful, producing a further nine children.

Trips to London, for weddings or otherwise, were no rarity for Day despite his supposed retirement from society. When he was not engaged in the task of improving his wife in their Essex home, Day was far from reclusive. Leaving Esther alone to ponder her faults, Day devoted as much time and energy to his social, political and literary interests as ever. He had finally been called to the bar in 1779, after one of the longest legal trainings on record, although he would never practice law. Renting new chambers in Furnival Inn, near Chancery Lane, as a convenient London refuge, he roved the country giving lectures on human rights and liberty while Esther stayed at home, effectively a captive to Day's authoritarian regime.

Having made a name for himself with his defiant stands on slavery and American independence, Day became a leading figure in the reform movement that was launched in 1780 to campaign for wider electoral suffrage, annual elections and reduced powers for the Crown. Day gave rousing speeches at public meetings in Cambridge and Chelmsford calling for a right to vote for all working men—though not, of course, for women— and he was even urged to stand for parliament. Although he refused to be drawn into the murky world of parliamentary politics he soon found himself further embroiled in the American war.

Ever since Day had pledged support for American independence, he had remained true to the cause. So when Henry Laurens, the slave owner who had become president of the American Congress in 1777, was captured at sea by British forces and charged with treason at the end of 1780, Day knew where his loyalties lay. Laurens was incarcerated in the Tower of London, but on his release, fifteen months later, following Britain's defeat at Yorktown, he immediately sought out Day on his Essex farm. They became firm friends, and Day used his parliamentary contacts to secure Laurens safe conduct to France in order to take part in the peace negotiations.

Laurens had just arrived in Paris when news came through that his son John had been killed in an assault on British forces. He asked Day to write an epitaph. And as the peace talks drew to a climax at the end of 1782, Laurens sent Day a complete transcript of the draft treaty still under secret discussion with British negotiators. Cautioning Day to "keep a proper reserve" on the details, Laurens pricked out the proposed new boundaries of the "United States" on a map and added: "We are at the threshold of Peace." When Laurens read almost identical details published in the *Morning Herald* in January 1783, he could not help harboring suspicions. It was, however, probably not Day who leaked the American peace treaty—although he had certainly read the entire contents of the draft agreement to Esther—and he earnestly assured Laurens that he had "shewn no one else." For all his double standards, Day made an unlikely double agent. With peace secured and independence inevitable—the Treaty of Paris would be signed in September 1783—Day applauded his American friends' climactic steps toward independence in the true spirit of Rousseau's ideals of liberty and equality.

Attempting to create a miniature version of Rousseau's utopian ideal in his little corner of England, Day ministered to the needs of the tenants

and workers on his Essex farm. When he bought a new estate, Anningsley Park near Chertsey in Surrey, where he and Esther moved in 1782,
he created a prototype welfare system that provided work, education, religious instruction and medical care for all the folk in the neighborhood.
Together the Days distributed blankets, food and medicine, held Sunday
school in their home for local children and invited the sick into their
kitchen to share meals.

Yet Day found no pleasure in his philanthropy and begrudged every
penny. Although he was still in his thirties, he was already a grumpy old
man. "I have never expected any thing romantic from my fellow creatures,
and have long confined myself to the lowest returns of good behaviour, or
the commonest attentions of civility," he grumbled to Edgeworth. "Yet
daily experience shews, that even this is too much to be expected from
those, who make the greatest professions, and have most experienced your
friendship."

Although it was a larger and more comfortable house than the Days'
former retreat, Anningsley Park looked if anything more forbidding. The
two-story house lay sunk in a hollow encircled by dense woods and
bounded by acres of barren heath. One visitor described walking toward
the house through silent trees so thick that scarcely any sunlight pene-
trated. When Maria Edgeworth came to stay, in holidays from her new
boarding school in London, she was struck by "Mr. Day's austere simplicity of life" and the "icy strength of his system." With a "stern voice" mixed
with "something of pity" Day made her drink a daily tumbler of tar
water—a popular medicine of the time—in a misguided effort to treat an
eye infection. Elizabeth Warburton-Lytton, whose father had made her
roll in snow as part of her toughening regime, later described her dread
when she arrived at Anningsley Park late one night to see "a tall man, with
a grave and precise face, much marked with the habits of authority and
the ravages of small-pox." While Day made her translate long tracts of
Latin, she was consoled by "cakes and caresses" from Esther.

Although they were still young and in relatively good health, the Days remained childless. But even though they would never have children of their
own, Thomas Day now applied himself diligently to educating the chil-

dren of the nation. Even though he had banned Esther from writing poetry, he would achieve lasting fame as a writer of children's books. And it
was Edgeworth, the prime mover as ever, who had revived Day's interest
in education.

Edgeworth remained convinced that children's education needed radical reform even though he acknowledged that his efforts to apply
Rousseau's theories to Dick had proved disastrous. After suffering miserably in boarding school, Dick had joined the merchant navy at the age of
fifteen, but finding naval discipline no less severe, he deserted ship in India
in 1783 and returned to England in disgrace. Unreliable and lazy—a child
who never grew up—Dick would become permanently estranged from
his father, who cut his eldest son out of his will apart from a nominal sum.
He would eventually settle in America, where he married and had children, but lived a life of dissipation and died young in 1796, aged only
thirty-two. His father shed few tears. Ultimately Dick would provide Jane
Austen with the model for the "very troublesome, hopeless son," Dick
Musgrove, "who had never done anything to entitle himself to more than
the abbreviation of his name, living or dead" in her novel *Persuasion*.

Determined not to spoil his other children as he had spoiled Dick,
Edgeworth had returned to Ireland with Elizabeth in 1782 and dedicated
himself to supervising his young family's upbringing. Although he now
insisted that his children respond to discipline and learn elementary skills
like reading and writing in formal lessons, he remained faithful to the
Rousseau principle that children learn best through experiment and discovery. Whether he was building a wall or attempting an explosive experiment, Edgeworth gathered his growing brood to watch and answer
questions appropriate to their age. "He would sit quietly while a child was
thinking of the answer to a question, without interrupting, or suffering it
to be interrupted, and would let the pupil touch and quit the point repeatedly," wrote Maria, his eldest daughter. When the shuffling bystanders
had given up hope of a response, their father's patience was rewarded "with
a perfectly satisfactory answer," and the pupil would glow with pride at
Edgeworth's praise.

As Maria grew older, she helped her father to educate the younger
children, and they would later jointly write an education manual, *Practical*

Education, setting down the approach they had found most successful. An immediate best seller when it was published in 1798, the book would be acclaimed as one of the most significant works on education ever. Child-centered and down-to-earth, the book recommends an ideal learning environment based in the family home, with a playroom containing educational toys, models, books, maps and scientific apparatus. The book devotes the first thirty-five pages to the importance of toys to children's development and emphasizes that a child much prefers a simple wooden cart "to carry weeds, earth, and stones, up and down hill" to the finest model coach or dolls' house.

As part of his lifelong interest in education, Edgeworth had written some short stories for children in 1778 with his then wife Honora when she could not find any books to teach her youngest to read. He had planned to publish a series of books for children and had the first in the collection, titled *Harry and Lucy*, printed privately, in Lichfield in 1779. Inspired by this venture, Day had offered to contribute a story. When Honora died two years later, the grief-stricken Edgeworth abandoned the project, but Day continued to write. Before long, his short story had grown into a full-length book, which Day called *The History of Sandford and Merton, A Work Intended for the Use of Children*. It was published in three volumes, the first in 1783, the next in 1786 and the last in 1789. The Edgeworths were among the first to write specifically for and about children, but it was Day who won lasting fame for his children's book.

Written in simple words with plentiful dialogue, *Sandford and Merton* tells the story of two boys, Tommy Merton, the pampered son of a rich plantation owner who lives a life of indolence and selfishness, and Harry Sandford, the honest son of a poor farmer who works hard, treats animals and fellow humans with kindness and enjoys a simple life. A local clergyman, Mr. Barlow, is given the role of teaching the two boys—much in the way that Day had undertaken the task of teaching two girls though with rather better results. With Barlow as the boys' wise mentor and Harry as the model pupil, Tommy gradually sees the error of his ways and evolves into a virtuous, generous and plain-living gentleman. During their adventures, the boys meet a variety of characters who treat them to a string of fables and cautionary tales, drawn from classical stories and other sources, which illustrate the path to virtue, as well as offering them lessons on such skills as making bread, building a house and using magnets. With its firm moral stance and sentimental tales, the book combined Day's belief in the traditional values of industry, stoicism and honesty with his attachment to the idea of sensibility.

Sandford and Merton became an immediate success and would remain one of the best-selling and best-loved children's books for more than a century. Hundreds of thousands of boys—and girls—throughout the nineteenth century and into the early twentieth would be captivated by Day's hero Harry and dream of meeting its celebrated author. Once, when Day visited the Midlands, he was mobbed by young readers who came to gawp at the writer of their favorite book. Tommy and Harry's adventures would be eagerly consumed in turn by writers from Robert Southey and Leigh Hunt to Charles Dickens, Oscar Wilde and P. G. Wodehouse. Leigh Hunt declared the book "a production that I well remember, and shall ever be grateful to" while Southey insisted that it should be read by all "with profit and pleasure."

Standing on the bookshelves of almost every Victorian nursery, Day's children's novel would be reprinted 140 times by 1870, with translations in French and German; a new edition was published as recently as 2009. The book was not only one of the first aimed at children, it launched an entire new genre in adventure books for boys that helped to stiffen British resolve in the face of danger whether in the playground or on the battlefield.

Inevitably the popularity of *Sandford and Merton* would eventually wane. Dickens would lead the way with a vociferous attack in 1869 on the story that had "cast its gloom over my childhood." Three years later, schoolboys everywhere could guffaw in relief at a spoof version of the book, *The New Sandford and Merton*, although Day's novel would continue to hold sway for several more decades before it was declared well and truly out of date and out of step.

It was a remarkable achievement. In his book, Day had created two boys who exactly fitted the mold he had so long aimed to fill. And although the book focuses almost solely on the education of boys, at one point Day even introduces a perfect girl, Sukey Simmons, who befriends Harry. Orphaned in childhood, Sukey has been raised by her uncle, just like Esther, but in a decidedly Rousseauvian fashion. While young, Sukey was woken by candlelight in winter, plunged into cold baths and made to ride or walk dozens of miles daily but had also been taught to read "the best authors" in English and a few in French. Through this "robust and hardy" education Sukey acquired "an excellent character" in Day's words. Even if Day had failed to educate his two female pupils to adopt his singular ideas, in fiction he would finally fashion the children of his dreams. Furthermore, Day's enduring literary success would ensure that his views on innocent virtue and stoical courage would be inculcated in innumerable boys and girls throughout the nineteenth century.

Busy educating the nation's children, Day gave little thought to his early educational experiment. If he did, according to Keir, he would now scoff at his earlier naïveté in pursuing "schemes, which, on account of the impracticality of their execution, were sometimes the subject of his own pleasantry in his maturer age." In other words, Sabrina's ordeal was now the subject of a joke. But when Edgeworth wrote to tell him that he was thinking of adopting a peasant boy in order to educate him as a gentleman in a bizarre imitation of Day's attempt to educate Sabrina, Day was aghast at the idea and strenuously warned Edgeworth against the notion.

Plainly speaking with bitterness born of his own experience, Day protested: "If we chuse to make a lady out of what fortune has intended for a serving wench, or a gentleman out of the materials of a blacksmith, we certainly have a very good right." But the child would grow up to "consider you as doomed to supply all its wants," and Edgeworth would have to "maintain for a gentleman him whom you have taken as a beggar." With an eye to his future reputation Day added gravely: "Or will you much relish, towards the decline of your life, the having manifestoes to publish about your own conduct, and to apologise to your fellow-creatures for not being a dupe, or an idiot?" Wisely, Edgeworth dropped the scheme and concentrated on educating his own family.

But one person at least had not given up on Sabrina.

TEN

VIRGINIA, BELINDA AND MARY

~ *Five Ways, Birmingham, May 1783* ~

F ar from the dizzying world of politics and publishing, Sabrina had grown into her twenties with only an occasional cold letter and her yearly £50 allowance from Day. Since her final rejection by him in 1775, she had spent eight years living in anonymous boardinghouses and family homes across the Midlands. For a while, after moving from the lodging house in Birmingham where Day had first placed her, she obtained work as a lady's companion in Newport in Shropshire. For an educated, single woman of slender means, becoming a companion to a wealthy woman or a governess to a well-to-do family were the only two respectable options. Part-chaperone and part-maid, the job of lady's companion meant being at the command of a mistress day and night. In theory this was a step up from working as a domestic servant; in practice it was often harder work than being the lowliest maid.

By 1780 this unenviable position had come to an end, and Sabrina had moved back to the outskirts of Birmingham. At that point Day had felt the need to write a will, which was almost entirely devoted to exonerating himself from any additional responsibility for his former pupil. Although he made sure to leave ample security for his mother, stepfather and Esther after his death, Day stipulated that "Sabrina Sidney an Orphan now living near Birmingham" should continue to receive her £50 allowance only so long as she remained single. If she married she would receive the £500 dowry Day had promised back in 1769, but only on the condition that the money "be accepted by her as a perfect acquittal of every promise engagement or contract which I have made with her or on her behalf." Day appointed his trusty friend Keir to ensure his orders regarding Sabrina would be carried out. But even if Day could cut Sabrina out of any inheritance, he could not cut her out of his life.

Charming and graceful with an easy manner and a ready rapport, Sabrina had continued to visit old friends in old haunts and attract new admirers in new places. "Wherever she resided, wherever she paid visits, she secured to herself friends," wrote Anna Seward. She often stayed with the Darwins on visits to Lichfield—at least until Darwin moved to Derby after marrying a second time in 1781—and she was a favorite guest with the Savilles too. In August 1780, she had been invited to the baptism of John Saville's grandson, the first child of his daughter, Sabrina's friend, now married as Eliza Smith. "We are unable to fix the time till Sabrina comes," Saville told a friend. "She is expected in a few days." Judging from the need to await her arrival, Sabrina was probably the baby's godmother; the baptism duly took place on August 25 when the baby was named Saville Smith.

With all traces of Sabrina's foundling past forgotten or obscured, she faced the world as a self-assured woman of independent means. According to Seward, "she passed the dangerous interval between sixteen and twenty-five without one reflection upon her conduct, one stain upon her discretion." Yet although Day was at pains to keep her out of his sight he maintained a hold on her life—and her marital fortunes. When in her early twenties Sabrina received a marriage proposal from an eligible young suitor she made the mistake of seeking Day's advice.

The proposal, written in verse, came from a surgeon apothecary, named Jarvis Wardley, who had served an apprenticeship in Newport before setting up business on his own in nearby Market Drayton. Traditionally apothecaries ground powders and mixed potions prescribed by physicians, but by the late 1700s they were becoming recognized as medical men in their own right—the future general practitioners. Wardley was highly regarded by Erasmus Darwin judging from the considerate reply Darwin sent to a letter from Wardley seeking advice on a patient. It was perhaps through Darwin that Wardley had met Sabrina. Charmed by the amiable young woman, Wardley, a year her senior, sent his marriage proposal in the form of an acrostic poem—a verse in which the first letter of each line spells out a message or name.

Wardley was a professional man with a secure income and romantic leanings, and so his proposal was not one to reject lightly; there were far worse fates than becoming an apothecary's wife. But Day was unequivocal in telling Sabrina to reject him—perhaps from a snobbish view that Wardley's vocation was too lowly for his erstwhile pupil; perhaps through reluctance to let her go. Applying his poetic talents to the task, Day composed a return acrostic spelling out Jarvis Wardley's name, with plentiful barbed allusions to the apothecary's profession, which he advised Sabrina to send with a stern rebuff. Day wrote, in part: "In ev'ry art you shine the first of men, / So well you wield the pestle and the pen! / When e'er with skilful hand, the lint you spread, / And smooth a plaister for a broken head; / Rollers & bandages confess your skill; / Doctors themselves resign the murd'ring pill." Day even drafted her rejection letter: "Miss Sydney hopes, that the above will appear a sufficient Recompense, to Mr. Wardley, for his elegant Acrostic, which she will by no means rob him of, as it may serve again with very little alteration." Further letters from Wardley would be returned unopened, Day wrote, since "such correspondencies are highly improper for young *women of any Character.*"

Spurned by Sabrina, Wardley soon found another bride. Sabrina, however, continued unmarried and unattached into her mid-twenties. Living in a boardinghouse at Five Ways, a hamlet of fine villas where five roads met a mile south of Birmingham, Sabrina grew close to a young woman who moved into the same house in early 1783. Born in Geneva, Françoise-Antoinette de Luc—known as Fanny to her friends—was the daughter of Jean André de Luc, a geologist who had become friendly with the Lunar Society. Fanny, aged twenty-eight, soon became a popular guest with her father's Lunar friends—not least for her entertaining stories about the oddest member of their circle.

Finding a friend in Fanny in their shared lodgings, Sabrina confided the bizarre ordeals she had suffered during her training with Day. And Fanny in turn repeated the shocking stories when she visited the home of Samuel Galton, one of the Lunar club's newest members, who lived in Hagley Row near Five Ways. Galton's eldest daughter, Mary Anne, was less than six at the time, but she would remember into her seventies Fanny de Luc's tales of Sabrina's torture by sealing wax and pistols. "We were very much interested in anecdotes she told us of Sabrina Sidney, the *élève* of Mr. Day, who was boarding at the same house as her," she wrote, although the revelations did not diminish her admiration for her favorite book, *Sandford and Merton*.

Living on the fringes of Birmingham as she turned twenty-six in spring 1783, Sabrina was in danger of being left on the edge of society. Her experimental education was the subject of tea table gossip and giggles. Her financial security was under the control of her reluctant benefactor. And her past connections with Day placed her reputation precariously in the balance. The expanding city that she could see from the windows of her lodgings provided a stark symbol of her ambiguous position. The tree-lined squares and tea gardens still offered a desirable location for Birmingham's well-heeled residents, but the cramped terraced houses and smoky workshops fast encroaching on every available space suggested an alternative future. Since Day had now married the woman he still hoped to mold into his perfect wife, Sabrina had probably given up hope that she would ever marry. Living at the junction of five roads, she had no idea in which direction her life would lead. And then a long forgotten visitor arrived on her doorstep. It was John Bicknell.

Years of carousing with his friends at Middle Temple had taken its toll on Bicknell. Like Day, he had always preferred to spend his time stirring up radical politics and producing literary works to reading law books and legal briefs. Unlike Day, Bicknell had no independent fortune to bankroll his leisure pursuits. His family's long predominance in the law had given him a helpful shove up the legal ladder. His positions as a barrister in the court of King's Bench and as a commissioner of bankrupts brought substantial fees. According to Edgeworth, Bicknell was a "man of shining talents" with "great wit and acuteness." But Bicknell had squandered his talents and good fortune through laziness, high living and licentiousness.

Instead of studying briefs for court cases, Bicknell studied his cards in gambling clubs and spent his winnings in Covent Garden brothels or forgot his losses in Fleet Street taverns. He was particularly fond of the game *chemin de fer*, which was popular with the aristocratic fast set, a variation of baccarat so named because the cards were dealt from an iron box. At one point he won a "considerable fortune," but as quickly as his winnings accrued they trickled through his fingers again. Before long the attorneys who referred clients to barristers like Bicknell were sending their business elsewhere. "He is said to have kept briefs an unconscionable time in his pocket, or on his table, unnoticed," wrote Edgeworth. "Attorneys complained, but still he consoled himself with wit, literature and pleasure, till health as well as attorneys began to fail." By the time he reached his thirties, Bicknell was suffering from "absolute palsies"—probably a stroke—and wrote to Day for advice. Day suggested his stock remedies of fresh air, plain food and exercise—sage words in Bicknell's case.

But if Day's prescription came too late to alleviate Bicknell's ailments, the connection with his old school friend suggested another idea to revive his ailing fortunes. With both his health and his finances in dire straits, Bicknell faced up to his future. It was not looking rosy. Having remained resolutely single so far, at thirty-six Bicknell resolved to settle down and get married. He wanted a companion, perhaps even children, to comfort and care for him in his remaining years. Casting around for possible candidates, he suddenly remembered the pretty twelve-year-old orphan that he had plucked from the line of girls at the Shrewsbury Foundling Hospital fourteen years earlier.

In the intervening years Bicknell had taken scant interest in Sabrina. Despite the fact that he had first selected her as Day's prospective wife, he later expressed surprise that Day was so smitten with her. He told Edgeworth "he could not, for his part, see any thing extraordinary about the girl, one way or other." When Edgeworth praised her melodious voice and gentle manner, Bicknell had "only shrugged his shoulders." When

Day rejected Sabrina and married Esther, Bicknell's indifference had turned to pity but nothing more. And since then Sabrina had apparently slipped completely from his mind.

Now Bicknell made discreet inquiries about her circumstances, probably through Edgeworth since he was careful not to alert Day to his interest. Having established that she was still single, he wanted to know whether she retained a taintless reputation. By Georgian double standards it was quite acceptable for Bicknell to sow his seeds but reprehensible for his potential wife. Satisfied to learn that Sabrina was alive and well, single and saintly, Bicknell obtained her address and set off hotfoot to find her. When he tracked her down to her lodgings at Five Ways, he was delighted to discover that the adolescent girl he remembered had matured into a beautiful and poised young woman.

According to Edgeworth, Bicknell now "saw her with different eyes from those, with which he had looked upon her formerly" and "fell desperately in love." Equally it may have been Sabrina's promised £500 dowry that Bicknell viewed with different eyes. Confident that he had found "a companion for middle life, and a friend, perhaps a nurse, for his declining years," Bicknell asked her to marry him. Sabrina, he was certain, would be perfect for his needs.

Sabrina weighed up the offer. She had rejected a young surgeon apothecary with a promising future and a literary flair. Now she was confronted by a middle-aged, down-at-the-heels lawyer in declining health. But she was alone, single, living in rented rooms and financially dependent on Day with no guarantees for her future. Bicknell was clever, charming, persuasive and belonged to a respectable family with immaculate connections. It was probably rational considerations, or "prudential" reasons in Seward's words, that prompted Sabrina to say yes. Later, Sabrina would let it be known that Bicknell was "the man of her dreams," and perhaps that was true. She had, of course, once told Edgeworth, "I love Mr. Day best in the world, Mr. Bicknell next, and you next." But before she could go ahead with the wedding, Sabrina insisted on consulting Edgeworth and Day.

Edgeworth responded with characteristic generosity and optimism. He confessed himself a trifle surprised to hear that Bicknell was suddenly in love with someone he had previously considered with indifference and more than a little concerned that Bicknell's poor health and poorer work ethic might leave Sabrina in financial straits. But ever the incurable romantic, he reasoned that "no motive could be stronger or more likely to make a man exert himself, than the desire of providing for a woman he loved," and he duly sent his approval with good wishes for their future happiness. Day's response was rather different.

If Sabrina had been surprised by Bicknell's proposal, she was far more astonished when he revealed the full ghastly truth of her relationship with Day. Until now Sabrina had accepted without question Day's story that he had taken her from the Foundling Hospital as an apprentice maid and educated and supported her out of sheer benevolence. Likewise she had believed that his desire to marry her had evolved over time by chance. But Bicknell now divulged that Day had specifically chosen her—and Lucretia—as his prospective future wife from the outset, and throughout her teenage years he had persevered—albeit sporadically—to train her for that purpose. All Day's acts of supposed kindness and paternalistic protection had been self-centered moves to train her as his bride. He had never legally been her guardian; she had never been his apprentice after all.

Sabrina was horrified. Not only had she been the unwitting subject of Day's bizarre experiment, but most of his circle, the friends she had come to know and love in Lichfield and beyond, had been fully aware of his grand plan all along. Furious and humiliated, she wrote to Day announcing her plans to marry Bicknell and demanding a full, candid and speedy explanation of all his past conduct.

Day's reply, on May 4, 1783, was a masterpiece of self-righteous indignation in which he attempted to justify his past relations with Sabrina while grudgingly giving his approval for her marriage. "My dear Miss Sidney," he began, "The subject you write to me upon, is of sufficient importance to engage me to give you as you desire an immediate answer." Day promised not only to give "my opinions upon the connections you are now forming" but also to explain "that more extraordinary one which has hitherto subsisted between you & me." At last he confessed his motives in selecting her at the Foundling Hospital and his plans to educate her as his wife. But protesting vehemently that he had no need to justify his past actions, Day proceeded to do just that.

"I need not mention what you were about fourteen years past," Day wrote—Sabrina's origins in the Foundling Hospital were still too shameful to put into writing—"when I first selected you as the object of my very extraordinary scheme." He now admitted: "I may now plainly acknowledge I took you, with a view of educating you according to my own opinions, & if you turned out agreeably to my wishes, to make you my wife, when I had attained a sufficient confidence in your character." He made no attempt to apologize for his conduct. "Whether those intentions were wild, chimerical, & extravagant, or rational & prudent it is not now necessary to inquire; that object relates to myself alone," he wrote, "& you are the last person in the world to whom I owe any apologies upon that head." He had embarked on his plan, he now confessed, in order "to obtain a wife that should be free from the common prejudices & extravagances in which women are now educated." He had felt fully entitled to attempt this experiment, he explained, since whatever Sabrina's fate she would still be better off than if she had remained in the orphanage. "In rescuing you from this situation, it appeared to me, that whether I married you or not, you would at least be a gainer provided I placed you in a more decent situation of life, & enabled you to live by an easy exertion of your own industry."

Day stuck rigidly to the fiction that Sabrina had originally been apprenticed to him—although she could easily have disproved this by asking Edgeworth—and he insisted that he had always behaved toward her with due decorum. While this was probably true in the sense that he had not debauched her, it failed to answer his cavalier attitude to her reputation. Day went on to confirm how he had tried to train her at Stowe House—though he neglected to mention his sadistic physical tests—then sent her away to school in Sutton Coldfield and later to her apprenticeship with the Parkinsons before finally embarking on the last decisive trial. He listed a catalog of her repeated failings—her inability to bend to domestic chores, her negligence in her behavior toward him, her indolence with the Parkinsons—culminating in her violation of his "particular injunctions," which had ultimately ended their relationship. Despite all her flaws, however, he had "supported you, educated you, & protected you to the best of my abilities through a period of thirteen years; during which space I call god to witness that I have always considered your own good, as an object of more importance than any gratification to myself."

Plainly anxious to absolve himself from any suggestion of immorality or mistreatment, Day asked Sabrina now to affirm his testimony of events in a declaration to Keir as an "irrefragable memorial" of his conduct "not to be disputed or set aside hereafter." Day sent his letter in an unsealed wrapper to Keir with the clear intention that he should read it too. It was plain that Day had come under attack for his treatment of Sabrina—certainly by Esther in their quarrels and most probably by Edgeworth too—from his plea to Sabrina that if she made a statement to Keir "I may at least have a friend in the world who understands the series of my behaviour towards you, & one person who will not abuse me for a conduct, the generosity & disinteredness of which, I believe few will imitate."

As to her proposal to marry Bicknell, Day sniffily pointed out that as Sabrina had asked for his consent rather than "my advice or opinion," she had obviously already made up her mind. Since Bicknell was "a man of undoubted sense and an affectionate disposition," she should count herself lucky that he "chuses you, from an hundred others your superior." But from the moment she married, Day stressed, she would be dependent solely on her husband. This letter, he told her, would be their last communication. He wished her "from the bottom of my soul every degree of good & happiness which the frail condition of human life admits." And with those final words, and an almost audible sigh of relief, Day said goodbye to his protégée forever.

If Sabrina had wanted more affectionate wishes and enduring concern she was sorely disappointed. When she had had the chance she had decided not to marry him; whether by defying his instructions or by running away, she had rejected Day. Now that she had chosen another man he felt entirely within his rights to cast her off forever; there was no possibility of friendship or any other connection. He had taken her into his life when she was just twelve and had no say in the matter; now that she was twenty-six he could drop her without a backward glance.

The following year, on April 16, 1784, Sabrina walked up the aisle of St. Philip's Church in Birmingham and married John Bicknell. Bicknell's sister

Catherine and Day's advocate Keir were the witnesses. In a small but significant assertion of her past identity and independence from Day, she signed her name in the register as Anna Sabrina Sidney. And then she adopted her fourth and final name: Sabrina Bicknell.

On the very same day, Day signed a bond to pay Bicknell the £500 dowry—worth more than £60,000 in today's terms—which he had promised to Sabrina; under Georgian law this immediately transferred to her husband. Financed by this windfall, the newlyweds moved to Shenfield, a village in Essex that was fast developing as a handy country base for professional men with jobs in the city. And contrary to Edgeworth's worries and Seward's insinuations, the marriage proved both companionable and fruitful. In eighteenth-century terms, for most married people, that was perfection indeed.

Sabrina gave birth to two sons within the next three years. The eldest, born in late 1785 or early 1786, was baptized John Laurens Bicknell, in memory of Bicknell's recently killed American friend. The second, born on December 18, 1786, was baptized Henry Edgeworth Bicknell, the middle name coming from Sabrina's lifelong friend and supporter. There was no such homage to Day. Despite Day's conviction that Sabrina fell short of matrimonial ideals, Sabrina made "an excellent wife," in Edgeworth's view, while Seward described her as "one of the most affectionate, as well as the best of wives."

Writing regularly to Edgeworth in Ireland, Bicknell described his life with Sabrina and the little changes in their sons, "with all the delight of the most happy husband and father." And even if Sabrina had married Bicknell out of prudence, she seemed contented too. One of her friends later said she "could hardly have been happier with the man of her dreams—a husband who idolised her" and brought her "joy and delight"; or at least that was the view Sabrina wanted to pass on to her sons.

At first Bicknell prospered in his career; marriage seemed to suit him. Applying himself to his legal work with renewed zeal, he was appointed a King's Counsel, one of the most senior members of the bar. When Boswell visited the King's Bench in 1786, he was introduced to "Counsellor Bicknell" by their mutual friend, William Seward. At the same time Bicknell shared his literary interests with Sabrina. They were both subscribers to the first collection of poems published in 1786 by Helen Maria Williams, a fellow campaigner against slavery.

Yet the responsibilities of marriage and late fatherhood did little to temper Bicknell's youthful excesses. Instead of saving money toward his sons' future, Bicknell spent most of what he earned on fine living and gambled away the rest at the card table. His health was no better than his luck. Sabrina's perfect marriage—or the closest she would ever get to it—was short-lived.

Just as they were coming up to their third wedding anniversary, Bicknell suffered another stroke, and a few weeks later, on March 27, 1787, he died. His death warranted only a small mention in the London newspapers in which he was finally given credit for cowriting *The Dying Negro* as well as being named the chief author of the less honorable *Musical Travels* under the pseudonym Joel Collier. Six days later, on April 2, 1787, Bicknell was buried in the family vault of St. Dunstan-in-the-West in Fleet Street, just a few hundred yards from Middle Temple and his family home in Chancery Lane.

After less than three years of married life Sabrina was alone again— only now she had no income and two small children to bring up on her own. Henry was three months old while John was barely one. Sabrina was unwell herself, perhaps as a result of giving birth to Henry or from the shock of her husband's death. But worse was still to come. Bicknell had left no will. Although this might seem an odd omission for a veteran lawyer, Bicknell had presumably felt there was no need to write a will, since he had nothing to bequeath except debts. He had left Sabrina penniless—nothing remained of his legal earnings or the £500 she had brought to the marriage—and there were several creditors demanding payment. Bicknell had squandered a fortune in less than three years. The commissioner of bankrupts was effectively bankrupt.

A widow at the age of thirty, with two infants and no means of support, Sabrina was entirely dependent on the kindness of friends and strangers. "She had absolutely nothing," said one acquaintance. It was in just such circumstances that women had given up their children to the Foundling Hospital, but since the charity had long since ceased to accept orphans, only the parish workhouse remained as the last resort for destitute mothers and their children. Sabrina had spent the first twelve years of her life dependent on charity; she was determined her sons would not suffer the same fate.

For many women in Georgian times, locked in miserable or abusive marriages, widowhood came as a happy release and even brought financial independence. Although wives were legally obliged to hand all their property and earnings to their husbands, widows were entitled to keep all they owned and earned. But for those women left destitute by a husband's death, widowhood could bring penury since no state provision existed apart from pitiful parish relief or the workhouse. Many widows had no option but to beg on the streets or turn to prostitution to feed themselves and their families.

Despite having severed all communications before her marriage, Day now grudgingly reinstated Sabrina's annual allowance but reduced the amount to £30 with a clear injunction that she must find work to boost her income. "To have been more bounteous must surely have been in his heart," wrote Seward, "but it was not in his system." This sum was matched by Edgeworth, who even offered to educate one of her sons and take her into his household for a year. Sabrina declined the offer, presumably unwilling to move to Ireland. While £60 a year was still several times the salary of a housemaid, it was far from sufficient to support her young family in any comfort or to pay for the education of her sons. The Bicknell family were even less help.

At sixty-six, Bicknell's mother Sarah was a steely matriarch who guarded the family coffers and reputation with an iron grip. Well aware of Sabrina's past, since she had looked after her on Day's return from Avignon, Mrs. Bicknell had never accepted her daughter-in-law into the fold. The taint of illegitimacy retained a pungent smell, and, according to one of Sabrina's friends, Mrs. Bicknell "always refused to love" her. With four sons struggling to make a name for themselves in the law, Mrs. Bicknell was determined to put the needs of her immediate family first. Bicknell's brothers likewise steadfastly ignored Sabrina's plight. Anxious to ensure Sabrina and her boys would not become a burden on their resources, the Bicknell family found her a job as a maid in a village school. She was all but neglected by those who might be regarded as having the clearest duty to help her, and now it was people she barely knew who came to her aid.

Just a few weeks after Bicknell's death, Sabrina received an unexpected letter. Charles Burney, the son of the composer Dr. Charles Burney, who had tried to introduce music lessons at the Foundling Hospital, wrote to offer a free place for Sabrina's son John at the school he ran in Hammersmith. Evidently bearing no grudge for her husband's satirical attack on his father, Burney had learned of Sabrina's misfortune through William Seward, the old schoolfriend of Bicknell and Day. A gifted classical scholar, who knew Bicknell from London's literary scene, Burney would have been well aware of Sabrina's irregular past. Just a few months younger than Sabrina, with a son the same age as her eldest, he had every reason to sympathize—since Burney was himself no stranger to scandal.

Having distinguished himself at Charterhouse School, Charles Burney had been admitted to Cambridge at nineteen. A few months later he had been expelled after thirty-five of the university library's priceless books were discovered in his room. A heavy drinker and inveterate gambler, Burney had been selling the books to service his debts. As Burney was sent home in shame, his father threatened to disown him while his sister, the novelist Fanny Burney, was said to have found him on the point of shooting himself. He was lucky. An earlier Cambridge book thief had been transported to a penal colony for his crime; Charles Burney was merely banished to the University of Aberdeen to finish his degree. Returning to London still cloaked in disgrace, Burney took lowly teaching jobs, first in Highgate and then in Chiswick, where he charmed and married the headmaster's daughter, Sarah Rose. On his father-in-law's death, Burney took over the Chiswick school, which later moved to Hammersmith. It was here that Burney now offered a place for young John.

Her reply to Burney, on May 16, 1787, is the earliest surviving letter in Sabrina's own hand. In a neat, rounded script and impeccable English grammar, Sabrina confessed that she had been "very unwell" since the death of her "dear dear lost friend." She thanked Burney profusely for his "great & friendly offer to me & my dear little boy" and added that she had often heard her late husband "express great regard & respect for you & your abilities." Regretting that her son was as yet too young for school—John was little more than a year old—she looked forward "with impatience" to the date when he could take up his place. In the meantime Sabrina had no choice but to accept the menial job the Bicknell family had arranged. With baby Henry looked after by a nurse and John playing at her feet, she worked on her hands and knees to feed and clothe her boys.

In October the following year Sabrina managed a few days' holiday to visit Eliza Smith in Lichfield. Now also a widow, with two children, Honora and Saville, to support, Eliza lived with her father and used her singing talents to make ends meet. Coached by Saville, Eliza sang at concerts at Lichfield, Birmingham and Bath. It may well have been the first time that Sabrina introduced John and Henry, now two years and one year old, to her Lichfield friends. Inevitably there was a trip to the palace. Having not seen Sabrina for several years, Anna Seward pronounced her "more graceful, more attractive, much more eloquent than ever" although she could not resist the rider "though less beautiful." But when Seward learned of Sabrina's situation, she was appalled.

Unable to resist some well-intentioned meddling, Seward dashed off a letter to a lawyer friend, George Hardinge, who was solicitor-general to Queen Charlotte and a former acquaintance of Bicknell, with an appeal to help his "sweet unfortunate" widow. Asking Hardinge whether he knew the "romantic circumstances" of Sabrina's youth, Seward lamented: "It is hard to be dependent upon the bounty of friends, especially after having married rather from discretion than from choice." Seward issued an acid condemnation of the Bicknell family. Bicknell's brothers were "prosperous, and tolerably affluent," yet it was "strangely unfeeling that they should suffer so amiable a sister-in-law to labour for her daily bread, in a situation scarce above that of a common servant, and much more harassing." Seward assumed—perhaps through Sabrina's delicacy—that Sabrina's job was akin to an assistant teacher; Fanny Burney would describe her as a "maid." But Seward saved her darkest thunder for Day, who dispensed two-thirds of his income to the local poor but left his former pupil with scarcely enough to survive. "Yet lives there one whose still more bounden duty it is to consider her as his child," she wrote, but "gloomy stoicism, and sour-headed infidelity" caused Day to "defy the claims of obvious duties."

Hardinge rose splendidly to the challenge and raised a remarkable £800 from Bicknell's fellow barristers within a few months. This nest egg, worth more than £100,000 or $165,000 in modern terms, ensured a regular income for Sabrina as well as a capital sum for her sons' inheritance. Reporting his success to Seward, Hardinge could not resist adding the revelations he had gleaned of Bicknell's "bachelor voluptuousness." Horrified and fascinated in equal measure, Seward replied: "I suppose Mr Day knew it not, or, with his general abhorrence of sensuality, he had spared to mention him with so much esteem." And she added: "but, Lord! what a pale, maidenish-looking animal for a voluptuary!—so reserved as were his manners!—and his countenance!—a very tablet, upon which the ten commandments seemed written." Her children's welfare now assured, Sabrina looked forward to the day when she could take advantage of Charles Burney's kindness.

If Day had helped Sabrina with a grudging miserliness, she was not alone. After ten years living the fantasy life he had so long envisaged he was more curmudgeonly and miserable than ever. Railing at the ungrateful poor, he vented his fury on Esther and their friends. He grumbled incessantly to Edgeworth, wrote lecturing letters to Esther's girlfriends and sent curt demands for repayment of loans to Boulton. Boulton paid up, but their friendship was ended. Day even lashed out at his publisher, John Stockdale, threatening in July 1789 not to deliver the final instalment of *Sandford and Merton* until he was paid the balance owing. Their mutual friend Keir had to smooth ruffled feathers. To the delight of Day's fans, Harry and Tommy's adventures continued, and the third book appeared in the shops in August. But Day would never see his book reach its pinnacle of success.

A month later, on September 28, 1789, Thomas Day was riding from Anningsley to Barehill when he was thrown from his horse and killed. Having reared, fed and tamed the horse himself, in accordance with his belief in animal rights, Day died a victim of his own benevolence, friends lamented. It was Day's commitment to Rousseau's gentle system of education—for animals if not for children—that finally destroyed him. He was just forty-one.

Esther, who had been staying at Barehill, rushed to the scene, but Day never regained consciousness. Far from feeling liberated from her program of perpetual correction, she was inconsolable. She told Edgeworth she was "overwhelmed" by the "weight of sorrow." From the moment she first met

Day, she said, "I seemed born to love & admire him; every circumstance about him was so peculiarly pleasing to me." According to one report Esther never again enjoyed a day's health, while another recorded that she spent the rest of her life in darkness, never opening the curtains during the day and only venturing out at night.

Friends—or those few who remained—were nearly as bereft. "He was dear to me by many names as friend, philosopher, scholar, and honest man," wrote Erasmus Darwin. When Edgeworth received the news he was numb with shock. Looking at the portrait of the podgy young man in his gold suit and red mantle that hung above the sofa in his sitting room and thinking back to the day he had first met the scruffy, lank-haired youth, Edgeworth remembered predicting that they would be lifelong friends. They had traveled together, lived together, competed for the same women, collaborated in bringing up Dick and educating Sabrina, and for all their differences they had indeed remained true friends. They had been, wrote Maria, "two friends, so different in tastes, yet so agreeing in principle; so opposite in all appearance, yet so attached in reality."

After a frantic search among Day's papers, the only will that could be found was that from 1780 largely devoted to excising Sabrina from his life. Day's accounts revealed a cool £20,000 less than expected. He had given away most of his fortune. Even if he had begrudged every penny, Day had been a genuine philanthropist in an age when charity was rare and a true enthusiast for social reform long before his time. What remained of his fortune, along with Anningsley, was left to Esther, and since she still retained her own independent income she was able to live comfortably.

There was, of course, no provision for Sabrina in Day's will, but Esther charitably continued her £30 allowance. Writing to Edgeworth, Esther explained that Day had not been "lavish" toward Sabrina in the hope that she would "exert herself." But Esther had no such qualms. "When I reflect that the circumstances which deprived Miss Sidney of Mr Day's confidence, were the means of all my happiness, she appears to me doubly entitled to *my* pity & assistance," she wrote. "You will perhaps my dear Sir think me very romantic, when I say, that I feel peculiarly interested about her from the belief that she once really loved the ever lamented Object of my fondness & veneration. Then without any fault of her own she has been peculiarly unfortunate, for as to the state of her husbands affairs, she is certainly acquitted of all blame."

The small band of Day's remaining friends competed to laud his virtues. One obituary described him as "the advocate of human kind" while another sang his praises in verse: "For never poet's hand did yet consign / So pure a wreath to Virtue's holy shrine." But it was not long before a contrary view surfaced. In reply to one hyperbolic eulogy, an anonymous correspondent wrote to the *General Evening Post* of London to correct "a little misinformation." Although Day was certainly a philanthropist, the writer noted, he frequently complained that those he fed would "cut his throat the next hour" if it benefited them, he had eschewed luxury to the point where he was "generally slovenly, even to squalidness" and had said that he lived in his retreat to avoid the "stink of human society." Furthermore, Day had forced his wife to sever all contact with her relations and sacrifice her comforts to his "unsocial spleen." The letter was signed C. L. But it took little ingenuity for Day's acquaintances to recognize the barbed pen of Anna Seward. Once Day's confidante, now embittered by his treatment of Sabrina and friendship with the despised Edgeworth, Seward relished her chance for revenge. But she would keep the bulk of her powder dry for a later date.

Well aware that Day's reputation hung in the balance, his family and friends moved quickly to counter further attacks. Indefatigable as ever, Edgeworth launched into writing a memoir. Inevitably, given his fond reverence for Day, he wanted to celebrate his friend's charitable acts and progressive philosophy. But at the same time, being Edgeworth, he intended to paint a frank and faithful picture of his friend's eccentricities, irregular ideas and—not least—his bizarre quest to secure marital bliss. Edgeworth planned to donate the profits of the book to Sabrina. "I propose publishing Mr Days life to be prefixed to a volume of his letters," he told his sister Margaret, "and I believe I shall give the Sale of the Book to Mrs Bicknel."

Edgeworth had half completed his book when he heard that Esther had asked Keir to write her husband's life. The rival biographers exchanged notes. It was clear they took entirely different views on committing their friend to memory. Anxious to bury any mention of Day's wife-training project, Keir bluntly told Edgeworth it would be "impossible" to mention Sabrina in any memoir. Edgeworth promptly laid down his pen and sent his notes to Keir with the comment: "The anecdotes which I send you are very few; but they are all that I could select to suit your plan, as we differ so materially in our ideas of private biography. You believing, that nothing but what concerns the public should be published; I thinking, that to entertain mankind is no inefficacious method of instructing them." Edgeworth added, "with the same materials you will do much higher honour to your friend's memory." The emphasis on "your friend" was significant; Keir's portrait would not be somebody recognizable to Edgeworth. To Darwin, Edgeworth complained: "What can the life of a private man consist of, but of private circumstances?"

Darwin agreed. When Keir sought his advice, Darwin urged that it would be "a great omission" in a biography of Day not to relate "so singular an affair as the education of his two foundlings." Now Keir admitted that obfuscating the truth would be problematic because "it could be easily contradicted," but he feared it would be equally difficult "to reconcile the making mention of this affair with the delicacy of Mrs. Day and of Mrs. Bxxx." Drafts shuttled between Keir, Darwin and Esther like an unwanted present.

When Keir's biography was finally published in 1791 it was a dull rendition of a saintly hero who resolved from boyhood to dedicate his life to the greater good—just like Day's fictional creation Harry Sandford. Never once deviating from these aims, Day deployed his literary talents "in the cause of humanity, freedom, and virtue" and devoted his fortune "to the service of his fellow creatures." Although strangers sometimes found his manner and remarks severe, Keir admitted, Day was really a kindly genius who loved to jest and enjoyed the company of children.

As to Day's relationship with two particular children, Keir described Day's "experiment on female education" with a careful economy with the truth. Without naming Sabrina or Lucretia or mentioning the Foundling Hospital, he said that Day "received into his guardianship two female children" and proceeded to educate them "during some years" and admitted coyly that it was "not improbable" that he "might entertain some expectation of marrying one of them." As the poet Robert Southey would later remark, Keir's biography "omitted all its most remarkable circumstances."

Yet just as Day's friends sought to protect his reputation after his death, so Day's future biographers would almost universally endeavor to promote him as a model of virtue—an ideal man. He would be lauded for his commendable efforts to abolish slavery, to campaign for wider suffrage and to promote American independence as well as his pioneering children's writing while his rather inconvenient wife-rearing experiment would be brushed under the carpet as merely a youthful aberration or a farcical sidetrack.

A year later, on June 12, 1792, Esther died. The medical cause of her death, at thirty-nine, was not recorded, but friends were in no doubt of the reason for her demise. "I think with you that she died of a broken heart," wrote Stockdale to Keir while the *Gentleman's Magazine* reported that she "fell a victim of conjugal affection." Despite all the criticisms, the arguments and the continual program of improvement that she had endured, for Esther at least, Day had proved the perfect partner. Without him she had no reason to live.

Blithely unaware of Keir's biography, Sabrina clung to her obscurity. She had taken up Charles Burney's offer of a place for her eldest son, which Burney had since extended to include both boys as well as a position for Sabrina, and moved with her sons to his school in Hammersmith in 1791. As John and Henry, aged five and four, squeezed behind their desks in the crowded schoolroom, Sabrina, now thirty-four, established herself as Burney's housekeeper and secretary. Proving herself capable and efficient, she soon became popular with generations of schoolboys as well as with all the Burney family. It was the beginning of a relationship with the extraordinary Burney clan that would change her life.

Although their father, Dr. Burney, had been born into fairly humble origins, the Burneys were a talented and engaging family who survived misfortune and scandal to achieve enduring success. Fanny braved the ignominy of writing fiction to win lasting fame for her breezy and witty novels; Charles redeemed his earlier disgrace at Cambridge by achieving scholarly acclaim; and their half sister Sarah Harriet followed in Fanny's footsteps and published five novels. Samuel Johnson, a family friend, enthused: "I love all of that breed, who I can be said to know, and one or two whom I hardly know I love upon credit, and love them because they love each other." Hester Thrale, another family friend—at least at first—declared: "The Family of the Burneys are a very surprizing Set of People."

For Sabrina the surprise was chiefly that the Burneys took her into their hearts and their homes without a moment's hesitation over her remarkable past. Meeting Sabrina for the first time in October 1791, Fanny was delighted with the new addition to her brother's household. "His wife was here on Sunday, with Mrs. Bicknell, whom I had never seen before," she wrote. "I was extremely pleased with her. She is gentle & obliging, & appears to be good & amiable." Few letters would be exchanged between Fanny and her brother from now on without fond remembrances to Sabrina; one such ended, "never forget for us Mrs. Bicknell—as we shall never forget her ourselves."

As an integral member of the Burney household, Sabrina provided vital support not only to Charles but also to his wife. Frequently ill with a series of vague symptoms, probably connected to manic depression, Sarah was known in the family as Rosette—or more commonly "poor Rosette." At times of severe depression Rosette sometimes insisted on living apart from Charles; at other times her behavior was evidently manic. During one such episode Charles's sister Susan reported that Rosette was "in her best humour, wch is overpowering enough but when one considers how she *can* appear, her noise and incessant rattle is even welcome." Susan was alarmed, however, when Charles poured a glass of medicine for Rosette, which she tasted and then flung out of the window.

Sabrina provided Rosette, who was two years her junior, with comfort and companionship during her recurrent depression, which often necessitated visits to the spas at Bath or Clifton, while at the same time giving sympathy and practical help to Charles. Since Rosette was frequently incapacitated or absent through her medical problems, Charles came to depend increasingly on Sabrina both in his business and his home; she was the pillar that propped up their difficult marriage.

When Charles moved his school and family from Hammersmith to Greenwich in 1793, Sabrina and her sons came too. That summer, Sabrina accompanied the Burneys to the spa at Clifton, but this time it was Charles's turn to fall ill and the role of nursing him fell to Sabrina. Burney would be plagued all his life by gout and headaches, which were not helped by his anxiety over his wife and his continuing addiction to fine wines and rich foods. While Rosette returned home, obviously needing to be alone again, Sabrina tended Charles for the ensuing month. When Sarah Harriet called on Charles in August, she came as "a sort of *assistant-nurse* to Mrs Bicknel" who had been "confined to the closest attention to him," she wrote. By this point, Rosette was now "very ill" in Greenwich, "in her old way." Anxious about her brother, Fanny begged him to ask Sabrina to write her a few lines and added: "I shall always love Mrs. Bicknel for the tender care she has shewn upon this occasion. Pray remember me to her very kindly."

Another time, when Rosette's problems recurred, it was Charles and his son who were dispatched to Bath while Sabrina stayed behind to look after Rosette and manage school business. In a postscript on a letter to Rosette, Charles asked Sabrina to forward all letters "which appear to be Bills" to his hotel. It was signed "your affectionate friend, C Burney."

If Sabrina was working twice as hard as ever she had for Day, in her demanding roles as housekeeper, school secretary, nursemaid and marriage prop for the Burneys, she was now treated with a degree of respect and equality that she had never enjoyed in her former benefactor's company. When the artist Joseph Farington came for dinner at the Burneys' house in Greenwich, he noted that across the table from him, next to the sculptor Joseph Nollekens, sat the family housekeeper Sabrina Bicknell. Ably running household affairs below stairs while being treated as an equal above stairs, Sabrina developed a close and significant relationship with Charles.

Quite how close, especially during the frequent and sometimes lengthy periods when Rosette's swinging moods sunk so low that she insisted on being apart from Charles, is open to conjecture. One acquaintance of the Burney family would suggest that Sabrina's role as housekeeper involved more than chaste domestic duties. Hester Thrale, Samuel Johnson's friend who had remarried in 1784 to become Hester Piozzi, would later describe Charles Burney as "living all but openly with a woman in his own *house.*" The reference was understood to point to Sabrina. However, Mrs. Piozzi was a distinctly unreliable witness. She had been estranged from the Burneys since an acrimonious split with Fanny at the time of Mrs. Piozzi's second marriage, and she erroneously believed that Charles had published malicious gossip about her. It is unlikely that her accusation was based on more than speculation.

Whether or not Mrs. Piozzi's suspicions were correct, Sabrina would certainly remain at Charles Burney's right hand throughout the entire time he ran his school, often in Rosette's absence. In some ways she fulfilled the role of a surrogate wife; in many ways it was a perfect partnership. "They understood between them very well that they both appreciated each other, that nothing could surpass the fondness or the usefulness of their liaison," wrote Fanny Burney. "He could entrust all his affairs to her, to her foresight, to her faithfulness, and she was always sure of being treated by him as his equal, his friend, and a person whose virtues are honoured as much as her talents are useful." He was truly her "affectionate friend."

Shielded by the high walls that encircled the Burney School in Greenwich and sheltered within the Burney family, Sabrina felt her secret past was safe. A sleepy town beside the Thames, ten miles downriver from London, Greenwich had rather degenerated since its heyday as a glorious setting for royal palaces and the birthplace of three Tudor monarchs. Now ragged children played in the sewage that ran through the huddle of dark, narrow streets down to the stinking river while the 2,500 invalid sailors quartered in the Royal Hospital for Seamen could often be seen downing beer in the smoky taverns or lying insensible on the pavements with their crutches abandoned by their sides. But away from the dank and dangerous quayside, the town provided a pleasant location for admirals and aristocrats in the imposing villas overlooking Greenwich Park.

Situated in a redbrick mansion at the bottom of Crooms Hill, Greenwich's oldest and most salubrious street, the Burney School accommodated around one hundred boarding pupils aged six to fifteen. Parents who deposited their boys at the blue wooden gates paid sizable fees of £100 a year for their sons to be coached for Oxford or Cambridge. As a renowned classical scholar, Charles Burney taught the boys traditional subjects using conventional methods, which were as far removed from the Rousseau philosophy as it was possible to stray. A fair but stern headmaster, who was reputed to buy birch rods "by the cartload," Burney seemingly treated his role as a form of atonement for his own misspent youth.

Helping to manage an establishment for one hundred boys, their teachers, the family, and the servants to look after them all was no mean feat. Yet Sabrina proved herself an indispensable housekeeper above and below stairs. On the ground floor and upper levels of the three-story house, where the family lived, a grand mahogany staircase led to sumptuously furnished rooms resplendent with ornate marble fireplaces and red velvet curtains. While the upper floors exuded an air of calm sophistication, the lower levels were a flurry of fevered activity. In the basement, servants sweated over a cast-iron "stewing stove," a vast range and two stone sinks while keeping an anxious eye on a bell-board with twelve "spring bells." A large housekeeper's room was stocked with linen presses and a revolving mangle. There would have been constant demand for water from the hydraulic pump connected to a well in the garden and for ice from the icehouse outside. An adjoining school building housed the pupils and their classrooms.

As housekeeper, Sabrina would have been in charge of a large fleet of servants, including cooks, kitchen maids, laundry maids and housemaids along with an impressive set of keys. Bills that survive for two pupils who attended the school reveal the press of activity. They itemize fees for lessons in fencing, drawing, geography and mathematics along with bills for the dentist, hatter, tailor and shoemaker and charges for copybooks, pens, slates and pencils. The bills each include one guinea, for "Mrs. Bicknell, at Christmas."

Writing to the Edgeworths, Sabrina gave some idea of the unending demands on her time and labor. In one letter, she complained that she could not take a day off because the approach of the school holidays "always *loads* me with an unconscionable accumulation of business." In another she apologized for writing "in the disagreeable expectation of being disturbed every moment" since her hope of finding a "quiet hour" had been continually frustrated. She certainly earned her guinea tips.

Yet the respectable middle- and upper-class parents who sent their sons to Greenwich for a rigorous education at the Burney School had no inkling that the busy housekeeper who welcomed their boys hid a sensational past. Although bland details of Thomas Day's experiment had appeared in Keir's biography, this sold poorly, and Sabrina's identity had remained concealed. As her two boys thrived in Burney's school, she hoped that John and Henry would never discover their mother's origins or the strange story of how she met their father. But even though Day's body had been interred in its grave, Sabrina's history refused to remain buried. Day's ghost would always stand at her shoulder; his crazed experiment would cast its shadow over the rest of her life.

It was hardly surprising that Maria Edgeworth should use her literary talents to wreak revenge on her father's friend, Thomas Day. Firstly, there was all that foul tar water he had forced her to drink as part of his "icy" system. Secondly, and more crucially, Day had tried to prevent Maria from writing at all. If Day had had his way, Maria Edgeworth would never have become a novelist.

With her father's encouragement, Maria had begun writing short stories at the age of twelve. Two years later he suggested she should translate from French a new book on education with a view to publication. Maria had just completed the task when another English translation appeared. When Day heard the news, he wrote to Edgeworth, not to commiserate on his daughter's disappointment but to congratulate him that she had been beaten to the press. According to Maria, Day had "such a horror of female authorship" that he was "shocked and alarmed" to hear that Edgeworth had allowed her to attempt the translation at all. Indeed, Day was so eager to deter women from writing that he often quoted lines from a poem, "Advice to the Ladies," which warned, "Wit like wine intoxicates the brain, / Too strong for feeble women to sustain." First published in 1731, the poem was dedicated to a mythical Belinda.

Although Edgeworth was as apprehensive as any Georgian father at the idea of his daughter becoming a publishing sensation, he had vehemently defended Maria's literary ambitions. But with Day's harsh words ringing in her ears, Maria waited until after his death to publish her first book, *Letters for Literary Ladies*, in 1795, when she was twenty-seven. A sharp riposte to Day's objections, it mounted a bold defense of women's right to pursue a literary career. Nothing could stop her now. After *Practical Education*, the child-care manual cowritten with her father, appeared in 1798, Maria's first novel, *Castle Rackrent*, was published to wide acclaim in 1800. Buoyed by her literary success, now Maria was ready to turn the tables on her erstwhile detractor Day.

First she limbered up for the task with a short story, "Forester," in a collection entitled *Moral Tales for Young People* in 1801. Plainly based on Day, the uncouth young Forester detests "politeness so much" that society appears to him "either odious or ridiculous." Arriving at his guardian's house, Forester refuses to wipe his shoes or change his "disordered dress" before bursting into the drawing room. "He entered with dirty shoes, a threadbare coat, and hair that looked as if it never had been combed; and he was much surprised by the effect, which his singular appearance produced upon the risible muscles of some of the company."

Now that she had developed a taste for literary revenge, in the same year Maria published her second novel, *Belinda*. She not only chose the name of her heroine, and the book's title, as a rebuff to Day's advice to would-be female writers, she used the story of Day's attempt to educate Sabrina as the kernel of her narrative. Maria Edgeworth's first "society" novel, *Belinda* tells the tale of the eponymous heroine's search for an ideal husband. At seventeen, Belinda is intrigued by the rich and aristocratic Clarence Hervey, but she eventually discovers that Hervey hides a scandalous secret. As an idealistic young man, Hervey had been "charmed" by the ideas of Rousseau and had "formed the romantic project of educating a wife for himself." Searching for a simple maid to suit his scheme, Hervey stumbles upon a young girl living with her grandmother in an isolated cottage. The girl, Rachel, is "a most beautiful creature" with a "sweet voice" and "finely shaped hands and arms" whose mother had been seduced by a rake. When her grandmother dies, Hervey takes charge of the girl and conceals her in a house with only a governess and a pet bullfinch for company. He renames her Virginia St Pierre, in a reference to another Rousseau fanatic Jacques Henri Bernardin de Saint-Pierre, the French writer and botanist whose novel *Paul et Virginie*, published in 1787, had imagined an idyllic romance for Rousseau's Émile and Sophie.

Testing Virginia's simple tastes, Hervey asks her to choose between a rosebud and a pair of diamond earrings. Unlike Day's erstwhile fiancée, Elizabeth Hall, Virginia picks the rose. Confused by her feelings for her benevolent captor in the same way Sabrina must have felt in her relationship with Day, Virginia says: "When he is near me, I feel a sort of fear, mixed with my love." Yet as Virginia warms toward Hervey, his passion fades in favor of the accomplished Belinda, just as Day had dropped Sabrina for Esther. "In comparison to Belinda, Virginia appeared to him but an insipid, though innocent child; the one he found was his equal, the other his inferiour," so that "at length, he became desirous to change the nature of his connexion with Virginia, and to appear to her only in the light of a friend or a benefactor." The tangle is happily resolved when Virginia is reunited with a childhood sweetheart, leaving Hervey free to marry Belinda.

Although the connection between Hervey and Day is never stated, at one point Belinda's friend reads from *The Dying Negro* and at another quotes directly from Keir's biography in an effort to flush out Hervey's secret. But Maria Edgeworth made no secret of the inspiration for her plot when later editing her father's memoirs. "Mr. Day's educating Sabrina for his wife suggested the story of Virginia and Clarence Hervey in *Belinda*," she wrote. "But to avoid representing the real character of Mr. Day, which I did not think it right to draw, I used the incident, with the fictitious characters, which I made as unlike the real persons as I possibly could." Appropriately enough, it was *Belinda* that firmly established Maria Edgeworth's literary career. Before long she had eclipsed Fanny Burney as the most popular novelist of her time, and her style would influence both Walter Scott and Jane Austen.

There was little surprise that Fanny Burney, always alert for a dramatic plot, was inspired by Sabrina's story too. After moving to France in 1802 to join her French husband, Alexandre-Jean-Baptiste Piochard d'Arblay, Fanny decided to improve her French by writing some short compositions for her husband to correct. As she was casting around for a suitable subject to divert him, their son Alex was reading aloud from Day's moral tales in

Sandford and Merton. She needed to look no further. Having heard all about the author's immoral past from Sabrina or Charles, Fanny decided to entertain her husband with Day's wife-training project in her shaky, self-taught French.

In a tiny notebook, which still survives, Fanny describes Sabrina's story with the cavalier approach to truth that only a novelist could bring to the tale. In Fanny's version, Day is so torn between his "two lambs" that he resolves to bring up both Sabrina and "Juliana"—as she calls Lucretia— to become "society ladies." When Day settles on marrying Sabrina and confesses his intentions to her, she runs away to marry Bicknell who "had desperately loved her since he first saw her and who was loved by her with adoration." But despite marrying "the man of her dreams," Sabrina never ceased to think of Day without "affection, gratitude, regret"—or so said Fanny.

Sabrina's story would continue to beguile novelists such as Henry James, with his racy 1871 novella *Watch and Ward.* His contemporary Anthony Trollope would tell a similar story about a young man who molds an orphan to become his wife as a central thread in his 1862 novel *Orley Farm.* Trollope's character, a young barrister named Felix Graham, who had left Oxford without taking a degree, is plainly based on Day. Graham is "tall and thin, and his face had been slightly marked with the smallpox. He stooped in his gait as he walked, and was often awkward with his hands and legs." As a naïve but well-intentioned youth, Graham takes under his care an orphan, Mary Snow, the daughter of an engraver, described as "drunken, dissolute, and generally drowned in poverty." Graham agrees to a written contract with the father to educate Snow with a view to marriage "if her conduct up to that age had been becoming." Rather than "take a partner in life at hazard," Graham was resolved "to mould a young mind and character to those pursuits and modes of thought which may best fit a woman for the duties she will have to perform."

But just like Day, at the last minute, Graham cannot bring himself to carry through his plan. Having fallen in love with another woman, a judge's daughter from his own rank in society, he discards Snow at the age of nineteen after discovering—to his relief—that she has secretly met with another man, an apothecary's assistant. Unlike Day, Graham then admitted "that he had made an ass of himself in this affair of Mary Snow" and wisely concluded: "This moulding of a wife had failed him, he said, as it always must fail with every man." Trollope's choice of profession for Mary Snow's lover was probably a coincidence; he was unlikely to have known of Sabrina's earlier marriage proposal. But Shaw would almost certainly have known of Trollope's book when writing his play *Pygmalion*, with Eliza Doolittle's similarly dissolute father and its almost identical ending.

Yet even though Sabrina's strange past had so far been aired in biography, in fiction and in French, she had still not been named in public, and her identity remained secure. As her sons grew into their teens and rose through the forms of Charles Burney's school she was anxious to keep it that way. In term-time, while Sabrina supervised the school's daily routine, the Bicknell boys must have lived as much in fear of the stern headmaster as any of the other pupils. But during the holidays, when they joined in lively Burney family gatherings with their mother, John and Henry had come to look on Charles Burney as a father figure. Reconciled with the Bicknell family too, John and Henry hoped to launch legal careers with the help of their Bicknell uncles. And at the dawn of the nineteenth century, the only obvious threat to Sabrina's happiness came from the cannons of the French army pointed at the white cliffs of Dover.

ELEVEN

GALATEA

❧ *Greenwich, January 1805* ❧

For nearly two years the British had lived with the fear of invasion. Ever since Napoleon Bonaparte had amassed a huge invasion force at Boulogne in 1803, the threat of occupation had filled the nation with dread. Village greens across England resounded to the noise of volunteers defiantly drilling, and taverns were filled with the strains of patriotic ballads. The people of Kent fully expected to bear the brunt of the assault whether by land or river, and the heath close to Greenwich had even been proposed as the likely battlefield for the first clash with French troops. Yet the blow that now rocked Sabrina's life did not come from Bonaparte's army, although its effect shattered her world just as surely as if Emperor Napoleon had stormed her home.

During the winter of 1804–5, Sabrina's eldest son, John Laurens Bicknell, had turned nineteen, and he was poised on the brink of a promising legal career in the footsteps of the father he had never known. When he picked up the book *Memoirs of the Life of Dr. Darwin*, he may well have been prompted to read about the genial physician, who died in 1802, because Darwin had been a friend to his mother in her youth. The biography, by Anna Seward, had been published in early 1804. As he started reading, John was probably as bewildered as any other reader to find that the beginning of the memoir was largely absorbed not with Darwin but the life of one of his eccentric friends.

After the briefest mention of Darwin, the book's next twenty-six pages were devoted entirely to detailing Thomas Day's early life, his comical romances and his bizarre decision to educate two orphans from the Foundling Hospital in a quest to create his perfect wife. John learned that Day renamed the orphans Lucretia and Sabrina, then took them to France where he decided to give up the willful Lucretia in preference for the pliable Sabrina. Reading on, he discovered that Day then lived alone with thirteen-year-old Sabrina in Lichfield for a year while he conducted some shocking and seemingly prurient trials until eventually he rejected Sabrina too.

But the tale did not end there. "Ere the principal subject of this biographical tract is resumed, the reader will not be sorry to learn the future destiny of Sabrina," Seward wrote. But young John was in fact extremely sorry to learn Sabrina's destiny. To his horror, he now read that Sabrina had married for "prudential" reasons the lawyer John Bicknell, who had first chosen her from the line of girls at the orphanage. Seward went on to reveal that Sabrina Bicknell had been left a penniless widow with two sons and had only been saved from destitution by charitable lawyers. If any doubt remained as to the identity of the subject of this appalling social experiment, Seward announced: "That excellent woman has lived many years, and yet lives with the good Dr. Burney of Greenwich, as his housekeeper, and assistant in the cares of his academy."

At first John refused to believe what he read. The thought that his mother had been abandoned at the Foundling Hospital was appalling; the idea that she was almost certainly illegitimate was unthinkable. Attitudes toward illegitimacy had if anything hardened since the days when the Foundling Hospital had first opened its doors. In law, as John would have known, illegitimate children were forbidden from inheriting property or titles since they were considered to be the son or daughter "of nobody." Novelists in Georgian times returned repeatedly to this negation of identity and the disgrace illegitimacy bestowed. "I am nobody; the child of nobody," laments the illegitimate heroine of one novel. "I am nothing,—a kind of reptile in humanity," says another.

In novels, salvation usually came with the discovery that the book's hero or heroine turned out to be legitimate after all—and usually rich to boot. Yet John's mother—according to Seward's shocking book—had apparently taken this journey in reverse: she was currently a respectable widow of modest means and had now been exposed as an illegitimate foundling. As if this was not sufficient shame, Seward had cast disgraceful aspersions on his mother's reputation by suggesting that she had lived alone with Day and entered a marriage of convenience with his father. Pale with shock and shaking with rage, Bicknell confronted his mother and demanded to know the truth.

At forty-seven, Sabrina was still a doughty housekeeper who was used to calming nervous boys and quieting fanciful fears. But when her eldest son burst in with a book gripped in his hand, his anger was so intense that she was frightened. He was in "such a state of irritation as [I] could not describe," she later said. Since she had never told John the details of her origins or her early life, he was "dreadfully shocked" and "violently enraged." Even though Sabrina now reluctantly confirmed the story, John refused to allow the slur on his mother's reputation to go unchallenged. Feverish with fury, he wrote to Seward demanding a retraction and apology.

Now sixty-two and pained by ill health, Seward lived alone in the Bishop's Palace after the deaths of her parents followed by the loss of her beloved John Saville in 1803. Having traveled together and received company just like a married couple for many years—despite Saville's wife still living next door to him in the Vicars' Close—Seward had grieved like a widow for the loss of "the dearest friend I had on earth." Heartily regretting that she had ever undertaken to write Darwin's biography, she had already been forced by his family to issue a correction over her unflattering portrait of the physician, in particular the claim that he had reacted with "hard and unfeeling spirit" to the suicide of his middle son, Erasmus Junior, when he drowned himself in 1799. When Seward now read John Bicknell's letter she was infuriated.

On January 22, 1805, Seward wrote to a friend that "a base and surely most unprovoked attack is made upon my truth by a son of Mrs. Bicknel's, Mr. Day's 'Sabrina'." She fumed: "His foolish pride is stung by the publicity of circumstances concerning his mother's singular story, which cast no shade of reflection upon her in any respect, viz. her being originally a foundling child, and having been left in straitened circumstances, and a subscription having been raised for her." Seward could not understand why John should complain. "Surely she appears in a very amiable light from my representation, and for that glowing testimony to her merit, this is my reward." Seward was adamant that every circumstance she had described was accurate "without a shadow of exaggeration," with the possible exception of the subscription raised for her as a widow, which had been related by George Hardinge. "The abusive letter states no particular complaint, but avers that all the anecdotes of the author's mother are falsehoods, and that as such he shall publicly brand them."

But Seward was not to be cowed. Replying to John Bicknell's letter she threatened to defend herself publicly by calling "several credible witnesses" who knew "all the circumstances I have stated to be true." And she added: "Mrs. Bicknel well knows that they are all unvarnished facts. If she has sanctioned this dark, malicious, and lying scroll, the virtues which I believed she possessed, and that which my memoirs have invested her, could not have been genuine." Exchanging increasingly angry letters, Seward and Bicknell battled for supremacy in a "furious paper war." But finally forced to accept the truth of Seward's story, young Bicknell had no choice but to come to terms with his mother's past.

To Sabrina's lasting distress and her son's mortification, the press's fascination with the story of the nation's best-loved children's author and the child he took to train as his wife would never completely subside. Taking a typically high moral tone, reviewers of Darwin's biography savaged Seward for exposing the innocent victims of Day's exploits while simultaneously reproducing the titillating details of his life at length. "There is a want of delicacy, and even of decorum, in publishing so much of the private history of the living as appears in this narrative," observed a critic in the *Annual Review*. Yet the reviewer had to admit that Day's "domestic history" formed the "most interesting part" of the volume.

If Seward felt the press's fury, the attack on Day was worse. "With regard to Mr. Day, language is deficient in terms to express his character: that he was either a madman or a fool is more than probable; that he acted infamously is beyond contradiction," raged a reviewer in the *Universal Magazine*. A writer for the *Critical Review* chimed in, "In short, the most puerile of mankind could not have formed a more absurd system, or pursued it with greater folly." And echoing the shock of thousands of parents up and down the country, the *British Critic*'s reviewer declared that the revelations were "very disgraceful to him, and much diminish any previous respect which might have been conceived for the author of *Sandford and Merton*."

Times had changed: what might have been casually dismissed as eccentric folly a few decades earlier was now viewed as dangerous irregularity that smacked of French radicalism. The absurd misanthrope who had been indulged for his unworldly ways at the end of the eighteenth century was condemned as a shameful brigand at the beginning of the nineteenth. Yet while none of the newspapers identified Sabrina directly—as Seward had done—there was evident sympathy for her plight. "What woman is there who does not feel a natural and proper indignation," asked a writer in the *Annual Review*, "if she knows that the secret history of her life, her courtship and her marriage, and her distress, has been made the subject of tea-table tittle-tattle?"

Always a highly strung character who was frequently in poor health, John Bicknell would never fully recover from the shock of discovering his mother's origins. Over the ensuing decades, any mention of Day or his children's book would reignite the stories of his quest for a perfect wife and prompt questions about the fate of his former pupil. One magazine article, relating "a half true, half false history," would even suggest that Sabrina was dead, causing John renewed upset and sickness. Sabrina would later confess that her elder son's ailments kept her *"anxious & unhappy"* and had played "greater havock with my constitution than 15 or 20 years labour would have done free from mental suffering."

As victory at Trafalgar in October 1805 decisively scotched all threat of a French invasion—and Admiral Nelson's body was brought back to lie in state for three days at Greenwich—the subject of the tea-table tittle-tattle continued to live in relative anonymity. For all the press interest and her son's neurosis, Sabrina continued quietly to devote herself to the demands of the Burney School and its pupils. Once at the center of a radical eighteenth-century educational experiment, now Sabrina helped to mold generations of schoolboys into some of the most famous—and infamous—figures of the nineteenth century.

Among the many pupils who benefited from Sabrina's efficient management at the Burney School was James Haliburton, an Egyptologist who excavated tombs in the Valley of the Kings; while working in Egypt, Haliburton purchased a Greek slave, twenty-five years his junior, whom he brought back to England as his wife. One of his fellow alumni was Thomas Fowell Buxton, who would become one of Britain's foremost campaigners against slavery. Rather less noble among the Burney School boys, however, was Thomas Griffiths Wainewright, who was suspected of poisoning his uncle, mother-in-law and sister-in-law. Escaping charges for murder, he would be convicted of forging documents to obtain money from his grandfather's will and transported in 1837 to a penal colony.

Most of the time Burney's pupils submitted meekly to his draconian discipline, just as his housekeeper had once submitted to her tutor's ordeals. But just as schoolboys elsewhere periodically rose up in rebellion, so the Burney boys at one point refused to toe the line. In February 1808 more than forty boys barricaded themselves in their dormitory in protest at Burney's liberal use of the birch rod. "The boys were very angry with Burney for being so strict & severe with them & thought they could put an end to it by rebelling," one boy, John Graham, told his mother. Armed with sticks and knives, the boys nailed shut the door and only finally let Burney in when he threatened to break it down. At that point, the boys "hit him with their sticks," said Graham, who had wisely kept out of the riot, but Burney hit the offenders back until finally they quieted down. Two of the ringleaders were expelled and the rest of the boys "forgiven."

For all the occasional protests, most of the Burney scholars seemed happy enough. As John Graham told his mother, "we play till we are quite tired & then lie down in the shade in a nice field at the bottom of the playground." In another letter home he wrote: "Mrs Bicknell is exceedingly kind to me & I am quite happy." Certainly Sabrina's sons viewed their schooldays with fondness. John and Henry became founder members of the Burney Club, whose former pupils met for convivial dinners in homage to their stern headmaster.

While Sabrina remained at the center of the school, her sons moved on. When they both announced plans to marry in 1808, Sabrina relayed the news to Edgeworth just as she had turned to him for advice over her own marriage more than twenty years earlier. "My Dear Sabrina," he replied, "If your sons marry to please you I wish you joy with all my heart." Promising to send her usual allowance by the next post, Edgeworth told her, "I assure you most sincerely of my esteem and affection."

Edgeworth had himself remarried, his fourth wife, in 1798. When Elizabeth had followed her sister Honora to the grave in 1797, leaving Edgeworth with ten children, he had been single for all of six months before marrying Frances Anne Beaufort, the twenty-nine-year-old daughter of an Irish clergyman. Twenty-five years his junior, Frances was nearly two years younger even than Maria. Frances would give Edgeworth six more children, bringing his total brood (including those who died in infancy) to twenty-two.

Of Sabrina's sons, Henry took the plunge first and married his first cousin, Mary Arnold, the daughter of his father's sister Mary, on August 23, 1808. Four months later, on December 28, John married Jane Willmott, the daughter of a paper manufacturer who lived not far from Greenwich. Grandchildren followed swiftly. Henry's wife Mary gave birth to a daughter, Marianna, a year after their marriage followed by five more daughters and two sons. Henry would marry a second time, after his first wife's death left him with five surviving daughters, to Caroline Gason, who gave birth to four more children, although only a daughter would survive infancy. John and Jane, however, would remain childless until 1824, when Jane gave birth to a daughter, their only child, named Mary Grant Bicknell.

Like his namesake, Henry Edgeworth Bicknell would always live life on a grand scale. Tall, good-looking and dapper, Henry rose effortlessly up the legal ladder and was soon established in the Court of Chancery. A portrait of Henry in later life shows a stylish, handsome man with a steady gaze. For John, life would always be a struggle, dogged by his ill health and reminders of the family shame that he endeavored to submerge. He too progressed up the legal ladder, but it was a hard and laborious haul. John would eventually become solicitor to both Greenwich and Chelsea Hospitals—the retirement homes for sailors and soldiers respectively—as well as private solicitor to the eccentric architect and collector John Soane. A portrait of John in later life shows a short, stout, respectable gentleman with a tight-set mouth and a deeply etched worry line between his eyes. While Henry moved with his large family into a smart townhouse in central London, John stayed close to his mother, leasing a house for himself and his new wife in Crooms Hill, two doors up from the Burney School.

When Charles Burney retired as headmaster in 1813, Sabrina continued in her job as school housekeeper, working for his son Charles Parr Burney. Worn out by hundreds of rebellious pupils and one unhappy wife, Charles Burney became rector of St. Paul's Church in nearby Deptford. Sabrina, now a fifty-six-year-old grandmother, escaped the flurry of school business during the interregnum to see the Edgeworths, who were visiting London for a few weeks. Worried they would return to Ireland before she could see them a second time, Sabrina wrote, "I *long* to see you *once* more."

As Henry's marriage might suggest, Sabrina's sons forged strong links with their Bicknell relatives despite their uncles' apathy to their childhood plight. Uncle Charles, who had acquired the lucrative positions of solicitor to the Admiralty and to the Prince of Wales, helped his nephews establish themselves in the legal world, and the boys were friendly with his daughter Maria. Cousin Maria came to stay with John and his wife, Jane, in Greenwich for a week in February 1816. Since Charles Bicknell was determined that none of his family would ever face the debts that had embarrassed his brother John and impoverished his sister-in-law Sabrina, he had forbidden Maria from seeing John Constable, a struggling artist with uncertain prospects who had courted her faithfully for seven years. But Maria smuggled him a furtive letter from Greenwich, complaining, "I walked out a very damp day, and have got a cold." Eight months later Maria defied her father and the couple were married. So John Constable, who would become one of the age's greatest painters, became Sabrina's nephew by marriage, and he took a close interest in her work and her sons.

If anything Charles Parr Burney was regarded as an even stricter headmaster than his father had been. Constable, at one point, told Maria that he had upset some friends with a "dictatorial" letter "demanding (almost)" that they return their unhappy son. Constable thought Burney "a heartless fellow" though he added dolefully "but all schools are woeful things at best." Passionately happy and perfectly devoted, the Constables would enjoy just twelve years of marital harmony before Maria died of consumption—tuberculosis—in 1828, leaving a heartbroken husband and seven children under eleven.

In the meantime, Sabrina had her own grief to deal with. In the three years up to 1817, her son Henry lost three children—his eldest daughter Marianna and two infant sons—and her son John was severely ill again. He continued an invalid and was "likely to remain so," Sabrina told Edgeworth in April. For herself, she was "still toiling on with Mr Burney" but hoped she could continue "enduring the labours of this situation" a few years longer before retiring "to some quiet retreat where I may have leisure to devote my mind to subjects necessary to prepare me for a better world."

The following month, she thanked Edgeworth for £50 that he had sent her but assured him that she no longer needed his bounty and had not done for several years past. Her sons were now settled and "are not the drag on my purse they used to be" so that she was able to put aside some savings in order to "make a reserve for my infirmities, which I feel daily approaching." Her ailments were less the result of old age, she said poignantly, than "the *many* trials I have had to encounter." And she added: "Whenever my life ends I trust I shall feel that it *has not* passed uselessly or intirely unprofitably." She was now sixty, and working as hard as ever, yet retirement remained a distant hope.

But in the midst of Sabrina's worries about her sons and her grandchildren, it was Edgeworth's ill health that now brought her distress. "Your account of yourself & declining health gives me great uneasiness & has sunk my spirits more than I can express," Sabrina wrote to him. "I had hoped for the happiness of seeing you once more—but should this blessing be denied me in this world God grant that I may be worthy of meeting in *that* World where *all* is peace & joy." It was only after sealing the letter that the realization truly hit home that this might be the last time she would ever write to the faithful friend and benefactor to whom she had written—in dictation to Day—her first-ever letter forty-eight years earlier, from Avignon, at the age of twelve. On the outside she added a hurried postscript: "Adieu dear dear Sir & again accept a thousand grateful thanks for all your goodness to me."

Her fears were realized. On June 13, 1817, Richard Lovell Edgeworth died. He was seventy-three. Throughout his long and grueling illness he had remained characteristically positive. He had continued performing his experiments and mechanical trials—he was still trying to create the perfect carriage—until just a year earlier. When he became too ill to continue his experiments unaided, his children had gathered around the bed to conduct them for him. Five days before he died, after a sleepless night spent in pain and sickness, Edgeworth wrote to his sister, Margaret Ruxton, bubbling with vigor and joy as much as ever, to assure her that "my mind retains its natural cheerfulness."

According to his wishes, Edgeworth was placed in a plain coffin "without velvet, plate or gilding." It was carried by his own laborers to the family vault where a simple marble tablet was erected recording just his name and the dates of his birth and death. He left behind his fourth wife, Frances, and thirteen surviving children of the twenty-two he had fathered; Maria, now the eldest, was forty-nine, and the youngest was only five.

True to his abiding interest, Edgeworth had left among his papers some plans for a school to be built in Edgeworthstown, where children of poor families could learn basic reading, writing and arithmetic, with opportunities to study mechanics, of course, for those inclined. He had insisted that the school should be open to Catholics and Protestants alike. And never forgetting his lifelong commitment to the Rousseau method—albeit with typical Edgeworth pragmatism—he had stipulated: "In this school the understanding should be cultivated and exercised, without loading the memory; and the constant object should be, to excite the pupils to think and to apply their understandings to their conduct." His eldest surviving son, Lovell, began work immediately building the school.

When Sabrina heard the news of Edgeworth's death in a letter from Maria sent a few days later, she was devastated. "By this loss I am deprived of my oldest friend, & *one* I have always found *most* ready, & prompt to assist me in *every* way in his power," Sabrina replied. "His kindness to me is deeply engraved on my heart, & while I have life I shall dwell with *grateful pleasure* on his *dear* & *loved memory*." Edgeworth had been presented unbidden with the responsibility for Sabrina when she was twelve, and all his life he had done his best to safeguard her welfare and happiness.

But just as with Day's death, so Edgeworth's demise reopened old wounds. Having acted as her father's business manager and personal secretary for most of her life, Maria began the task of sorting through his letters—"those to and from Mr. Day especially," she told Sabrina in August—with a view to publishing his unfinished memoirs. Now she asked Sabrina to return "a little manuscript life of Mr. Day" that she believed her father had sent her. Dictated by Edgeworth to Maria, it was probably a draft of the biography that Edgeworth had originally planned to publish before Keir assumed that task; with his customary deference to her feelings Edgeworth had evidently invited Sabrina to peruse the details. Now Maria was desperate to have it back. "I am particularly anxious to have it because it was in fact not mine but *his*. It was all spoken by him to me," she told Sabrina. She added: "I entreat you to look carefully before you give me the pain of answering NO."

But before she had time to contemplate the effect of Edgeworth's memoirs being published, Sabrina had to bear the loss of a second close friend. After years of painful gout and debilitating headaches, Charles Burney suffered a stroke on Christmas Eve 1817 and died three days later, aged sixty. The loss in a single year of both Burney and Edgeworth—her two most loyal friends and allies—was inestimable.

Sabrina had now turned sixty herself, and her heavy duties at the Burney School began to take their toll on her. Her eyesight had deteriorated to the extent that she could no longer read unaided, and in the spring of 1818 she became ill with an abscess on her back, which took more than six months to heal. As well as the ebb and flow of pupils, there were new additions in the Burney family, making demands on her time too. Charles Parr Burney had married in 1810, and the first of six children, Frances

Anne, arrived two years later. Growing up amid hordes of rowdy boys, little Fannittina, as she was known, took refuge with the housekeeper she called Bicky. When a third daughter arrived to the Burneys in February 1818, Sabrina was asked to become godmother, and the baby was named Susan Sabrina in her honor. Working on despite her ailments, Sabrina had probably forgotten all thoughts of Edgeworth's impending memoirs when a letter arrived in October from Maria.

Having begun writing his memoirs in his sixties, Edgeworth had broken off midsentence in 1809 when illness had struck him down. At that point he had made Maria promise she would complete the work after his death. Scrupulously honest and disarmingly humble, Edgeworth's memoirs related his miserable first marriage and subsequent three happier marriages, his failed efforts at educating Dick and his rather more successful attempts with his younger children, his wild inventions and his Lunar club connections, and, of course, his recollections of his lifelong friend Thomas Day along with a full and frank account of Day's mission to educate Sabrina.

Now that she faced the daunting task of finishing and editing her father's memoirs for publication, Maria vowed to stay faithful to his commitment to simplicity and truth. Yet she was well aware that digging up her father's past could prove highly uncomfortable for those few friends left alive. Having already published her fictionalized version of Day's educational experiment in her novel *Belinda*, Maria approached the factual retelling with trepidation. In August she had sailed for Bristol with her half sister, twenty-seven-year-old Honora, and the draft manuscript of her father's memoirs carefully stowed in a sturdy boxfile. It was, in effect, Edgeworth's last trip to England.

Arriving in London in October Maria was feted as a literary celebrity. Admirers of her big, bold Irish novels were surprised to meet the tiny, self-effacing, mild-mannered, middle-aged woman. One described her as "a little, dark, bearded, sharp, withered, active, laughing, talking, impudent, fearless, outspoken, honest, whiggish, unchristian, good-tempered, kindly ultra-Irish body." Seeking a break from the social whirl she retreated to Hampstead and from there she wrote to Sabrina in Greenwich with a request to meet and "look over the parts of *the* MS. in which she and her husband" were mentioned. Sabrina wrote back immediately: "I cannot come to you my dear Miss E for I have had these 5 months an abscess in my back which prevents me from bearing the motion of a carriage." Despite her discomfort Sabrina was busy preparing and packing clothes for a boy who was leaving for university. "There she is with an abscess in her back doing all this mending and packing," Maria told her stepmother. "Well may it be said that half the world don't know how the other half live."

In the meantime Maria set out to find the Essex farm where the Days had once lived in grim austerity. Vaguely remembering the place from her holidays enduring Day's icy system, Maria was disappointed to find that the house with its windowless dressing room had been razed to the ground and replaced with a tiny cottage. But she was gratified when the new resident, one of Day's former laborers, recalled his old employer with warmth and declared: "Oh Mr. Day was a *good* man and did a power of good to the poorer sort." Her faith in her father's fondest friend as a "good man" was sorely shaken, however, the following day, October 15, when she and Honora ventured to Greenwich to meet Sabrina.

Having met Sabrina fleetingly when Maria stayed in Stowe House as a small child and Sabrina had been in her early teens, Maria was astonished when she came face to face with the doughty sixty-one-year-old widow who was managing a school for one hundred boys. "I was struck with a great change in Mrs. Bicknells manner and mind," Maria wrote home. "Instead of being as Mr. Day thought her helpless and indolent she is more like a stirring housekeeper—all softness and timidity gone!"

It was a difficult and disturbing visit for all concerned. Maria now produced her father's manuscript of his memoirs with the detailed story of Sabrina's selection and education. When Sabrina told her that she was unable to read the handwritten text on account of her poor eyesight, Maria had no choice but to recite the passages out loud herself. "It was disagreeable to me as you may guess—especially to read about the *foundling hospital*." When Sabrina then told her the harrowing effect on her son John when he had first discovered his mother's origins thirteen years earlier, Maria was aghast. "She wishes that part to be left out on account of her sons," Maria wrote home. "So much for the wisdom of concealment!" she added, although she immediately agreed to further concealment by removing all mention of the Foundling Hospital from her script. "I can easily alter a sentence or two so as to avoid repeating or tearing open the wound."

Although John Bicknell was now thirty-three, a successful solicitor earning £2,000 a year—"in a good house, with garden—greenhouse," Maria said—he was still so ashamed of his mother's past that he erupted in fury whenever the secret resurfaced. He had only lately been "enraged" again when a magazine retold the story, Sabrina told Maria. To Maria's surprise neither John nor Sabrina had any knowledge of Keir's biography although Sabrina now spoke of the Keirs with "great resentment." The intensity of her feelings after so many years attested to the central role that Keir had played as Day's agent in orchestrating her relationship with him. But this was nothing to the bitterness that Sabrina now expressed for her erstwhile teacher. Day had "made her miserable—a slave &c!" exclaimed Maria; the association with Day's antislavery contributions was plainly deliberate. By contrast, when Maria mentioned her father's generosity toward Sabrina, she replied: "You have not said enough—You *cannot* say enough of your father's kindness to me."

True to her word, Maria excised any mention of the Foundling Hospital in her father's memoirs and sent a copy of the amended draft to Sabrina for approval. Finally recovering from her back complaint at the end of October, Sabrina responded with mixed emotions. There was nothing in the document that "I *ought* to object to" she told Maria, "on the contrary I feel sincere sentiments of gratitude for your friendly attention & caution not to wound my feelings & for this your goodness, I beg you to accept my *heartiest* thanks." Sabrina was grateful Maria had omitted "the circumstance of my having been taken from the Foundling Hospital," and she urged her "to say as little as possible respecting Mr. Days having given me the name of Sabrina Sydney."

Yet she had to confess "that I do wish the life of my very dear & excellent friend your father could have been compleat without introducing the events of my checker'd & adventurous history." She added: "These romantick fancies do well enough in youth but in age they are repugnant & distressing to ones feelings." And although she looked forward to reading the book, she told Maria she would do so with "very painful sensations of pleasure." It was a perfect choice of phrase.

When Edgeworth's memoirs were published in 1820, the book duly made no mention of Sabrina's origins in the Foundling Hospital, revealing only that Day and Bicknell had selected "from a number of orphans, one of remarkably promising appearance." But the fact that the book went on to describe how Day chose a second orphan from the Foundling Hospital in London would have left few readers in any doubt of Sabrina's past. Although the book attempted to obfuscate Sabrina's origins, it provided new and shocking revelations about her subsequent relationship with Day including his revival of interest in her when she was seventeen and Day fully expected they would marry before the final showdown abruptly ended their connections, as well as the circumstances of Sabrina's marriage to Bicknell. Inevitably the book triggered renewed press interest in Sabrina's story with further outrage about eighteenth-century "crack-brained absurdities," which shocked nineteenth-century sensibilities and brought fresh pain to John Bicknell.

It was five more years before Sabrina was finally released from her job at the Burney School. Now sixty-eight, the grandmother of seven little girls, she moved into a fine new house around the corner from the school, at 9 The Circus. Built at the turn of the century, on land sliced from the Burney School grounds, the semicircular terrace of twenty-two grand four-story houses had been modeled on The Circus in Bath. Having labored almost all her life in the service of others, now Sabrina had two servants to wait on her. Learning of his aunt's retirement, John Constable assured his wife that he understood Sabrina's replacement to be "as fully competent as Mrs. Bicknell was to the conducting the domestic affairs of the school."

It was not Constable, obsessively perfecting landscapes, but one of the period's most popular portrait artists, Stephen Poyntz Denning, who painted Sabrina's picture in 1832 as a memorial for the hundreds of former pupils she had cared for during thirty-three years at the Burney School. Charles Parr Burney commissioned the portrait from Denning, who was best known for his picture painted in 1823 of a four-year-old girl who would grow up to become Queen Victoria. Although Denning's original portrait of Sabrina has disappeared, the prints that Burney ordered for distribution among his former pupils, from engravings by Richard James Lane, whose lithographic pictures featured the celebrities of the time, survive still. Denning was delighted with the prints and wrote to thank Lane "for your beautiful drawing of Mrs. Bicknell," which was "much beyond my most sanguine expectation, and most successful."

The only known portrait of Sabrina, it shows a buxom, rosy-cheeked, self-assured woman, looking younger than her seventy-five years, with abundant, glossy curls still springing willfully from a white cap and mischievous shining eyes looking directly ahead. The ring on her finger may be a mourning ring for her long-gone husband. She wears a handkerchief around her neck, although it is highly unlikely that it is adjusted according to her former teacher's precise directions. And she is smiling enigmatically as if she has a story to tell. Fanny Burney was delighted with her copy of the portrait "which is so strong a likeness I should have recognized it on any part of the Globe." But it was not long before even Sabrina began to look her age.

When Charles Parr Burney's eldest daughter, now married as Fanny Anne Wood, visited "Bicky" in 1837 she confided to her diary: "She is, alas! much changed." It seemed, indeed, as eighteen-year-old Victoria took the throne that year, that the old world was being swept away. The Burney School closed in 1838, and the following year, to Fanny Anne Wood's dismay, the "dear old house and garden" were demolished to make way for "little brick shops and Houses." From her windows in The Circus, Sabrina would have been able to watch as the stewing stove, stone sinks and linen presses that she had known so well were all dismantled, and the old house and school were torn down to make way for a new terrace named Burney Street.

All around, previously unimaginable changes were taking place. The riverside slums were cleared, the old marketplace was demolished, a new workhouse was erected and in 1841 the railway reached Greenwich, reducing an hour's coach journey to fifteen minutes by steam train and bringing hordes of sightseers to the previously isolated town. While Sabrina remained in The Circus, Fanny Anne moved away from the river with its threat of cholera to more salubrious Blackheath, and lamented the decay in buildings and people around her. "I see grey hairs upon brows where I have never noticed them before; and limbs have grown feeble, faces wrinkled, steps less elastic, spirits less gay and buoyant;—in short, many of my acquaintances seem to have aged by magic." That was certainly true when she called that summer on "dear old Mrs. Bicknell (a very old friend indeed)."

Two years later, on September 8, 1843, Sabrina died at her home in The Circus, aged eighty-six. Her death certificate recorded the cause of death as asthma—perhaps the legacy of five decades of damp Greenwich surroundings—and gave her name as Sobrina Ann Bicknell. She had accumulated a tidy sum. In her will she left £2,000 (worth about £365,000 today) to John and £1,000 to Henry; the difference was not due to any wish to discriminate, she had written, but on the grounds that John's health was "by no means good" and his professional duties "anxious & laborious" while Henry was settled in a well-paid position. There were small sums for Charles Parr Burney, his daughters Fanny Anne and Susan Sabrina, and her two servants, not forgetting her seven granddaughters.

Although she died only eight miles from the parish where she had been born, Sabrina had come a long way. She had been born into utter poverty, almost certainly illegitimate, an orphan without possessions, identity or even a token to suggest her origins, at the very bottom of the eighteenth-century social scale. And she had died a respectable, well-loved and well-off Victorian matron and grandmother, with two servants under her command, at one of the most desirable houses in Greenwich. She had been renamed three times—from Monimia Butler, to Ann Kingston, to Sabrina Sidney and finally to Sabrina Bicknell—yet although the records of her arrival had been faithfully preserved in the Foundling Hospital she had never learned her original name or her place of birth.

With no known family history, no known ties or connections, Sabrina represented the archetypal anonymous orphan, the supposedly blank slate on which others could imprint their beliefs and ideas. She had been shaped by the institutional system of the Foundling Hospital into a compliant, industrious and pious young girl; she had been fashioned by Thomas Day into a hardy, bright and curious teenager; and she had been educated at her Sutton Coldfield boarding school to acquire the refinements and graces of an elegant and amiable young woman. She had touched the lives of some of the most brilliant minds of the eighteenth century—including Richard Lovell Edgeworth, Erasmus Darwin, Anna Seward, Maria Edgeworth, Fanny Burney and, of course, Thomas Day, and—with the exception of Maria Edgeworth—she had outlived them all. Each of them had in some way affected and influenced her life and her outlook.

Yet for all these various efforts to transform her, to impose nurture upon nature, to change her name, her beliefs, her appearance and her behavior, Sabrina had remained essentially true to herself. The little girl who had once stood out in a row of identically uniformed orphans, the spirited teenager who had rebelled against Day's domestic enslavement and perverse trials, the penniless young widow who had struggled to bring up her two sons alone, had ended her life as a formidable housekeeper who insisted upon her own version of events. She had been selected as the candidate for one man's idea of the perfect woman, and she had refused to accept her fate.

Sabrina Bicknell was buried six days after her death in All Souls Cemetery, Kensal Green, in northwest London, the most prestigious final resting place in all Victorian England. John Laurens Bicknell survived his mother by only two years before he died, exhausted by work and anxiety, on August 3, 1845, aged fifty-nine. He was buried beside her. His only daughter, Mary Grant Bicknell, lived into the twentieth century before she died at the age of eighty-one in 1905. Henry Edgeworth Bicknell retired on a pension of £2,500 a year—decried as an example of government profligacy—and lived until the age of ninety-one before he died in 1879. Although four of his six surviving girls died unmarried, and another daughter emigrated to Germany, his daughter Mary Henrietta gave birth to two sons who produced a long line of descendants still flourishing in Britain today: Sabrina's great-great-great-great-grandchildren. Sabrina, meanwhile, would live on in fiction in perpetuity under the guises of Virginia St Pierre, Mary Snow, Nora Lambert, Eliza Doolittle and many more further and future incarnations of Galatea waiting to be molded according to the Pygmalion myth.

The story of Thomas Day's quest to create a perfect wife symbolizes an eternal human desire: to craft a supreme being. The quest to find a perfect other half will always retain its seductive appeal. It is no surprise that storytellers have always been mesmerized by the idea. From Ovid's myth of Pygmalion carving his ivory girl to Mary Shelley's tale of Doctor Frankenstein summoning to life a monster, from Shaw's play about the professor turning a flower girl into a duchess to maverick inventors producing robots and cyborgs, the fantasy of creating a perfect being exudes a powerful allure. For most people, of course, such a notion stays firmly in the realm of fiction.

Day took the quest for fashioning a perfect human being further perhaps than anyone before or since. While most of us might idly imagine meeting or molding a sublime soulmate, Day was convinced he could turn that dream into reality. His methods might nowadays strike us as absurd, sadistic or obscene. Anyone today who attempted to abduct two girls from an orphanage in order to train one to become his future wife would doubtless be branded a pervert and charged as a criminal. Yet at a time when people were locked in debate over the significance of nature over nurture, Day's project did not seem quite so outlandish or immoral. As a product of his time, his gender and his rank, he possessed the power and money to pursue his quest, and he therefore believed he had every right to subvert another person to meet his ideals. He was, perhaps, more deluded than wicked.

Yet Day's story also provides a sobering lesson. His attempt to bend Sabrina to suit his fantasy proved a disaster. His efforts to train other women to suit his fads and fancies resulted in various degrees of comedy and farce. And even as he tried endlessly to correct Esther to meet his strictures he was forever disappointed. As Day discovered, striving for perfection is a thankless task. Creating a perfect woman is an unattainable goal. Galatea is, of course, a mythical being.

FINDING MY FOUNDLING

Researching and writing this book has been a delight and a challenge. Finding my foundling proved to be one of the biggest and most delightful of those challenges. I began my search with little hope of success in the voluminous records of the Foundling Hospital kept at London Metropolitan Archives. All I knew from previous books was that Thomas Day was said to have chosen a foundling who was apprenticed to Richard Lovell Edgeworth in the latter part of 1769 and renamed her Sabrina Sidney. I had no idea of her name in the Foundling Hospital or before she arrived. It was entirely possible that the whole story was apocryphal and that Day had never taken Sabrina—or for that matter Lucretia—from the Foundling Hospital at all.

Previous writers describing Day's story had asserted or repeated that there was no record of a girl being apprenticed by Day in the archives of the Shrewsbury Foundling Hospital. This was true. But I quickly discovered that all orphans from the branch hospitals were apprenticed centrally through the charity's London headquarters—and of course it was Edgeworth not Day to whom Sabrina had been apprenticed. With trepidation I scoured the charity's apprenticeship register for 1769. There, to my amazement, it was plainly written that two girls were apprenticed to Richard Lovell Edgeworth on August 17 and September 20, 1769. Their names—and even more important their numbers—were given as Ann Kingston, no. 4579, and Dorcas Car, no. 10,413. I had found my foundlings.

Armed with their numbers—those numbers that were stamped on lead tags tied around their necks—I could now trace their lives from the moment they entered the Foundling Hospital gates until the moment they left. Almost holding my breath, I found their original admission forms, filled out nearly 250 years ago, giving their date of arrival and original names, in the hospital's remarkable billet books. Following the paper trail, through the bundles of letters and giant ledgers, the rushed scrawls of hospital inspectors and the unfortunately named Shrewsbury "Waste Book," I tracked Sabrina's footsteps as she toddled in the fields around Dorking, trundled in the wagon heading for Shrewsbury, thrived with her second foster family near the town, walked through the doors of the Shrewsbury Foundling Hospital at the age of seven and walked out again with Thomas Day and John Bicknell five years later. That was the easy part.

Following Sabrina through the rest of her life was at times infuriatingly difficult. Since she was never very wealthy, she left few legal documents or financial transactions. Since she was not well connected—except through Day—she cropped up rarely in other people's correspondence or documents. Because she was female she lived her life under the patronage of men, her movements, actions and views all subsumed under their command. And, of course, Day and his acolytes tried their utmost to erase Sabrina from their records while she and her family tried their best to conceal her origins. Only a few letters in her hand, to her benefactor Charles Burney and lifelong friends the Edgeworth family, have survived. The only portrait, an engraving of a lost oil painting, reputed to depict Sabrina seemed dubious. And so Sabrina disappeared and reappeared, vanishing in the fogs and smoke of the industrial Midlands and reemerging in Lichfield, London and Greenwich.

Yet many of the places where she lived, where she ate, drank, slept and talked, survive. The Shrewsbury Foundling Hospital stands virtually unchanged at the top of the hill overlooking the River Severn. Stowe House still hovers ghostly white beside the banks of Stowe Poole. And the house in Greenwich, where her life ended, still sits in the middle of the stately crescent now renamed Gloucester Circus. Frustrated by these blank walls, the places where she had spent her life, I doubted that the portrait that was supposed to show Sabrina was truly her. It was almost identical to another with a different name. On my last day of research I visited the archives of the National Portrait Gallery and there discovered firm proof that the portrait of the smiling, self-confident, curly-haired woman was indeed Sabrina.

Finding Sabrina's final resting place proved nearly as tantalizing as tracking down her beginnings. The records of the General Cemetery Company, which manages Kensal Green Cemetery, are as well kept as those of the Foundling Hospital. Armed with another number, designating her burial place, I arrived at the vast cemetery on an icily cold February morning eager to find her grave. But searching among the broken and sunken gravestones crowded into the corresponding corner of the cemetery I could not find Sabrina's name anywhere. On the point of giving up, I spotted a stone cross—newer than all the rest—which bore the name Bicknell. It was a memorial to Sabrina's granddaughter, Jane Grant Bicknell, who had lived until 1905. On either side of the cross were two headstones. On the right I could just make out the name of John Laurens Bicknell. The gravestone on the left therefore had to belong to Sabrina. All the writing had been worn completely smooth, and the headstone was totally blank. I had found her, but she remained as elusive and silent as ever. Walking back to the cemetery gates, I realized that I had lost an earring. I could have turned back to look for it, but it was bitterly cold. And it seemed only right to leave behind one of a pair, a token, for my foundling.

ACKNOWLEDGMENTS

This book owes its existence to the help and generosity of many people and many organizations. In particular I would like to pay tribute to librarians and archivists everywhere, the unsung heroes who safeguard our past, for their unstinting devotion and priceless work at a time when their resources have been and are still under severe threats and pressures.

For permission to use the archives of the Foundling Hospital, which were so crucial to this story, I wish to thank the Coram Foundation. I am indebted to the staff at the London Metropolitan Archives, where the Foundling Hospital records are kept, for their guidance. Permission to quote from the Edgeworth Papers is due to the courtesy of the National Library of Ireland, where I would like to thank James Harte and Berni Metcalfe for their prompt help. I am grateful to Middle Temple Archives for permission to use the records held there and especially to the curator Lesley Whitelaw for her invaluable knowledge and kind hospitality. I wish to thank the Samuel Johnson Birthplace Museum, Lichfield, for permission to use the letters of Anna Seward and particularly curator Joanne Wilson, who went out of her way to make my visits such a pleasure. For permission to quote from Fanny Burney's notebooks I thank the Henry W. and Albert A. Berg Collection of English and American Literature at New York Public Library, Astor, Lenox and Tilden Foundations. For access to the Burney Family Collection in the James Marshall and Marie-Louise Osborn Collection I wish to thank the Beinecke Rare Book and Manuscript Library at Yale University. I would like to thank Lichfield Record Office for permission to use their archives. For permission to use the Barrington Family archives I wish to thank Essex Record Office. My thanks are due to Birmingham Central Library for permission to quote from the Boulton Papers and Watt Papers in the Soho Archives held there. I am grateful to the National Portrait Gallery for permission to quote from Joseph Wright's account book, Richard James Lane's account books and other archive material held there, and especially to assistant curator Alexandra Ault. I am grateful to University College London Special Collections for access to the

Pearson Papers. I would like to thank Staffordshire Record Office for access to letters and diaries belonging to the Sneyd family. My thanks are due to the William Salt Library for permission to quote from letters between Thomas Day and Anna Seward and especially to assistant librarian Dominic Farr. For permission to quote from the Darwin papers I wish to thank the Syndics of Cambridge University Library and would like to record my particular thanks to Adam Perkins. I wish to thank Lambeth Archives Department for permission to quote from John Graham's letters. In addition I want to thank staff at Greenwich Heritage Centre for their help in researching the Burney School and Greenwich history. I am grateful to staff at the John Soane Archives at Sir John Soane's Museum for help researching John Laurens Bicknell's connections with John Soane. I would also like to record my thanks to staff at the British Library (especially for the warm and efficient help in the Rare Books and Music reading room), the Wellcome Library, the Foundling Hospital Museum, the Royal Society of Arts, the Society of Genealogists, the Victoria and Albert Museum, the Household Cavalry Archive, Islington Local History Centre, Surrey History Centre, Manchester Art Gallery, Derby Museums and Art Gallery, Bath Record Office and Sutton Coldfield Library.

Among the great pleasures in researching this book have been my visits to Lichfield and the generous help of various people based there. I want to thank Alan Baker for taking the time to show me around Stowe House, now owned by the Institute of Leadership and Management. I am grateful to Jenny Arthur and all the staff of Erasmus Darwin House for their help and to Pauline Duval at The Bogey Hole for her kind hospitality. Likewise it was a delight to visit Shrewsbury School, where the former Shrewsbury Foundling Hospital survives intact as the main block, and I am grateful to Mike Morrogh for taking time to show me around.

So many individual people have played a vital role in helping me to research and write this book. I feel privileged to have been welcomed into the Burney Society and will always have fond memories of the society's conference in Paris in 2010. It is impossible to pay tribute to everyone within the society who has provided me with advice, support and encouragement, but I particularly want to say thank you to Hester Davenport, Lorna Clark, Peter Sabor, Nick Cambridge, Kate Chisholm, Helen Cooper, Catherine Dille, Jacqueline Grainger, Zandra O'Donnell, Elizabeth Burney Parker and Sophie Vasset. Cynthia Comyn, the widow of John Comyn, a descendant of Charles Burney, kindly answered my requests for information. Desmond King-Hele, biographer of Erasmus Darwin, generously gave me his help and in particular pointed me toward Day's brief engagement to Elizabeth Hall. Peter Rowland, author of the last biography of Thomas Day, was extremely kind in sharing with me new sources of information that had come to light since his book was published as well as directing me toward Henry James's *Watch and Ward*. Eric Stockdale brought eighteenth-century Middle Temple Hall to life for me and kindly treated me to lunch under the wonderful double hammerbeamed roof as well as answering my queries on legal history. Mick Crumplin gave me his usual prompt and impeccable advice on weaponry. Elizabeth E. Barker helped with trying to date Joseph Wright's portrait of Day, and Kate Barnard gave me valuable advice on Anna Seward. Rachel Hall and Sophie Kilic were both fantastic aides in French translation and especially in helping me to decipher Fanny Burney's untidy, eccentric and inaccurate eighteenth-century French. Mike Cudmore gave his unstinting and uncomplaining help as always in sorting out the usual technological issues.

Jacky Worthington was an invaluable help in tracing descendants of Sabrina Bicknell and others, often burning the midnight computer screen to follow a promising lead down the centuries. It was through Jacky that I managed to contact some of Sabrina's living descendants, including Elizabeth Kiddle and Julia Wells, who helped further with my research and took a keen interest in the story. I am also grateful to Marcus Bicknell, who runs the current Bicknell family tree website, for his aid.

As ever I count myself extremely lucky to benefit from the unerring support, guidance and friendship of my agent, Patrick Walsh. My editor Kirsty Dunseath, at Weidenfeld and Nicolson in the UK, has played an invaluable and inspiring role, as she always does, in helping me to shape, improve and polish this book. Somehow Kirsty seems to know exactly what I meant to do even if I haven't yet done it. At Weidenfeld & Nicolson, Jennifer Kerslake gave timely and efficient help in picture records. I am extremely grateful too to Lara Heimert, my editor at Basic Books in the United States, for her enthusiasm and commitment to this project, to Katy O'Donnell for her guidance and to Norman MacAfee, for his meticulous and wise editing.

Finally I want to thank my family and friends for giving me the practical, emotional and physical help that has been essential in writing this book from beginning to end. Most of all, my thanks are to Sam and Susie, for their usual forbearance and patience, and to my husband, Peter, my first reader and my constant support.

ILLUSTRATION CREDITS

1. Thomas Day by Joseph Wright, 1770 (Manchester Art Gallery)
2. *top left* Richard Lovell Edgeworth by Antoine Cardon, 1812 (National Library of Ireland); *top right* Erasmus Darwin by Joseph Wright, c. 1770 (The Erasmus Darwin Foundation, Lichfield); *bottom left* Jean-Jacques Rousseau by Allan Ramsay, 1766 (Scottish National Gallery); *bottom right* James Keir, engraving by W. H. Worthington, after L. de Longastre (Wellcome Library, London)
3. *top left* Anna Seward by Tilly Kettle, 1762 (British Library/Robana via Getty Images); *top right* Honora Sneyd, medallion from Josiah Wedgwood's factory, 1780 (Victoria and Albert Museum, London); *bottom left* Esther Milnes by James Millar, c. 1780 (the Samuel Johnson Birthplace Museum, Lichfield); *bottom right* Maria Edgeworth by unknown engraver, c. 1754 (Universal History Archive/ Getty Images)
4. *top* The London Foundling Hospital, engraving by B. Cole, 1755 (Coram, in the care of the Foundling Museum, London); *bottom left* Thomas Coram by William Hogarth, 1740 (Coram, in the care of the Foundling Museum, London); *bottom right* Tokens left at the Foundling Hospital (the Foundling Museum, London)
5. *top left* Billet form for Monimia Butler, 1757 (City of London, London Metropolitan Archives/Foundling Hospital Deposit); *top right* Apprenticeship indenture for Ann Kingston, 1769 (City of London, London Metropolitan Archives/Foundling Hospital Archives Deposit); *bottom* Shrewsbury House of Industry, colored aquatint published by C. Hulbert, c. 1830 (Shropshire Archives)
6. *top* The Bow and The Minuet, from Leith Davis, *The Polite Academy*, London, 1762 (British Library); *bottom* The Temple, 1722 (by kind permission of the Masters of the Bench of the Honourable Society of the Middle Temple)
7. *top left* Charles Burney by William Sharp, 1821 (National Portrait Gallery, London); *top right* Fanny Burney by Edward Burney, 1782 (the Collection at Parham Park, West Sussex); *bottom* Dr Burney's House by R. B., 1839 (Greenwich Heritage Centre)
8. *top* Sabrina Bicknell by Richard James Lane, after Stephen Poyntz Denning, 1833 (National Portrait Gallery, London); *bottom left* Henry Edgeworth Bicknell by Charles Baugniet, 1853 (National Portrait Gallery, London); *bottom right* John Laurens Bicknell, lithograph by Charles Baugniet, 1845 (Wellcome Library, London)

NOTES

A NOTE ON MONEY AND WEATHER

Comparing sums of money between the eighteenth century and today is fraught with problems. However, where comparisons are given these are based on the Bank of England inflation calculator using figures for 2011: http://www.bankofengland.co.uk/education /Pages/inflation/calculator/index1.aspx.

All references to weather are taken from meteorological reports in the *Gentleman's Magazine* and other contemporary records.

CHAPTER 1: MARGARET

1 *Thomas Day read the letter:* Edgeworth, RL and M, vol. 1, pp. 208–9. Edgeworth describes the visit to Ireland on pp. 196–99. RLE states that they left for Ireland in "spring 1768." However, the Buttery Books at Middle Temple for that year show that RLE dined there until the week of May 8–14. And since the travelers met Darwin on their route this must have been before Darwin's carriage accident, which laid him up for several weeks, on July 11 that year. They must have left, therefore, between late May and early July. The family history, family house and surrounding countryside are described in *The Black Book of Edgeworthstown and Other Edgeworth Memories*, which was handed down in the Edgeworth family. See Butler, Harriet Jessie and Harold Edgeworth.

2 *One acquaintance would later say that if Margaret appeared:* Edgeworth, FA, p. 18.

2 *Even his close friend Edgeworth:* Edgeworth, RL and M, vol. 1, p. 175.

2 *At the dinner table Day's manners:* Edgeworth, RL and M, vol. 1, p. 197.

4 *As Day told a friend at the time:* TD to JB, n.d. (postmarked October 11 and must be 1768, but mostly written three weeks earlier, i.e., September 20) Essex RO, D/DBa C10. Day describes the on-off relationship with Margaret in this 11-page letter as well as her previous romance with the English officer.

5 *He had suffered rejection before:* TD to JB, n.d. (c. 1765), three letters and three fragments from Day at Oxford to Bicknell, Essex RO, D/DBa C10.

5 *He would later describe Margaret:* TD to AS, March 14, 1771, SJBM, 2001.71.17. Although this letter is dated 1771, it was probably written in 1772 since it refers to events—such as Elizabeth Sneyd's arrival in Lichfield and Day's winter of being groomed—which had not happened until then.

6 *"These my Friend are the Prejudices":* TD to JB, n.d. Essex RO, D/DBa C10.

CHAPTER 2: LAURA

9   *The crowded room hushed:* Keir, pp. 108–9.

10   *Thomas Day was born on June 22:* Day's early years are described in Keir, pp. 4–5; Kippis; and Gignilliat, pp. 1–2. Gignilliat says Day's mother was 27 when she married in 1746, but Keir states that she was 70 in 1791 so she was actually 25. A correspondent writing to the *Gentleman's Magazine* in 1791, signing himself "E" and describing Day as "my old playfellow," says Day Sr. was deputy collector of customs outward (not collector as Keir states) and gives his date of death as July 24, 1749. This writer, probably RLE, states that Phillips was an usher in the same office. GM, 1791, vol. 61, part 1, p. 401.

10   *Baby Thomas was baptized:* Parish register, St. George-in-the-East, LMA.

10   *From his mother—who once stared down a bull:* Keir, p. 16.

10   *Soon after she was widowed:* Keir, p. 5.

11   *Thomas and his stepfather would never see eye to eye:* Seward (1804), p. 27.

11   *Barehill, near Wargrave, in Berkshire:* The area, neighboring Kiln Green, five miles south of Henley-on-Thames, was called either Bare or Bear Hill in the eighteenth century but is now known as Bear Lane.

12   *One of about a hundred boarding pupils:* Anon, *Charter-House, Its Foundation and History* (London, 1849); Thornbury, Walter, *Old and New London* (London, 1897), vol. 2, pp. 380–404; Wheatley, Henry Benjamin, *London, Past and Present*, vol. 1, pp. 362–66; Quick, Anthony, *Charterhouse, A History of the School* (London, 1990). General background on eighteenth-century education is from Fletcher.

12   *He even gained a reputation:* Keir, p. 11. Keir cites William Seward as giving the anecdote about boxing.

13   *Indeed one version of the boxing story:* Stephen.

13   *it was published in a London newspaper: Gazetteer and New Daily Advertiser*, May 5 and August 15, 1764. The verses were published in two parts so Day and Bicknell were actually 16 and 18 by the time the second verses appeared. Gignilliat attributes the poem to Day, but it was almost certainly a collaboration since Day asked Bicknell in a letter from Oxford (n.d.), "I suppose Knife & Fork is consign'd to Rust." Essex RO, D/DBa C10.

13   *Bicknell was "in the strictest sense":* Kippis.

14   *Gibbon described the few classes:* Gibbon, Edward, *Memoirs of My Life*, ed. Radice, Betty (Harmondsworth, UK, 1984), pp. 77–86. General background on Oxford University is from Midgley, Graham, *University Life in Eighteenth-Century Oxford* (New Haven; London, 1996); details on Corpus Christi are from Fowler, Thomas, *Corpus Christi* (Oxford, 1898).

15   *Arriving in Oxford in his black silk gown:* University of Oxford, *Alumni Oxonienses, 1715–1886* (London; Oxford, 1887–88), vol. 1, p. 357. The college architecture is largely unchanged today.

16   *Day liked to "descant at large":* Edgeworth, RL and M, vol. 1, pp. 248 and 341; vol. 2, p. 86. The second comment is from Maria Edgeworth.

16   *Alone in his rooms, he poured:* Letters, TD to JB, Essex RO, D/DBa C10. Three letters sent by Day to Bicknell from Oxford have survived. All are undated, but events mentioned suggest they were written in 1765 and 1766. The succeeding quotes are all from these letters. No replies from Bicknell survive.

17   *Instead he made friends with other misfits:* Kippis; Cannon, pp. 21–22.

18   *Engaged on a path of solo research:* Keir, p. 6.

18   *Briefly considering a career in law:* Students' Ledger, Middle Temple archives. Day was admitted on February 12, 1765.

18   *Virtue was a noble ideal:* Morse, pp. 155–57 re Day and passim.

20   *Day dedicated himself to "the unremitting practice":* Keir, p. 8.

20   *Day's contempt for "modern refinements":* Keir, p. 34; *and "Want of Elegance:* TD to JB, n.d. (c. 1765–66), Essex RO, D/DBa C10.

21   *Although Day loved to declaim:* Keir, pp. 88–89.

21   *"With his customary frankness":* Keir, p. 41.

22   *At one point, as a seventeen-year-old:* Keir, pp. 21–22.

23   *During the long university holidays:* Keir, pp. 32–33.

24   *Day judged that by the "manly exercise of walking":* Kippis.

24   *Alone on these country expeditions:* TD, Commonplace book, Essex RO, D/DBa Z40.

25   *Day was "wounded by the caprice":* Seward (1804), pp. 20–23. Seward reproduces the elegy to Laura. Day's friend at Oxford, William Jones, was also inspired by Petrarch to write an elegy entitled Laura. Cannon, ed., pp. 26–27.

25   *"O gentle Lady of the West":* TD, Commonplace book, Essex RO, D/DBa Z40; the poem is reproduced in Keir, pp. 42–44.

26   *"the Habits of the Mind":* TD to JB, n.d. [c. September–October 1768] Essex RO, D/DBa C10.

26   *As the second eldest son:* Baptism register, St. Andrew's Holborn, July 28, 1746. John Bicknell was not baptized with the middle name Laurens, as is commonly stated; this is a confusion with his son John Laurens Bicknell. General family background is from Bicknell, although this is inaccurate in places.

27   *Originally the base for the Knights Templar:* Williamson, J. Bruce, *The History of the Temple* (London, 1925); *Middle Temple Hall: Notes Upon Its History* (London, 1928); and *Notes on the Middle Temple in the Nineteenth Century* (London, 1936); Bellot, Hugh H. L., *The Inner and Middle Temple: Legal, Literary and Historic Associations* (London, 1902); Herber, Mark, *Legal London: A Pictorial History* (Chichester, 2007); Blackham, Robert James, *Wig and Gown, The Story of the Temple* (London, 1932).

27   *Bicknell duly enjoyed his dinners:* Buttery Book, 1759–1772, MT archives, MT7 /BUB/2.

27   *James Boswell, the lawyer, diarist and notorious libertine:* Boswell, James, *Boswell's London Journal, 1762–1763*, ed. Pottle, Frederick A. (Edinburgh, 1991), pp. 234 and 49.

27   *One female acquaintance would later:* AS to George Hardinge, March 5, 1789. Seward (1811), vol. 2, p. 250. The Buttery Book for the time shows Hardinge dined at the same time as JB. Buttery Book, 1759–72, MT archives, MT7 /BUB/2.

28   *Born in 1744, the second son:* Edgeworth, RL and M, vol. 1, pp. 21–22. Details of Edgeworth's life are from his memoirs unless otherwise stated. Other sources include Butler, Harriet Jessie and Harold Edgeworth; and Clarke, although the latter is mostly culled from the memoirs.

29   *So Edgeworth was packed off:* Alumni Oxonienses, 1715–1886, p. 408.

29 *She was pregnant:* Black Bourton parish records, February 21, 1764. Edgeworth and Anna Maria were married by license with the consent of her parents. She was then 20. The baptism register shows Anna Maria was born on October 20, 1743. In 1761, when Edgeworth arrived in the household, her sisters were aged 16, 15, 7 and 6. Dick was "received" into the parish church on December 25, 1765, having been "previously privately baptised," according to the baptism register.

30 But although she was "prudent": Edgeworth, RL and M, vol. 1, p. 179.

30 *Anna Maria as "always crying":* Butler, Marilyn (1972), p. 37. The description was crossed out of the original manuscript of Edgeworth, Frances Anne, *A Memoir of Maria Edgeworth,* which was edited by her stepmother and sisters.

30 *The tireless inventor bombarded the newly founded Society for the Arts:* Letters RLE to the RSA, RSA archives PR.GE/110/14/134; 22/146; 23/7 and 32 and 54; 24/86; 26/75; 30/136 and 137. The society is now the Royal Society for the Encouragement of Arts, Manufactures and Commerce, known as the RSA. RLE was awarded the silver medal in 1768 and the gold medal in 1769.

31 *Having heard that Darwin shared his interest:* Edgeworth, RL and M, vol. 1, pp. 156–58.

31 *They took the name the Lunar Society:* Edgeworth, RL and M, vol. 1, pp. 180–81. For more information on the Lunar Society see Uglow; Schofield; Robinson; Herbert L. Ganter, "William Small, Jefferson's Beloved Teacher," in *The William and Mary Quarterly,* 4 (1947), pp. 505–11; King-Hele (2007). Dr. Small taught mathematics to Thomas Jefferson when he was professor of natural philosophy at the College of William and Mary in Virginia. More background on Darwin can be found in King-Hele (1999).

32 *Dashing off a letter:* ED to Matthew Boulton, n.d. [summer 1766], in King-Hele (2007), p. 74. Darwin meant Edgeworth's father-in-law's home at Black Bourton when he referred to Oxfordshire.

32 *Into Edgeworth's exhilarating:* Edgeworth, RL and M, vol. 1, pp. 175–79; vol. 2, p. 102.

32 *Edgeworth would later compare:* Edgeworth, RL and M, vol. 1, pp. 175–77.

34 *"calculating the vibrations":* TD to RLE, Nov 1769, from Avignon, in RLE, *Memoirs,* vol. 1, p. 214.

CHAPTER 3: SOPHIE

35 *Enjoying a stroll in the gardens:* The story of Darwin's ruse to meet Rousseau is told by his grandson, the naturalist Charles Darwin, in Darwin, p. 47. The story is also described, slightly differently, in Howitt, p. 513. Background on Rousseau generally and his visit to England specifically is from Edmonds and Eidinow; Damrosch; Broome; and Rousseau (2008). Letters between JJR, Hume and Davenport are in Rousseau (1965–2012), vols. 29–33. Born in Geneva in 1712, Rousseau was brought up by his father, a watchmaker. He enjoyed no formal education until the age of 10, when he was sent to live with a pastor in a nearby village. Although he was apprenticed to an engraver, he ran away at 16, and for the next 14 years he traveled Europe and drifted from one menial job to another with no apparent ambition until settling in Paris at

the age of 30. He was 38 when he was suddenly propelled to literary and philosophical acclaim by winning first prize in a provincial writing competition for his essay *Discourse on the Arts and Sciences.*

36   *"All the world are eager to see":* Quoted in Edmonds and Eidinow, p. 120. Rousseau was called "John James Rousseau" in *London Evening Post,* January 31, 1766.

36   *Thérèse Lavasseur until she was escorted across the Channel:* During the 10-day journey to Dover, Boswell enjoyed intimacies with Thérèse on 13 occasions— or so he would boast in his diary. Edmonds and Eidinow, pp. 144–45.

36   *Rousseau rightly suspected:* In typically paranoid fashion, Rousseau had decided that Hume's efforts to negotiate a pension for him from George III was a trick to humiliate him and that Hume and Davenport were both involved in a spoof letter published in London in the *St. James's Chronicle* of April 1–3, 1766. The letter, purported to be written by the king of Prussia, was actually concocted by Horace Walpole. Walpole confessed himself the author in a letter to Horace Mann. Rousseau (1965–2012), vol. 30, p. 83.

37   *As a father, who gave up all five children:* Rousseau (2008), p. 335. The children were born in the late 1740s and early 1750s. Rousseau would later try to justify giving away his offspring, but it was an act that would haunt him all his life.

37   Émile *has been described as the most important work:* Wokler, p. 2; Darling, p. 17. Darling offers a clear and inspiring exposition of the evolution of educational systems from Rousseau to the present day.

37   *at birth children's minds resemble "white Paper":* Locke, John, *Some Thoughts Concerning Education* (London, 1693) p. 261.

37   *"Everything is good":* Rousseau, (2010), p. 161. I have used the most recent translation of *Émile,* edited by Bloom and Kelly and published in 2010, for quotations except in a few places where the Boyd translation, which is an abridged version, seemed more expressive.

38   *"I hate books":* Rousseau (2010), p. 331.

38   *Although* Émile *was not the first parenting manual:* Rousseau's visionary belief in placing children at the center of education and his advocacy of teaching through demonstration and experiment—essentially "learning by doing"— have remained pillars of educational theory. After his death, early Rousseau disciples set up pioneering schools based on his methods across Europe. Their ideas crossed the Atlantic to America in the twentieth century and were exported from the US to Asia. Then two centuries after his memorable visit to England, during the 1960s Rousseau's teaching methods were adopted in Britain and remain—despite countercampaigns—the prevailing educational system. The Rousseau vision of children as innocent individuals with distinct characteristics and rights is still the dominant world view. See Darling; Jimack; and Moncrieff.

39   *The Prince and Princess of Wurtemberg:* Douthwaite, pp. 134–45. Douthwaite also describes the experiments by Edgeworth and Day as well as the story of Madame Manon Roland, who brought up her daughter Eudora, born in 1781, according to the Rousseau system. The letter from Prince Louis-Eugène to JJR, October 4, 1763, is in Rousseau (1965–2012), vol. 18, pp. 13–16.

39 *Another enthusiast, a Swiss banker*: Rousseau (1965–2012), vol. 46, pp. 235–37. The notes in Rousseau's *Correspondance Complète* identify one of the girls, the source of the story, as Marie de Bourdeille (née Roussel) who was born in 1758 and married le comte de Bourdeille in 1781. She related the story to a friend of Rousseau's, Mme de Gauthier, in 1790.

39 *When* Émile *was published in English:* Background information on the changes in children's education and upbringing can be found in Stone, pp. 254–99; Fletcher; Cunningham; and Jimack. *Émile* was published in English in two rival translations: *Emilius, or an essay on education by John James Rousseau*, translated by Thomas Nugent, and *Emilius and Sophia, or a new system of education*, translated by William Kenrick. Both books give 1763 as their date of publication although one at least was in the shops by late 1762.

39 *In one painting,* An Experiment on a Bird: Wright, *An Experiment on a Bird in the Air Pump*, 1768. The figure in the foreground with a stopwatch is thought to be Darwin and the two boys his eldest sons, Charles and Erasmus. See Daniels, Stephen, *Joseph Wright* (London, 1999), pp. 37–39, and King-Hele (1999), p. 83.

40 *Richard Davenport, who had placed:* Broome, pp. 22–23; Howitt, p. 514. A letter describing the effects on Davies, from his son Edward Davies Davenport to his grandson, Arthur Henry Davenport, July 7, 1838, is given in Rousseau (1965–2012), vol. 33, pp. 272–75.

40 *Rather more successfully, Emily Kildare*: Emily Kildare's experimental school is described in Tillyard, Stella, *Aristocrats: Caroline, Emily, Louisa and Sarah Lennox 1752–1832* (London, 1994), pp. 244–46.

40 *Edgeworth devoured* Émile: Edgeworth, RL and M, vol. 1, pp. 172–73.

41 *Dick had been pampered and indulged:* Edgeworth, FA, p. 37.

42 *Having been dressed in petticoats:* The experiment on Dick is described in Edgeworth, RL and M, vol. 1, pp. 177–180, and the subsequent quotes from RLE are from these pages.

43 *"the plague of childhood":* Rousseau (2010), p. 253.

43 *Only if Dick himself picked up a book:* Edgeworth, RL and M, vol. 1, p. 221. Day was echoing Rousseau's advice. In *Émile*, he wrote: "I am almost certain that Emile will know how to read and write perfectly before the age of ten, precisely because it makes very little difference to me that he knows how before fifteen." Rousseau (2010), p. 254.

43 *"a Waggon drawn by Fire":* ED to Josiah Wedgwood, June 14, 1768, in King-Hele (2007), pp. 87–88.

43 *winning a silver medal:* Clarke, p. 52.

44 *"I cannot believe that you took the book":* JJR to Philibert Cramer, October 13, 1764, in Rousseau (1965–2012), vol. 21, pp. 248–49.

45 *The educational program had been progressing:* RLE states that he and Day left for Ireland in "spring 1768."

45 *Anna Maria, who had given birth to a daughter, baptized Maria:* Maria's date of birth has been contentious. It has variously been given as January 1, 1767, and January 1, 1768; the latter is correct. She states categorically in a letter written on January 1, 1819: "This is my 51st birthday." See Edgeworth, Maria, p. 153.

The Black Bourton parish register states that she was baptized Mary on October 31, 1768.

45 *Eager to provide some light entertainment:* Edgeworth, RL and M, vol. 1, pp. 188–92. The play, by George Farquhar, was first staged in 1707.

47 *Rousseau had recognized as he wrote* Émile: Rousseau (2010), pp. 499 and 531.

47 *In the quest to find Sophie:* Rousseau (2010), p. 529.

47 *"Let us give Émile his Sophie":* Rousseau (1960), p. 152. The Bloom version gives this as: "Let us render his Sophie to our Emile. Let us resuscitate this lovable girl." Rousseau (2010), p. 587.

48 *Rousseau has no hesitation in asserting:* Rousseau (2010), p. 531.

48 *"the time will come when she will be her own doll":* Rousseau (1960), p. 137.

48 *"almost all little girls learn to read and write with repugnance":* Rousseau (2010), p. 543.

48 *"From this habitual constraint":* Rousseau (2010), p. 546.

48 *The poet and socialite Frances Greville praised* Émile: Lady Caroline Holland to Emily, Duchess of Leinster, December 7, 1762, in Emily, Duchess of Leinster, *Correspondence of Emily, Duchess of Leinster (1731–1814),* ed. Fitzgerald, Brian (Dublin, 1949), vol. 1, p. 353.

48 *Mary Wollstonecraft would later condemn*: Wollstonecraft, pp. 56–57.

49 *"I have been disappointed in a Manner":* TD to JB, n.d. (c. September–October 1768), Essex RO, D/DBa C10.

51 *Back in London, Day moved into lodgings:* Edgeworth states that Day and Bicknell lodged together "in town." Edgeworth, RL and M, vol. 1, p. 204.

51 *Day might well have accompanied Edgeworth:* Edgeworth, RL and M, vol. 1, pp. 202–4.

52 *"such a society, as few men have had the good fortune to live with":* Edgeworth, RL and M, vol. 1, pp. 180–81.

53 *a comfortable income of £1,200 a year:* Seward (1804), p. 18.

54 *Built as a country branch of the Foundling Hospital:* Ionides, Julia, *Thomas Farnolls Pritchard of Shrewsbury: Architect and "Inventor of Cast Iron Bridges"* (Ludlow, 1999); Oldham, J. Basil, *A History of Shrewsbury School 1552–1952* (Oxford, 1952), pp. 135–39. The £16,960 cost of the building, given in Ionides, would today equal nearly £3m ($4.8 million). The iron bridge over the Severn at Coalbrookdale, the first iron bridge in the world, was designed by Pritchard in 1775 but not built until 1777–79 after his death. The former orphanage is now part of Shrewsbury School and largely intact. My thanks to Mike Morogh of Shrewsbury School for a guided tour of the building.

55 *At its peak, in 1766, the Shrewsbury orphanage:* The daily routine at Shrewsbury is described in Regulations for the Government of the Orphan Hospital at Shrewsbury, FHA: A/FH/M01/13. Figures for the number of children in August 1769 are given in State of the Orphan Hospital (Shrewsbury), FHA: A/FH/D2/15/1. There were 58 boys and 299 girls in August. Instructions to send 100 boys to Ackworth were given in Shrewsbury Letter Book 4, 21 June 1768, FHA: A/FH/D/5/4.

55 *"girls will be harder to be placed out":* London Letter Book 4, August 31, 1769, FHA: A/FH/A/6/2/2.

55 *Earlier in 1769, the governors had prosecuted:* Shrewsbury Letter Book 4, 2 Jan 1767, FHA: A/FH/D/5/4. The court case is described in London Letter Book 4, 11 Feb 1769, FHA: A/FH/A/6/2/2. In August 1769, two girls, aged 13 and 17, ran back to the orphanage from their apprenticeships in a factory making wood saws near Burton upon Trent, because the owner had beaten them if they refused to come to his bed.

56 *As he walked up and down the parade:* Edgeworth, RL and M, vol. 1, p. 209. Seward (1804), p. 36. Edgeworth says Day chose Sabrina "from among a number of orphans." Seward states that Day and Bicknell chose both girls from "a little train" at Shrewsbury although Lucretia was in fact selected in London. ME states that it was Bicknell who originally chose Sabrina, Edgeworth, RL and M, vol. 2, p. 110. The visit must have taken place between June 22, when Day turned 21, and June 30, when the Shrewsbury Committee ratified the apprenticeship.

56 *"chestnut tresses" and dark eyes "expressive of sweetness":* Seward, p. 26; Edgeworth, RL and M, vol. 1, p. 213.

57 *A few days later, on June 30:* Shrewsbury Committee Minutes, June 30, 1769, FHA: A/FH/D2/1. Apprenticeship indenture for Ann Kingston, August 17, 1769, FHA: A/FH/A/12/4/60/1.

58 *The following day, the London office:* Thomas Collingwood to Samuel Magee, October 5, 1769, correspondence, FHA: A/FH/D2/3/16; SM to TC, October 9, 1769, Shrewsbury Letter Book 4, FHA: A/FH/D2/5/4.

CHAPTER 4: ANN AND DORCAS

60 *"I had such well merited confidence":* Edgeworth, RL and M, vol. 1, p. 210. RLE stated that Day placed Sabrina in lodgings near Chancery Lane.

60 *Then even though he had flouted:* Minutes of FH General Committee, 1769–70, FHA: X041/17; lists of governors 1784 and 1786, FHA: A/FH/A/2/1/2 and A/FH/A/2/1/4.

61 *Thomas Day was not the first to dream of:* Ovid, "Pygmalion," in *Metamorphoses,* trans. Melville, A. D., ed. Kenney, E. J. (Oxford, 2008), pp. 232–34. Fascination with the Pygmalion myth and its influence on other works are discussed in Hersey; Stoichita; and Sheriff.

61 *With its simple but timeless theme:* Works reputed to have been inspired by the Pygmalion myth include Shakespeare's *The Winter's Tale,* the Willy Russell play and later film *Educating Rita,* Alfred Hitchcock's film *Vertigo,* "The Galatea Affair" in the television series *The Man from UNCLE* and the sci-fi novel by Richard Powers, *Galatea 2.2.* See Stoichita for a fascinating discussion.

61 *Probably the best-known and best-loved version:* There is no direct evidence that Shaw knew of Day's story although it was certainly well known when he wrote *Pygmalion* and there are many parallels in his text. He may well have absorbed details from Anthony Trollope's novel, *Orley Farm,* published in 1862. The quotes are from pp. 32, 30 and 65.

62 *In 1762, he composed a poetic drama:* JJR, *Pygmalion, A Poem* (Eng. trans., London, 1779); Damrosch, p. 462. Rousseau first staged his play in Lyon, in spring 1770, in collaboration with a friend, Horace Coignet, who wrote the music.

63 *Founded in 1741, the Foundling Hospital:* Chief sources for the history of the Foundling Hospital and the biography of Thomas Coram are anon, *An Account of the Foundling Hospital* (1826); Wray and Nicholls; Pugh; Levene (2007); McClure; Clark; Allin. Allin provides comprehensive information on the early years and the General Reception; McClure is extremely helpful on Coram's life and the early history of the charity. Other general information is gleaned from the Foundling Hospital archives and the Foundling Hospital Museum.

63 *the sight of abandoned babies:* McClure, p. 19.

64 *"the Expressions of Grief":* Pugh, p. 39.

64 *few children were ever reunited:* It has been estimated that 1.2 percent of babies were reclaimed between 1741 and 1799. Levene (2007), p. 18.

64 *Carefully stored under lock and key, the billet forms:* Clark, p. xxxii; exhibit in FH Museum; FHA: Billet Books. Some women left poems with their abandoned babies. One began: "Pity the Offspring of a Youthful Pair, / Whom folly taught, and Pleasure did Ensnare." Another reads: "Here I am brought without a name / Im' sent to hide my mothers' shame, / I hope youll say, Im' not to Blame, / Itt seems my mothers' twenty five / and mattrymonys Laid a side." Both poems are quoted in Wray, p. 121. Many mothers left plaintive instructions as to how they wished their child to be named or brought up. One note, attached to a tiny gold hoop, begged, "pleas to continue the yearring in the right year"—Billet Book, no 10,416, FHA: A/FH/A/9/1/117—while another asked "please to call her Molly Collins not Marey." Levene (2006), pp. 133. Both directions were, of course, ignored.

64 *"This Little Innocent":* Levene (2006), pp. 142.

64 *Upon reception each child:* Pugh, p. 35. Billet books passim.

65 *The General Reception, as it became known:* Wilson; Levene (2007), p. 41; Allin, pp. 4 and 7. Wilson suggests that the babies admitted during the General Reception accounted for 10 percent of all babies born in London in that period; Levene plausibly counters that the figure is more like 7 percent—still a staggering proportion.

66 *One child was described as:* Allin, p. 112.

66 *Mortality rates leapt from an already tragic:* Of the total 14,934 admitted during the General Reception, only 4,400 (29.5 percent) lived to be apprenticed. George, p. 57. McClure gives the figure 81.29 percent for mortality between June 24, 1758, and September 29, 1760, but Allin points out that a disproportionate number of these babies in later years died before they were even sent to nurse, i.e., they were already on the verge of death when admitted. Mc-Clure, pp. 102, 261; Allin, p. 95. Levene states that from 1741 to 1799, nearly 65 percent died before they were apprenticed. Levene (2007), p. 18.

66 *Thursday, May 24, 1757, dawned: Gentleman's Magazine,* 27 (1757), p. 252.

66 *According to the hospital regulations:* The system for admitting babies is described in Regulations of the Foundling Hospital, 1757, FHA: A/FH/A/06 /015/002.

67 *The billet form, which survives to this day:* Billet Book 1757, FHA: A/FH/A/9 /1/56, no 4579. The other six babies admitted the same day were numbered 4574, 5, 6, 7, 8 and 4780. A contemporary survey of the origins of babies ad-

mitted to the FH revealed that 100 babies came from St. James's Clerkenwell and 28 from St. John's Clerkenwell between June 2, 1756, and June 2, 1757, "as those persons declared who delivered them at the said hospital." FHA: A /FH/M/1/8/39–42

67   *Despite the assertion on the billet form:* Baptism registers, St. James's Church and St. John's Church, Clerkenwell, LMA, X027/029 and X097/244. Both registers were checked for 12 months previously. Curiously there is also no record in the billet books of other foundlings said to have been baptized at St. James's so it is possible there was an alternative baptism system in place. The original St. James's church was demolished and the existing church built between 1788 and 1791. Otway's play was being staged at the Theatre Royal in Drury Lane at the beginning of 1757 with celebrated actors Susannah Cibber and David Garrick in the lead roles. Also in 1757, the play was published, as part of Otway's *Works*. With their usual gift for inventing witty names, the Foundling Hospital governors baptized one baby Monimia Orphan.

67   *Clerkenwell was home:* George, pp. 175–76; Ackroyd, Peter, *London the Biography* (London, 2000) pp. 461–74. By 1798 about 7,000 artisans worked in the watchmaking trade producing an estimated 120,000 watches a year.

68   *Illegitimacy rose throughout the eighteenth century:* Zunshine, p. 1; Adair, Richard, *Courtship, Illegitimacy and Marriage in Early Modern England* (Manchester, 1996), pp. 5–11; Laslett, Peter, *Family Life and Illicit Love in Earlier Generations* (Cambridge, 1977), p. 113; Wilson. According to Laslett, illegitimacy rose between 1650 and 1800 from about 1 percent of all births to more than 5 percent. The figure was about 3 percent in 1757. There is a counterview that it was the recording of illegitimacy that rose—rather than illegitimacy itself—because people were keen to ensure their babies were baptized in order to qualify for poor relief at a later stage. Personal communication, Else Churchill, genealogist, Society of Genealogists.

68   *The enigma mattered little:* General Register, FHA: A/FH/A9/2/1–2 (microfilm X41/3). Babies numbered 4574 (an unnamed girl, baptized Elizabeth Temple) and 4576 (a boy previously baptized John, renamed James Bickerstaff) lived to be apprenticed. The other four babies died before they reached five.

69   *Her stay in the hospital was short:* Receipt, in Inspectors' accounts, FHA: A/FH /B1/18/10; Nursing Book A/FH/A/10/3/5. The receipt gives the wet nurse's name as Mary Pemble, but on the reverse, this has been amended to Penfold so the initial name was presumably an error. No Mary Pemble can be found in parish records. The Inspections Book, microfilm X041/1, shows five babies were sent to Dorking that day, including no. 4576, James Bickerstaff, who was admitted the same day as AK. It was the usual custom for wet nurses to travel to the hospital to receive babies, then accompany them back home. The nursing book records that Ann was breast-fed.

69   *Although the charity's legion of wet nurses:* For information on the Foundling Hospital wet nurses see Fildes. All the Foundling Hospital infants were breast-fed if they were still able to suckle thanks to the enlightened zeal of the physician William Cadogan, a governor of the charity who provided med-

ical services free to the orphans from 1753. See William Cadogan, *An Essay upon Nursing* (1948).

70 *Living in the hamlet of Wotton:* Mary Penfold was born Mary Potter. She married Thomas Penfold on July 1, 1740, when both were living in the parish of Horley, in southeast Surrey. Following traditional courting custom, Mary was at least five months pregnant when she walked down the aisle. Her first son, James, was born soon after. The Penfolds had seven children baptized—James (1740?), Mary (1742), Betty (1749), Thomas (1751; died before 1757), John (1755), Thomas (1757) and Sarah (1758), according to the parish registers of Horley and Charlwood. There were six surviving children in 1757. All records are at Surrey History Centre. For background on English country life see Horn, Pamela, *Life and Labour in Rural England, 1760–1850* (Basingstoke, UK, 1986), especially pp. 12–19.

70 *Of all babies sent to wet nurses:* Allin, p. 142. Excluding those who died before being sent to nurse, a total 53.5 percent died under the age of two from 1757 to 1760.

70 *Ann's survival, in the face of such odds:* Hugh Kerr supervised an impressive 601 foundlings during his total service to the hospital, making him the charity's second busiest inspector. His voluminous correspondence in the FH archives testifies to his industrious dedication. See "A list of the places where the children were nursed," FHA: A/FH/M/1/8/1–371; and Allin, pp. 127–28.

71 *"The poor Women think it Extreamly hard":* Letters Hugh Kerr to the governors, correspondence, K, 1759, FHA: A/FH/A/6/1/12/10/1–73.

71 *"shewed the most lively sorrow":* John Grant to the governors, read to the General Committee on July 18, 1759, FHA: A/FH/A/M/1/5/57–62.

71 *No sooner had she said goodbye:* Shrewsbury vouchers (bills) 1759, FHA: A/FH /D/2/46.

72 *Ann was presented to a new nurse, Ann Casewell:* Receipts, AK and DV, August 24, 1759, FHA: A/FH/A/10/1/8/1. Ann Davies married John Casewell on March 19, 1752, and had two children, Mary born April 6, 1755, and Robert born October 5, 1757: Pontesbury Parish Register. They lived in the hamlet of Longden.

72 *Growing up with her new foster family:* Ann and Deborah were brought to the hospital on April 6, 1765. Shrewsbury Waste Book, FHA: A/FH/D2/29/2.

72 *The Shrewsbury governors:* Regulations for the Government of the Orphan Hospital at Shrewsbury, FHA: A/FH/M01/13. The comment from a spot check is from April 9, 1763, Visitors Book, FHA: A/FH/D2/6/1.

73 *Pressed by the board in London:* December 20, February 3, 1762, Letter Book 2, FHA: A/FH/D/5/2. The comment was made by Roger Kynaston, who chaired the governors, to Taylor White, the London treasurer, December 6, 1760, correspondence K 1760, FHA: A/FH/A/6/1/13/11/1–42.

73 *When one of the girls:* Thomas Morgan to Taylor White, April 24, 1762, July 30, 1763, Letter Book 2, FHA:A/FH/D/5/2. TW was the first Shrewsbury secretary, who was sacked in 1765 for misconduct. Although he was kindly and well-meaning his organization was chaotic. It was discovered that the records of 30 children sent from London were missing from the Shrewsbury

files. Several children were without names, some had the names of children
recorded as dead, some had disappeared without trace and there were two girls
with the name Mary Bennet and another two called Ann Edwards.

73   *She seems to have been selected:* Children in the House 1763–8, FHA: A/FH
      /D2/9/3.

74   *The following year, when she turned twelve:* Letter London to Shrewsbury,
      March 4, 1769, London subcommittee minutes, March 4, 1769 to June 2,
      1770, FHA: A/FH/A/3/5/8.

74   *the charity's "Instructions to Apprentices":* Instructions to Apprentices, 1754, cited
      in McClure, pp. 263–64.

75   *The tale had been evoked by Edmund Spenser:* Day certainly alluded to Milton's
      play in one of his own verses, "A Ballad," written in his journal in 1767 or
      1768. Telling the story of a simple shepherd who kills himself beside the River
      Severn for unrequited love, Day's poem invokes the pagan river goddess with
      fraught words that would resonate in the future: "And thou forgive a simple
      Swain, / O fair Sabrina honor'd Flood! / If by thy Banks untimely slain, / He
      tinged thy virgin Stream with Blood!" TD, Commonplace book, Essex RO,
      D/DBa Z40.

75   *Day added the surname Sidney:* Other writers—e.g., Scott—have suggested
      that Day named Sabrina after the seventeenth-century republican martyr Al-
      gernon Sidney. But Sir Philip Sidney (1554–86) is the more likely inspiration.
      In Day's children's book, *Sandford and Merton,* the hero Harry relates the story
      of Sir Philip being fatally wounded on the battlefield; when he is offered a
      drink of water he directs his servants to offer it instead to a poor English sol-
      dier who is likewise dying. Harry describes this sacrifice as an example of "the
      greatest virtue and humanity." Day, *Sandford and Merton,* ed. Bending and By-
      grave, pp. 271–72. Sabrina's surname is variously spelled Sidney or Sydney
      (even by Day and Sabrina herself) as spelling of names often varied during
      the eighteenth century.

76   *Once again Day told the charity's officials:* Apprenticeship indenture for Dorcas
      Car, FHA: A/FH/A/12/9/58. In contrast to Sabrina's certificate, this bears
      Edgeworth's genuine signature.

76   *Like Sabrina she was described as "beautiful":* Seward (1804), p. 26.

76   *Each possessed an "extraordinary beauty":* Burney, French Exercise Book (Berg).
      My thanks for translation to Sophie Kilic and Rachel Hall.

77   *A year younger than Sabrina, Lucretia:* Billet Book 1758, FHA: A/FH/A/9/1
      /117, no. 10413. As with Sabrina, there is no trace of Ann's baptism in the
      baptism register of St. James's, Clerkenwell.

78   *"They were eleven and twelve years old":* Edgeworth, RL and M, vol. 1, pp. 209–
      10.

78   *Day's plan was spelled out:* Seward (1804), pp. 26–27.

CHAPTER 5: SABRINA AND LUCRETIA

81   *Like fugitives evaporating into the London fog:* Day describes the journey in his
      letter to his mother from Paris. He describes the girls as model travelers in
      his second letter to Edgeworth from Avignon. TD to Jane Phillips, November

18, from Paris, Essex RO, D/DBa C9; TD to RLE, 1769 (2nd letter from Avignon, c. December 1769) given in Edgeworth, RL and M, vol. 1, pp. 217–22. For background on Britons traveling abroad at the time see Black (Stroud, UK, 2003) and (Basingstoke, UK, 2003).

82   *In his comic novel* A Sentimental Journey: Sterne, Laurence, *A Sentimental Journey through France and Italy* (Harmondsworth, 1967, first pub. 1768), pp. 144 and 154n.

83   *"Mr. Day had as large a portion":* Edgeworth, RL and M, vol. 1, p. 211.

83   *Day would later attribute his move to France:* TD to RLE, 1769 (2nd letter from Avignon, c. December 1769), in Edgeworth, RL and M, vol. 1, pp. 217–18.

83   *To make doubly sure that the girls:* Seward (1804), p. 27.

84   *Having settled himself and the girls:* TD to Jane Phillips (his mother), November 18, from Paris, Essex RO, D/DBa C9.

85   *Samuel Johnson's friend Hester Thrale:* Thrale, Hester Lynch (afterward Piozzi), *Observations and Reflections Made in the Course of a Journey Through France, Italy and Germany* (Ann Arbor, MI, 1967, first published 1789), p. 11.

85   *Another seasoned traveler, Robert Wharton:* Black (Stroud, UK, 2003), pp. 254–55.

86   *One British traveler who had braved:* Cited in Black (Basingstoke, UK, 2003), pp. 88–89.

86   *Day and his wards traveled by the* diligence: Day describes the journey in his two letters to Edgeworth from Avignon. TD to RLE, 1769 (1st letter, November 1769; 2nd letter, c. December 1769) given in Edgeworth, RL and M, vol. 1, pp. 214–17 and 217–22.

87   *One exasperated traveler exclaimed:* Elizabeth, Lady Craven (later Margravine of Brandenburg-Ansbach-Bayreuth), cited in Black (Basingstoke, UK, 2003), p. 85.

87   *It was here, in the Church of Sainte-Claire:* Girard, p. 64.

87   *Day, at least, survived the rigors:* TD to RLE, 1769 (1st letter, November 1769), given in Edgeworth, RL and M, vol. 1, pp. 214–17. Edgeworth comments, on p. 214, "The following are given merely as specimens of his early style, and as almost the only instances of gaiety of manner, which ever appeared in his correspondence." Succeeding quotes from Day are taken from this letter. Background on Avignon history is from Girard.

88   *Sterne poked fun at:* Sterne, Laurence, *The Life and Opinions of Tristram Shandy, Gentleman* (Harmondsworth, UK, 1967, first published 1759–67), p. 508.

89   *Day . . . rented a house:* Day gives his address in his first letter to Edgeworth as "chez M. Fréderic, vis-à-vis la Madeleine, Avignon." TD to RLE, 1769 (1st letter, November 1769), in Edgeworth, RL and M, vol. 1, pp. 214–217. The church, known both as Sainte Madeleine and Saint Étienne, stood on the corner of the rue Petite-Fusterie and rue St-Étienne but was abandoned after 1792 and later demolished. Girard, pp. 23–28 and 230–35.

89   *The novelist Tobias Smollett scorned extravagant:* Smollett, Tobias, *Travels Through France and Italy* (London, 1766), pp. 97–98.

91   *By the time Day replied a few weeks later:* This second letter from Avignon is dated by RLE as simply 1769. Since it obviously follows the first, dated

November, it was written at the very end of that year. Succeeding quotes by Day are from this second letter. TD to RLE, 1769 (2nd letter from Avignon, c. December 1769), in Edgeworth, RL and M, vol. 1, pp. 217–18.

94 *"Give me a child of twelve":* Rousseau (2010), p. 497.
95 *"He taught them by slow degrees":* Edgeworth, RL and M, vol. 1, p. 212.
95 *"Dear Mr. Edgeworth," the letter began:* Edgeworth, RL and M, vol. 1, p. 220.
96 *Day "excited much surprise":* Edgeworth, RL and M, vol. 1, p. 211.
96 *On one excursion beyond the city walls:* Seward (1804), p. 27.
96 *In an almost equally reckless escapade:* Keir, p. 110.
97 *Like Pygmalion sculpting his ivory girl:* For more discussion of the ideal woman embodied in representations of Galatea and the enduring Pygmalion myth see Hersey; Stoichita; and Sheriff.
98 *Indeed, the cult of the living statue:* Anna Seward related the story of a neighbor who abandoned his interest in Anna's sister Sarah when he met a woman who resembled the statue of Venus at a dinner party. He insisted on measuring her waist, throat and ankles to assure himself they exactly matched the proportions of the revered statue. Cited in Barnard, p. 52.
98 *Edgeworth summed up his friend's singular recipe:* Edgeworth, RL and M, vol. 1, p. 212.
99 *With Sabrina, said one acquaintance:* Burney, French Exercise Book (Berg).
99 *Or as Edgeworth put it:* Edgeworth, RL and M, vol. 1, p. 212.
100 *One writer, who knew Sabrina in later life:* Burney, French Exercise Book (Berg).
100 *"They teized and perplexed him":* Seward (1804), pp. 27–28.
100 *Lucretia had been inoculated:* Inoculation Book, girls 1766, FHA: A/FH/A/18 /8/10. Although no records survive describing Sabrina's inoculation, it was the Shrewsbury Hospital's practice to inoculate children immediately after they returned from their nurses.
101 *Arriving back in London, Day immediately:* Edgeworth, RL and M, vol. 1, pp. 212–13; Seward (1804), pp. 27–28.
101 *he placed her in temporary accommodation with Bicknell's mother:* Seward (1804), p. 28. It is not clear where Sabrina stayed in the countryside if, indeed, she did stay with Mrs. Bicknell. Bicknell's mother, Sarah, was living in the family home in Chancery Lane at this time. Her family also hailed from London. She has been erroneously given the maiden name of Sarah Breadelbane Campbell in the family history by Algernon Sidney Bicknell, *Five Pedigrees.* Her maiden name was Ansted or Anstead, according to her will, proved 1806. She was a twin, baptized with her brother Joseph, on October 2, 1750, at St. Dunstan-in-the-West, Fleet Street, London. Will of Sarah Bicknell, proved September 22, 1806, NA, prob/11/1452. St. Dunstan-in-the-West parish register, LMA.

CHAPTER 6: ANNA AND HONORA

103 *Growing up in the plush Bishop's Palace:* Biographical information on Anna Seward is chiefly from Barnard; Stapleton; Lucas; Oulton; and Anna Seward's voluminous correspondence in the published collections of her letters—the 6

volumes edited by Constable in Seward (1810) and the poems and letters edited by Scott in Seward (1811)—and her unpublished letters in the archives
at SJBM. My thanks to Joanne Wilson, curator of the SJBM, Lichfield. See
also Kelly, Jennifer, *Bluestocking Feminism: Writings of the Bluestocking Circle,
1738–85* (London, 1999), vol. 4; and Faderman, Lilian, *Surpassing the Love of
Men* (New York, 1981).

103   *Dr. Johnson would always say:* Hopkins, p. 210.

104   *Encouraged by her father, at nine Anna:* AS to "Emma," juvenile correspondence,
in Seward (1810), vol. 1, p. lxviii. Barnard suggests that Seward's correspondent
"Emma" was an imaginary friend. Barnard, p. 9, and personal communication.

104   *Anna's youth in the happy company:* AS gives the dates for Honora's time spent
with the Seward family in a letter, AS to Mrs T [Temple], June 19, 1796, Seward (1811), vol. 4, pp. 214–20. There had been 10 girls and 2 boys in the
Sneyd family, but 4 of the girls died before their mother.

104   *Within days of her sister's burial:* AS to Mary Powys, December 11, 1784, SJBM
2001.77.10. Sarah Seward was buried on June 16, 1764. Parish register, The
Close, Lichfield 1744–97, LRO.

105   *"This child seems angel":* AS to "Emma," April 1764, Seward (1810), vol. 1, p. cxvii.

105   *the "lovely infant-girl,"; "the oval elegance":* AS, "The Anniversary," written June
1769, Seward (1810), vol. 1, pp. 68–73; AS to Court Dewes, March 30, 1786,
in Seward (1811), vol. 1, p. 144.

106   *Taking a year's lease on a substantial:* The exact date that Day moved to Lichfield is unclear. Edgeworth said that he himself was not in the country when
Day returned from Ireland. This must have been after April 1770, when Seward recorded that Edgeworth was visiting Lichfield. Seward said Day arrived
in spring 1770. It was probably May.

106   *Situated at the crossroads of the main:* Background on Lichfield is from Hopkins;
Anon, *A Short Account of the Ancient and Modern State of the City and Close of
Lichfield* (Lichfield, 1819); Jackson, John, *History of the City and Cathedral of
Lichfield* (London, 1805); and Upton, Chris, *A History of Lichfield* (Chichester,
2001).

106   *Standing on its own in a secluded spot:* Stowe House survives today almost unchanged in external appearance and largely unchanged on the ground floor.
The house was built, in about 1750, for Elizabeth Aston, who lived farther
up the hill in another house. Details of the history and interior of Stowe
House are from Dorothea Mary Benson, Baroness Charnwood, "A Habita-
tion's Memories," in *The Cornhill Magazine*, 63, no. 378 n.s. (November 1927),
pp. 535–47; and *Call Back Yesterday* (London, 1937). Dorothea Charnwood
grew up in Stowe House. Stowe House is now a management training college,
owned by the Institute of Leadership and Management. I am grateful to Alan
Baker for showing me around. Information on the area is from Greenslade,
M. W., *The Victoria History of the County of Stafford*, "Lichfield" (Oxford, 1990),
vol. 14, pp. 67–72.

107   *the "watry mirror" of Stowe Pool:* Barnard, p. 67.

107   *The "villa, rising near the lake":* AS, "Lichfield, an elegy, written May 1781," in Seward (1810), p. 89.

107   *In Shaw's play* Pygmalion: The quotes are from Shaw, pp. 29, 33, 34 and 38.

108   *"without a protectress":* Edgeworth, RL and M, vol. 1, p. 240.

109   *he should teach her "everything he knows":* Rousseau (1960), pp. 156–57.

110   *Even Edgeworth thought that this relaxed:* Edgeworth, RL and M, vol. 1, pp. 234–35 and 231–32.

110   *"Every stranger, who came well recommended":* Edgeworth, RL and M, vol. 1, p. 232.

111   a *"whole cluster of Beaux":* AS to Mary Powys, April 25, 1770, SJBM, 2001.76.1.

111   *regarded as something of a social climber:* Walpole described Canon Seward as a social climber. Hopkins, p. 63.

111   *Sabrina was "received at the palace":* Edgeworth, RL and M, vol. 1, pp. 234–35.

111   *From the start Anna Seward was fascinated by the "eventful story":* Seward (1804), p. 19.

112   *She was a "beauteous girl":* Seward (1804), p. 26.

112   *"Mr. Day looked the philosopher":* Seward (1804), pp. 13–16.

112   *A portrait of Day:* It is difficult to date Wright's portrait of Day precisely. Anna Seward states that it was painted in 1770. Seward (1804), pp. 14–15. Wright's account book gives no date for the portrait, but it is included in a list of others painted in 1771 and 1772. Joseph Wright, Account Book, Heinz Archive and Library, NPG. More information on Wright and his portrait of Day is from Nicolson, Benedict, *Joseph Wright of Derby: Painter of Light* (2 vols., London; New York, 1968); Egerton, Judy, *Wright of Derby* (London, 1990); Barker, Elizabeth E., "Documents Relating to Joseph Wright of Derby (1734–97)," in *Walpole Society Journal*, 71 (2009), pp. 1–181. My thanks to Elizabeth Barker for her help. The first portrait, initially owned by Edgeworth, is currently in the National Portrait Gallery; the second portrait, previously owned by the Strutt family, is now in Manchester Art Gallery. My thanks to both galleries for advice. Seward states that the book in Day's hand is open at the oration of "that virtuous patron in the senate, against the grant of ship-money"—a reference to Sir Algernon Sidney opposing Charles II—but no writing can be discerned in the actual paintings. It seems more likely the book was *Émile*.

114   *Day was "a rigid moralist":* Seward (1804), pp. 24–25 and 13.

114   *Since Honora, the usual target for her affections:* AS referred to Honora's return from Bath, in autumn 1770, in a letter in 1786. AS to Mary Powys, June 25, 1786, Seward (1811), vol. 1, pp. 156–57.

114   *When Rousseau's novel* Julie, or The New Héloïse: AS to Dorothy Sykes, December 10, 1775, SJBM, 2001.72.8. Honora attended a school run by the Latuffière couple who moved to Lichfield in 1766 before uprooting for Derby in 1775.

114   *When* Émile *appeared, Anna read:* AS to Henry Cary, May 29, 1789, Seward (1811), vol. 1, p. 282. Seward described to Cary how her views had changed since reading *Émile* 20 years earlier.

114   *On Day's repeated trips to the palace:* Seward (1804), pp. 24–25.

115   *Seward described the contract Day signed with Bicknell:* Seward (1804), pp. 26–27.

115   *Darwin was devastated:* King-Hele (2007), pp. 42–43; and King-Hele (1999), p. 91. Mary Darwin was buried on July 4, 1770: Parish register, The Close, Lichfield 1744–97, LRO.

116   *John Saville had arrived in Lichfield from Ely:* Hopkins, pp. 105–12; Barnard, pp. 74–76 and passim. The Lichfield parish register gives Saville's age as 67 when he was buried in 1803, suggesting that he was born c. 1736; Mary Saville was buried in 1817, aged 80, suggesting she was born c. 1737. Their eldest daughter Elizabeth was buried in 1839, aged 84, suggesting she was born c. 1755–56. She married on November 25, 1777, with her father's consent, meaning that she was then under 21, and was therefore born after late 1756. In other words she was probably born at the end of 1756. Burials register, The Close, Lichfield 1744–97, LRO; marriage register, The Close, Lichfield, November 25, 1777.

117   *Following one musical soirée in 1764:* AS to "Emma," in Seward (1810), vol. 1, p. cvi.

117   *"the vilest of Women":* AS to Dorothy Sykes, May 1773, SJBM, 2001.72.1.

118   *"He cannot be my husband":* AS to Dorothy Sykes, May 1773, SJBM, 2001.72.1.

118   *fifteen love poems:* AS, Seward (1810), vol. 1, pp. 25–64.

118   *It was not long before rumors began:* King-Hele (1999), p. 96; King-Hele (2007), p. 140n.

118   *Darwin's grandson, the future naturalist Charles Darwin, would even suggest:* King-Hele (1999), p. 105. Charles Darwin suggested that his grandfather fathered a girl baptized Lucy Swift on July 29, 1771, i.e., she was conceived in late 1770.

119   *When Samuel Johnson made his "annual ramble":* Samuel Johnson to Hester Thrale, July 7, 11 and 14, 1770, in Johnson, vol. 1, pp. 344–45. Johnson stayed in Lichfield between July 2 and 18.

120   *"Harden their bodies"; "When reason begins to frighten them":* Rousseau (2010), pp. 173 and 192.

120   *Richard Warburton-Lytton, Day's friend:* Bulwer, (1883), vol. 1, p. 20.

120   *the surgeon John Hunter curtly demanded of one father:* Ottley, Drewry, *The Life of John Hunter, FRS,* in *The Works of John Hunter,* ed. Palmer, James (4 vols., London, 1834), vol. 1, p. 29.

121   *Behind the closed doors of Stowe:* Details of these trials in varying descriptions are from Seward (1804), pp. 29–30; Rev. Richard George Robinson quoted in Hopkins, p. 148; Anon (1819), p. 155; and Schimmelpenninck, p. 10. Although AS states that Day dropped wax on Sabrina's arms, Schimmelpenninck said it was her back and arms. There is no trace of the letter from Robinson cited in Hopkins.

122   *He had even suggested accustoming children to loud noises by firing pistols:* Rousseau (2010), p. 192. Many thanks to Mick Crumplin for his advice on eighteenth-century pistols.

123 *"I always discouraged every appearance of indolence & finery":* TD to SS, May 4, 1783, ERO, D/DBa C13. This letter was probably a draft as it contains various crossings-out and amendments.

124 *she was petrified of horses:* Rev. Richard George Robinson quoted in Hopkins, p. 148.

125 *"I never thought I had a right to sacrifice another being":* TD to SS, May 4, 1783, ERO, D/DBa C13.

125 *Dates and details of early Lunar Society:* Uglow; Robinson; Schofield.

125 *At one point he would reject an offer from Boulton:* TD to Matthew Boulton, October 29, 1780, Soho archives: Boulton Papers, MS 3782/12/81/104.

126 *Or as Boulton would delicately put it:* Matthew Boulton to Matthew Robinson Boulton (his son), October 26, 1789, Soho archives: Boulton Papers, MS 3782 /12/57/37.

126 *Day lent significant sums to Small, Keir and Boulton:* Day lent £400 to Small, which the doctor passed on to a friend, and £3,000 to Boulton to help weather his extensive losses following the credit collapse in 1772. He lent an unknown sum to Keir, according to Rowland. TD to Matthew Boulton, March 17, 1775, Soho archives: Boulton Papers MS 3782/12/81/84; Schofield, p. 53; Rowland, p. 100.

126 *The Lunar men would exchange views on education as their children grew:* King-Hele (1999), p. 83; Uglow, p. 124. King-Hele suggests that in Wright's painting, ED is the figure in profile on the left foreground and the boy behind him is his son Erasmus, then 8, while the boy on the right holding the cage is his son Charles, 9. Sukey Wedgwood and Maria Edgeworth both stayed with Day.

126 *Mary Anne Schimmelpenninck would certainly be:* Mary Anne Schimmelpenninck (née Galton), *Life of Mary Anne Schimmelpenninck,* ed. Christiana A. Hankin (London, 1860), p. 31.

127 *He had just bought a lease:* Moilliet and Smith; Moilliet, A.; Uglow, pp. 155–62; Smith, Barbara M. D., "Keir, James (1735–1820)," *Oxford Dictionary of National Biography* (Oxford University Press, 2004) online edition, accessed April 14, 2008. For more on Keir's glassmaking business and glass manufacture generally in eighteenth-century Staffordshire see Timmins, Samuel, "James Keir, FRS, 1735–1820," in *Transactions, Excursions and Report for the Year 1898, Birmingham and Midland Institute Archaeological Section,* 24, no. 74 (1899), pp. 1–5. The Stourbridge area boasted numerous glasshouses, which had first been established by French Protestant refugees in the seventeenth century. The glasshouse that Keir took over had been operating since that period.

127 *"some Lichfield fair":* JK to ED, August 20, 1766, cited in Moilliet, A., p. 48.

127 *"Nothing surely can be more absurd":* Keir, pp. 20–28.

127 *True to his name, Dr. Small:* Lane, Joan, "Small, William (1734–1775)," *Oxford Dictionary of National Biography* (Oxford University Press, 2004), online edition, accessed April 14, 2008.

128 *the doctor held "paramount" influence over Day:* Edgeworth, RL and M, vol. 1, p. 331.

128 *Small tried to persuade Day to abandon his Pygmalion project:* Keir, p. 31.

128 *"He never saw any woman":* Edgeworth, RL and M, vol. 1, pp. 331–32.

128 *"She betrayed an averseness to the study of books":* Seward (1804), p. 29.

128 *As Day would later put it:* TD to SS, May 4, 1783, ERO, D/DBa C13.

129 *The problem, as Seward acutely:* Seward (1804), p. 29.

129 *Sabrina herself would later tell a friend:* ME to Frances Edgeworth, October 13 and 15, 1818, in Edgeworth, M, p. 122.

129 *He would later tell Sabrina:* TD to SS, May 4, 1783, ERO, D/DBa C13.

130 *The ambiguity of Sabrina's situation: Watch and Ward* was initially published as a serialized story in 1871 and then as James's first book in 1878. The quotes are from pages 72 and 81. My thanks to Peter Rowland for drawing my attention to this work.

131 *It was Richard Lovell Edgeworth, bringing:* Edgeworth Senior died August 4, 1770. Johnston-Liik, E. M., *History of the Irish Parliament, 1692–1800* (Belfast, 2002), vol. 4, pp. 104–5. Emmeline was baptized "Emely" at Wargrave parish church on November 29, 1770. Wargrave parish register 1770.

131 *"curious to see how my friend's philosophic romance would end":* Edgeworth, RL and M, vol. 1, p. 213.

131 *She had "a beauty":* Edgeworth, RL and M, vol. 1, p. 213.

131 *Sabrina was "now too old to remain":* Edgeworth, RL and M, vol. 1, p. 240.

132 *he had found "a woman that equalled the picture of perfection":* Edgeworth, RL and M, vol. 1, p. 235.

132 *While she had been away with her father and sisters in Bath:* AS to Mary Powys, April 25, 1770, SJBM, 2001.76.1; AS to Mary Powys, June 25, 1786, Seward (1811), vol. 1, pp. 156–57.

132 *she told him he was the "first person":* Edgeworth, RL and M, vol. 1, p. 236.

133 *"Sabrina Sydney had, perhaps":* Edgeworth, RL and M, vol. 1, p. 240.

133 *After nearly twelve months of lessons:* AS said that the trials lasted twelve months; RLE stated that Sabrina was sent away in early 1771. Seward (1804), p. 29.

133 *he promptly "renounced all hope":* Seward (1804), pp. 29–30.

134 *If she worked hard, Day told her:* TD to SS, 4 May 1783, ERO, D/DBa C13.

134 *on no account to allow her to learn either music or dancing:* Edgeworth, RL and M, vol. 1, p. 240.

CHAPTER 7: ELIZABETH

135 *Named Sutton:* Main sources for background on Sutton Coldfield are Jones, Douglas, *The Royal Town of Sutton Coldfield* (Sutton Coldfield, 1984); Lea, Roger, *The Story of Sutton Coldfield* (Stroud, 2003); Anon, *The History of Sutton-Coldfield . . . by an impartial Hand* (London, 1762); and Riland, William Kirkpatrick, *Three Hundred Years of a Family Living, Being a History of the Rilands of Sutton Coldfield* (Birmingham, 1889).

137 *His trust in the power of education:* Seward (1804), pp. 29–30.

137 *Utterly confounded by his friend's indifference:* Edgeworth, RL and M, vol. 1, p. 241.

138 *A powerful dynasty, the Sneyd family:* Burke, vol. 2, pp. 1259–61; flyleaf of family bible belonging to Charlotte Sneyd, 1766, with dates of birth of children, Edgeworth Papers, MS 10166/3; Edward Sneyd's diaries, containing dates of birth of the family, Staffordshire Record Office, HM37/40. The first ten children were all girls. Four children, Eliza-Maria, Honora (the first with this name), Susanna and Harriet, did not survive childhood. Anne died in 1765, aged 19. The others were Lucy born February 9, 1748; Mary August 7, 1750; Honora (the second with this name) September 29, 1751; Elizabeth January 24, 1753, and Charlotte May 2, 1754. There were then two boys, Edward born September 28, 1755 and William February 28, 1757. Lucy married William Grove on September 19, 1768, and had five children. Mary was sent to live with an unmarried cousin Ann Sneyd, Edward's niece, who left a lively collection of household accounts detailing trips to assemblies, payments for gloves, gowns and shoes for herself and Mary, as well as presents for the other Sneyd girls.

138 *Three of the girls—Lucy, Honora and Elizabeth:* Sherwood, p. 10.

138 *Courted by a succession of admirers, Honora:* Sargent, Winthrop, *The Life and Career of Major John André* (New York, 1902); Garnett, Richard, "André, John, 1750–1780," *Oxford Dictionary of National Biography* (Oxford University Press, 2004) online edition, accessed July 26, 2011. The ODNB gives André's date of birth as May 2, 1750, but he describes himself as 18 in his letter to AS of October 3, 1769, suggesting that he was born in 1751. Three letters from André to AS are published in Seward, *Monody on Major André* (Lichfield, 1781), pp. 29–47.

139 *During his Christmas break with Day, Edgeworth:* Edgeworth, RL and M, vol. 1, p. 236.

140 *"marriage is often the grave of love":* Seward (1804), p. 24.

140 *In a letter to a friend, Seward divulged her scheme:* AS to Mary Powys, n.d. [c 1771], SJBM, 2001.76.2.

141 *Finally, Day wrote to Edgeworth:* Edgeworth, RL and M, vol. 1, pp. 241–43.

142 *"I saw him continually in company with Honora Sneyd":* Edgeworth, RL and M, vol. 1, pp. 242–43.

143 *Written out laboriously over several sheets of paper:* Edgeworth, RL and M, vol. 1, pp. 243–45. Day's marriage proposal and Honora's reply have not survived, but they are described in detail by RLE in his memoirs.

143 *Explaining her decision to Anna, Honora:* Seward (1804), p. 30.

144 *A few weeks later Major Sneyd:* Edward Sneyd's diaries, Staffordshire RO HM37/40. The third diary, for 1782, shows that Sneyd had accumulated £9,371.1.5 ½ by Christmas 1773 from shares in the Trent and Mersey Canal.

144 *"The domestic separation proved very grievous":* AS to Mrs T[emple] June 19, 1796, Seward (1811), vol. 4, p. 217; AS, "Time Past," written January 1773, in Seward (1810), vol. 1, pp. 87–88.

145 *a summer archery contest:* Edgeworth, RL and M, vol. 1, pp. 246–49.

145 *He had drawn swooning debutantes; jump clear over a dining table:* Edgeworth, RL and M, vol. 1, p. 92; Harriet Butler to Michael Pakenham Edgeworth, September 13, 1838, cited in Butler (1972), p. 41.

146 *It was as the air of a country dance:* Edgeworth, RL and M, vol. 1, pp. 247–49.

146 *Elizabeth was "very pretty, very sprightly":* Seward (1804), pp. 30–31.

147 *Having grown up with cousins:* Elizabeth Sneyd had been brought up in Shrewsbury in the care of her cousin Susannah Powys and her husband Henry, whose daughter Mary Powys—or "Po"—was AS's friend and regular correspondent.

147 *Anna Seward captured one such gathering in late July:* AS to Mary Powys, July 13 and 19, 1771, SJBM, 2001.76.3.

147 *Watching his friend fall under Elizabeth's spell:* Edgeworth, RL and M, vol. 1, p. 249.

148 *In the same way that artists, writers and philosophers:* Carter; Barker-Benfield; Davis, Leith, *The Polite Academy, or School of Behaviour for Young Gentlemen and Ladies* (London, 1762); Towle, Matthew, *The Young Gentleman and Lady's Private Tutor* (Oxford; London, 1770); Philpot, Stephen, *An Essay on the Advantages of a Polite Education Joined with a Learned One* (London, 1747). Barker-Benfield discusses Day specifically on pp. 149–53.

150 *"It is the graceful Motion of the Body in Walking":* Philpot, p. 68.

150 *Laurence Sterne had fun depicting a French peasant:* The books by Sterne, Mackenzie and Brooke are discussed in Barker-Benfield, pp. 142–49.

150 *It was Day's favorite novel:* Gignilliat, p. 264. Brooke, Henry, *The Fool of Quality, or the History of Henry Earl of Moreland* (5 vols., London, 1765–70). Day and Brooke had much in common besides a shared penchant for sentimental tales. Brooke trained as a lawyer at the Temple but was recalled to Ireland at the age of 17 by an aunt on her deathbed who begged him to become guardian to her beautiful 12-year-old daughter, Catherine. Brooke placed the orphan in a boarding school in Dublin, but within two years he eloped with her and they secretly married. The couple had 23 children, of whom only two lived to adulthood, before Catherine herself died, leaving Brooke heartbroken for the remaining ten years of his life. Brooke's tragic life is described by his daughter Charlotte in the preface to his poetical works. Brooke, Henry, *The Poetical Works . . . of Henry Brooke*, ed. Brooke, Charlotte (Dublin, 1792).

151 *Leaving Elizabeth to her books:* TD to AS, August 31, 1771, SJBM, 2001.71.60. In this letter Day refers to having left Lichfield 2 weeks before.

151 *Having returned to Paris the previous year:* Rousseau lived on the 5th floor (by British reckoning; the 6th floor in American and Continental terms) of 60 rue Plâtrière, since renamed rue Jean-Jacques Rousseau. Damrosch, pp. 466. His assimilation back into Parisian intellectual society and his lifestyle in Paris are described in Damrosch, pp. 463–76.

152 *Climbing the steep, dark stairs:* Edgeworth, RL and M, vol. 1, pp. 252–54. RLE describes the visit to Rousseau and Rousseau's walk with Dick.

152 *One visitor who was struck by this picture:* Bentley, p. 67.

153 *Rousseau returned to his visitors:* Edgeworth, RL and M, vol. 1, pp. 252–54.

153 *Moving rapidly on, the party:* Edgeworth, RL and M, vol. 1, p. 255.

153 *Since his father was busy directing teams:* Edgeworth, RL and M, vol. 1, pp. 268–74. Edgeworth describes the fluctuations of Dick's education in France.

155 *Meanwhile, lessons were proving equally:* Day's education is described by RLE and AS. Edgeworth, RL and M, vol. 1, pp. 255–56, 267–68 and 308–9; Seward (1804), p. 31.

155 *One acquaintance later said that Day:* Kippis.

156 *Writing from Lyon, he complained:* TD to AS, November 13, 1771, William Salt Library, S.MS 478/4/46.

156 *"I am a lac'd coat, a bag":* TD to AS, December 18, 1771, LRO, D262/1/6.

157 *In a rambling, almost incoherent letter:* TD to AS, begun December 31, 1771, finished January 1, 1772, SJBM, 2001.71.16.

158 *The correspondence at least brought some:* AS to Mary Powys, n.d. (c. 1771–72), SJBM, 2001.76.4.

158 *Anna's fortunes had taken a tumble:* Barnard, pp. 69–71; Hopkins, pp. 112–18.

158 *For the moment Seward had little:* AS to Dorothy Sykes, SJBM, May 1773 2001.72.1.

159 *Meanwhile, Edgeworth, at least, seemed ready:* Edgeworth, RL and M, vol. 1, p. 267; Butler, Marilyn (1972), p. 43. RLE wrote a contrite letter to Anna Maria in December 1771 in which he insisted he had already written to tell her he had decided to remain in Lyon. She must have joined him soon after in early 1772.

159 *After nearly a year of being groomed, coached and bullied:* Edgeworth, RL and M, vol. 1, p. 268; Seward (1804), pp. 31–32; TD to AS, dated March 14, 1771 (but probably 1772), SJBM, 2001.71.17. It is hard to date with certainty when Day returned from France to claim the hand of Elizabeth Sneyd. The various accounts conflict, in particular the letter from Day to AS, which he dated March 14, 1771, but which must have been written at a later date, most probably March 14, 1772. In this he refers to having been rejected by Elizabeth (and undergoing his training in polite manners); since she had not appeared in Lichfield before the summer of 1771, he could not have written the letter before then. He also discusses AS's misery over her parents' refusal to let her see Saville and the contempt shown by some people in Lichfield for Saville; these events erupted in early 1772. Day dated other letters erroneously too. The letter is cited in Hopkins, p. 156, where it is also dated March 14, 1772, without any discussion over the discrepancy.

159 *Some of them merely "lamented, very pathetically":* Kippis.

159 *"The studied bow on entrance":* Seward (1804), pp. 31–32.

160 *A furious and tearful row:* Domestic accounts of Mrs. Anne Sneyd, 1765–1782, Staffordshire RO, HM24/3. Anne Sneyd was a niece of Edward Sneyd, who looked after his daughter Mary when her mother died. Her accounts refer to "assembly for myself and Miss E Sneyd" in March 1772. Day's poem, "Celia," at the end of his letter to AS describes the angry words and tears. TD to AS, dated March 14, 1771 [but probably 1772], SJBM, 2001.71.17.

160 *Even Darwin's son, also named Erasmus:* Erasmus Darwin Jr. to Robert Waring Darwin [1776], cited in Uglow, p. 321.

160 *a mock court case entitled "The Trial of A. B.":* Day, Thomas and Esther (1805), pp. 75–90.

161 *Retreating back to Paris:* TD to Anna Seward, dated March 14, 1771 [but probably 1772], SJBM, 2001.71.17.

161 *Mixing in Parisian intellectual circles, Day met Amélie Suard:* ME (1979), pp. 31 and 40, citing letters from RLE to Charlotte Sneyd, November 18, 1802, and ME to Margaret Ruxton, December 1, 1802. Meeting M. and Mme Suard, RLE wrote: "Would you believe it, Mr. Day paid his court to her thirty years ago?" ME wrote that she had met Mme Suard "with whom *it is said* Mr. Day was in love—."

162 *Stopping at an inn in the town:* "An Ode supposed to have been written on an Inn Window in Sutton-Coldfield, and signed T. D., July 24, 1772," Pearson papers, 577, UCL Special Collections. I am indebted to Desmond King-Hele for drawing my attention to this poem, which he found among a collection of papers belonging to Erasmus Darwin.

162 *Rousseau, for one, had scribbled:* Damrosch, pp. 457–58.

163 *Soon afterward, Edgeworth was warned:* Edgeworth, RL and M, vol. 1, pp. 310–12.

163 *In the New Year Edgeworth made one last:* RLE to Anna Maria Edgeworth, January 12, 1773, cited in Butler, Marilyn (1972) p. 45.

163 *It was probably the last letter:* Anna Maria Edgeworth was buried on March 30, 1773, at Black Bourton. Black Bourton parish register.

163 *Maria, now five, would remember:* Edgeworth, FA, pp. 1–2.

163 *Edgeworth received the news:* AS wrote to Dorothy Sykes in May 1773 to say that Edgeworth was still in France "unless this event has brought him over within the last fortnight." AS to Dorothy Sykes, May 1773, SJBM, 2001.72.1.

164 *Poor little Maria, bereft:* Harriet Butler to Michael Pakenham Edgeworth, January 3, 1838, cited in Butler, Marilyn (1972), p. 46.

164 *A letter from Day awaited him:* Edgeworth, RL and M, vol. 1, pp. 318–21; AS to Dorothy Sykes, May 1773, SJBM, 2001.72.1.

164 *Scandalizing many of their friends and relations:* AS describes the wedding and the reactions of friends and family in two letters. AS to Dorothy Sykes, July 27, 1773, and AS to Mary Powys, n.d. (c. July 1773), SJBM, 2001.72.3 and 2001.76.5.

165 *she now enjoyed "the utmost happiness":* AS to Dorothy Sykes, July 27, 1773, SJBM, 2001.72.3.

165 *Her beloved Saville had now left his family home:* Hopkins, p. 114; Sherwood, p. 80.

165 *Destined therefore to live a single life:* AS to Dorothy Sykes, July 27, 1773, SJBM, 2001.72.3.

166 *Day suffered more stoically:* Edgeworth, RL and M, vol. 1, pp. 321–25.

CHAPTER 8: SABRINA

169 The Dying Negro *related the true story:* TD and JB, *The Dying Negro* (W. Flexney, London, 1773). All quotes are taken from the first edition of 1773 unless otherwise stated. The original news item was published in the *Morning Chronicle* on May 28, 1773. The 1793 edition denotes which lines were written by Bicknell and which by Day, according to a manuscript in Esther Day's pos-

session. Of the 441 total lines in the 1793 edition, Bicknell wrote 181 and Day 260. The poem was reviewed in the *Monthly Review*, July 1773, p. 63. The poem and its contribution to the abolition movement are discussed in Carey, pp. 73–84, and Kitson, Peter J., and Lee, Debbie et al., eds, *Slavery, Abolition and Emancipation: writings in the British romantic period* (8 vols., London, 1995), vol. 4, pp. 9. Brycchan Carey hosts a useful website on British abolitionists: http://www.brycchancarey.com/. General information on slaves in London in the eighteenth century is from Gerzina.

170   *Bicknell had just become a commissioner of bankrupts:* Bicknell's appointment as one of the commissioners of bankrupts was announced in July 1773: *Lloyd's Evening Post,* July 19, 1773. He surrendered his chambers at 1 Garden Court on May 15, 1773: MT archives, Box 93, bundle 4, 27. Bicknell advertised his services from chambers at New Court in various London newspapers from 1774 onward.

170   *Middle Temple had been a magnet for settlers from the American colonies:* For background information on the history of Middle Temple and its American connections see Stockdale and Holland; Stockdale; Macassey. Many thanks to Eric Stockdale for his hospitality and help in exploring Middle Temple's colorful past.

171   *"Pray have you read the dying Negro":* AS to Mary Powys, n.d. (c. July 1773), SJBM, 2001.76.5.

174   *he took lodgings with his old university chum William Jones:* Cannon, pp. 55–56. Middle Temple archives have no record of Day living at Pump Court—he was probably an unofficial tenant of Jones. Records show Day later leased chambers in Elm Court.

174   *"the practice of rearing and killing animals for food":* Keir, pp. 131–32. The spider anecdote is described in Cannon, pp. 55–56.

174   *He had met Benjamin Franklin:* Franklin was a friend of Darwin and Small; he had originally introduced Small to Boulton in 1765. Franklin first met Day on a tour of the Midlands and north in May 1771, in Lichfield. He had originally arrived in England in 1757 with two slaves, named Peter and King, but when King absconded Franklin seemed happy to hear that he had been adopted by a kindly Englishwoman who was educating him in Suffolk. By 1772 Franklin had become an ardent critic of slavery. In a letter to the *London Chronicle* of June 18–20, 1772, he attacked the British for celebrating the freeing of one slave when 850,000 more were enslaved in England and its colonies. Labaree, Leonard W., ed., *The Papers of Benjamin Franklin* (40 vols., New Haven; London, 1959–1973), vol. 18, pp. 113–16 and 187–88; and vol. 19, pp. 210–12; King-Hele (1999), p. 100. For more on Franklin see Isaacson's biography and Skemp, Sheila L., *Benjamin and William Franklin: father and son, patriot and loyalist* (Boston, 1994).

174   *Meeting at Franklin's lodgings in Craven Street:* Williams; Robinson, Eric, "R. E. Raspe, Franklin's 'Club of Thirteen,' and the Lunar Society," *Annals of Science,* 11 (1955), pp. 142–44. The quotes from Williams are from his wonderful autobiography with additional research by Peter France.

175   *he would later set up the Royal Literary Fund:* The Literary Fund was established by Williams in 1790 and became the Royal Literary Fund in 1842. It survives to this day.

176   *Mounting anger at Britain's determination to tax:* See Isaacson, pp. 249–50 and 276–78 for Franklin's dressing down by the Privy Council and passim for the slow evolution of his support for complete independence from Britain. For general background on the American war of independence see Ferling; Rakove; and Black, Jeremy, *War for America: the fight for independence 1775–1783* (Stroud, UK; New York, 1994).

176   *Discussing the vexed question of independence with American friends:* The Middle Temple Buttery Book shows that Day began dining in the hall from April 1774 at the same time as various American students including John Laurens, Thomas Pinckney and John F. Grimké. MT Buttery Book 3, 1773–76, MT7 /BUB/3.

176   *hundreds of thousands of slaves were working cotton:* Rakove, p. 206.

176   *Many of the most prominent Americans lobbying for independence:* Ferling, *Setting the World Ablaze,* pp. 44, 48 and 54; Bernstein, R. B., *Thomas Jefferson* (New York, 2003), p. 111. Re Jefferson see also http://www.monticello.org/site /plantation-and-slavery/thomas-jefferson-and-sally-hemings-brief-account.

176   *walking the streets of Georgian London with black slaves:* For fascinating background on Americans living in London in the eighteenth century and specific details on their ownership of slaves see Flavell, p. 91 and passim; and Gerzina. Also see Flavell, Julie, "A New Tour of Georgian London's Fleet Street Shows: Its mixed race American side" at http://yalepress.wordpress.com/2011/11/16/.

177   *reprint of the popular poem:* TD and JB, *The Dying Negro* (2nd edn., London, 1774). And see Carey, pp. 73–84. Day wrote 44 of the extra 54 lines and Bicknell 10. The preface to the 1793 edition states that Day wrote the entire dedication, but it seems likely that he consulted Bicknell, judging from his references to it in his letter to JB from The Hague, which is included in the third edition. TD and JB, *The Dying Negro* (3rd edn., London, 1793).

178   *she had "gained the esteem" of her teachers:* Seward (1804), p. 36; AS states that Sabrina was at school for three years.

178   *Instead Day brusquely informed her:* TD to SS, May 4, 1783, ERO, D/DBa C13. There is no trace of any Parkinsons working as dressmakers in surviving records. My thanks to archivists of the Victoria and Albert Museum for checking. For background information on the work of mantua-makers see Buck, Anne, *Dress in Eighteenth-century England* (London, 1979); and same, "Mantuamakers and Milliners: women making and selling clothes in eighteenth-century Bedfordshire," in *Bedfordshire Historical Miscellany,* 72 (1993), pp. 142–55.

179   *Day made plain both to Sabrina and to the Parkinsons:* TD to SS, May 4, 1783, ERO, D/DBa C13. The following quotes are all from this letter, which was probably a draft.

179   *According to Seward, Sabrina had matured:* Seward (1804), p. 36.

180 *"a beauty" in the words of Dr. Small:* William Small to James Watt, October 19, 1771, Soho archives: Boulton Papers, MS 340/17.

181 *Sending letters back to Bicknell and his mother:* TD to JB, August 4, 1774, printed in TD and JB, *The Dying Negro* (3rd edn., London, 1793), pp. v–viii; TD to Jane Phillips (his mother), August 10, 1774, printed in Lowndes (1825–27), vol. 2, pp. 3–5.

182 *they published a satirical attack on plans to provide music lessons:* Collier, Joel (pseudonym for John Bicknell), *Musical Travels through England* (London, 1774); Lonsdale, Roger, "Dr. Burney, 'Joel Collier,' and Sabrina," in Ribeiro, Alvaro and Wellek, René, eds., *Evidence in Literary Scholarship: essays in memory of James Marshall Osborn* (Oxford, 1979), pp. 281–308. In this fascinating essay, Lonsdale suggests that Bicknell alone wrote the first and second editions, on the basis that Day was abroad when they were published, and that the pair collaborated on the third edition. A friend of Bicknell, Francis Douce, however, stated that Day and Bicknell wrote the tract together. Since the pamphlet smacks so plainly of their combined views, it seems highly likely it was a collaboration in some form.

184 *"a spirit of discord pervading the country":* Williams, p. 17.

184 *John Laurens enrolled as a student at Middle Temple:* John Laurens to Henry Laurens, January 20, 1775, in Laurens, vol. 9, pp. 587–88; vol. 10, p. 34. John Laurens described Charles Bicknell as "the merest machine in the world—the most barren in Conversation and least calculated to improve, of any Man I ever was connected with" but he found John Bicknell far more likable. "The elder brother is a sensible Fellow, and I cultivate his acquaintance as much as possible." When Henry Laurens arrived in London in 1771, he brought a slave called Scipio, who changed his name to Robert to blend in better with English domestic life. Other information on Henry and John Laurens is from Laurens; Jones, E. Alfred, *American Members of the Inns of Court* (London, 1924); Massey, Gregory D., *John Laurens and the American Revolution* (Columbia, SC, 2000); Stockdale (2005), Stockdale and Holland; Flavell, pp. 7–113; Rakove, pp. 198–238, especially pp. 200–218.

185 *In an eloquent and forceful letter to Henry Laurens:* TD, *Fragment of an Original Letter on the Slavery of the Negroes, written in the year 1776* (London, 1784). This tract was published by Day's usual publisher John Stockdale. The recipient of Day's letter is anonymous. In the preface Day wrote that he was induced to write the letter by John Laurens to an American slave owner. It seems most likely that it was Henry Laurens.

185 *"America is our child":* Elizabeth Montagu to Elizabeth Vesey, February 3, 1776, in Montagu, Elizabeth, *Mrs. Montagu "Queen of the Blues": her letters and friendships from 1762 to 1800*, ed. Blunt, Reginand (London, 1923), vol. 1, p. 139.

186 *Day told Boulton to "give a sigh to the dead":* TD to Matthew Boulton, March 17, 1775, Soho archives: Boulton Papers, MS 3782/12/81/84.

186 *"My loss is as inexpressable":* Matthew Boulton to James Watt, February 25, 1775, Soho archives: Watt Papers, MS 3219/4/62 and MS 3219/4/66; Keir, pp. 92–93; Uglow, pp. 249–50.

186 *Finding himself dazed and adrift in Lichfield, after Small's funeral:* Edgeworth states that Day reignited his relationship with Sabrina before Small died, but he was almost certainly trying to blur events to protect Day's reputation in view of his later marriage. Edgeworth, RL and M, vol. 1, p. 332. Day told Sabrina that he revived their relationship "upon the death of Doctor Small."TD to SS, May 4, 1783, ERO, D/DBa C13.

186 *Day would refer to them when writing to Sabrina as "your friends":* TD to SS, May 4, 1783, ERO, D/DBa C13. The ensuing quotes are from this letter, which was probably a draft.

188 *"I therefore determined," wrote Day:* TD to SS, May 4, 1783, ERO, D/DBa C13. The details of this final trial are taken from the letter from Day to Sabrina in which he describes his whole experiment on her, Edgeworth's memoirs and the description of Sabrina's story by Fanny Burney, written as a French exercise for her husband. Edgeworth, RL and M, vol. 1, pp. 332–35; Burney, French Exercise Book (Berg).

189 *Seward noted that Day:* Seward (1804), p. 37.

189 *Sabrina would later regard the Keirs "with great resentment":* ME to Frances Edgeworth, October 15, 1818, in Edgeworth, M (1971), p. 122.

189 *She was either pregnant:* JK to Charles Darwin (ED's son), May 2, 1776, in Moilliet, A., p. 54. Keir refers to "your godson." The baby died in infancy. Day was still spending much of his time at his law studies in London; records show him dining in Middle Temple Hall with Bicknell, William Jones and John Laurens on numerous occasions in 1775. MT Buttery Book 3, 1773–76, MT7 /BUB/3.

190 *As Eliza miserably told Professor Higgins:* Shaw, p. 101.

190 "She surpassed all his ideas": Burney, French Exercise Book (Berg).

191 *Since there were few neighbors and fewer diversions:* Edgeworth, RL and M, vol. 1, pp. 326–29.

191 *"If it is happy for us, which it certainly is":* Honora Edgeworth to Mary Powys, May 5, 1775, Edgeworth Papers, MS 10,166/9.

191 *Life was not quite so joyful:* Butler, HJ and HE, p. 159. The sofa belonged to her Aunt Fox, RLE's eldest sister.

192 *Edgeworth had seriously doubted she could ever become "sufficiently cultivated":* Edgeworth, RL and M, vol. 1, pp. 332–35. Succeeding quotes by RLE are from these pages.

193 *"I studiously avoided the word marriage to you":* TD to SS, May 4, 1783, ERO, D/DBa C13.

193 *"He finally explained to Sabrina":* Burney, French Exercise Book (Berg).

195 *It was a "trifling" consideration:* Edgeworth, RL and M, vol. 1, pp. 334–35.

195 *"She completely disappeared for a few hours":* Burney, French Exercise Book (Berg). FB may well be embroidering events here. She said that Sabrina had run off to get married to Bicknell although this only happened many years later.

196 *He dispatched Sabrina immediately to a boardinghouse:* Seward (1804), p. 36. Picard gives the annual wage of a housemaid as between £6 and £8; the American law student John Dickinson estimated £120 was needed to live frugally.

Picard, Liza, *Dr. Johnson's London* (London, 2000), p. 297; Colbourn, H. Trevor, "A Pennsylvanian Farmer at the Court of King George: John Dickinson's London Letters, 1754–1756," in *The Pennsylvania Magazine of History and Biography*, 86, no. 3 (1962), pp. 241–85, specifically p. 275.

196 *"my checker'd & adventurous history"*: Sabrina Bicknell to ME, October 29, 1818, Edgeworth Papers, MS 22470/15.

197 *Edgeworth would feel concerned that he had somehow "betrayed"*: Edgeworth, RL and M, vol. 1, pp. 345–46.

CHAPTER 9: ESTHER

199 *Clever, amiable and wealthy, at twenty-three, Esther Milnes:* Information on the Milnes family is from Walker, John William, *Wakefield, Its History and People* (Wakefield, 1934), pp. 345 and 397–98; Burke, vol. 2, pp. 868–69; Glover, Stephen, *The History and Gazetteer of the County of Derby* (Derby, 1831), p. 323; Betham, William, *The Baronetage of England* (5 vols., London, 1803–5), vol. 5, p. 449–50; TD and Esther Day (1805). Much of the family history information in printed sources is inaccurate; for example, Elizabeth was not the eldest daughter. Esther was baptized on October 15, 1752: Chesterfield parish records. My thanks to Jacky Worthington for help in tracing the Milnes nephews.

200 *Esther addressed flattering odes to her best friends:* Some of Esther's poems, hymns and juvenile letters are reproduced in TD and Esther Day (1805).

200 *Writing to one friend, who was about to travel to India:* EM to Caroline Purling, September 2, 1767, Essex RO, D/DBa C14; and EM to Frances Sewell, November 11, 1769, Essex RO, D/DBa C15. After persuading her family to let her marry Matthew Lewis in 1772, Frances later ran off with a music teacher.

201 *Exhorting one friend to avoid the "giddy, fantastick whirl of amusements":* EM to Caroline Purling, c. 1768, in TD and Esther Day (1805), pp. 139–44.

201 *In a juvenile essay, on "Politeness," Esther scorned:* TD and Esther Day (1805), pp. 151–52.

201 *Esther sent Robert a tender poem:* EM, "To Miss M.'s brother in law Mr. L," in TD and Esther Day (1805), pp. 47–48.

202 *Esther's Aunt Ann urged her to tell Robert:* Ann Wilkinson to EM, March 6, April 8 and October 25 (1769), Essex RO, D/DBa C16. Ann Wilkinson was married to Richard Wilkinson of Chesterfield, a cousin of Esther's father Richard Milnes. The Wilkinsons acted as guardians to EM.

202 *Aunt Esther admitted it was "a very difficult question":* Esther Milnes (EM's aunt) to Esther Milnes, February 3, 1773, Essex RO, D/DBa C18.

202 *promising a bequest for a young girl, a foundling:* EM's incomplete will, 1777, leaving £5 annuity to a foundling called Tabitha Parker, who lived with her aunt, also named Esther Milnes, Essex RO, D/DBa F65.

203 *Esther had first met Day in 1774:* Edgeworth says EM was 22 or 23 when she met TD. He describes the conversation between TD and Small. The meeting must have taken place before Small's gradual decline from the end of 1774. It

was obviously, therefore, before Day took up with Sabrina for the second time. Edgeworth, RL and M, vol. 1, p. 336. RLE describes the romance with EM. Edgeworth, RL and M, vol. 1, pp. 335–38.

203 *She sometimes stayed with relatives in Temple Row:* Fanny Sewell to EM (at Joseph Wilkinson's, Temple Row, Birmingham), November 5, 1772, ERO, D /DBa C15.

203 *According to Edgeworth, the doctor waited:* Edgeworth wrote that Day met Esther before Small's death, but Day plainly stated that he took up with Sabrina a second time soon after Small died. Edgeworth, RL and M, vol. 1, pp. 336–37; TD to SS, May 4, 1783, ERO, D/DBa C13.

203 *Day demanded to know whether the talented Miss Milnes possessed:* Day's inquisition regarding Esther's virtues is described by Edgeworth. Edgeworth, RL and M, vol. 1, pp. 335–38.

204 *"My affection for you was the spontaneous effusion":* Esther Day to TD, n.d. (c. 1782), Essex RO, D/DBa C12.

205 *"no more than esteem & friendship," she would later say:* Esther Day to TD, n.d. (c. 1782), Essex RO, D/DBa C12.

205 *At one point Esther sent Day some verses:* TD and Esther Day (1805), pp. 1–5. There are preceding pages that are unnumbered.

206 *he wrote another of his many poems on unrequited love:* TD, "Verses Addressed to a Young Lady, 1775," in TD and Esther Day (1805), p. 25.

206 *a fiercely pro-American poem,* Ode for the New Year: TD, *Ode for the New Year 1776* (J. Almon, London, 1776); Day, *The Devoted Legions* (J. Ridley, London, 1776). Day published a further poem, *The Desolation of America*, which reprised his attack on the British government's war with America, in 1777.

206 *Day sauntered along to a meeting of the Club of Thirteen:* Williams, pp. 20–22; Bentley, pp. 59–66. Bentley describes the trip to visit Rousseau and Williams describes its consequences.

208 *A silver paper tray, which Day ordered:* MB to TD, December 18, 1776, Letter book G, p. 780, Soho archives: Boulton Papers, MS 3782/1/10. The story of Day's engagement to Elizabeth Hall is described in a letter, Emma Sophie Galton to Charles Darwin, November 12, 1879, Cambridge University Library, DAR 210.14.34, quoted by permission of the Syndics of Cambridge University Library. I am indebted to Desmond King-Hele for directing me to this reference to Elizabeth Hall. King-Hele suggests that the tray was meant for Darwin's sister Susannah, his housekeeper, who was 48 in 1777, which is also plausible.

209 *hasty marriage with Roger Vaughton:* Smith, E., "Vaughton family history" (1995), transcript at SOG, p. 18. Desmond King-Hele has suggested that the hurry over the marriage could have been due to Elizabeth being already pregnant by Day. Her first child, Elizabeth Anne, was baptized on July 8, 1778, ten months after the wedding although of course the baptism could have been delayed to guard her mother's reputation. King-Hele, personal communication.

209 *Day was pressing Matthew Boulton to pay the interest:* TD to MB, various letters 1776 and 1777, for example, January 29, 1777, December 13, 1777, Soho

archives: Boulton Papers MS 3782/12/81/88 and 95; TD to MB, December 21, 1777, MS 3782/12/81/97.

210 *"With Mr. Day there were a thousand small preliminaries":* Edgeworth, RL and M, vol. 1, pp. 337–38; Keir, p. 46.

210 *During their courtship she wrote:* EM to TD, scrap of letter, n.d.; and TD to EM, n.d., ERO, D/DBa C12.

211 *Writing to the Wilkinsons in the first half of 1778, Day:* TD to Richard Wilkinson, n.d. (1778), ERO, D/DBa C10.

211 *The novelist Tobias Smollett described the mixed bathing:* Smollett, Tobias, *Humphrey Clinker* (London, 1967, first published 1771), p. 75.

212 *Day would later tell his old chum Bicknell:* TD to JB, n.d., cited in *European Magazine*, 2 (1795), pp. 21–22.

212 *Thomas Day finally married Esther Milnes:* Marriage of TD and EM, August 7, 1778, Marriage register St. James's Church, Bath Record Office. Richard Warburton Lytton was one of the witnesses.

212 *"I hope he will contrive to be happy":* Josiah Wedgwood to Thomas Bentley, August 24, 1778, Wedgwood, Josiah, *Letters of Josiah Wedgwood*, ed. Farrar, Katherine Euphemia, Lady (3 vols., Manchester, 1903), vol. 2, p. 443.

212 *A month later, Keir:* JK to MB, October 20, 1778, Boulton Papers, MS 3782 /12/65/24.

213 *She pronounced Esther "extremely engaging":* AS to Mary Powys, n.d. (1788) SJBM, 2001.76.18.

213 *All their friends at least were in no doubt that Day and Esther:* Keir, p. 46; Edgeworth, RL and M, vol. 2, p. 122; TD and Esther Day (1805), p. 34.

214 *"by living in inconvenient lodgings":* Edgeworth, RL and M, vol. 1, pp. 339–40. The succeeding quotes by RLE are from here.

214 *he told Darwin's son Erasmus Junior:* TD to Erasmus Darwin Jr., January 29, 1779, BL Add. MS 29300 f 55.

214 *a silver coffeepot and steak dish:* MB (Boulton and Fothergill) to TD, March 13, 1779, Soho archives: Boulton Papers MS 3782/1/11/387.

215 *"The house was indifferent and the land worse":* Edgeworth, RL and M, vol. 1, p. 342.

215 *continued to pay them during the winter:* Keir, p. 48.

215 *One laborer would later remember:* Edgeworth, M (1971), p. 111. This is related by ME when she visits the farm in 1818.

215 *Edgeworth was paying his friend a visit:* Edgeworth, RL and M, vol. 1, p. 343.

216 *Day proudly boasted to Bicknell:* TD to JB, n.d., cited in *European Magazine*, 2 (1795), pp. 21–22.

216 *It was probably an exaggeration when Anna Seward:* Seward (1804), pp. 34–35.

216 *"the dearest object to me, which this world affords"; "my whole soul":* TD to Richard Wilkinson, n.d., ERO, D/DBa C10; Esther Day to TD, n.d. (c. 1782), ERO, D/DBa C12.

217 *a sequel to* Émile: Rousseau (1783).

217   *she even contemplated separating from Day forever:* Esther Day to TD, n.d. (c. 1782) and same to same, March 21, 1783, ERO, D/DBa C12. The following quotes about the Days' rows are all from these letters.

219   *As the telltale symptoms of consumption weakened Honora's health:* Edgeworth, RL and M, vol. 1, pp. 358–69. Honora's last letter, to unnamed recipient, n.d. (1780), Edgeworth Papers, MS 10,166/25. The letter is also reproduced in RLE's memoirs, vol. 1, p. 369. The poem quoted is "The Fireside" by Nathaniel Cotton, a physician who was also a poet popular at the time.

220   *"She now lies dead beside me":* RLE to ME, May 2, 1780, Edgeworth Papers, MS 10166/31.

220   *He attended the funeral in a trance:* Edgeworth, RL and M, vol. 1, pp. 367–68. RLE also relates the visit to the Days.

221   *When the Edgeworths had called at the palace:* AS to Mary Sykes, June 1, 1776, SJBM, 2001.72.9.

221   *The phantom of her idealized woman:* AS, "Lichfield, An Elegy," in Seward (1810), vol. 1, p. 89–100.

221   *"the specious, the false, the cruel, the murderous Edgeworth":* AS to Thomas Sedgewick Whalley, September 3, 1791, in Whalley, vol. 2, p. 56.

221   *Elizabeth had previously described Edgeworth:* Edgeworth, RL and M, vol. 1, pp. 371–74.

222   *Edgeworth wrote to Boulton:* MB to RLE, February 25, 1781, Soho archives, Boulton Papers, MS 3782/12/5/3.

222   *"To my inexpressible concern my Daugr. Elizabeth":* Edward Sneyd's diaries, Staffordshire RO, HM37/40. Will (canceled) of Edward Sneyd of Lichfield 1780, Staffordshire RO, HM37/37.

222   *Edgeworth wrote in an uncharacteristic fury:* RLE to Margaret Ruxton, November 28, 1780, Edgeworth Papers, MS 10166/36.

222   *Edgeworth and Elizabeth headed for London:* Note, Harriot Edgeworth's hand, Edgeworth Papers, MS 10166/38.

222   *He had finally been called to the bar in 1779:* Day was called to the bar on May 14, 1779. MT archives, Barristers Ledger, MT3/BAL/2. Day's letters to Walter Pollard, a lawyer friend, describe his tenancy at 10 Furnival Inn: BL Add. MS 35655. Pollard was the son of a physician who had a large practice in Barbados until it was destroyed by a tornado. With his access to fellow Americans, he played a key role in providing Day with information on the American campaign.

222   *Day became a leading figure in the reform movement:* Day also helped found the Society for Constitutional Information, which began publishing and distributing subversive propaganda, including Day's speeches, in support of sweeping constitutional reforms. For background on this and the reform movement in general see Christie, Ian R., *Wilkes, Wyvill and Reform: the parliamentary reform movement in British politics, 1760–1785* (London, New York, 1962), pp. 68–115; Butterfield, Herbert, *George III, Lord North and the People, 1779–80* (London, 1949), pp. 256, 284–88, 295 and 350–51; TD, *Two Speeches of Thomas Day, Esq, at the General Meetings of the Counties of Cambridge and Essex*

(London, 1780). The speeches were published by the Society for Constitutional Information. Day was encouraged to stand for Parliament by the physician Dr. John Jebb and Erasmus Darwin, but Day insisted he was not one of the "bought and buying tribe." Keir, pp. 121–23.

223 *Ever since Day had pledged support for American independence:* The letters between Day and Laurens are all from Laurens as follows: TD to HL, September 1, 1782, in vol. 15, p. 604; HL to TD, December 23, 1782; TD to HL, January 5, 1783; and TD to HL, June 29, 1783, in vol. 16, pp. 94–97, 116–123 and 221–223. TD briefly considered emigrating to the new United States but told Laurens that he would "rather be buried in the ruins of this my native country, than transplant my fortunes to another." For general information on Day's friendship with Henry Laurens see Stockdale (2005).

224 *Anningsley Park near Chertsey in Surrey:* Kippis. Anningsley Park is described in Blackman, pp. 100–101; and WCB and TJR, *Handbook of Chertsey and the Neighbourhood* (Chertsey, 1870), pp. 76–79.

224 *"I have never expected any thing romantic":* TD to RLE, 1788, and RLE to TD, 1788, in Edgeworth, RL and M, vol. 2, pp. 87–91.

224 *"Mr. Day's austere simplicity of life":* Edgeworth, FA, pp. 11–12.

224 *"a tall man, with a grave and precise face":* Bulwer, pp. 20–21.

225 *He would eventually settle in America:* Dick settled on the border of North Carolina and South Carolina and married Elizabeth Knight in 1788. They had three sons, Nathanial Lovell, Achilles Sneyd and Richard Lovell. Dick's many descendants are scattered across America. See Edgar E. MacDonald (ed.), *The Education of the Heart: the correspondence of Rachel Mordecai Lazarus and Maria Edgeworth* (Chapel Hill, NC, 1977), p. 320.

225 *Dick would provide Jane Austen with the model:* Austen, Jane, *Persuasion* (Harmondsworth, UK, 1965, first published 1818), pp. 76–77; Douthwaite, pp. 136–38. Douthwaite provides a fascinating portrait of Dick's education as well as discussing Day's efforts to educate Sabrina and Manon Roland's attempt to educate her daughter Eudora according to Roussueau's ideas.

225 *"He would sit quietly while a child":* ME fondly describes her father's methods of educating his children and their work together writing their educational manual in Edgeworth, RL and M, vol. 2, pp. 180–84. Their commonsense approach is described in their enduringly valuable book, RLE and ME, *Practical Education* (2 vols., London, 1798). See also Douthwaite, Julia, "Experimental Child-rearing After Rousseau," in *Irish Journal of Feminist Studies*, 2, no. 2 (1997), pp. 35–56; and Uglow, pp. 315–16. ME and RLE developed a loving and fruitful partnership. In letters to Maria, RLE would describe himself as "Your critic, partner, father, friend." See RLE to ME, August 4, 1804, in Edgeworth, RL and M, vol. 2, p. 353.

226 *As part of his lifelong interest in education:* Edgeworth, RL and M, vol. 2, pp. 334–36; Josiah Wedgwood to ED, 1779, cited in Schofield, p. 132.

226 The History of Sandford and Merton: TD (1783, 1786, 1789). I am indebted to Peter Rowland for his work in tracing references by various writers to Day's book. Rowland, preface, pp. ix–x, 207–48 and 351. Thomas Beddoes describes Day being mobbed by young fans in Beddoes to Davies Giddy, November 21,

1791, cited in Stock, John Edmonds, *Memoirs of T. Beddoes, MD, with an analytical account of his writings* (London, Bristol, 1811), p. 38. For general information on Day as a children's writer and his book see Doyle, Brian, *The Who's Who of Children's Literature* (London, 1969), pp. 70–72; and Immel, Andrea, "Thomas Day" in Zipes, Jack, ed., *The Oxford Encyclopedia of Children's Literature* (4 vols., Oxford, 2006), vol. 1, p. 390. Barker-Benfield discusses how *Sandford and Merton* reflects contemporary ideas of sensibility: Barker-Benfield, pp. 150–53.

227 *Day's children's novel would be reprinted 140 times by 1870:* Uglow, p. 322. The latest edition, with a new introduction and notes on the text, is TD, *The History of Sandford and Merton*, ed. Bending, Stephen and Bygrave, Stephen (Peterborough, ON, 2009).

228 *"the subject of his own pleasantry":* Keir, p. 27.

228 *thinking of adopting a peasant boy:* TD to RLE, two letters, n.d., in Edgeworth, RL and M, vol. 2, pp. 95–100.

CHAPTER 10: VIRGINIA, BELINDA AND MARY

229 *she obtained work as a lady's companion:* Seward, p. 36; Edgeworth, RL and M, vol. 2, p. 109. The subsequent quote by Seward is from here.

229 *Day had felt the need to write a will:* Will of Thomas Day, May 26, 1780, probate 11/1188.

230 *"We are unable to fix the time till Sabrina comes":* John Saville to Henry White, August 16, 1780, SJBM, 2001.71.30. Baptism register, Lichfield, St. Mary's, August 25, 1780, LRO. Eliza had married Thomas Smith in Lichfield Cathedral on November 25, 1777, with her father's consent. Marriage register, The Close, Lichfield, November 25, 1777, LRO.

230 *Sabrina received a marriage proposal from an eligible young suitor:* TD to Sabrina Sidney (n.d.), acrostic and draft letter, ERO, D/DBa C13. The letter must have been sent before 1783. There is no trace of Wardley's acrostic, only Day's draft reply. Wardley's details are from the apprentice register, Newport, Shropshire, January 3, 1771. The letter from Darwin is ED to Mr [Jarvis] Wardley, November 28, 1786, in King-Hele (2007), pp. 263–64.

231 *Sabrina grew close to a young woman:* Schimmelpenninck, p. 10; Jean-André de Luc, sometimes spelled Deluc, visited Soho in 1782 when he was shown around by Watt. The following year he performed some experiments with Watt. Schofield, pp. 240–41. Fanny arrived from Switzerland in 1783. De Luc told a friend he was going to visit his daughter in Birmingham in February 1783. De Luc to Gen Haldimand Courlet, February 16, 1783, BL Add. MS 21731 f 29. My thanks to Lorna Clark for mutual detective work to track down Fanny.

232 *The expanding city that she could see from the windows:* Background on eighteenth-century Birmingham is from Skipp, Victor, *A History of Greater Birmingham: down to 1830* (Birmingham, 1980); Hutton, William, *An History of Birmingham* (2nd edn., Birmingham, 1783); Langford, John Alfred, *A Century of Birmingham Life* (Birmingham, 1870); Hutton, William, *The Life of William Hutton*, ed. Chinn, Carl (Studley, 1998).

233 *"man of shining talents":* Edgeworth, RL and M, vol. 2, pp. 110–13; Seward (1804), pp. 37–38.

233 *At one point he won a "considerable fortune":* Burney, French Exercise Book (Berg).

233 *Day suggested his stock remedies of fresh air:* TD to JB, n.d., cited in *European Magazine,* 2 (1795), pp. 21–22.

233 *Bicknell had taken scant interest in Sabrina:* The story of Bicknell's proposal to Sabrina is told in Edgeworth, RL and M, vol. 2, pp. 110–13 and Seward (1804), pp. 37–38.

234 *Bicknell was "the man of her dreams":* Burney, French Exercise Book (Berg).

235 *Day's reply, on May 4, 1783:* TD to SS, May 4, 1783, ERO, D/DBa C13. This letter was probably a draft as it contains various crossings-out and amendments.

237 *Sabrina walked up the aisle of St. Philip's Church:* Marriage register, St Philip's Church, Birmingham, April 16, 1784, Birmingham record office. Bicknell's application for a marriage license, which enabled the couple to marry without the usual church bans being read, was cosigned by William Withering, the physician who later discovered digitalis in foxgloves, who had recently joined the Lunar Society. John Bicknell, marriage license application, April 16, 1784, Lichfield RO. Bond between JB and TD, April 16, 1784, ERO, D/DBa L86.

238 *Sabrina gave birth to two sons:* The exact date and place of birth of John Laurens Bicknell is unknown. He later stated that he was born in Middlesex. JLB was said to have been "almost one year old" and HEB was "only just born" in March 1787. Henry Edgeworth Bicknell was baptized on April 2, 1787, when his name was misspelled as Henry Edgeworth Bricknell and his date of birth given as December 18, 1786, in St. Pancras Church. St. Pancras baptism register 1783–93, X102/074, LMA. He may have been named Henry after Henry Laurens, the father of John Laurens. Curiously, Henry was baptized on the same day that his father was buried but in a different church on the northern edge of London. The timing may have been due to differences with the Bicknell family or to Sabrina's own illness.

238 *"with all the delight of the most happy husband and father":* Edgeworth, RL and M, vol. 2, p. 113.

238 *"could hardly have been happier with the man of her dreams":* Burney, French Exercise Book (Berg).

238 *When Boswell visited the King's Bench in 1786:* Boswell, James, *Private Papers of James Boswell from Malahide Castle,* ed. Scott, G. and Pottle, Frederick A. (18 vols., New York, 1928–34), vol. 17, p. 11.

238 *subscribers to the first collection of poems:* List of subscribers in Williams, Helen Maria, *Poems* (2 vols., London, 1786).

239 *a small mention in the London newspapers: Whitehall Evening Post,* April 3, 1787; *European Magazine,* April 1787, p. 296.

239 *Bicknell was buried in the family vault:* Burial register, St. Dunstan-in-the-West, April 2, 1787, LMA.

239 *Bicknell had left no will:* No will has been discovered. It is likely he did not feel the need to write one since he was in such dire financial straits.

239 *"She had absolutely nothing":* Burney, French Exercise Book (Berg).

240 *"To have been more bounteous":* Seward, p. 38.

240 *This sum was matched by Edgeworth:* RLE to Sabrina Bicknell, August 28, 1808, BL Add. MS 70949 f. 280; Esther Day to RLE, January 21, 1790, Edgeworth Papers, MS 22470.

240 *Mrs. Bicknell "always refused to love" her:* Burney, French Exercise Book (Berg).

241 *Burney had been admitted to Cambridge at nineteen:* Venn, J. A., *Alumni Cantabrigienses,* part II, 1752–1900 (Cambridge, 1953), p. 459; Troide, Lars, "Burney, Charles (1757–1817)," *Oxford Dictionary of National Biography* (Oxford, 2004) online edn., accessed April 14, 2008; Scholes, Percy A., *The Great Dr. Burney* (Oxford, London, New York, Toronto, 1948), pp. 344–48. Hester Thrale later asked Burney Senior whether a scene from his daughter's novel *Evelina*, describing an attempted suicide, had been "founded on fact." The doctor had "changed Colour" at the assertion. Thrale, Hester Lynch, *Thraliana: the diary of Mrs Hester Lynch Thrale (later Mrs Piozzi) 1776–1809*, ed. Balderston, Katherine C. (Oxford, 1942), vol. 1, p. 360.

241 *Her reply to Burney:* Sabrina Bicknell to Charles Burney, May 16, 1787, Burney Family Collection, The James Marshall and Marie-Louise Osborn Collection, Beinecke Rare Book and Manuscript Library, Yale University.

242 *"more graceful, more attractive, much more eloquent than ever":* AS to Sophia Weston, February 4, 1789; and AS to George Hardinge, October 19, 1788, November 19, 1788, and March 5, 1789, Seward (1811), vol. 2, pp. 234, 176, 195 and 250. The story of Seward's prompting to raise funds through Hardinge is told through the above letters.

243 *He grumbled incessantly to Edgeworth:* TD to unknown correspondent (part of letter), n.d. (after 1782), BL Add. MS 70949, ff. 275–78; TD to Mary Evans, July 29, 1787, BL Add. MS 52540, ff. 25–28; and TD to MB, June 8, 1785, Soho Archives, Boulton Papers MS 3782/12/115.

243 *Day even lashed out at his publisher, John Stockdale:* TD to John Stockdale, July 28, 1789, cited in Stockdale (2005), pp. 205–6; Keir to TD, September 29, 1789, in Moilliet, A., p. 100.

243 *he was thrown from his horse and killed:* Keir, pp. 97–98; Edgeworth, RL and M, vol. 2, pp. 103–5.

243 *she was "overwhelmed" by the "weight of sorrow":* Esther Day to RLE, January 21, 1790, Edgeworth Papers, MS 22470.

244 *According to one report Esther never again enjoyed:* Death notice of Esther Day, *Gentleman's Magazine*, 1792, p. 581; Seward (1804), pp. 35–36. It was not, in fact, true that Esther never left her house again; she met with the Edgeworths in later years.

244 *"He was dear to me by many names":* ED to Robert Darwin, in Darwin, p. 81.

244 *When Edgeworth received the news:* Edgeworth, RL and M, vol. 2, pp. 103–5. Elizabeth Edgeworth was on the point of giving birth to RLE's twelfth child. They named the baby Thomas Day Edgeworth.

244 *the only will that could be found:* Notes by Milnes Lowndes on finding Day's will, ERO, D/DBa L96/10. JB's brother, Charles Bicknell, was also involved in looking for Day's will, presumably as TD's lawyer.

244 *Esther explained that Day had not been "lavish":* Esther Day to RLE, January 21, 1790, Edgeworth Papers, MS 22470/3.

245 *One obituary described him as "the advocate of human kind":* Gentleman's Magazine, 1789, p. 958.

245 *an anonymous correspondent wrote to the* General Evening Post: Anon (AS) to the Editor of the *General Evening Post*, October 11, 1789. The letter is given in full in Seward's collected letters so presumably it was found among her papers after her death. Seward (1811), vol. 2, pp. 329–31.

245 *"I propose publishing Mr Days life":* RLE to Margaret Ruxton, n.d. (1789), Edgeworth Papers, MS 10166/65.

245 *The rival biographers exchanged notes:* RLE to ED, 1790, in Edgeworth, RL and M, vol. 2, pp. 133; RLE to JK, January 6, 1790, and March 31, 1790, and RLE to Esther Day, December 18, 1790, Edgeworth Papers, MS 22470/1, 5 and 8.

246 *"a great omission" in a biography of Day:* JK to RLE, March 31, 1790, Edgeworth Papers, MS 22470/5 [citing Darwin's view]; JK to ED, March 15, 1790, in Moilliet, A., pp. 108–9.

246 *Keir admitted that obfuscating the truth:* Notes on manuscript, ERO, D/DBa F68/4. Esther further amended Keir's draft to remove a reference to "one pupil"—Lucretia—having married "without consulting her protector" and to Bicknell having been "entrusted from the beginning with the secret of the intention & execution of the experiment on female education." Any mention of a secret plan would have indicated that Day had fully intended to marry one of the girls.

247 *As the poet Robert Southey would later remark:* Rowland, p. x.

247 *"I think with you that she died of a broken heart":* John Stockdale to JK, 15 June 1792, cited in Moilliet, A., p. 115; *Gentleman's Magazine*, June 12, 1792, p. 581.

248 *"I love all of that breed":* Samuel Johnson to Hester Thrale, November 14, 1781, in Johnson, vol. 3, p. 373; Hester Thrale cited in Burney, Charles, *The Letters of Dr. Charles Burney*, ed. Ribeiro, Alvaro (Oxford, 1991), vol. 1, p. xxv. General background on Fanny Burney and the Burney family is from Harman, Claire, *Fanny Burney, a biography* (London, 2000) and Chisholm, Kate, *Fanny Burney, her life* (London, 1999).

248 *"His wife was here on Sunday, with Mrs. Bicknell":* FB to Charlotte Ann Francis (her sister; later Broome), October 10, 1791, in Burney, vol. 1, p. 70. The postscript is in FB to CB, June 16, 1803, in Burney, vol. 6, p. 474.

248 *Frequently ill with a series of vague symptoms:* For references to Rosette's illness see Burney, vol. 7, p. 52n; vol. 1, pp. 81–82 and 82n; and vol. 2, pp. 378–79.

249 *When Sarah Harriet called on Charles:* Sarah Harriet Burney to Mary Young, August 2–4, 1793, in Burney, SH, pp. 9–10.

249 *"I shall always love Mrs. Bicknel":* FB to CB, August 8, 1793 in Burney, vol. 2, p. 182.

249 *In a postscript on a letter to Rosette:* Charles Parr Burney to Rosette Burney with postscript from CB to Sabrina, January 17, 1799, Burney Family Col-

lection, The James Marshall and Marie-Louise Osborn Collection, Beinecke Rare Book and Manuscript Library, Yale University, OSB MSS 3, box 7.

249 *When the artist Joseph Farington came for dinner:* Farington, vol. 6, p. 2054.

250 *"living all but openly with a woman in his own* house*":* Hester Lynch Piozzi (née Thrale) to John Salusbury Piozzi Salusbury (her stepson), July 27, 1810, in Piozzi, vol. 4, pp. 296 and 298n. Mrs. Piozzi wrongly believed that CB was editor of the *European Magazine,* which had published gossip about her. She also described CB as "a habitual Drunkard." The editors of her letters erroneously suggest that Sabrina went to live with CB and Rosette after his retirement to Deptford rectory in 1813. She remained at the Burney School.

250 *"They understood between them very well":* Burney, French Exercise Book (Berg).

250 *A sleepy town beside the Thames:* Background on Greenwich history is from Platts, Beryl, *A History of Greenwich* (London, 1986); Lysons, Daniel, *The Environs of London* (London, 1792); Aslet, Clive, *The Story of Greenwich* (London, 1999); Silvester-Carr, Denise, *Greenwich: a history and celebration of the town* (Salisbury, 2005).

250 *Situated in a redbrick mansion:* Background information on the Burney School is from various documents in the Burney School Folder at Greenwich Heritage Centre. The fees are mentioned in a letter from James Watt to James Davies Kington, October 17, 1811, copy GHC. The reference to birch rods is from Farington, vol. 3, p. 35n.

251 *On the ground floor and upper levels:* Details of the house are from descriptions by Fanny Anne Wood, CB's granddaughter, and an auction catalog of 1839 before the house was demolished. The latter is within an album of Greenwich archive material held in the British Library (Rare Books). The catalog was available from John Laurens Bicknell, among others. Miscellaneous papers relating to Greenwich, BL; Wood, p. 61.

251 *Bills that survive for two pupils:* CB to Robert Gray, December 28, 1805, in George IV, *The Correspondence of George, Prince of Wales, 1770–1812,* ed. Aspinall, A. (8 vols., London, 1970), vol. 5, pp. 285–87. The two boys were orphans whose tuition was paid by the Prince of Wales, the future King George IV.

251 *she complained that she could not take a day off:* Sabrina Bicknell to Frances Edgeworth, June 9, 1813 and same to Maria Edgeworth, October 29, 1817, Edgeworth Papers, MS 22470/9 and 15.

252 *she should translate from French a new book:* Edgeworth, RL and M, vol. 2, pp. 341–43. The book was *Adèle et Théodore, ou les Lettres sur l'Éducation,* by Madame de Genlis. Genlis's book had been acclaimed as a more moderate version of Rousseau's educational ideas. The poem "Advice to a Lady" is by George, Lord Lyttelton. See Lyttelton, George, *The Poetical Works of George Lord Lyttelton* (London, 1801), pp. 56–62.

253 *a short story, "Forester":* Edgeworth, Maria, "Forester" in *Moral Tales for Young People* (London, 1801), pp. 1–258. For more discussion about Day's effect in stifling ME's writing career see Myers. Myers describes Day as "the patriarch who stopped the young woman's career cold" until ME was "freed" by Day's

fall from his horse. Myers also provides an illuminating portrait of Day's wife-training experiment. For further discussion of Day's influence on ME see Butler, M.

253 *Maria Edgeworth's first "society" novel,* Belinda: Edgeworth, Maria, *Belinda* (first pub. 1801; Oxford, 1999). The quotes are from pp. 362–77.

254 *Maria Edgeworth made no secret of the inspiration:* Edgeworth, RL and M, vol. 2, p. 349.

254 *it was* Belinda *that firmly established Maria Edgeworth's literary career:* Butler, Marilyn, *Romantics, Rebels and Reactionaries: English literature and its background, 1760–1830* (Oxford, 1981), p. 96.

254 *Fanny decided to improve her French by writing some short compositions:* Burney, French Exercise Book (Berg).

255 *Trollope would tell a similar story:* Trollope, Anthony, *Orley Farm* (2 vols., London, 1935). The quotes are from vol. 1, pp. 176, 330, 226 and vol. 2, p. 137. In a key element of the plot, Graham is also thrown from his horse although, unlike Day, he survives with just a broken arm. My thanks to Tilli Tansey for drawing my attention to Trollope's book.

CHAPTER 11: GALATEA

257 *the British had lived with the fear of invasion:* Information on the expected French invasion is from Fortescue, Sir John William, *A History of the British Army* (13 vols., London, 1910), vol. 5, pp. 167–244; Schom, Alan, *Trafalgar: Countdown to Battle 1803–1805* (London, 1990); Pocock, Tom, *The Terror before Trafalgar* (London, 2002).

257 *he picked up the book* Memoirs of the Life of Dr. Darwin: It is not possible to date exactly when John Laurens Bicknell read Seward's biography of Darwin and wrote to her—his letter has not survived—but she referred to his letter in January 1805. AS had been away from Lichfield for five months up to December 1804. It has also not been possible to date his birth precisely, but he was born in the winter of 1785–86. The descriptions and quotes relating to Day in Seward's memoir are from Seward (1804), pp. 12–38.

258 *In law, as John would have known, illegitimate children:* William Blackstone, in his *Commentaries on the Laws of England,* states that an illegitimate child "can inherit nothing, being looked upon as the son of nobody." Blackstone, William, *Commentaries on the Laws of England* (2 vols., London, 1765–69), vol. 1, p. 447. Literary references are from Zunshine, pp. 133–34. Fanny Burney, in her novel *Evelina,* wrote that illegitimacy would bring "shame and dishonour" on her heroine. Fanny Burney, *Evelina* (first published 1778; Oxford, 2008), p. 337.

259 *"such a state of irritation":* Sabrina later described her son's reactions to ME who related the story to her stepmother. ME to Frances Edgeworth, October 13 and 15, 1818, in Edgeworth (1971), pp. 121–22.

259 *"the dearest friend I had on earth":* AS to R. Fellowes, August 31, 1803, Seward (1811), vol. 6, p. 101.

259 *forced by his family to issue a retraction:* Robert Darwin to AS, March 5, 1804, LRO, D262/1/34; Darwin, pp. 70–75.

259 *"a base and surely most unprovoked attack":* AS to Rev. Thomas Sedgewick Whalley, January 22, 1805, in Whalley, vol. 1, pp. 263–64. AS describes her reply to JB in her letter to Whalley.

260 *reviewers of Darwin's biography savaged Seward: Annual Review,* January 1804; *Universal Magazine,* April 1804; *British Critic,* October 1804.

261 *"a half true, half false history:"* ME to Frances Edgeworth, October 13 and 15, 1818, in Edgeworth (1971), pp. 121–22.

261 *Sabrina would later confess that her elder son's ailments:* Sabrina Bicknell to RLE, April 21 and May 13, 1817, Edgeworth Papers, MS 22470/10 and 12.

262 *Thomas Griffiths Wainewright, who was suspected:* Peach, Annette, "Wainewright, Thomas Griffiths (1794–1847)," in *Oxford Dictionary of National Biography* (Oxford, 2004) online edn., accessed December 29, 2011.

262 *more than forty boys barricaded themselves:* John Graham to his mother, Mrs. Graham, February 24, 1808, transcript at GHC. Twenty years later, CB's sister, Sarah Harriet, met one of the boys involved in the riot, Willoughby Crewe, who had become a curate. See SHB to Charlotte Barratt and Charlotte Broome, February 17, 1828, in Burney, SH, p. 273. Background on the rebellions in other schools is from Moncrieff, pp. 210–11. Riots erupted at Winchester, Rugby, Harrow and Eton schools on a number of occasions during the late eighteenth and early nineteenth centuries. Charles Dickens did not exaggerate when he created the sadistic Wackford Squeers as headmaster of Dotheboys Hall in *Nicholas Nickleby.* Squeers was based on a real headmaster, William Shaw, who was prosecuted when several boys in his school, the Bowes Academy in Yorkshire, went blind due to the unhygienic and inhumane conditions.

262 *As John Graham told his mother:* John Graham to his mother, Mrs. Graham, September 22 and August 29, 1805, Lambeth Archives, IV/4/50 and IV/4/48.

263 *"If your sons marry to please you":* RLE to Sabrina Bicknell, August 28, 1808, BL Add. MS 70949 f 280.

263 *Grandchildren followed swiftly:* I am indebted to Jacky Worthington for her help in tracing John and Henry Bicknell's descendants and to the Bicknell family descendants for their interest in my book.

264 *A portrait of Henry in later life:* Portrait of Henry Edgeworth Bicknell by Charles Baugniet, 1853, NPG D31757. Portrait of John Laurens Bicknell by Charles Baugniet, 1845, Wellcome Library.

264 *leasing a house for himself and his new wife in Crooms Hill: Hughes New Law List,* 1809, p. 47; Rates Books, Greenwich West, from 1814, at GHC.

264 *Worried they would return to Ireland before:* Sabrina Bicknell to Frances Edgeworth, June, 9, 1813, Edgeworth Papers, MS 22470/9.

264 *Maria smuggled him a furtive letter from Greenwich:* Maria Bicknell to John Constable, February 24, 1816, in Constable, vol. 2, p. 178. For the full story of Constable's relationship with Maria Bicknell see Gayford, Martin, *Constable in Love: love, landscape, money and the making of a great painter* (London, 2009), pp. 295–302.

265 *Constable, at one point, told Maria:* John Constable to Maria Constable (née Bicknell), January 21, 1825, in Constable, vol. 2, pp. 372–73.

265   *her son Henry lost three children; John was severely ill again:* Sabrina Bicknell to RLE, April 21, Edgeworth Papers, MS 22470/10.

265   *The following month, she thanked Edgeworth:* Sabrina Bicknell to RLE, May 13, 1817, Edgeworth Papers, MS 22470/12.

266   *Throughout his long and grueling illness:* Edgeworth, RL and M, vol. 2, pp. 445–53.

267   *"By this loss I am deprived of my oldest friend":* Sabrina Bicknell to ME, June 30, 1817, Edgeworth Papers, MS 22470/13.

267   *Maria began the task of sorting through his letters:* ME to Sabrina Bicknell, August 17, 1817, BL Add. MS 70949 f. 271.

268   *the housekeeper she called Bicky:* Wood, p. 123.

268   *Sabrina was asked to become godmother:* Susan Sabrina Burney was born on February 25, 1818, and baptized December 21, 1818: St. Alfege baptism register, LMA. Sabrina described her as her goddaughter in her will.

268   *and the draft manuscript of her father's memoirs carefully stowed in a sturdy boxfile:* Edgeworth (1971), pp. 75–99. On her way to London ME stayed with various friends to whom she showed the manuscript of her father's memoirs. Étienne Dumont, a Geneva-born writer and editor who was an old friend of RLE, "hates Mr. Day in spite of all his good qualities," according to ME. She wrote: "He says he knows and *cannot bear* that sort of man 'who has such pride and misanthropies about trifles and who raises a great theory of morals upon an amour propre blessé.'" Lady Louisa Lansdowne, her hostess in Wiltshire, took an opposite view. "She admires and loves Mr. Day as much as Dumont dislikes him," Maria wrote but added shrewdly: "Had she seen him she would not have endured his manners however 24 hours."

268   *"a little, dark, bearded, sharp, withered, active":* Butler, M, p. 3.

268   *she wrote to Sabrina in Greenwich with a request to meet:* ME to Frances Edgeworth, October 13 and 15, 1818, in Edgeworth (1971), pp. 109–11 and 121–22. Sabrina's reply is related by ME to her stepmother. ME stayed in Hampstead with the poet Joanna Baillie and her sister Agnes, who were nieces of the surgeon John Hunter. Her visits to Essex and to Greenwich are described in her letters home.

270   *"enraged" again when a magazine retold the story:* The offending article may have been a column in the journal *La Belle Assemblée, or Bell's Court and Fashionable Magazine*, published the previous month and headed "Curious particulars of Mr. Day, the author of 'Sandford and Merton,'" which replayed the details from Seward's *Life of Erasmus Darwin* at length. *La Belle Assemblée, or Bell's Court and Fashionable Magazine*, September 1818, pp. 105–6.

270   *Day had "made her miserable—a slave &c!":* Edgeworth, RL and M, vol. 2, p. 114.

270   *There was nothing in the document:* Sabrina Bicknell to ME, October 29, 1818, Edgeworth Papers, MS 22470/15.

271   *"from a number of orphans, one of remarkably promising appearance":* Edgeworth, RL and M, vol. 1, p. 209.

271   *"crack-brained absurdities," which shocked nineteenth-century sensibilities:* Quarterly Review, July 1810, p. 523.

271 *a fine new house around the corner from the school:* Greenwich Rates Books at GHC. The terrace is now called Gloucester Circus and the house is numbered 29. For information on building Gloucester Circus see Bonwitt, W., *Michael Searles: a Georgian architect and surveyor* (London, 1987), pp. 20–22; Bonwitt, W., "Gloucester Circus," in *Transactions of the Greenwich and Lewisham Antiquarian Society*, vol. 10, pp. 21–30.

271 *"as fully competent as Mrs. Bicknell was":* John Constable to Maria Constable, January 21, 1825, in Constable, vol. 2, p. 373.

271 *Denning, who painted Sabrina's picture in 1832:* "Mrs Bicknell," by Richard James Lane, after Stephen Poyntz Denning, lithograph, 1833 (1832), NPG D22174; Richard James Lane, account books, NPG MS 56, vol. 1, pp. 34 and 36; S. P. Denning to Richard James Lane, April 1, 1833, in RJL, correspondence, NPG MS 61, vol. 1, p. 22. My thanks to Alexandra Aault, assistant curator at the NPG, for helping me to verify the sitter of the portrait as Sabrina Bicknell.

272 *"so strong a likeness I should have recognized it":* FB to Charles Parr Burney, May 3, 1836, in Burney, vol. 12, p. 890.

272 *"She is, alas! much changed":* Wood, p. 123. The sale of the contents and fittings is described in the auction catalog of the Burney School, May 14, 1839, in Miscellaneous papers relating to Greenwich, BL (Rare Books).

273 *"I see grey hairs upon brows":* Wood, pp. 306 and 326–27.

273 *Sabrina died at her home in The Circus:* Death certificate of Sabrina Bicknell, September 9, 1843, GRO, 1231703–1; Will of Sabrina Bicknell, Prob 11/1986. Sabrina's grave is plot no. 4371 in square 108. Her son John Laurens Bicknell is buried on the right of her grave and her granddaughter Mary Grant Bicknell is to the right of her father.

274 *John Laurens Bicknell survived his mother by only two years:* Death certificate of John Laurens Bicknell, August 9, 1845, GRO 1408910–1.

BIBLIOGRAPHY

ABBREVIATIONS

AS   Anna Seward
CB   Charles Burney Jr. (1757–1817)
ED   Erasmus Darwin
EM   Esther Milnes
ERO   Essex Record Office
FB   Fanny Burney
FHA   Foundling Hospital Archives
LRO   Lichfield Record Office
GHC   Greenwich Heritage Centre
JB   John Bicknell
JJR   Jean-Jacques Rousseau
JK   James Keir
LMA   London Metropolitan Archives
LRO   Lichfield Record Office
MB   Matthew Boulton
ME   Maria Edgeworth
MT   Middle Temple
NPG   National Portrait Gallery
RLE   Richard Lovell Edgeworth
SJBM   Samuel Johnson Birthplace Museum
SOG   Society of Genealogists
SS   Sabrina Sidney (later Bicknell)
TD   Thomas Day

MANUSCRIPT SOURCES

Barrington Family Papers, Essex Record Office
Burney Family Collection, The James Marshall and Marie-Louise Osborn Collection, Beinecke Rare Book and Manuscript Library, Yale University
Burney, Fanny, Fanny Burney Notebooks, in the Berg Collection (Henry W. and Albert A. Berg) of English and American Literature, New York Public Library, Astor, Lenox and Tilden Foundations
British Library Add. MSS

Darwin Papers, Cambridge University Library
Edgeworth Papers, National Library of Ireland
Egerton Papers, British Library
Foundling Hospital Archives, London Metropolitan Archives
Greenwich Heritage Centre (Burney School documents)
Heinz Archive and Library, National Portrait Gallery, London
Lambeth Archives Department (Graham family correspondence)
Lichfield Record Office
Middle Temple Archives, London
Pearson Papers, University College London Special Collections
Royal Society of Arts (Letters of Richard Lovell Edgeworth)
Samuel Johnson Birthplace Museum, Lichfield
Sir John Soane Archives, Sir John Soane's Museum, London
Soho Archives (Boulton Papers and Watt Papers), Birmingham Reference Library
Staffordshire Record Office (Edward Sneyd and Ann Sneyd papers), Stafford
William Salt Library (Letters of Thomas Day and Anna Seward), Stafford

BIOGRAPHIES OF THOMAS DAY
(IN CHRONOLOGICAL ORDER)

Keir, James, *An Account of the Life and Writings of Thomas Day, Esq.* (London, 1791)
Kippis, Andrew, "Thomas Day" in *Biographia Britannica* (London, 1793), vol. 5, pp. 21–32.
Seward, Anna, *Memoirs of the Life of Dr. Darwin, chiefly during his residence in Lichfield, with anecdotes of his friends, and criticisms on his writings* (London, 1804)
Blackman, John, *A Memoir of the Life and Writings of Thomas Day, author of "Sandford and Merton"* (London, 1862)
Stephen, Sir Leslie, ed., *Dictionary of National Biography* (London, 1888), vol. 14, pp. 239–41
Sadler, Sir Michael, *Thomas Day, an English disciple of Rousseau* (Cambridge, 1928)
Gignilliat, George Warren, *The Author of Sandford and Merton, a life of Thomas Day, Esq* (New York, 1932)
Scott, Sir Samuel Haslam, *The Exemplary Mr. Day, 1748–1789, author of "Sandford and Merton"* (London, 1935)
Rowland, Peter, *The Life and Times of Thomas Day, 1748–1789, English philanthropist and author, virtue almost personified* (Lewiston, NY; Lampeter, 1996)

WORKS BY THOMAS DAY REFERRED TO IN THE TEXT
(IN CHRONOLOGICAL ORDER)

TD and JB, *The Dying Negro* (London, 1773)
TD, *The Devoted Legions* (London, 1776)
TD, *Ode for the New Year 1776* (London, 1776)
TD, *The Desolation of America* (London, 1777)
TD, *Fragment of an Original Letter on the Slavery of the Negroes, written in the year 1776* (London, 1784)
TD, *The History of Sandford and Merton, A Work Intended for the Use of Children* (3 vols., London, 1783, 1786 and 1789)

TD and Esther Day, *Select Miscellaneous Productions, of Mrs Day, and Thomas Day, Esq in verse and prose . . .* , ed. Lowndes, Thomas (London, 1805)

TD et al., *Tracts in Prose and Verse*, ed. Lowndes, Thomas (2 vols., Dover; London, 1825–27)

OTHER PUBLISHED SOURCES
(Texts that are mentioned only once are given in full in the endnotes but not here.)

Allin, D. S., *The Early Years of the Foundling Hospital, 1739/41–1773* (London, 2010)

Anon, *A Short Account of the Ancient and Modern State of the City and Close of Lichfield* (Lichfield, 1819)

Anon, *An Account of the Foundling Hospital* (London, 1826)

Barker-Benfield, G. J., *The Culture of Sensibility: sex and society in eighteenth-century Britain* (Chicago; London, 1992)

Barnard, Teresa, *Anna Seward: a constructed life* (Aldershot, UK, 2009)

Bentley, Thomas, *Journal of a Visit to Paris, 1776*, ed. France, Peter (Brighton, 1977)

Bicknell, Algernon Sidney, *Five Pedigrees* (London, 1912)

Bicknell, John (under pseudonym Joel Collier), *Musical Travels Through England* (London, 1774)

Black, Jeremy, *The British Abroad: the Grand Tour in the eighteenth century* (Stroud, UK, 2003)

———, *France and the Grand Tour* (Basingstoke, UK, 2003)

Boswell, James, *Boswell's London Journal, 1762–1763*, ed. Pottle, Frederick A. (New Haven; London, 1991)

Broome, Jack Howard, *Jean-Jacques Rousseau in Staffordshire, 1766–1767* (Keele, UK, 1966)

Bulwer, Edward, Baron Lytton, *The Life, Letters and Literary Remains of Edward Bulwer, Lord Lytton*, ed. Bulwer-Lytton, Edward (his son) (2 vols., London, 1883)

Burke, John, *A Genealogical and Heraldic Dictionary of the Landed Gentry of Great Britain and Ireland* (3 vols., London, 1846)

Burney, Fanny, *The Journals and Letters of Fanny Burney (Madame d'Arblay), 1791–1840*, ed. Hemlow, Joyce et al. (12 vols., Oxford, 1972–84)

Burney, Sarah Harriet, *The Letters of Sarah Harriet Burney*, ed. Clark, Lorna J. (Athens, GA; London, 1997)

Butler, Harriet Jessie and Edgeworth, Harold (eds.), *The Black Book of Edgeworthstown and Other Edgeworth Memories, 1585–1817* (London, 1927)

Butler, Marilyn, "Edgeworth's Stern Father: Escaping Thomas Day, 1795–1801" in Ribeiro, Alvaro, and Basker, James G. (eds.), *Tradition in Transition: women writers, marginal texts, and the eighteenth-century canon* (Oxford, 1996), pp. 75–93.

———, *Maria Edgeworth: a literary biography* (Oxford, 1972)

Cannon, Garland, *The Life and Mind of Oriental Jones: William Jones, the father of modern linguistics* (Cambridge, 1990)

———, ed., *The Letters of Sir William Jones* (Oxford, 1970)

Carey, Brycchan, *British Abolitionism and the Rhetoric of Sensibility: writing, sentiment, and slavery, 1760–1807* (Basingstoke, UK, 2005)

Carter, Philip, *Men and the Emergence of Polite Society, Britain, 1660–1800* (New York, 2000)

Clark, Gillian, *Correspondence of the Foundling Hospital Inspectors in Berkshire, 1757–68* (Reading, UK, 1994)

Clarke, Desmond John, *The Ingenious Mr. Edgeworth* (London, 1965)

Constable, John, *John Constable's Correspondence*, ed. Beckett, R. B. (4 vols., London, 1964)

Cunningham, Hugh, *The Invention of Childhood* (London, 2006)

Damrosch, Leo, *Jean-Jacques Rousseau: restless genius* (New York, 2007)

Darling, John, *Child-Centred Education and Its Critics* (London, 1994)

Darwin, Charles, *Charles Darwin's The Life of Erasmus Darwin*, ed. King-Hele, Desmond (Cambridge, 2002)

Douthwaite, Julia, *The Wild Girl, Natural Man, and the Monster: dangerous experiments in the Age of Enlightenment* (Chicago; London, 2002)

Edgeworth, Frances Anne, *A Memoir of Maria Edgeworth, with Selections from Her Letters* (London, 1867)

Edgeworth, Maria, *Letters from England, 1813–1844*, ed. Colvin, Christina (Oxford, 1971)

———, *Maria Edgeworth in France and Switzerland: selections from the Edgeworth family letters*, ed. Colvin, Christina (Oxford, 1979)

Edgeworth, Richard Lovell and Maria, *Memoirs of Richard Lovell Edgeworth, Esq. Begun by Himself and Concluded by His Daughter* (2 vols., London, 1821)

Edmonds, David, and Eidinow, John, *Rousseau's Dog: two great thinkers at war in the age of enlightenment* (London, 2006)

Evans, Tanya, *Unfortunate Objects: lone mothers in eighteenth-century London* (Basingtoke, UK, 2005)

Farington, Joseph, *The Farington Diary*, ed. Greig, James (8 vols., London, 1922)

Ferling, John E., *Setting the World Ablaze* (Oxford, 2000)

Fildes, Valerie, *Wet Nursing* (Oxford, 1988)

Flavell, Julie, *When London Was Capital of America* (New Haven; London, 2010)

Fletcher, Anthony, *Growing Up in England: the experience of childhood, 1600–1914* (New Haven, 2008)

Girard, Joseph, *Évocation du Vieil Avignon* (Paris, 1958)

George, M. Dorothy, *London Life in the Eighteenth Century* (Harmondsworth, UK, 1976)

Gerzina, Gretchen, *Black London: life before emancipation* (New Brunswick, NJ; London, 1995)

Hare, Augustus J. C., *The Life and Letters of Maria Edgeworth* (2 vols., London, 1894)

Hersey, George L., *Falling in Love with Statues: artificial humans from Pygmalion to the present* (Chicago; London, 2008)

Heywood, Colin, *A History of Childhood: children and childhood in the West from medieval to modern times* (Cambridge, 2001)

Hopkins, Mary Alden, *Dr. Johnson's Lichfield* (London, 1956)

Howitt, William, *Visits to Remarkable Places* (London, 1840)

Inglis-Jones, Elisabeth, *The Great Maria: a portrait of Maria Edgeworth* (London, 1959)

Isaacson, Walter, *Benjamin Franklin: an American life* (New York; London, 2003)

Jaeger, Muriel, *Experimental Lives from Cato to George Sand* (London, 1932)

James, Henry, *Watch and Ward* (Boston, 1878)

———, *Watch and Ward*, ed. Edel, Leon (London, 1960)

Jimack, Peter, *Rousseau: Emile* (London, 1983)

Johnson, Samuel, *The Letters of Samuel Johnson*, ed. Redford, Bruce (3 vols., Princeton; Oxford; 1992)

King-Hele, Desmond, *The Collected Letters of Erasmus Darwin* (Cambridge, 2007)

———, *Erasmus Darwin: a life of unequalled achievement* (London, 1999)

Laurens, Henry, *The Papers of Henry Laurens*, ed. Hamer, Philip M. et al. (16 vols., Columbia, SC, 1968–2002)

Lemire, Beverly, *Dress, Culture and Commerce: The English clothing trade before the factory, 1660–1800* (Basingstoke, UK, 1997)

Levene, Alysa, *Childcare, Health and Mortality at the London Foundling Hospital, 1741–1800: "left to the mercy of the world"* (Manchester, UK, 2007)

———, ed., *Narratives of the Poor in Eighteenth-Century Britain*, vol. 3 (London, 2006)

Lucas, E. V., *A Swan and Her Friends* (London, 1907)

McClure, Ruth K., *Coram's Children: The London Foundling Hospital in the eighteenth century* (New Haven; London, 1981)

Macassey, Sir Lynden, *Middle Templars' Associations with America* (London, 1998)

Moilliet, Amelia, *Sketch of the Life of J. Keir, with a Selection from His Correspondence*, ed. Moilliet, J. K. (London, 1868)

Moilliet, J. L. and Smith, Barbara M. D., *"A Mighty Chemist": James Keir of the Lunar Society* (Birmingham, UK, 1982)

Moncrieff, Ascott Robert Hope, *A Book about Schools, Schoolboys, Schoolmasters, and Schoolbooks* (London, 1925)

Morse, David, *The Age of Virtue: British culture from the Restoration to Romanticism* (Basingstoke, UK, 2000)

Myers, Mitzi, "My Art Belongs to Daddy? Thomas Day, Maria Edgeworth, and the Pre-Texts of Belinda: Women Writers and Patriarchal Authority," in Backscheider, Paula, ed., *Revising Women: eighteenth-century "Women's Fiction" and social engagement* (Baltimore, 2000), pp. 104–46

Nicholls, Reginald Hugh, and Wray, F. A., *The History of the Foundling Hospital* (Oxford, 1935)

Oulton, W. C., *The Beauties of Anna Seward* (London, 1813)

Pearson, Hesketh, *Extraordinary People* (London, 1965)

Picard, Liza, *Dr. Johnson's London: life in London, 1740–1770* (London, 2000)

Piozzi, Hester Lynch, *The Piozzi Letters: correspondence of Hester Lynch Piozzi 1784–1821 (formerly Mrs Thrale)*, ed. Bloom, Edward A. and Lillian D. (4 vols., Newark; London; 1996).

Pugh, Gillian, *London's Forgotten Children: Thomas Coram and the Foundling Hospital* (Stroud, 2007)

Rakove, Jack, *Revolutionaries: a new history of the invention of America* (London, 2010)

Robinson, Eric, "The Lunar Society: its membership and organisation," in *Transactions of the Newcomen Society*, vol. 35 (1962–3), pp. 153–77

Rousseau, Jean-Jacques, *Confessions*, trs. Scholar, Angela; ed. Coleman, Patrick (Oxford, 2008)

———, *Correspondance Complète de Jean-Jacques Rousseau*, ed. Leigh, R. A. (52 vols., Geneva; Oxford, 1965–2012)

———, *Emile, or on Education*, trs. Nugent, Thomas (London, 1763)

———, *Emile, or on Education, includes Emile and Sophie, or, The solitaries*, ed. Bloom, Allan and Kelly, Christopher (Hanover, NH; London, 2010)

———, *Emile for Today: The* Emile *of Jean Jacques Rousseau*, ed. Boyd, William (London, Melbourne, Toronto, 1960)

———, *Emilius and Sophia; or, The solitaries* (London, 1783)

Schimmelpenninck, Mary Anne (née Galton), *Life of Mary Anne Schimmelpenninck*, ed. Hankin, Christiana A. (2 vols., London, 1860)

Schofield, Robert, *The Lunar Society of Birmingham: a social history of provincial science and industry in eighteenth-century England* (Oxford, 1963)

Scholes, Percy Alfred, *The Great Dr. Burney* (Oxford, 1948)

Seward, Anna, *Letters of Anna Seward, Written Between the Years 1784 and 1807*, ed. Constable, Archibald (6 vols., Edinburgh, 1811)

———, *The Poetical Works of Anna Seward, with Extracts from Her Literary Correspondence*, ed. Scott, Walter (3 vols., Edinburgh, 1810)

Shaw, George Bernard, *Pygmalion*, ed. Laurence, Dan H. (London, 2003)

Sheriff, Mary D., *Moved by Love: inspired artists and deviant women in eighteenth-century France* (Chicago; London, 2004)

Sherwood, Martha Mary, *The Life and Times of Mrs. Sherwood from the Diaries of Captain and Mrs. Sherwood (1775–1851)*, ed. Darton, F. J. Harvey (London, 1910)

Stapleton, Martin, *Anna Seward and Classic Lichfield* (Worcester, UK, 1909)

Stockdale, Eric, *'Tis Treason, My Good Man! four revolutionary presidents and a Piccadilly bookshop* (New Castle, DE; London, 2005)

Stockdale, Eric and Holland, Randy J., *Middle Temple Lawyers and the American Revolution* (Eagan, MN, 2007)

Stoichita, Victor, *The Pygmalion Effect: from Ovid to Hitchcock*, trs. Anderson, Alison (Chicago; London, 2008)

Stone, Lawrence, *The Family, Sex and Marriage in England 1500–1800* (London, 1990)

Uglow, Jenny, *The Lunar Men: the friends who made the future* (London, 2002)

Whalley, Thomas Sedgewick, *Journals and Correspondence of Thomas Sedgewick Whalley*, ed. Wickham, Reverend Hill (2 vols., London, 1863)

Williams, David, *Incidents in My Own Life Which Have Been Thought of Some Importance*, ed. France, Peter (Brighton, UK, 1980)

Wilson, Adrian, "Illegitimacy and Its Implications in Mid-18th Century London," in *Continuity and Change*, vol. 4 (1989), pp. 103–64

Wokler, Robert, *Rousseau: a very short introduction* (Oxford, 2001)

Wollstonecraft, Mary, *A Vindication of the Rights of Woman*, ed. Brody, Miriam (London, 2004)

Wood, Frances Anne, *A Great-Niece's Journals: being extracts from the journal of Fanny Anne Burney, Mrs Wood, from 1830 to 1842*, ed. Rolt, Margaret S. (London, 1926)

Zipes, Jack, ed., *The Oxford Encyclopedia of Children's Literature* (4 vols., Oxford, 2006)

Zunshine, Lisa, *Bastards and Foundlings: illegitimacy in eighteenth-century England* (Columbus, OH, 2005)

INDEX